Personal Injury and the
Law of Torts for Paralegals

ASPEN PUBLISHERS

Pesonal Injury and the Law of Torts for Paralegals

Emily Lynch Morissette, ESQ.

Wolters Kluwer

Law & Business

AUSTIN   BOSTON   CHICAGO   NEW YORK   THE NETHERLANDS

Aspen Publishers
Attn: Permissions Department
76 Ninth Avenue, 7th Floor
New York, NY 10011-5201

To contact Customer Care, e-mail customer.care@aspenpublishers.com, call 1-800-234-1660, fax 1-800-901-9075, or mail correspondence to:

Aspen Publishers
Attn: Order Department
PO Box 990
Frederick, MD 21705

Printed in the United States of America.

1 2 3 4 5 6 7 8 9 0

ISBN 978-0-7355-6957-7

Library of Congress Cataloging-in-Publication Data

Morissette, Emily Lynch.
 Personal injury and the law of torts for paralegals / Emily Lynch Morissette.
  p. cm.
 Includes index.
 ISBN 978-0-7355-6957-7
1. Torts — United States. 2. Personal injuries — United States. 3. Legal assistants — United States — Handbooks, manuals, etc. I. Title.
 KF1250.Z9M667 2009
 346.7303 — dc22

                                                          2008038457

About Wolters Kluwer Law & Business

Wolters Kluwer Law & Business is a leading provider of research information and workflow solutions in key specialty areas. The strengths of the individual brands of Aspen Publishers, CCH, Kluwer Law International and Loislaw are aligned within Wolters Kluwer Law & Business to provide comprehensive, in-depth solutions and expert-authored content for the legal, professional and education markets.

CCH was founded in 1913 and has served more than four generations of business professionals and their clients. The CCH products in the Wolters Kluwer Law & Business group are highly regarded electronic and print resources for legal, securities, antitrust and trade regulation, government contracting, banking, pension, payroll, employment and labor, and healthcare reimbursement and compliance professionals.

Aspen Publishers is a leading information provider for attorneys, business professionals and law students. Written by preeminent authorities, Aspen products offer analytical and practical information in a range of specialty practice areas from securities law and intellectual property to mergers and acquisitions and pension/benefits. Aspen's trusted legal education resources provide professors and students with high-quality, up-to-date and effective resources for successful instruction and study in all areas of the law.

Kluwer Law International supplies the global business community with comprehensive English-language international legal information. Legal practitioners, corporate counsel and business executives around the world rely on the Kluwer Law International journals, loose-leafs, books and electronic products for authoritative information in many areas of international legal practice.

Loislaw is a premier provider of digitized legal content to small law firm practitioners of various specializations. Loislaw provides attorneys with the ability to quickly and efficiently find the necessary legal information they need, when and where they need it, by facilitating access to primary law as well as state-specific law, records, forms and treatises.

Wolters Kluwer Law & Business, a unit of Wolters Kluwer, is headquartered in New York and Riverwoods, Illinois. Wolters Kluwer is a leading multinational publisher and information services company.

To my mom,
who supported and encouraged me in realizing this dream; without you
this book would not have been possible.

Summary of Contents

Contents

Chapter 10   **Intentional Torts to Property 165**

Chapter 11   **The Defenses to Intentional Torts and Immunities 177**

Chapter 12   **Strict Liability and Products Liability 197**

Preface

Focus

Personal Injury and the Law of Torts for Paralegals meets the growing need for a personal injury textbook with an emphasis on medical information useful in litigating all types of tort cases. Included in the book is a guide on how to obtain medical records and how to understand those records. Paralegals are provided with a sample medical authorization to assist them in obtaining medical records in compliance with HIPAA. The textbook gives tips on what to look for in the medical records and gives an example of a medical summary. Students are provided with some medical records that they must review and summarize. An appendix with basic medical information is provided, including medical terms, basic anatomy, common prescription drug types, and medical tests that may be encountered when reviewing personal injury medical records.

This information is of benefit to many of the subjects included in the book, such as premises liability, medical malpractice, intentional torts to persons, strict liability, products liability, and workers' compensation. In addition, the book provides a comprehensive overview of the remaining torts outlined in the American Association for Paralegal Education's Model Tort Law Syllabus.

- Negligence
- Defenses to Negligence
- Defenses to Intentional Torts
- Immunities
- Vicarious Liability
- Nuisance

The final section of the book goes through the litigation process, beginning with complaints, then discovery, and ending with the trial itself. Insurance is discussed in detail due to the importance of insurance in tort litigation. Samples of the discussed pleadings and discovery are included, such as a complaint, affirmative defenses, an answer, interrogatories, requests for production of documents, and requests for admissions. A deposition of a plaintiff in a torts case is provided and the students are given a sample summary of the deposition so they can learn how to prepare deposition summaries. In addition, this chapter instructs the paralegal on how to produce a trial notebook, which is one of major functions of paralegals in the field of tort litigation.

Overview

The book starts by introducing the concept of torts and then moving into each element of negligence. Although intentional torts might be an easier concept to understand for paralegals, the majority of the paralegal's work experience will be negligence-related. Thus, negligence is placed in the beginning of the book to give it greater emphasis, and each element of negligence has its own separate chapter. After discussing each element of negligence, issues related to negligence, and the defenses to negligence, the book tackles medical malpractice as a type of negligence.

Next, intentional torts are covered. Intentional torts to persons and intentional torts to property are divided into two chapters for easier learning. Strict liability and products liability also receive separate chapters.

Workers' compensation is discussed close to the end of the book. While workers' compensation is an area of law many beginning paralegals go into, it does not fit nicely into the above categories and thus merits its own chapter.

Chapter 15 discusses how to discover medical records, especially with the issues raised by the Health Insurance Portability and Accountability Act ("HIPAA"). In addition, paralegal students will learn how to review and summarize medical records.

The last chapters address the litigation process from a torts standpoint. Chapter 16 starts with complaints, answers, and affirmative defenses. The chapter also covers discovery. Students learn how to summarize a deposition and examples of each type of discovery are provided. In Chapter 17, students learn how to prepare a trial notebook.

Appendix A, An Introduction to Medicine, presents a short introduction to medical terms, basic anatomy, common prescription drug types, and medical tests that may be encountered when reviewing personal injury medical records. This appendix is a jumping-off point for the paralegal, who will have to learn much more about medicine if he decides to work in personal injury.

Chapter Format and Features

- Chapter Outline
- Chapter Objectives: Every chapter begins with the objectives of the chapter, so a student will know precisely what he should be learning as he reads the chapter.
- Introduction
- Body of Chapter
  - Marginal definitions: Legal terminology is defined in the text and in the margins to assist with reading comprehension. Marginal definitions are

included even for the cases, as cases often have words a beginning paralegal would not know.

○ Examples and answers within the text: Difficult concepts are discussed and then shown through examples. The examples within the text are substantial and provide the answer with the example.

○ Tables: The elements of the torts are placed into a table, at the beginning of the discussion for the tort, for easier reference.

○ Plain English: The textbook uses plain English to describe complex legal terms and concepts.

○ Case Summaries: Cases have been redacted for the key facts, discussion, and the holding so the paralegal student, who is very busy, does not have to wade through irrelevant material. Each case is directly on point and provides the paralegal student with a variety of old standards and new cases to give the student a well-rounded view of torts.

○ Legal Documents: The textbook provides many of the forms, pleadings, and complaints a beginning paralegal will use in his employment.

■ Professional Contributor Essay: Each chapter has a professional contributor who discusses various topics, such as how to study torts, a career as a paralegal, becoming a paralegal as a second career, networking, life as a new paralegal, document review, or the steps in a lawsuit.

■ Ethics Section: Each chapter also has a section on ethics as it pertains specifically to paralegals.

■ Chapter Summary: At the end of each chapter is a concise chapter summary, along with key words, so students will know the legal language they should be learning.

■ Key Terms: Key words from the chapter are placed together at the end of the chapter.

■ Review Questions: The review questions are basic questions to determine whether the student read the chapter, and the exercises are more in-depth applications of the concepts of the chapter, so the student can apply what he has learned.

■ Web Links: Every chapter has web links related to the subject matter in the chapter or to tort law in general.

■ Exercises: The exercises are in-depth fact scenarios where the student must apply what he has learned. Exercises also include the use of the Internet and whenever possible tie the concepts of torts law to real life. For instance, the Consumer Product Safety Commission is discussed in the context of products liability. The CPSC has regulations for pacifiers, which are included in this book, and which the student is required to read and apply.

Supplemental Teaching Material

■ Sample Syllabus
■ Additional Websites/Using the Internet for Legal Research

- Each Chapter:
  - *Summary*
  - *Outline*
  - *Further Exercises*
  - *Answers to Review Questions*
  - *Answers to Exercises*

One of the best features of this book is the combination of so many examples, with answers, included in the Plain English text, along with further, more-detailed exercises at the end of the chapter. The answers to these exercises are included in the Instructor's Manual. The book focuses on the elements and defenses of the different torts and then uses numerous fact situations to illustrate and reinforce the concepts.

- Using the Appendices
  - Additional Medical Information
- Test Bank with sample test questions for chapters 1-16
- Sample Exams
  - Mid-Term: true-false, multiple choice, short answer, and essay questions
  - Answer Key to Mid-Term
  - Final: true-false, multiple choice, short answer, and essay questions
  - Answer Key to Final
- Further Reading List and Bibliography
- On CD
  - PowerPoint Slides

Emily Lynch Morissette

September 2008

Acknowledgments

This was my first book and I simply could not have accomplished it without the help of so many dedicated people. Thank you especially to Betsy Kenny, Developmental Editor, and Dave Herzig, Acquisitions Editor, for bringing this book to fruition. Thank you to Sue Sullivan, Program Director at the University of San Diego's Paralegal Program for vouching for my ability to write such a work!

Again, thank you to the professional contributors to this book: Brian Decerda, Doreen Vega, Bonnie Arms, Nicole Winn, Rami Haddad, Annie Parrish, Michael Frazier, Vanessa Lu, Josh Davis, Carole Mahn, Jennifer Mashini, Don Garcia, Anthony Matson, Barbara Bing, Irena Ainza, Laura Glennon, Theresa Labban, and Olga Gonzalez. Your contributions added a special touch to this work.

I had particular help from two former students who helped me research this book: Lise Bretton and Dorota James, thank you.

Additional thanks to the reviewers of this book. You offered so many wonderful suggestions in improving this first work.

Thank you to the National Institute of Arthritis and Musculosketetal and Skin Diseases (NIAMS) and the National Heart, Lung, and Blood Institute, of the National Institutes of Health, for allowing the use of their reprinted diagrams.

Doy gracias por Blanca Gonzalez. Se ayudame con las cosas al dentro de la casa y entonces yo tengo tiempo para escribir.

Finally, thank you to my husband, Gregg Morissette, for supporting me through the seemingly never-ending writing sessions.

Foreword

How to Be a Successful Paralegal Student
By Michael Frazier, Paralegal

In order to be a successful paralegal student there are a variety of factors that must be considered. While there is no single right way to approach an education, the factors that determine a student's level of success can generally be categorized as attendance, attention, participation, and studying. Every student has his own methods and learning curves, which makes determining the right formula for any one student quite difficult. The following are my suggestions on the aforementioned categories of success.

Attendance is the first and most obvious step toward being a successful student; in order to be successful you have to attend class. However, there is more to attendance than just showing up. A successful student will arrive early and be prepared for the day's lecture or activity. This not only shows a desire to learn but allows for time to get organized before the start of the lecture. Though it should go without saying, it is worth mentioning the importance of attending every class session. There is vital information discussed in every lecture and missing one could make a noticeable difference, not only in the class grade but in the workforce as well. If it is necessary to miss a class, arrange to copy the notes of another success-oriented student.

Once class starts, pay attention. For many students, it has been quite some time since they were last in school. Remembering how to stay attentive for a long period of time can be a daunting task at first. The best way to maintain focus is through taking notes. Even if printed notes are provided by the instructor, taking down notes of what is discussed in the lecture may provide added information that is not in the handouts or textbooks. Additionally, since learning is such an individualized process, taking down personally significant notes will increase the likelihood of being successful.

Another way to maintain focus, other than note taking, is to participate in class discussions and activities. Contributing to class discussions is a litmus test for both the student and professor to gauge whether the material is being absorbed and retained. Participation can also bolster confidence and help students to understand the material more thoroughly. Also, learn from other students' participation. Most of the time students will have the same questions and struggle in the same areas of the material. The instructor's interaction with each student then becomes quite valuable to the class as a whole, whether as a clarification for similar confusion or as a reinforcement of the fundamentals.

The most important tool for success is to study. There is much to be done outside of class in order to be a successful student. Assignments and required readings should be completed BEFORE the start of class. Being punctual with assignments is a fundamental aspect of being successful in school as well as in the workforce. Having required readings done is necessary in order to participate in class discussions, take accurate and meaningful notes, and staying current with lectures and activities. Most course material builds from beginning to end with the fundamentals being taught first, then more difficult concepts coming later. As the concepts become more complex, students who have not kept up with the assignments and readings will find themselves slipping further behind. It is recommended to spend two hours studying and reviewing outside of class for every one hour spent in class. While this is not a hard and fast rule, it serves to show the dedication and commitment that is required to be a successful student.

There is no specific model for being a successful paralegal student. Nevertheless, all successful students share many of the same practices. They all attend class, take meaningful notes, participate in class discussions and activities, and spend a good amount of time outside of class studying and preparing. Using these fundamental categories will put any student on the path to success!

Personal Injury and the Law of Torts for Paralegals

Introduction to Torts and Negligence

"The precepts of the law are these: to live honestly, to injure no one, and to give everyone his due."[1]

Chapter Outline

Chapter Objectives

- Define a tort
- Explain the difference between a criminal cause of action and a tort cause of action
- Identify the major sources of tort law
- Discuss the public policy behind tort law
- Discuss how negligence is different from other types of torts

---

1. Justinian I, *Justinian Code*, A.D. 533.

- Define negligence
- Introduce the four elements of negligence
- Explain why unavoidable accidents are not negligence
- Contrast gross negligence with normal negligence

1.1 Introduction

Defining a tort is difficult because tort law keeps evolving and adding new types of lawsuits under the category of "tort." When reading the definition, pay attention to what types of law a tort is not (for example, a crime). The sources of tort law are common law, statutes, Restatements of Torts, constitutional law, and administrative law. Public policy shapes the laws making up tort law. Therefore, it is important to understand some of the public policy objectives behind tort law. This chapter defines negligence and compares negligence to intentional and strict liability torts. Negligence is the most likely type of tort you, as a paralegal, will work on. Thus, negligence is covered at the beginning of this book.

To better understand negligence, you should learn what a prima facie case of negligence is. The plaintiff must have a prima facie case of negligence to bring a negligence lawsuit. This chapter lays out a prima facie case of negligence, which consists of four elements. Each of these elements is then further discussed in its own chapter. Unavoidable accidents are also addressed in this chapter to compare them with negligence. A defendant will not be found negligent for unavoidable accidents. In contrast to negligence, gross negligence is a particularly egregious, or severe, type of negligence.

1.2 Definition of a Tort

Defining exactly what a tort *is*, is difficult in part because the definition of a tort constantly changes as society evolves.

> New and nameless torts are being recognized constantly, and the progress of the common law is marked by many cases of first impression, in which the court has struck out boldly to create a new cause of action, where none had been recognized before. . . . The law of torts is anything but static, and the limits of its development are never set. When it becomes clear the plaintiff is entitled to legal protection against the conduct of the defendant, the mere fact a claim is novel will not of itself operate as a bar to the remedy.[2]

Tort
a wrong done by one person (A) to another (B) that results in injury to the other person (B) or his property, and involves obtaining monetary compensation for the injury or damage.

The word "**tort**" has Latin and French roots. In Latin, tortus means twisted and in French, the word translates into English as "wrong." A tort is a wrong done by one person (A) to another (B) that results in injury to the other person (B) or his

---

2. *Prosser and Keeton on the Law of Torts* §1, 3 (W. Page Keeton et al. eds., 5th ed., West 1984).

Tortfeasor
the person who causes the harm, also known as the defendant.

Defendant
the party from whom compensation is sought for the injury or damage.

Injunction
an order from a court telling the defendant to refrain from or stop performing certain act(s).

property, and involves obtaining monetary compensation for the injury or damage. A **tortfeasor** is the person who causes the harm. A tortfeasor is also referred to as the defendant. A **defendant** is the party from whom compensation is sought for the injury or damage.

A tort is a civilly addressed wrong, rather than a criminally addressed wrong. Nor is a tort a contract. Typically, a tort must be an injury that can be compensated for monetarily, although there are some nonmonetary remedies as well, such as an injunction. An **injunction** is an order from a court telling the defendant to refrain from or to stop performing certain act(s). Injunctions are normally granted when money will not adequately solve a problem, such as a person building construction that crosses from his property line onto his neighbor's property.

What is the Standard of Proof in a:

Tort Case?	Criminal Case?
Preponderance of the Evidence* *(also known as more likely than not)	Beyond a Reasonable Doubt

Plaintiff
the person who files the lawsuit.

Prosecutor
the person who brings and pursues a criminal action against a criminal defendant on behalf of the government.

Who brings the lawsuit is another way in which torts and crimes are different. In general, the wronged individual brings the tort lawsuit and is called the **plaintiff**. A plaintiff is the person who files the lawsuit. A crime harms the public at large and is prosecuted by the government in criminal court. With a criminal case, a **prosecutor**, as a representative of the government, brings the case against the defendant. The prosecutor works for the government, not the victim of the crime. Thus, an individual brings a tort case, but the "People," represented by the prosecutor, bring a criminal case.

Who is the Plaintiff in a:

Tort Case?	Criminal Case?
An individual	The People, represented by the Prosecutor

Assault
an act committed with the intent to cause another person to be apprehensive he is going to be harmfully or offensively touched, which does cause the other person to be apprehensive.

Battery
a harmful or offensive contact with a person, caused by the defendant's intent to cause the harmful or offensive contact.

Some acts can be both a crime and a tort, such as in the cause of assault and battery. As you will learn in Chapter 9, an **assault** is an act committed with the intent to cause another person to be apprehensive he is going to be harmfully or offensively touched, which does cause the other person to be apprehensive. **Battery** is harmful or offensive contact with a person, caused by the defendant's intent to cause the harmful or offensive contact. The government might prosecute the defendant in criminal court for an assault and battery, and the victim of the assault and battery might sue the defendant in civil court for monetary damages.

Working in Criminal Law
By Irene Ainza

My career at the District Attorney's ("DA") Office resulted from a chance meeting with a county recruiter while accompanying my husband to a job fair. I took the opportunity to work for the DA to satisfy my curiosity. I was intrigued to find out more about the process and people whose decisions define the rules which govern our society's behavior.

I have seen first hand the challenges on prosecutors and judges to effect change in the life of a criminal through rehabilitation, but we cannot forget the innocent victims whose lives have been affected. Their stories are tragic and often heartbreaking. Through the collective efforts of prosecutors, investigators, paralegals, and support staff, we make a difference. It is our duty, as public servants, to see justice served and we have a huge responsibility to our citizens to make sure the guilty are held accountable for their actions.

I am proud to tell people that I work for the District Attorney's Office.

What is the purpose of a:

Tort Case?	Criminal Case?
Compensation to the plaintiff	Punishing the defendant
Justice	Justice
Deterrence	Deterrence

Torts include negligence, personal injury, and medical malpractice, along with many other areas addressed by this book. The injured party is typically looking for monetary damages to make him whole again.

1.3   Sources of Tort Law

There are several sources of tort law, such as common, statutory, constitutional, Restatements of Torts, and administrative law. (See Figure 1.1)

Figure 1.1

Sources of Tort Law

Source of Tort Law	Definition
Common Law	Hundreds of years of courts' written decisions, applying the law to the facts.
Statute	A law passed by a legislature; typically prohibiting conduct
Restatement of Torts	A secondary authority, while not technically law, is often relied upon by courts to reach decisions.

Constitution	Body of law creating the judicial, executive, and legislative branches of government, as well as providing for basic rights of citizens.
Administrative	Law handed down from administrative agencies, such as workers' compensation.

a. Common Law

Common law
hundreds of years of judicial law making; started in England and then carried over to the United States of America.

Common law is derived from the hundreds of years of judicial law making. Common law is law made by judges through cases. Case law is common law. In general, common law started in England and then carried over to the United States of America, with one state as an exception. Louisiana was settled by both the French and the Spanish, so its common law differs from the rest of the United States. This exception illustrates why it is always important to research the specific law of the state a case is in. Each state has its own courts, and thus, each state's laws will differ from each other's. Each of the fifty states has at least slightly differing views on tort law. This text is a general guideline to tort law and additional research is necessary to determine the specific rules in a particular state.

Courts are supposed to follow statutes (see below) where there are statutes on certain topic matters, but even when there are statutes, unanswered questions remain. The courts must step in and answer those questions through case law. Much of tort law is derived from case law and this text includes major cases affecting the law of torts.

b. Statutory Law

Statutory law
law made by politicians.

Legislatures pass statutes on behalf of the people. Thus, **statutory law** is law made by politicians. Statutes are constitutions, Acts of Congress, state laws, and county or city ordinances. The vehicle code in your state is statutory law. An example of a statute is the following California vehicle code statute. The statute states a person who operates a motor vehicle must have proof of insurance in the amount of $15,000.00 per person, $30,000.00 per accident.

> Proof of financial responsibility when required by this code means proof of financial responsibility resulting from the ownership or operation of a motor vehicle and arising by reason of personal injury to, or death of, any one person, of at least fifteen thousand dollars ($15,000), and, subject to the limit of fifteen thousand dollars ($15,000) for each person injured or killed, of at least thirty thousand dollars ($30,000) for the injury to, or the death of, two or more persons in any one accident, and for damages to property (in excess of seven hundred fifty dollars ($750)), of at least five thousand dollars ($5,000) resulting from any one accident. Proof of financial responsibility may be given in any manner authorized in this chapter.[3]

---

3. Cal. Veh. Code Ann. §16430 (2008).

Primary authority
the most persuasive type of legal authority; includes statutes and is the first place a paralegal should look to answer a legal question.

Annotated statutes
statutes along with references to cases that interpret the statutes.

Statutes of limitations
the time frame in which a tort lawsuit can be brought.

Restatement of Torts
a set of reference books on the principles of tort law which many courts refer to when formulating decisions.

Constitutional law
law consisting of the constitution, the amendments to the constitution, and all the cases interpreting the constitution.

Administrative law
law handed down from the administrative agencies that are part of the executive branch (e.g., presidential branch) of our government.

Statutes are **primary authority**. Primary authority is the first place a paralegal should look to answer a legal question. Primary authority is the most persuasive type of legal authority. Sometimes a statute will be interpreted by a court. **Annotated statutes** are statutes along with references to cases interpreting the statutes.

Many tort statutes are related to products liability and medical malpractice statutes. **Statutes of limitations**, or the time frames in which different tort lawsuits can be brought, are also statutes. Much of the rest of tort law is not made up of statutes.

c. Restatements of Torts

The **Restatements of Torts** are a reference set of books outlining the different principles of torts. The Restatements of Torts are published by the American Law Institute ("ALI"). The ALI is made up of judges, attorneys, and legal scholars. While the restatement is not binding on a court of law, many courts refer to the Restatement (Second) of Torts when formulating their decisions. Therefore, the Restatements, while not law themselves, have an important impact on tort law.

The Restatement (Second) of Torts is still the most widely used restatement, though the Restatement (Third) of Torts is gaining popularity. The "Second" in the Restatement (Second) of Torts stands for the second edition. The "Third" in the Restatement (Third) of Torts stands for the third edition. The Restatement (Third) of Torts addresses products liability, which is broad and complex enough to warrant several volumes in and of itself. In this textbook, products liability is discussed in Chapter 12.

d. Constitutional Law

Constitutional law consists of the Constitution, the amendments to the Constitution, and all the cases interpreting the Constitution. Constitutional law is the highest source of law in the United States of America. If the Constitution does not address a particular issue, then the individual states may address those particular issues. Constitutional law has an impact on tort law, in particular through the First Amendment regarding free speech. Freedom of speech has a big impact on whether a plaintiff can sue for defamation.

e. Administrative Law

Administrative law is law handed down from the administrative agencies that are part of the executive branch (e.g., presidential branch) of our government. Administrative law influences only certain parts of tort law, in particular workers' compensation. Most states have a workers' compensation board that hears workers' compensation cases. Workers' compensation is discussed in Chapter 14.

Administrative agencies at a state or national level can make rules, which are administrative law. Examples of federal administrative agencies are the Environmental Protections Agency ("EPA"), the Internal Revenue Service ("IRS"), and the Social Security Administration ("SSA"). Administrative law governs conflicts arising between people or business entities and an administrative agency. The rules govern administrative hearings and are particular to each administrative agency.

1.4   The Public Policy Objectives Behind the Law of Torts

One purpose of tort law is to impose liability on people who commit wrongs. The motivation for this purpose is fairness. Who should fairly pay for the plaintiff's injury? Fairness demands the plaintiff be restored, as closely as possible, to the position she was in before she was injured. Society does not want injured persons to have to rely on the government to support them while recovering because this imposes the costs of the plaintiff's injury on taxpayers. Thus, the goal of tort law is, in part, to make a defendant pay for the cost, rather than have the plaintiff resort to governmental assistance.

Tort lawsuits can act as a deterrent to wrongdoers. If a potential defendant knows he could face paying money for his wrongful actions, this may discourage him from taking wrongful actions. Thus, our society is safer if it deters people from taking injurious action.

A third purpose of tort law is to allocate or distribute losses. Who is in the best position to bear the cost? The plaintiff who was injured or the defendant who injured the plaintiff? Take the example of a defective product. Typically, the cost is placed upon the manufacturer or seller of the defective product, rather than upon the user of the defective product. Part of this analysis looks at whether the cost of taking precautions to avoid the accident was cheaper than the cost of the accident. If it was cheaper for the defendant to take a precaution, then the defendant may be in the better position to have prevented the accident and should thus be responsible for the accident.

Tort law helps establish minimum standards of conduct among society. It holds people responsible for their actions, even negligent actions, such as an automobile accident. One characteristic almost all torts share is that torts involve behavior which is not a benefit to society.

1.5   Categories of Torts

Negligence
actions that cause unreasonable risks of harm to another person.

The three main types of torts are negligence, intentional torts, and strict liability. (See Figure 1.2) This chapter introduces negligence and the following chapters discuss each element of negligence in detail. **Negligence** involves actions that cause unreasonable risks of harm to another person.

Individuals need to use reasonable care to avoid injury to another. With negligence, the defendant failed to use reasonable care to avoid causing injury to another person. Negligence is different from intentional torts because negligence does not require intent to commit a wrong. Negligence equates to carelessness. An example of negligence is a car accident.

Intentional tort
the defendant acts with the intent to cause the injury or with substantial certainty the injury will occur.

In an **intentional tort**, the defendant wants to cause an injury or is substantially certain the injury will occur as a result of the defendant's action. Intentional torts to people include assault, battery, false imprisonment, intentional infliction of emotional distress, fraud, misrepresentation, invasion of privacy, defamation, and malicious prosecution. Intentional torts to persons are discussed in Chapter 9. Intentional torts to property include conversion, trespass to land, and trespass to chattels/personal property. Intentional torts to property are discussed in Chapter 10.

Figure 1.2

Types of Torts

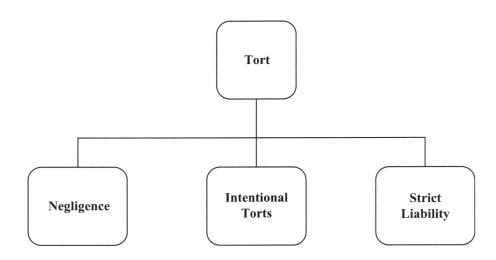

Strict liability
a tort where fault is not the issue; conduct which has liability imposed upon it even when there was no intent or negligence in committing the conduct.

With **strict liability**, fault is not the issue. Some types of conduct have liability imposed upon it even when there was no intent or negligence. Some types of activities are unreasonably dangerous to undertake no matter how much care is exercised in undertaking them, such as using explosives. Strict liability is different from negligence because no matter how careful the tortfeasor was, the tortfeasor will still be responsible under strict liability. Strict liability is discussed in Chapter 12.

1.6   Prima Facie Case of Negligence

Prima Facie
Latin term meaning "on its face."

To make a negligence claim (or any tort claim), a plaintiff must have a prima facie case. **Prima facie** is a Latin term meaning, "on its face." On its face, the case looks like negligence. The four separate prima facie elements of negligence, each of which will be addressed in its own chapter, are duty (Chapter 2), breach of duty (Chapter 3), causation (Chapter 4), and damages (Chapter 5). (See Figure 1.3)

Figure 1.3

The Elements of Negligence

The Elements of Negligence:

Duty	The defendant must owe a duty to the plaintiff.
Breach	The defendant must have breached the duty to the plaintiff.
Causation	Causation is the connection between the defendant's act and the resulting injury to the plaintiff.
Damages	Damages are the plaintiff's monetary damages, which can include missing time from work and medical expenses.

Chapter 1 Introduction to Torts and Negligence

9

Each tort has elements, whether the tort is a negligent, intentional, or strict liability tort. In order to win a tort case, each element must be proven. To see if the plaintiff can meet each element, apply the facts of the case to each element. For negligence, the plaintiff must show duty, breach, causation, and damages. The plaintiff will draft a cause of action, or claim, alleging those elements, as in the following example.

Example: Cause of Action for Negligence

- Defendant owed a legal duty of due care to Plaintiff.
- Defendant breached that legal duty to the Plaintiff.
- Plaintiff has been injured by said breach.
- The detriment caused to the Plaintiff was caused by Defendant's breach of duty.
- Plaintiff has suffered damages, due to Defendant's breach, in $_____ amount.

1.7 Unavoidable Accidents

Proximate cause
an uninterrupted sequence which causes an injury and without this cause, the injury to the plaintiff could not have happened.

Unavoidable accident
a freak accident, not caused by the defendant.

An unavoidable accident is not negligence and a defendant will not be liable for an unavoidable accident. An unavoidable accident is "an event not proximately caused by the negligence of any party to it."[4] **Proximate cause** is an uninterrupted sequence that creates an injury. Without this cause, the injury to the plaintiff could not have happened. The **unavoidable accident** must be caused by a physical condition, such as the weather, and not the people involved in the accident. Another way of stating an unavoidable accident is it is a freak accident. An unavoidable accident occurs despite precautions taken to prevent it. Some accidents are simply no one's fault, and thus, there will be no liability for them.

1.8 Gross Negligence

Gross negligence
the failure to exercise care or to act with so little care as to show indifference to the safety of others.

Gross negligence is much greater type of negligence than regular negligence. Remember, regular negligence is normally caused by careless behavior. Gross negligence occurs when a person acts recklessly or with a willful disregard for another person's safety. Gross negligence is the failure to exercise care or to act with so little care so as to show indifference to the safety of others. Gross negligence raises the presumption that the defendant acted with a conscious disregard to the safety others. An example of gross negligence is flying a plane when intoxicated. If a defendant flies a plane while intoxicated, the defendant is consciously disregarding the safety of others.

4. *Dallas Ry. & Terminal Co. v. Bailey*, 151 Tex. 359, 370, 250 S.W.2d 379, 385 (1952).

E   T   H   I   C   S

Model Rules of Professional Conduct Law Firms and Associations

Rule 5.3 Responsibilities Regarding Nonlawyer Assistants

With respect to a nonlawyer employed or retained by or associated with a lawyer:

(a) a partner, and a lawyer who individually or together with other lawyers possesses comparable managerial authority in a law firm shall make reasonable efforts to ensure that the firm has in effect measures giving reasonable assurance that the person's conduct is compatible with the professional obligations of the lawyer.

(b) A lawyer having direct supervisory authority over the nonlawyer shall make reasonable efforts to ensure that the person's conduct is compatible with the professional obligations of the lawyer. . . .[5]

Attorneys are responsible for the work product of paralegals. Attorneys who supervise paralegals are required to ensure a paralegal is fulfilling the attorney's ethical obligations. A paralegal must review the ethical obligations of attorneys under the Model Rules of Professional Conduct because these ethical duties apply to paralegals as well. These legal ethical obligations are not necessarily the same as moral ethics. The legal ethical obligations are not always commonsensical; therefore, a paralegal must review the rules to assure compliance with the rules.

Chapter Summary

A tort is a civil wrong wherein the victim of the tort is compensated, usually in the form of monetary damages. The person committing the wrong is known as the tortfeasor. Major sources of tort law include common law and statutory law. Common law is made up of cases rendered by judges. Statutory law is written by legislators. Although not technically law, the Restatements of Torts help guide judges in making decisions.

There are many different purposes behind tort law, perhaps the most important purpose is determining who should pay for an injury. One public policy is the government should not have to pay for the injury caused by a private defendant. As between the injured and the injurer, the law holds the injurer is typically in a better position to pay for the costs of the injury.

The three major areas of tort law are negligence, intentional torts, and strict liability. Negligence is the failure to utilize reasonable care so as to avoid causing injury to other people. In essence, negligence is an accident. Negligence consists of four elements: duty, breach, causation, and damages. Each of these elements must be proven by the plaintiff for the plaintiff to win his case. Intentional torts occur when a tortfeasor has the intent to injure another person or another person's property. Strict liability is imposed without regard to fault.

---

5. Model R. Prof. Conduct 5.3 (ABA 2004).

Unavoidable accidents are accidents caused by nature and are freak accidents. The defendant will not be held liable for these accidents. In contrast to unavoidable accidents is a defendant's gross negligence. Gross negligence is worse than regular negligence. Gross negligence is acting with a disregard for other people's safety.

Key Terms

- Administrative Law
- Annotated statutes
- Assault
- Battery
- Case law
- Civil law
- Common law
- Constitutional law
- Conversion
- Criminal law
- Defamation
- Defendant
- False imprisonment
- Fraud
- Gross negligence
- Harm
- Injunction
- Injury
- Intentional infliction of emotional distress
- Intentional tort
- Invasion of privacy
- Libel
- Malicious prosecution
- Medical Malpractice
- Misrepresentation
- Monetary damages
- Negligence
- The "People"
- Personal Injury
- Plaintiff
- Prima facie
- Primary authority
- Products liability
- Proximate cause
- Prosecutor
- Restatement of Torts
- Statute
- Statute of limitations
- Strict liability
- Tort
- Tortfeasor
- Trespass to chattels
- Trespass to land
- Unavoidable accidents

Review Questions

- What is a tort?
- Who is the plaintiff in a tort case? Who is the plaintiff in a criminal case?
- What is the purpose of tort law?
- How is tort law made?
- What are the differences between tort and criminal law?
- How are Restatements related to tort law?
- What are the elements that comprise negligence?
- How is an unavoidable accident different from typical negligence?
- How is gross negligence more extreme than regular negligence?

Web Links

- In general, the Cornell University's website is excellent for researching legal issues. The website, http://library.lawschool.cornell.edu/, has the United States Code, Federal Rules of Civil Procedure, U.S. Supreme Court opinions, other Federal Court opinions, and also includes state laws by topic. It is currently one of the best free sites for obtaining law, but depending upon future donations, it may or may not stay free. To specifically search this website for recent opinions on tort law, go to http://www.law.cornell.edu/supct/search/search.html?query=tort+injury+negligence/. For an overview of tort law look at the following section: http://www.law.cornell.edu/wex/index.php/Tort/.

- The United States Government Printing Office's website is located at http://www.gpoaccess.gov/. Congressional bills are cataloged here from 1993 on. The Supreme Court's website is actually hosted by GPO Access. The Code of Federal Regulations and United States Code can be accessed from this website.

- LexisNexis offers a free service at www.lexisONE.com that will provide you with United State Supreme court cases, and some federal and state cases.

Exercises

- Determine where your local county courthouse is physically located and determine whether the courthouse has a website. If the courthouse has a website, research the records you can obtain from the website.

First Element of Negligence: Duty

. . . [L]et us dare do our duty as we understand it.[1]

Chapter Outline

Chapter Objectives

- Define the general rule on duty
- Discuss the unforeseeable plaintiff
- Determine when a duty arises
- State the legal ramification of when a duty arises
- Explain why some relationships cause a higher standard of care

2.1 Introduction to Duty

The first element of negligence is duty. Determining whether the defendant owed the plaintiff a duty of care is necessary to determine whether the defendant is negligent. The duty people normally owe each other is a duty of reasonable care to

---

1. Abraham Lincoln, *Address at Cooper Union*, New York (February 27, 1860).

avoid injuring one another. Reasonable care is discussed further in Chapter 3. The duty of reasonable care is not owed to all people; to determine to whom a duty is owed, the scope of duty must be looked at. Next, in order for a defendant to have a duty, the injury must also be foreseeable.

The general rule is people are *not* legally required to help others. However, if there is a special relationship, such as parent-child or employer-employee, then the parent or employer has a duty to help the child or employee.

Finally, negligence per se is an act that is obviously negligence on its face or an act in violation of a statute. In understanding negligence per se, it is important to read examples of negligence per se.

2.2   The First Element of Negligence: Duty

Duty
an obligation for a person to meet a certain standard of care.

Duty of reasonable care
the duty to exercise the same care a reasonably prudent person under similar circumstances would to avoid or lessen the risk of harm to others.

In order for negligence to exist, the defendant must have owed the plaintiff a duty. A **duty** is an obligation for a person to meet a certain standard of care. Every person is under a duty to use reasonable care not to injure other people. The **duty of reasonable care** is the duty to exercise the same care a reasonably prudent person under similar circumstances would exercise to avoid or lessen the risk of harm to others. Reasonable care, and what this type of care constitutes, will be discussed in more detail in Chapter 3. In general, the duty of reasonable care applies to all people at all times.

Example of Failing to Use Reasonable Care

If a pedestrian is walking on the sidewalk, she is under a duty to look around and make sure she does not bump into another pedestrian. If she were reading a book and knocked another pedestrian off the sidewalk and into traffic because she was not looking, then she would not be exercising her duty of reasonable care.

The duty of reasonable care is the minimum duty owed to other people. A defendant could assume a higher level of duty than reasonable care. However, some classes of people (such as children) have lesser levels of duty than reasonable care. Other ways of referring to duty of reasonable care are the standard of ordinary care, the standard of due care, and/or the reasonably prudent person standard.

2.3   Scope of Duty

Scope of duty
the people to whom one has a duty.

Scope of duty refers to the people to whom one has a duty. A person does not owe everyone in the world a duty to act reasonably. If Janet is skiing down an Aspen, Colorado mountainside, she has a duty to the people below her to not run into them. However, Janet does not owe a duty to skiers in Switzerland. Her movements while skiing in Aspen should not affect skiers in Switzerland. The question of whom a duty is owed to is determined by looking at foreseeability.

Foreseeability
how much something can be known before it occurs.

Foreseeable risk
a risk a reasonable person could have anticipated.

Foreseeability is the question of how much something can be known before it occurs. The issue of foreseeability is assessed prior to — not after — the injury. The defendant owes the plaintiff a duty to act reasonably if the defendant's conduct created a foreseeable risk to the plaintiff. A **foreseeable risk** is one a reasonable person could have anticipated.

Using the skiing example from above, if Janet suddenly swerved on the Aspen, Colorado hillside, without checking behind or beside herself to make sure she was not cutting someone off, it is foreseeable she could have cut off another skier and caused a collision. However, a defendant is not expected to avoid risks that cannot be foreseen. Thus, foreseeability limits the scope of the duty owed to other people. The foreseeability of a potential injury is a good factor to use in imposing a duty upon a defendant.

This theory is also called the foreseeable plaintiffs theory. Was it reasonably foreseeable the plaintiff would be injured as a result of the defendant's conduct? An unforeseeable plaintiff would therefore be someone who a defendant could not have reasonably anticipated would be harmed by her actions.

Example of an Unforeseeable Plaintiff

Janet is skiing and cuts off another skier. The skier is injured and Anton, a volunteer paramedic, is called into work to help the skier off the mountain. Anton was eating lunch before he was called into work. He left his lunch on the kitchen counter, uneaten. Anton's roommate comes home eight hours later and sees the food on the kitchen counter, but no Anton. Anton is still working on getting the skier off the mountain. Anton's roommate thinks Anton left the food for him, so he eats it. The roommate develops food poisoning. The injury to the roommate was not a foreseeable injury: therefore Janet will not be legally responsible for the roommate's food poisoning. Note: it might have been foreseeable if an injury had happened to Anton while rescuing the skier.

2.4　Duty to Act or Failure to Act

Commission
an act.

Omission
a failure to act.

A defendant can usually only be found negligent for his **commissions** or acts. If a person acts, the person has a duty to use reasonable care to avoid injuring anyone else. An example of a commission is driving at dangerous speeds and causing an accident. Typically, however, a person is not responsible for a failure to act, also known as an **omission**. In general, a person does not have a legal duty to help another person. Whether a person has a moral duty to help another person is another issue. This general rule holds true even when a person can render help without causing injury to himself. "The fact that the actor realizes or should realize that action on his part is necessary for another's aid or protection does not of itself impose upon him a duty to take such action."[2] One of the justifications given for this rule of

2. Restatement (Second) of Torts Section 314 (1965).

law is if a bystander were to attempt to help a victim, then the victim might actually be placed into a worse situation.

Example of Failing to Act

Charlene is standing in line at the cafeteria when she notices someone in front of her drop his tray, spilling food all over the floor. Charlene walks around the food, but does nothing to pick the food up. Cynthia, who was standing behind Charlene, does not see the spilled food and slips on it. Did Charlene owe Cynthia a duty of care? No. Charlene does not have a duty to act, so she does not owe Cynthia a duty of care.

However, if a special relationship with the victim exists, then a defendant can be found responsible for failing to act to protect another against the negligent and/or intentional actions of third parties. Some of these special relationships include the relationship among family members, the relationship between a common carrier and passenger, the relationship between a correctional institute and a prisoner, and the relationship between an employer and employee. For example, if a prisoner becomes ill, it is the responsibility of the prison to make sure the prisoner receives medical care, as the prisoner is unable to do so herself.

However, a person can also have a duty, depending upon a special relationship, to prevent someone from committing a tort. This most frequently occurs when one person takes over the care of another with "dangerous propensities."[3] The police have a duty, when the police stop drunken drivers, to get those drivers off the road.[4]

In addition, a psychiatrist, whose patient specifically makes a physical threat towards someone else, has a duty to warn the potential victim. This is the subject matter of the next case. Since this is your first torts case, here are some tips to help you read the case effectively.

Studying Torts
By Vanessa Lu, Paralegal

For torts, it is important for the student to be able to read a case, understand the rules applied [meaning be able to apply those rules to a different set of facts], and the adaptations of those rules. Torts involve applying the rule of law to the facts and students must show the professor how the facts and rules work together. On the final, the professor will probably give a [new] fact scenario and ask the rule of law. It is the student's responsibility to analyze the fact pattern in terms of the rules given.

---

3. Restatement (Second) of Torts Section 319.
4. *Irwin v. Town of Ware,* 467 N.E.2d 1292, 1302 (Mass. 1984).

Pay particular attention, in the following case, to the discussion regarding when a legal duty arises. A court decides whether there is a legal duty based upon "(1) the magnitude of the risk, (2) the relationship of the parties, (3) the nature of the attendant risk, (4) the opportunity and ability to exercise care, (5) the foreseeability of the harm, and (6) the policy interest in the proposed solution."

Carol K. Munstermann, Representative of Jodi Sue Rowe, Deceased v. Alegent Health — Immanuel Medical Center and Hudson Hsieh, M.D.

Supreme Court of Nebraska
271 Neb. 834,
716 N.W.2d 73 (2006)

Marty Nuzum murdered his estranged girl friend, Jodi Sue Rowe. . . . The question presented . . . is whether Nuzum communicated a serious threat of physical violence against Rowe to the defendants, Nuzum's treating psychiatrist and health care facility, such that the defendants were under a duty to take reasonable precautions to prevent the murder. . . .

Nuzum was admitted to inpatient care at Alegent on February 4, 2002, when he checked himself in, suffering from depression and suicidal ideations. Nuzum was treated by Hsieh. Nuzum had been treated as an inpatient at Alegent in January 2002, following a suicide attempt. Nuzum had attempted suicide in 1990, 2000, and 2002.

When Nuzum was admitted in January 2002, he was not found to exhibit any homicidal tendencies. Nuzum was examined and observed for homicidal risk factors during his week as an inpatient, and none were found. When Nuzum checked himself back in on February 4, he again denied having homicidal ideations or assaultive behavior.

Nuzum was seen by Hsieh on February 5, 2002, with several medical students present, and one of those students, Rebecca Gurney (who is now a medical doctor), transcribed notes for Hsieh.

> Pt was last here . . . 1 mo ago. . . . Pt is having problems with girlfriend — she doesn't understand depression. . . . Pt was thinking of hurting girlfriend also since she is hurting him. Girlfriend doesn't want to talk about his depression. She won't participate here. . . .
>   Pt doesn't trust himself. . . .

Nuzum was discharged from Alegent on February 7, 2002. His discharge summary indicated that he had recovered from this instance of severe depression and that his suicidal ideations had subsided. Nuzum had been consistently assessed during his stay for homicidal risk factors, and none were present. . . .

On February 12, 2002, Nuzum murdered Rowe after she came to his apartment to retrieve a set of car keys. Neither Hsieh nor any employee of Alegent acted to warn Rowe or law enforcement that Nuzum might be dangerous.

The primary issue at trial was how to interpret the indication in Gurney's February 5, 2002, notes that Nuzum "was thinking of hurting girlfriend also since she is hurting him." Gurney testified that she never thought that Nuzum was a threat to Rowe. Gurney said that Nuzum had been consistently worried about losing Rowe, because he thought Rowe would leave him because of his depression. Gurney testified that after Nuzum said he was thinking of hurting Rowe, the medical students and Hsieh went into more detail with Nuzum to find out what he meant by the remark. Gurney recalled that Nuzum was asked why he would want to do that, what he meant by it, and [Nuzum] kind of said that he was saddened and frustrated that his girlfriend was not more supportive of him while he was depressed. Kind of wanted him to snap out of it, just be happy, and that really made him feel bad. And because of that, [Nuzum] wanted her to feel the same pain that he was feeling.

Gurney said that when she wrote that Nuzum was thinking of hurting Rowe, it indicated "an emotional hurt. . . ."

Hsieh explained that Nuzum's statement that he was "thinking of hurting girl-friend" was actually in response to direct questioning from Hsieh. [W]e also talk about — well, now, would it hurt when you injure yourself, and we talk about that he has overdosed on the antifreeze two years before, a month ago. Why would you do that? That was my question. And what were you thinking about when you were injecting the — ingesting the antifreeze? And that's when he said I was thinking about hurting her because she hurt me so much.

Hsieh further explained that this was a common question asked of a suicidal patient — what the patient was thinking when making a suicide attempt. According to Hsieh, Nuzum said that Rowe had hurt him, "[s]o when he took an overdose, it's a way to say — see what you are doing to me? You're hurting me." Hsieh explained that when Nuzum said Rowe was hurting him, Nuzum meant that she had hurt him in an emotional way, [a]nd so this is how [Nuzum] presented to let her know and get back at her by his taking an overdose. And we did also talk about it on different occasions. And not why would anybody go that far to do it, and his response was it worked. Every time he attempted suicide, she came back to him. . . .

The threshold inquiry in this appeal is whether the defendants owed the plaintiff a legal duty. . . . This is our first opportunity to address the issues most closely associated with the California Supreme Court's decision in *Tarasoff v. Regents of University of California.* . . . In *Tarasoff,* the plaintiffs alleged that the defendant therapist had a duty to warn their daughter of the danger posed to her by one of the therapist's patients. The court recognized the general rule that a person owes no duty to control the acts of another. But the court adopted Restatement (Second) of Torts §315 at 122 (1965), which provides:

> There is no duty so to control the conduct of a third person as to prevent him from causing physical harm to another unless
>
> (a) a special relation exists between the actor and the third person which imposes a duty upon the actor to control the third person's conduct, or
>
> (b) a special relation exists between the actor and the other which gives to the other a right to protection.

Applying this exception, the *Tarasoff* court held that the relationship between the patient and her therapist was sufficient to support the imposition of an affirmative duty on the defendant for the benefit of third persons. The *Tarasoff* court further held that a therapist's duty to act arises when the therapist determines, or pursuant to the standards of the profession should determine, that the patient presents a serious danger of violence to another. . . .

In the wake of *Tarasoff*, however, the California Legislature restricted the scope of *Tarasoff* liability. See Cal. Civ. Code §43.92. . . . Under §43.92(a), a duty to warn of and protect from a patient's threatened violent behavior arises only "where the patient has communicated to the psychotherapist a serious threat of physical violence against a reasonably identifiable victim or victims." Several states have enacted similar statutes based upon California's example, including Nebraska. . . .

Neb. Rev. Stat. §71-1,336 (Reissue 2003) provides, in relevant part:

(1) There shall be no monetary liability on the part of, and no cause of action shall arise against, any person who is licensed or certified [as a mental health practitioner] for failing to warn of and protect from a patient's threatened violent behavior or failing to predict and warn of and protect from a patient's violent behavior except when the patient has communicated to the mental health practitioner a serious threat of physical violence against himself, herself, or a reasonably identifiable victim or victims. (2) The duty to warn of or to take reasonable precautions to provide protection from violent behavior shall arise only under the limited circumstances specified in subsection (1) of this section. The duty shall be discharged by the mental health practitioner if reasonable efforts are made to communicate the threat to the victim or victims and to a law enforcement agency.

. . . [T]he defendant in this case, Hsieh, is a psychiatrist — a physician. . . . The Nebraska statutes specify the scope of *Tarasoff* liability for psychologists and "mental health practitioners," but do not provide corresponding statutory language for psychiatrists. . . .

The defendants now assert that in the absence of a specifically applicable statute, they owed no duty at all to warn and protect Rowe. The plaintiff insists that in the absence of a statute, the case should have been tried as an ordinary medical malpractice action. We do not accept either of these contentions. . . .

The threshold inquiry in any negligence action, including those involving a duty to warn and protect, is whether the defendant owed the plaintiff a duty. . . . A duty is defined as an obligation, to which the law will give recognition and effect, to conform to a particular standard of conduct toward another. . . . Whether a legal duty exists for actionable negligence is a question of law dependent on the facts in a particular situation. . . . When making that determination a court considers (1) the magnitude of the risk, (2) the relationship of the parties, (3) the nature of the attendant risk, (4) the opportunity and ability to exercise care, (5) the foreseeability of the harm, and (6) the policy interest in the proposed solution. . . .

Given our prior endorsement of Restatement (Second) of Torts §315 (1965), and the clearly articulated public policy expressed in §§71-1,206.30(1) and 71-1,336, we conclude that in some circumstances, a special relation may exist between a psychiatrist and patient which imposes a duty upon the psychiatrist to warn or protect a reasonably identifiable victim when a patient has communicated a serious threat of physical violence against that potential victim. However, given the Legislature's decision to limit *Tarasoff* by enacting §§71-1,206.30(1) and 71-1,336, we find that the limitations set forth in those sections should also be applied to psychiatrists. . . .

Risk-utility test
a formula used to weigh the risk versus the utility of conduct, to determine whether the conduct was negligent.

Moreover, the analysis of California's identical statutory language, from which the Nebraska statutes were derived, has revealed that the statute is based upon public policy concerns to which our familiar **risk-utility test** is applicable. . . . The intent of limiting a *Tarasoff* duty to situations in which the patient communicates a serious threat of physical violence was not to overrule *Tarasoff*, but, rather, to preempt an expansive ruling that a therapist can be held liable for the mere failure to predict potential violence by his or her patient. . . . The statutory language represents an effort to strike an appropriate balance between conflicting policy interests. . . .

On the one hand, the need to preserve a patient confidence recognizes that effective diagnosis and treatment of a mental illness or an emotional problem is severely undermined when a patient cannot be assured that a statement made in the privacy of his or her therapist's office will not be revealed. . . . On the other hand is the recognition that under limited circumstances, preserving a confidence is less important than protecting the safety of someone the patient intends to harm . . . In other words, the statutory language is the result of balancing risk and utility, considering the magnitude of the risk, relationship of the parties, nature of the risk, opportunity and ability to exercise care, foreseeability of the harm, and public policy interest in the proposed solution. . . .

Considering our risk-utility test, and the relevant public policy determinations made by the Legislature, we conclude the same duty should be required of psychiatrists as is required of psychologists and other mental health practitioners. We hold . . . that a psychiatrist is liable for failing to warn of and protect from a patient's threatened violent behavior, or failing to predict and warn of and protect from a patient's violent behavior, when the patient has communicated to the psychiatrist a serious threat of physical violence against himself, herself, or a reasonably identifiable victim or victims. The duty to warn of or to take reasonable precautions to provide protection from violent behavior shall arise only under those limited circumstances, and shall be discharged by the psychiatrist if reasonable efforts are made to communicate the threat to the victim or victims and to a law enforcement agency. . . .

a. Families

The law holds that parents and children have a special relationship. If a child is injured, then a parent has a duty to exercise reasonable care to help the child. This is true no matter who caused the injury to the child. If a parent sees his child start to drown, the parent has a duty to attempt to rescue the child. In addition, a parent has a duty to his child to protect her from foreseeable harm. This relationship changes the general rule of not having to act.

b. Jobs

The law holds there are special relationships between employers and employees. Employers have a duty to protect their employees from dangers the employees are not able to protect themselves from while working. If an employee is injured on the job, then the employer has a duty to exercise reasonable care to aid the employee. This is true no matter who caused the injury to the employee. However, if the special relationship did not exist, the employer would not have to aid the employee as long as the employer did not injure the employee.

2.5 Negligence Per Se

Negligence per se
negligence in and of itself; conduct which is inarguably negligence because it is either a violation of a statute or it is obvious reasonable care was not used.

Negligence per se means negligence in and of itself. Negligence per se is often a violation of a statute. (See Figure 2.1.) Frequently state legislatures write statutes prescribing the appropriate standard of care in certain instances. A reasonable person would obey those standards of care, unless there is a legally compelling excuse not to obey the standard of care set by statue.

Negligence per se by statute is particularly applicable when discussing standards of care while driving. Most states have vehicle codes. For instance, in some states, the person who rear-ends another is presumed to be at fault for the accident. Per those statutes, a driver has a duty of care not to rear-end another driver. Certain statutes are designed to provide safety standards. In the above example, the vehicle code section promotes drivers' safety.

Other Examples of Safety Statutes

Speed limits are other examples of safety statutes. However, speeding does not necessarily establish negligence, although it could. If Marie was driving on a highway, going 100 miles per hour in a 65 miles per hour zone, and she lost

Figure 2.1

Elements of Negligence Per Se

Elements of Negligence Per Se:	Short Explanation of Elements:
There was a viable safety statute at the time the plaintiff was injured.	"Viable statute" means the statute has to apply to the facts of the case.
The defendant violated the statute.	The act that caused the injury must be the same type of act prohibited by the statute.
The defendant's violation was the cause of the plaintiff's injuries.	Causation is discussed in Chapter 4.
The statute was created for safety reasons.	The harm that occurred as a result of the accident must be the same type of harm that was supposed to be prevented by the statute.
The statute was designed for a certain class of people, and the plaintiff falls into the class.	To show a breach of duty, the statute violated must have been enacted to protect the class of people the plaintiff falls into.

control of her car, causing an accident, then her negligence in causing the accident may be presumed. Police reports help establish negligence per se by indicating a violation of a vehicle code section and by stating the violation was the cause of the accident.

If a tortfeasor violates one of these statutes, then this is negligence in and of itself, or negligence per se. The concept of negligence per se allows plaintiffs to establish a prima facie case of negligence. Negligence per se carries the presumption of the defendant's duty and breach. A **presumption** is an inference tending to prove the truth of or a falsehood of a fact. Presumptions can be rebutted to show a person acted as she should have, even if she acted in violation of statute. If a defendant cannot rebut the presumption or show a valid excuse for not complying with the statute, then the defendant may be found negligent.

Presumption

an inference tending to prove the truth of or falsehood of a fact.

Violations of a statute can be excused. The Restatement (Second) of Torts describes the situations in which a violation of statute might be excused. Section 288A states a violation of statute might be excused due to incapacity, lack of knowledge, not being able to comply, emergency, or when complying would cause greater harm than not complying. An example of incapacity is a minor who is not held to the same level of care as an adult. Lack of knowledge is a very specific excuse. For instance, it is not sufficient for a driver to tell the police officer who pulls him over for speeding that he did not know the speed limit. The driver is supposed to know the speed limit. However, if driver's tire becomes flat after she starts to drive it and it is not yet noticeable, she did not have the knowledge about the flat tire necessary to pull over. The statute states a driver should not drive on flat tires, but since the driver did not have knowledge of the flat tire, she is excused from violating the statute.

Sometimes circumstances make it impossible to comply with statutes. Drivers should drive on the right side of the road in the United States. But what if there is construction and a driver is not able to stay in the right lane? If a cop pulls the driver over and writes the driver a ticket for not driving in the right lane, the driver has the excuse of the cones making it impossible to comply. The impossible circumstances excuse is similar to the excuse of an emergency. In an emergency, a person is not expected to use the same degree of care as they would under normal conditions. If a dog darts in front of a car, and there is no crosswalk, then the driver might be justified in swerving to avoid the dog, even though a driver should not swerve without signaling. Finally, if complying with a statute would be more dangerous than violating the statute, then this qualifies an excuse for violating the statute.

Example of Negligence Per Se

Sal was involved in a motor vehicle accident at Glendale Avenue and the intersection of Trent Road. Felix was operating the other motor vehicle. There was a heavy rain and Sal had his headlights and wipers on at the time of the accident. Felix was driving north on Trent Road, in the number one lane. Sal was driving west on Glendale Avenue. Felix entered the intersection on a red light for his direction of travel. Sal saw Felix, but did not have time to apply his brakes. The front of Sal's truck ran into the right side of Felix's truck.

The police report identified Felix as the cause of the accident. In Felix' deposition he stated he was in an unfamiliar area at the time of the accident; he was driving in heavy downpour but his windshield wipers were only going at medium speed; and he was searching for a driveway when he entered the intersection. Felix also stated in his deposition that he paid the citation for running the red light.

There are a number of examples of negligence in the above example. What are they? What is the example of negligence per se? Examples of negligence: Felix was unfamiliar with the area, only had his wipers going at medium speed during a downpour, and was not paying sufficient attention to the road. The example of negligence per se is Felix running the red light.

Vega v. Eastern Courtyard Associates illustrates negligence per se in real life. The court is concerned whether the statute, in this case building code, is meant to regulate this type of defendant and this type of injury. Vega was injured when she tripped and fell on a ramp leading into a building. She alleged the slope of the ramp exceeded the slope allowed in the building code and thus the slope was negligent per se. The case goes through the process of Figure 2.2 to determine whether there has been negligence per se.

Figure 2.2

Determining Negligence Per Se by Violation of a Statute

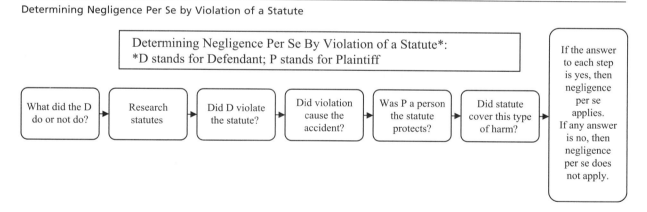

Vega v. Eastern Courtyard Assocs.

117 Nev. Adv. Op. No. 39

. . . We are asked to determine whether the violation of a validly adopted building code provision constitutes negligence per se. We conclude that the violation of a building code provision adopted by a county ordinance is negligence per se if the plaintiff belongs to the class of persons the building code provision is intended to protect, and the injury the plaintiff suffered is of the type the provision was intended to prevent. . . .

On September 10, 1993, appellant Wendy Vega had a scheduled appointment at respondent Eastern Courtyard Associates' medical facility in Las Vegas. While attempting to negotiate a ramp leading to the main entrance, Vega slipped, fell and was injured. Vega commenced suit, claiming Eastern Courtyard was negligent.

. . . Vega argued that Eastern Courtyard, as owner of the premises, had violated a provision of the Uniform Building Code ("UBC"), which had been adopted as part of the Building Code of Clark County. Vega claimed that the slope of the ramp leading into the entrance of the medical complex exceeded the slope allowed under the UBC, and that such a violation constituted negligence as a matter of law, or negligence per se. . . .

Vega . . . raised the theory of negligence per se in her trial brief. Vega proposed that the jury be charged with Nevada Jury Instruction 4.12, which reads:

> There was in force at the time of the occurrence in question [a law] [laws] which read as follows:
>
> > A violation of the law[s] just read to you constitutes negligence as a matter of law. If you find that a party violated a law just read to you, it is your duty to find such violation to be negligence; and you should then consider the issue of whether that negligence was a . . . cause of injury or damage to the plaintiff. . . .

Whether a particular statute, administrative regulation or local ordinance is utilized to define the standard of care in a negligence action is clearly a question of law to be determined exclusively by the court. . . . Although we have never ruled on the applicability of an alleged violation of a building code provision in a plaintiff's negligence action, we have consistently held that the violation of a statute constitutes negligence per se if the injured party belongs to the class of persons that the statute was intended to protect, and the injury suffered is of the type the statute was intended to prevent. In *Barnes v. Delta Lines, Inc.,* we held that where a plaintiff adduced evidence at trial showing that the defendant violated a statute designed to protect a class of persons to which the plaintiff belonged, the district court erred by failing to instruct the jury regarding the negligence per se doctrine. And later, in *Del Piero v. Phillips*, we applied the same analysis to a municipal ordinance. In that case we determined that a violation of the Reno Municipal Code, along with the defendant's failure to yield to pedestrians as required by the "rules of the road," required that the jury be instructed regarding negligence per se. . . .

. . . [W]e conclude that an alleged violation of a provision of the UBC may be utilized as part of a plaintiff's negligence per se theory if the plaintiff belongs to the class of persons that the provision was intended to protect, and the injury suffered is of the type the provision was intended to prevent. We see no reason not to apply the reasoning and analysis we employed in *Barnes* and *Del Piero* to an alleged violation of a building code provision. Other jurisdictions that have addressed this issue are in accord with this ruling.

Accordingly, we hold that if (1) a violation of a building code provision adopted by local ordinance is established, (2) an injured party fits within the class of persons that a particular provision of a building code was intended to protect, and (3) the injury suffered is of the type the provision was intended to prevent, the alleged violation constitutes negligence per se. We also hold that whether an injured party belongs to the class of persons that the provision at issue was meant to protect, and whether the injury suffered is the type the provision was intended to prevent, are questions of law to be determined by the court. . . .

The violation of a building code provision may serve as the basis for an action brought under a negligence per se theory if the plaintiff belongs to the class of persons that the provision was intended to protect, and the injury the plaintiff suffered is of the type the provision was intended to prevent. . . .

E T H I C S

**Model Rules of Professional Conduct
Client-Lawyer Relationship**

Rule 1.4 Communication
  (a) A lawyer shall: . . .
    (2) reasonably consult with the client about the means by which the client's objectives are to be accomplished;
    (3) keep the client reasonably informed about the status of the matter;
    (4) promptly comply with reasonable requests for information. . . .[5]
  (b) A lawyer shall explain a matter to the extent reasonably necessary to permit the client to make informed decisions regarding the representation.

Rule 1.4 requires an attorney to talk or write to his client directly. In addition, the attorney needs to provide the client with the information necessary for the client to make informed decisions on her case. The client needs to receive enough information to be able to participate in the decision-making process on the case in an effective manner.

An attorney cannot allow the paralegal to provide a legal opinion to the client. The attorney can ask the paralegal to provide other information to the client, but only if the attorney still maintains her relationship directly with the client. In addition, the attorney must keep abreast of the information the paralegal is providing to the client. In any event, the attorney is responsible, ethically, for the paralegal's contact with the client.

Chapter Summary

Duty is the first element to prove in negligence. Duty is an obligation for a person to meet a standard of care. Normally, this standard of care is the reasonable person standard. Reasonable care is the minimum amount of care owed to others. A duty of reasonable care is owed when an injury to a person is foreseeable. Foreseeability refers

---

5. Model R. Prof. Conduct 1.4 (ABA 2004).

to whether an injury to a plaintiff could have been anticipated. When a person's conduct creates a foreseeable risk of harm to another, then the duty of reasonable care arises.

People have duties when they act, but normally a person does not have a duty to act. For instance, if a person were choking in a restaurant, a fellow diner is not under an obligation to perform the Heimlich maneuver. A person does not have a duty to act unless there is a special relationship between the parties, such as the relationship between family members and employers and employees. A parent does have a duty to help a child and an employer does have an obligation to help an employee. These are two exceptions to the general rule that there is not a duty to act.

Negligence per se is conduct that is inarguably negligence because it is either a violation of a statute or it is obvious reasonable care was not used. There are five elements to proving negligence per se by violation of a statute. The statute must apply to the facts of the case. The defendant must have violated the statute and the violation must have been the cause of the injury to the plaintiff. Finally, the statute must have been enacted for safety purposes and the plaintiff must be a person who was meant to be protected by the statute.

Key Terms

- Breach of duty
- Commission
- Due care
- Duty
- Foreseeability
- Foreseeable plaintiff
- Negligence per se

- Omission
- Ordinary care
- Reasonable care
- Scope of duty
- Special relationship
- Unforeseeable plaintiff

Review Questions

- Define legal duty.
- What is the relationship between duty and foreseeability?
- Do you owe a duty to a person you do not know?
- What is a special relationship? What are some examples of a special relationship?
- What is negligence per se? How is negligence per se used to prove a defendant behaved negligently?

Web Links

- www.abanet.org/. This is the website of the American Bar Association. This website is geared towards lawyers, but is still useful for a paralegal because it contains "Lawlink." The best way to describe Lawlink is as a legal research jump

station. If in need of more websites or suggestions
research without Lexis-Nexis or Westlaw, this is tl

 ■ http://www.abanet.org/tips/home.html/. This is th
practice section of the American Bar Association. l
publications and continuing legal education classes
paralegal, go into personal injury law, you will need
the field.

 ■ www.alllaw.com/. This site is divided in part by topic and includes personal injury
articles. One article of particular importance is "What To Do After an [Auto]
Accident."

Exercises

■ Look up special relationships, other than families and jobs, that apply in
your state.

■ Bruce claims he is a doctor. He is not a doctor licensed by any state in the
United States of America. He sent away for medications on the Internet and
he "prescribes" them to his patients. He provides the medication to his patients
for a small fee, so the patients do not have to be inconvenienced by going to
the pharmacy. One of his patients takes the drugs he dispensed to her and she
suffers an adverse reaction. Is Bruce negligent per se?

■ Theo decides to start the New Year off right, by getting out his rusty bicycle
and riding it to work in order to exercise away his holiday meals. He has not
ridden in years and when he goes to put his bike helmet on, it does not fit. He
shrugs it off and goes biking anyway. On the way to work, a car comes very
close to Theo in the bike lane, forcing him off the road. He and his bike take
a tumble and he hits his head on a rock. If Theo attempts to sue the driver for
his injuries, what issues could the driver raise?

■ For the following hypothetical, assume your state has a mandatory disclosure law
for reporting sexually transmitted diseases ("STD"). The reporting requirement is
placed upon medical professionals and facilities. Clarence goes to a free clinic to
get tested. The test results show he does in fact have an STD. Clarence provides
the free clinic with a list of his recent sexual partners' names and addresses so the
clinic can notify his partners. However, due to budget cutbacks, the past sexual
partners are not notified for two months. Amanda was one of Clarence's past
sexual partners and she contracted the STD from Clarence. One month after
Clarence went to the free clinic, Amanda has sex with a third party, Ruben, who

6. http://www.abanet.org/tech/ltrc/lawlink/; American Bar Association's Lawlink: The Legal Research Jump-
station (last accessed Dec. 22, 2007).

contracts the same STD from her. Did the free clinic have a duty of care to Ruben? What about to Amanda?

- Oliver is leaving his house one morning when he sees his neighbor Eileen backing out of her garage. Richard, Eileen's two-year old, is playing in the yard, close to the car Eileen is backing up. Oliver starts to wave or scream, but then decides to do nothing. Eileen, who does not have a back-up camera on her car, runs over Richard. Eileen sues Oliver for failing to warn her about Richard being behind her car. Did Oliver have a legal duty to warn Eileen her son was playing behind her car?

- Gary is a child of five. He likes to climb trees, and one day he gets stuck in a tree. Kenneth, an adult, is passing by and sees Gary stuck in the tree. Kenneth decides to scale the tree and bring Gary down. However, when Kenneth is about to reach Gary, Gary becomes scared and climbs even higher in the tree. While reaching for the next limb of the tree, Gary slips and falls 15 feet. If Gary's parents sue Kenneth for negligence, how would the parents phrase the complaint?

C H A P T E R

3

Second Element of Negligence: Breach of Duty

The Common Law of England has been laboriously built upon a mythical figure — the figure of "The Reasonable Man."[1]

Chapter Outline

3.1 Introduction to Breach of Duty
3.2 Breaching the Duty of Reasonableness
3.3 The Learned Hand Formula
3.4 The Restatement (Second) of Torts' Risk-Utility Test
3.5 Good Samaritan Law

Chapter Objectives

- Discuss the standard of care, which is reasonableness
- Define breach of duty as unreasonableness
- Identify the criteria used to determine reasonableness
- Explain how a defendant's acts do not meet the standard of care
- Illustrate the Learned Hand Formula
- Point out the limited protection for Good Samaritans

3.1 Introduction to Breach of Duty

Breach of duty is the second element of negligence. Chapter 2 already covered the duty owed to others. To be found negligent, the defendant must also breach the duty he owed to the plaintiff. The breach of duty is a failure to comply with a certain standard of care. The standard of care is usually reasonableness.

---

1. Sir Alan Patrick Herbert, 1890-1971, Uncommon Law (1935) 1.

What is considered reasonable care depends upon the circumstances. You will learn what reasonableness is and who judges whether the conduct was reasonable. There are two main formulas used in determining whether there has been a breach of the duty of reasonable care: the Learned Hand formula or the Restatement's risk-utility formula. While the two tests are similar, you should note the slight differences between the two tests. Finally, the chapter discusses laws protecting Good Samaritans.

3.2   Reasonableness

Reasonable person standard
a test to evaluate whether the defendant acted as a reasonable person, under similar circumstances and with similar abilities, would have acted.

Breach of duty
the use of unreasonable actions towards a third party to whom the defendant owes a duty of care.

Reasonable person
an ordinary and prudent person who avoids injuring other people by using reasonable care.

The duty, discussed in Chapter 2, is to act with care to avoid injuring other people. A defendant's conduct will be compared to the conduct of a reasonable defendant under similar circumstances. When applying the **reasonable person standard**, ask whether a reasonable person, under similar circumstances and with similar abilities to the defendant, would have acted in the same manner as the defendant did. If the defendant's conduct does not meet the conduct of a reasonable defendant under similar circumstances, then the defendant has **breached his duty**. If the trial is a jury trial, then the jury will decide whether a defendant acted as a reasonable person. If the trial is a bench trial, then the judge will make the determination.

A reasonable person is often compared to a good citizen.[2] The reasonable person is one who always looks where he is going. A **reasonable person** is an ordinary and prudent person who avoids injuring other people by using reasonable care. A reasonable person does not create unreasonable risks of injury to another person.

Is, however, a reasonable person expected to be a "perfect" person? No. A perfect person would never cause an accident. A reasonable person does cause accidents, but those accidents are not caused by his own carelessness. Hindsight is not used to determine whether the defendant acted as a reasonable person. The knowledge available to the defendant at the time of the incident is used to determine whether the defendant acted as a reasonable person. If hindsight were used to evaluate reasonableness, almost all accidents would be negligence because hindsight provides much greater knowledge after the accident than the knowledge available before the accident.

A reasonable person is held to have the same knowledge as a layperson, or the same knowledge common to the general public. An example of knowledge a reasonable person knows is icy roads require more caution when driving upon them than clear roads. Jurors can use their life experiences to evaluate whether a defendant acted as a reasonable person. The reasonable person standard is an objective standard, meaning it is not a standard determined by whether a particular defendant personally thought his behavior was reasonable. It is not enough that a defendant acted as well as he was able to — the question is what a reasonable person would have done under the circumstances at the time.

If a defendant has certain skills, such as a carpenter, then the defendant is compared to a reasonable carpenter in similar circumstances. Similarly, if the defendant

---

2. Prosser & Keeton, Section 32 at 174.

has a physical or mental disability, the defendant is compared to a reasonable person with the same disability. For instance, consider a blind person who comes over to a plaintiff's home: using his cane, the blind man accidentally strikes a table and knocks over a priceless vase. Would a reasonable person who was also blind have caused the same accident?

Another Example of a Reasonable Person with a Disability

A deaf person, driving down the road, fails to pull over to the side of the road because he cannot hear the sirens of the ambulance. The deaf person would not be acting negligently. However, once the ambulance becomes visible, the deaf person needs to act as a reasonable person with sight would. That is, he needs to be aware of the flashing lights and pull over.

Standard of care
the amount of care required under the particular circumstances.

There are different standards of care for children. A **standard of care** is the amount of care required under the particular circumstances. Previously, the standard has been reasonable care. In general, children are not expected to act like reasonable adults, but rather like other children of similar age. An exception to the general rule is children who participate in adult activities; they are expected to act with the same care as an adult. Outside of adult activities, a child will be held to using the same amount of care a reasonable child (of similar age) would use under similar circumstances. A second exception to the general rules is children under five years old are considered too young to act with care at all.

3.3 Learned Hand Formula

Learned Hand formula:
formula which weighs the burden of taking precautions versus the likelihood and potential severity of an injury, to determine whether the conduct was negligent.

In determining whether a defendant has acted reasonably, it is helpful to have a formula. The **Learned Hand formula** is named after Judge Learned Hand. The formula is one way of determining whether there has been a breach of the legal duty of care. This formula is used to weigh the burden of taking precautions versus the likelihood and potential severity of an injury, to determine whether the conduct was negligent. If the likelihood and potential severity of the injury occurring are small, then the burden of taking the precautions may outweigh the need to take those precautions.

Judge Hand wrote the opinion expressing his formula in *United States v. Carroll Towing Co.*[3] In the *Carroll Towing* case, a barge broke loose from where it was moored in a harbor and caused damage. If a caretaker had been on the barge 24 hours a day, seven days a week ("24/7"), this injury could have been avoided. The question was whether it was negligent not to have a 24/7 caretaker. To answer this, Judge Hand decided to weigh the risk versus the utility. Whether the owner of the barge should have had a 24/7 caretaker is based on three factors, as shown in Figure 3.1.

3. 159 F.2d 169 (2d Cir. 1947).

Figure 3.1

Factors of the Learned Hand Formula

Factors of the Learned Hand Formula:	Short Explanation of Factors:
The likelihood of harm	In the *Carroll Towing* case how likely was it that the barge would break loose?
The severity of the harm	How much damage would the barge cause if it broke loose?
The value of the action performed to reduce the risk of this harm or burden of taking precautions	What is the burden on the owner of having a 24/7 caretaker?

The Learned Hand Formula is abbreviated as B<PL. The B stands for the burden of taking precautions against causing injury. The P stands for the probability someone will be injured and the L stands for how severe the loss will be.

Burden < Probability x Severity of Loss

If the probability of loss multiplied by the gravity of the loss is greater than the burden of taking precautions, then a defendant has a duty of due care (to avoid causing the injury by taking precautions). If the cost of keeping a caretaker for 24 hours a day, seven days a week was cheaper than the cost the barge was likely to cause in damages, then the owner of the barge should have paid for a caretaker.

To illustrate this concept, we need to look at it from a monetary standpoint. A diaper-changing table has a pad on top of it, but the pad is not attached in any way to the top of the table. The probability that babies can fall off the table as a result is extremely high; one in three babies fall off. The top of the changing table is over three feet off the ground and babies have a soft spot on their head, which could be injured in the fall. The injury to a baby could be hundreds of thousands of dollars. The pad could be attached to the table with heavy duty Velcro, which would cost two dollars and fifty cents ($2.50) per changing table. The Learned Hand formula would compel a reasonable person to attach the heavy duty Velcro to the diaper-changing pad. While this is an extreme example, and there are child safety rules already in place through the Consumer Products Safety Act, the Learned Hand formula uses the monetary costs of the risks versus the costs of precautions.

United States v. Carroll Towing Co.

United States Circuit Court of Appeals, Second Circuit
159 F.2d 169 (1947)

. . . The facts, as the judge found them, were as follows. On June 20, 1943, the Conners Company chartered the barge, "Anna C," to the Pennsylvania Railroad

Company at a stated hire per diem, by a charter of the kind usual in the Harbor, which included the services of a bargee, apparently limited to the hours 8 a.m to 4 p.m. On January 2, 1944, the barge, which had lifted the cargo of flour, was made fast off the end of Pier 58 on the Manhattan side of the North River, whence she was later shifted to Pier 52. At some time not disclosed, five other barges were moored outside her, extending into the river; her lines to the pier were not then strengthened. At the end of the next pier north (called the Public Pier), lay four barges; and a line had been made fast from the outermost of these to the fourth barge of the tier hanging to Pier 52. . . . The Grace Line, which had chartered the tug, "Carroll," sent her down to the **locus in quo** [location in question] to "drill" out one of the barges which lay at the end of the Public Pier; and in order to do so it was necessary to throw off the line between the two tiers. On board the "Carroll" at the time were not only her master, but a "harbormaster" employed by the Grace Line. Before throwing off the line between the two tiers, the "Carroll" nosed up against the outer barge of the tier lying off Pier 52, ran a line from her own stem to the middle bit of that barge, and kept working her engines "slow ahead" against the ebb tide which was making at that time. The captain of the "Carroll" put a deckhand and the "harbormaster" on the barges, told them to throw off the line which barred the entrance to the slip; but, before doing so, to make sure that the tier on Pier 52 was safely moored, as there was a strong northerly wind blowing down the river. The "harbormaster" and the deck-hand went aboard the barges and readjusted all the fasts to their satisfaction, including those from the "Anna C" to the pier.

After doing so, they threw off the line between the two tiers and again boarded the "Carroll," which backed away from the outside barge, preparatory to "drilling" out the barge she was after in the tier off the Public Pier. She had only got about seventy-five feet away when the tier off Pier 52 broke adrift because the fasts from the "Anna C," either rendered, or carried away. The tide and wind carried down the six barges, still holding together, until the "Anna C" fetched up against a tanker, lying on the north side of the pier below — Pier 51 — whose propeller broke a hole in her at or near her bottom. Shortly thereafter: i.e., at about 2:15 p.m., she careened, dumped her cargo of flour and sank. The tug, "Grace," owned by the Grace Line, and the "Carroll," came to the help of the flotilla after it broke loose; and, as both had syphon pumps on board, they could have kept the "Anna C" afloat, had they learned of her condition; but the bargee had left her on the evening before, and nobody was on board to observe that she was leaking. . . .

. . . [T]he question arises whether a barge owner is slack in the care of his barge if the bargee is absent.

It appears . . . that there is no general rule to determine when the absence of a bargee or other attendant will make the owner of the barge liable for injuries to other vessels if she breaks away from her moorings. . . . Since there are occasions when every vessel will break from her moorings, and since, if she does, she becomes a menace to those about her; the owner's duty, as in other similar situations, to provide against resulting injuries is a function of three variables:

(1) The probability that she will break away;
(2) the gravity of the resulting injury, if she does;
(3) the burden of adequate precautions.

Locus in quo:
latin phrase meaning the place where the accident occurred.

Possibly it serves to bring this notion into relief to state it in algebraic terms: if the probability be called P; the injury, L; and the burden, B; liability depends upon whether B is less than L multiplied by P: i.e., whether B less than PL. Applied to the situation at bar, the likelihood that a barge will break from her fasts and the damage she will do, vary with the place and time; for example, if a storm threatens, the danger is greater; so it is, if she is in a crowded harbor where moored barges are constantly being shifted about. On the other hand, the barge must not be the bargee's prison, even though he lives aboard; he must go ashore at times. . . . In such circumstances we hold — and it is all that we do hold — that it was a fair requirement that the Conners Company should have a bargee aboard (unless he had some excuse for his absence), during the working hours of daylight.

The following case is a more recent case on breach of duty than *Carroll Towing*. The plaintiff in *Boykin* contended the timing of a traffic light did not leave her enough time to cross the street, and therefore she was injured by the Department of Transportation and Development's ("DOTD") breach of duty to provide enough time to cross the street by timing the traffic lights longer. The Supreme Court of Louisiana uses a risk-benefit analysis, like the Learned Hand formula, to determine the DOTD did not breach its duty of care to the plaintiff. The Supreme Court weighed the benefit to highway safety versus pedestrian safety. The Supreme Court concluded the timing of the intersection was to prevent highway collisions with stopped cars. Compared to the number of pedestrians who crossed the highway at the intersection, the benefit of reducing highway collisions was greater.

Tammie Jo Boykin v. Louisiana Transit Company

Supreme Court of Louisiana
707 So. 2d 1225 (1998)

This is a tort action arising from an accident in which plaintiff, a pedestrian crossing a highway at a controlled T-intersection, was struck by a vehicle that entered the intersection on a red traffic signal. The principal issue is whether the Department of Transportation and Development (DOTD), the lone remaining defendant at trial, was liable for failing to set the cycle for the traffic signal so as to afford pedestrians a longer period of time to cross the highway under the protection of a red signal stopping highway traffic. . . .

. . . [D]aytime accident occurred at the "T" intersection of U.S. Highway 61 and North Howard Avenue in suburban Jefferson Parish. Highway 61 was a main traffic artery for vehicular traffic into and out of New Orleans. At that intersection, which was controlled by a functioning traffic signal, Highway 61 was an east-west divided four-lane highway with an twenty-three-inch-wide median. The posted speed limit was forty-five miles per hour. . . . Located on the south shoulder of the highway was a stop for eastbound transit buses, which picked up and discharged most of the pedestrians who crossed the highway at that point. . . .

The daylight accident occurred in the late afternoon on a clear dry day. Plaintiff was crossing Highway 61 from north to south. . . . She first had to cross the two westbound lanes of Highway 61 and then the two eastbound lanes. As the traffic light turned red for Highway 61 traffic, a vehicle driven by Clyde Lindsey was approaching from plaintiff's left, westbound on Highway 61 in the lane closest to the median. Plaintiff started across the westbound lanes and was struck by the left front of the Lindsey vehicle, which had passed a vehicle stopped for the light in the right lane and entered the intersection on a red light. After the accident, Lindsey told the investigating trooper that the setting sun blinded him and that he ran the red light, but did not know what he had hit. . . .

Plaintiff filed this action against Lindsey, [and] the DOTD. . . .

Plaintiff subsequently died from unrelated causes. Prior to her death, she gave two depositions. . . . When asked to identify problems at the intersection, she complained that it was "too busy", there was no marked pedestrian cross-walk, and the "cars go too fast. . . ."

Plaintiff's counsel asserted several theories of recovery, all of which were based on the DOTD's alleged violations, in several ways, of its duty to provide a signal-controlled intersection that did not present an unreasonable risk of harm for motorists and for pedestrians. This opinion focuses on that duty . . . namely, the DOTD's failure to set the timing of the traffic signal so as to allow pedestrians sufficient time to complete the forty-eight-foot crossing of the highway in which the median was not of sufficient width to provide a safe haven.

. . . [T]he DOTD received frequent complaints about highway motorists' having to stop for a red signal at the intersection when there was no crossing traffic from Howard. . . . [T]he DOTD determined that an actuated [motion-activated] signal would eliminate unnecessary stops for the 24,000 vehicles on the highway at that intersection daily and accordingly would reduce the risks of collisions with unnecessarily stopped vehicles.

With the actuated signal, the light remained green for highway traffic as long as there were no vehicles on Howard. When a vehicle approached on Howard to cross the intersection . . . , the light turned red . . . for highway traffic for a period varying between 10.9 and 20 seconds. Thus the new timing cycle changed the time for pedestrian crossings protected by a red highway signal from sixteen seconds to eleven to twenty-one seconds.

The DOTD did not install a push-button for crossing pedestrians to push to activate the side street green light because studies revealed no significant pedestrian activity at that intersection and no previous pedestrian accidents. The purpose of the DOTD's reducing the time of the red signal for highway traffic was to reduce the significant risk of collisions by highway motorists with stopped vehicles by reducing the number of stops of highway traffic. The DOTD did not consider the reduced time for pedestrian crossing protected by a red highway signal to present an unreasonable risk of harm for pedestrians, since some pedestrians crossed at intersections without traffic lights all along the highway in that area, and there had never been a pedestrian accident or a complaint about difficulty for pedestrians to cross at this particular intersection.

DUTY-RISK ANALYSIS

This negligence case is properly examined under the duty-risk analysis. . . . [The court determines whether there is]

(1) proof that the defendant had a duty to conform his conduct to a specific standard (the duty element);

(2) proof that the defendant's conduct failed to conform to the appropriate standard (the breach element). . . .

Many cases presenting a duty-risk analysis do not adequately distinguish the duty element and the breach of duty element. In a proper duty-risk analysis, it is helpful to identify

(1) the duty imposed upon the defendant by statute or rule of law and
(2) the conduct by defendant that allegedly constituted a breach of that duty.

In the present case, the duty of the DOTD was to design and provide a signal-controlled intersection that did not present an unreasonable risk of harm to motorists and pedestrians. The conduct by DOTD that allegedly constituted a breach of that duty was the failure to set the timing cycle of the signal so as to provide an adequate period of time for a pedestrian to cross the entire highway while the signal was red for highway vehicles.

. . . THE DUTY INQUIRY

There is an almost universal duty on the part of the defendant in negligence cases to use reasonable care so as to avoid injury to another. In some cases, the duty is refined more specifically that the defendant must conform his or her conduct to some specially defined standard of behavior. . . .

The duty at issue in the present case, as previously stated, was the DOTD's duty to design and provide a signal-controlled intersection that did not present an unreasonable risk of harm to motorists and pedestrians. There is no dispute that a duty for the DOTD to conform its conduct to this standard existed in this case.

. . . THE BREACH OF DUTY INQUIRY

The alleged breach of duty in this case was the DOTD's failure to set the signal timing so as to allow pedestrians sufficient time to complete the crossing of the entire highway, in the absence of a median that offered a safe haven. . . .

. . . On the breach issue, the experts presented by the plaintiff opined that there was insufficient protected time for a pedestrian to cross the highway completely and that this deficiency was a breach of the DOTD's duty. They pointed out that a pedestrian walking at four feet per second would take twelve seconds to cross the highway, in addition to the perception and reaction time between the changing of the signal and the pedestrian's beginning to walk. The principal expert, who attempted several crossings in preparing for trial, observed that "the only way I found I could safely go across this intersection is to break the law and pass . . . when the gaps in traffic occur."

The determination of whether the DOTD violated its duty of reasonable care to pedestrians includes balancing the probability and seriousness of any expectable injury with the burden of taking adequate precautions against the risk of such injury and any adverse consequences of such precautions. In making this determination, one must keep in mind the nature of the area (a suburban highway as opposed to a downtown business district street) and the nature of *all* of the risks at the particular intersection.

Prior to the DOTD's installing the signal initially at the intersection, pedestrians presumably crossed the highway without the protection of a red signal for highway traffic by timing their crossings between "gaps in traffic." Moreover, at the intersections one block in either direction, and at numerous other intersections in the area, there are still no traffic control devices which might assist pedestrian crossings by stopping traffic. The signal at the pertinent intersection was installed initially to prevent the risk to vehicular traffic of right angle collisions, and the timing was subsequently changed to prevent the risk of collisions with stopped vehicles. The design change of the timing of the red signal for highway traffic to as little as eleven seconds balanced the benefit to highway traffic safety against concerns for pedestrian safety. Such concerns are significant where there are pedestrian dangers. At this intersection, however, there was a very low volume of pedestrian traffic and a total absence of previous pedestrian injuries.

Of course, there are always risks to pedestrians who must cross the path of vehicular traffic. Under the timing cycle set by the DOTD, an average pedestrian could reach the last of the four lanes while the light was red for highway traffic. However, when the pedestrian has legally entered the fourth lane of the unmarked cross-walk at the intersection, a highway motorist is required to yield the right of way to the pedestrian to complete the crossing. . . .

Finally, a risk-benefit analysis undermines plaintiff's theory and supports the DOTD's design decision. The principal concern of a design engineer in setting the timing cycle at this intersection was to avoid the hazards created by unnecessary stopping of vehicles traveling the busy highway. The longer the red signal for highway traffic, the greater the number of vehicles stopped; and the greater the number of vehicles stopped on the highway, the greater the risk of a collision with a stopped vehicle. A timing design that increased the length of the red signal for highway traffic may have enhanced slightly the safety of the few pedestrians who crossed at that intersection, but clearly would have created greater dangers for the heavy volume of highway traffic. Considering the very low volume of pedestrian traffic . . . and the total absence of any history of pedestrian accidents or complaints at this particular crossing, we conclude that the DOTD was not negligent in its design of the timing cycle for the traffic light cycle at this intersection — that is, the DOTD did not breach its duty to provide a signal-controlled intersection that was reasonably safe for motorists and pedestrians. . . .

3.4   The Restatement (Second) of Torts' Risk-Utility Test

The Restatement (Second) of Torts' Risk-Utility Test
an act is negligent if the magnitude of risk caused by the act outweighs the utility of the act.

The Restatement (Second) of Torts states an act is negligent if the magnitude of risk caused by the act outweighs the utility of the act.[4] This section of the Restatement is stating that a reasonable person looks at the risks of his action versus the utility of his actions. For instance, if a homeowner decides to cut down a tree in his yard, the homeowner must consider whether the tree might fall onto his neighbor's property, causing damage. The magnitude of the risk is judged by the following factors shown in Figure 3.2.

---

4. Restatement (Second) of Torts Section 291 (1965).

Figure 3.2

Judging the Magnitude of Risk

Factors of Restatement of Tort's Risk-Utility Test/Formula	Comparison to the Learned Hand Formula
The social value given by the law to the people or property who might be injured.	The emphasis in the Restatement is on how valued are the people or property that might be injured. The emphasis in the Learned Hand formula is on the burden of taking precautions.
How likely it is the person or property will be injured.	Both formulas determine how likely an injury is.
The extent of the harm.	Both formulas look at how much damage could be done.
The number of persons who will be affected.[5]	The Restatement brings up the number of people who might be injured, while the Learned Hand formula does not have this as a specific factor.

On one hand are the likelihood the harm will occur and the seriousness of the harm. As the chance the harm will occur increases, then so does the utility required to justify the harm.[6] These factors mean the reasonable person looks at how great the potential harm will be. If the risks of a person's behavior are small, then it may be reasonable for the person to take those risks. For instance, using the tree example above, the homeowner measures the tree and the distance from the tree to his neighbor's property. The homeowner has two to three extra feet even after his tree is felled. The risk of damaging the neighbor's property is a lot less than if the homeowner does not have any extra feet. Also, the potential harm is to property, not people. The harm to property is weighed less heavily than the harm to people.

On the other side of the risk-utility test is the burden of reducing the risk. This burden is evaluated by:

1. how important the activity is which the Defendant's conduct is a part of;
2. the usefulness of the conduct towards the end goal;
3. how feasible it would be to use another, cheaper type of conduct.[7]

If there were alternatives to the risky behavior that would have achieved the same result but would have caused less risk, then the defendant will have breached his duty of care.

---

5. Restatement (Second) of Torts Section 293 (1965).
6. *Id.*
7. Restatement (Second) of Torts Section 292 (1965).

3.5 Good Samaritan Law

Good Samaritan
a person who aids another when he is under no legal obligation to help.

As a general rule, a person does not have a duty to help another person in a time of crisis. However, a person does have a duty to not take any actions which will make an emergency situation worse. If someone decides to aid a person, then he is considered to have voluntarily assumed the responsibility of helping the person. If the helper did not use reasonable care to protect the person, the helper can be found liable. A Good Samaritan who tries to help another can find himself paying damages, while a person who looks the other way while passing someone in need suffers no consequences. A **Good Samaritan** is a person who aids another when he is under no legal obligation to help. The general rule gives no incentive under the law to help people in need.

Good Samaritan laws were created to foster a willingness to help one another in a time of crisis. However, the end result is Good Samaritan laws are usually aimed at providing limited liability for off-duty medical professionals who render aid. The majority of states now have Good Samaritan laws protecting doctors at least.

Example of a Good Samaritan Law for Citizens with Emergency Medical Training

To encourage citizens to provide emergency medical services to fellow citizens, no person who has completed a basic cardiopulmonary resuscitation course, and who, in good faith, renders emergency cardiopulmonary resuscitation at the scene of an emergency, shall be liable for any civil damages as a result.

The above example applies to those who have CPR training. Some states also allow people without CPR training to aid another so long as there is no one present who does know CPR. However, most states hold if a person had never had CPR training before, it is not reasonable to attempt CPR. The rationale behind the majority view is if a citizen did not have CPR training and attempted to help a victim, the citizen could potentially make the situation worse. If a citizen does decide to help another, the majority view is he can be liable for acting negligently.

Becoming a Paralegal as a Second Career
By Theresa Labban, Paralegal

I finally went forward with my desire to change careers, and have just graduated with my Paralegal Certificate from an ABA-approved school. I was one of the older students in the Paralegal Certificate Program, at a time when I was a wife and a mother.

My first career was in the engineering field. I got my engineering bachelors degree, and have worked a total of 10 years as a Software Quality Assurance (QA) Engineer in a large corporate environment. As a QA Engineer, I tested computer software applications, which I liked doing.

I continued working full-time after our son was born, but when he was in preschool, I chose to quit working, and was a stay-at-home mom for a few years. I enjoyed the quality time I had with my son, but I missed having the added income and adult interaction.

I saw a career counselor, re-evaluated my interests, and identified some new career options. From those options, I chose the Paralegal profession to be my second career because it aligned with my interests of office management and law.

At first, I got nervous about switching careers. I spoke with, and was encouraged by, a mom who was already working part-time as a Paralegal. I also searched for and found several part-time Paralegal job postings, with job descriptions that appealed to me. This opportunity to work part-time as a Paralegal is what finally propelled me to start the Paralegal Certificate.

Throughout my Paralegal Certificate Program, I realized that there are some skills I used and enjoyed as an engineer that I will also use as a Paralegal. These transferable skills include, for example, thinking logically, paying close attention to the details, analyzing data, and using computer applications. I also found enjoyment in learning new tasks that Paralegals often perform, such as cite checking, legal research, and document organization. The challenge I encountered, however, was adapting my writing style from an engineering style. In general, making the legal argument was difficult for me. During exams, if I did not know the essay topic ahead of time, I felt rushed and often did not perform as well on the essay portion as I would have liked to. I hope that in time, and with practice, legal writing and making legal arguments will get easier.

E T H I C S

Model Rules of Professional Conduct Client-Lawyer Relationship

Rule 1.5 Fees

(a) A lawyer shall not make an agreement for, charge, or collect an unreasonable fee or an unreasonable amount for expenses. . . .

(b) The scope of the representation and the basis or rate of the fee and expenses for which the client will be responsible shall be communicated to the client, preferably in writing, before or within a reasonable time after commencing the representation, except when the lawyer will charge a regularly represented client on the same basis or rate. Any changes in the basis or rate of the fee or expenses shall also be communicated to the client.[8]

The attorney cannot delegate the attorney-client fee agreement to the paralegal. The attorney a paralegal is working for is required to make the fee agreement with the client. The attorney has to communicate with the client about what the legal services will entail. In addition, the attorney has to explain how the fees will be calculated. If the attorney does not sign the fee agreement with the client, there is a potential for the law firm to not be paid.

Ethics Exercise: Overbilling clients is one of the most important ethical issues, though it is seldom talked about. Watch the movie *The Firm* and note how the firm is finally "taken down."

---

8. Model R. Prof. Conduct 1.5 (ABA 2004).

Chapter Summary

The second element of negligence is breach of duty. The duty is one of using reasonable care to avoid injuring others. A defendant has breached this duty if his conduct is not what a reasonable person's conduct under similar circumstances would have been. A reasonable person is a person who always looks where he is going, but not a perfect person. If a defendant has a disability or is a child, then the defendant should have acted like a reasonable defendant with a disability or a reasonable child would have acted under similar circumstances.

There are two formulas for evaluating whether there has a breach of duty. The first is the Learned Hand formula and the second is the Restatement's risk-utility test. Both formulas are very similar. The Learned Hand formula states that the burden of taking precautions is greater than the probability someone will be injured multiplied by the severity of the loss. If the likelihood of the harm occurring and the severity of the harm are outweighed by the burden on the defendant of having to avoid the harm, then the defendant has not breached his duty. The Restatement (Second) of Torts formula states that an act is negligent if the magnitude of the risk caused by the act outweighs the utility of the act.

In general, people do not have a legal duty to aid one another in an emergency. To encourage people to aid one another, some states have enacted Good Samaritan laws. These laws protect the person who aided from being held negligent for injuries resulting from the aid.

Key Terms

- Breach of duty
- Good Samaritan law
- Learned Hand formula
- Locus in quo
- Objective standard
- Reasonable care
- Reasonable person

- Reasonable person standard
- Restatement of Torts Risk-Utility Test
- Standard of care
- Subjective standard
- Unreasonable

Review Questions

- How is it determined whether a breach of duty has occurred?
- What is the reasonable person standard?
- Why is an objective standard better than a subjective standard when assessing the reasonableness of a defendant's conduct?
- What level of knowledge is a reasonable person supposed to have?
- Is a reasonable person a perfect person?
- Explain the Learned Hand formula.

Web Links

- http://blawgsearch.justia.com/ contains over one thousand different blogs of legal professors, attorneys, judges, law librarians, and other legal professionals on a wide variety of legal topics. There are several blogs dedicated to paralegal issues, and over 100 injury and accident blogs.

- www.lawguru.com is a helpful website because a user can look at questions and answers on a variety of legal topics, including torts.

- The following is a good article explaining breach of duty: http://www.weitzlux.com/breachduty_398.html.

Exercises

- A 14-year-old gets into her parents' car with her little sister and drives. The 14-year-old causes an accident. Her little sister and another driver are injured. Will the 14-year-old be liable for the injuries she caused?

- Christine is a property owner. She has a historical home and on her property there is an abandoned well. She places ½-inch thick wooden boards over the well, but does not mark the well, which is level with the surrounding ground. If her friend Heidi comes onto her property and falls through the boards, will Christine be found negligent?

- Anywhere, USA owns and maintains a golf course within its city limits, adjacent to a busy street. The city erects 14-foot fences. However, golfers routinely hit balls over the fence. If a golf ball hits Jason's car, causing an accident, will Anywhere, USA be found negligent to Jason?

Third Element of Negligence: Causation of Injury

To find a fault is easy; to do better may be difficult.[1]

Chapter Outline

Chapter Objectives

- Explain when a defendant's acts are the proximate cause of the plaintiff's injuries
- Introduce cause-in-fact, including the but-for test and substantial factor test
- Introduce joint tortfeasors and contribution
- Define foreseeability
- Discuss the seminal case in causation, *Palsgraf*
- Explain intervening cause
- Illustrate res ipsa loquitur

---

1. Louis Nizer.

4.1 Introduction to Causation

The third element of negligence is causation. A defendant's actions must be the cause of the plaintiff's injury for the defendant to be found negligent. The defendant must be both the actual and proximate cause of the plaintiff's injuries. Actual cause is assessed by using one of two tests: the but-for test or the substantial factor test.

Proximate cause addresses how closely connected the defendant's conduct is to the victim's injuries. The victim's injuries must be foreseeable and there should not be an intervening cause between the defendant's act and the plaintiff's injury.

Finally, res ipsa loquitur is discussed in this chapter because even when a plaintiff cannot prove what caused her injury, she may still be able to recover under this theory.

4.2 Cause-in-Fact

Cause-in-fact
without the defendant's action or inaction, the incident would not have happened.

Actual cause
another term for cause-in-fact.

But-for test
one test for determining the cause-in-fact of an injury; stated as but for the defendant's negligence, the plaintiff would not have been injured.

Sine qua non
also known as the but-for test; a Latin phrase meaning a necessary requirement.

The defendant must have *caused* the plaintiff's injuries to be found negligent, meaning the defendant must have contributed to the plaintiff's injury. The concept of **cause-in-fact** states that without the defendant's action (or inaction), the incident would not have happened. Cause-in-fact is also known as **actual cause**. With actual causation, the defendant's acts were directly related to the plaintiff's injuries.

a. But-for Test

The **"but-for" test** is one way to determine the cause-in-fact of an injury. The but-for test is worded as follows: but for the defendant's negligence, the plaintiff would not have been injured. In other words, without the defendant's negligence would the plaintiff have still be injured? If the answer is no then the defendant was not a cause of the injury. If the answer is yes, then the defendant was a cause of the injury. The but-for test is also called the **"sine qua non"** test. Sine qua non is a Latin phrase meaning a necessary requirement. The defendant's action (or inaction) was a necessary requirement for the plaintiff to be injured. If the defendant's action was not a necessary requirement for the injury to occur, then the defendant was not the cause-in-fact of the injury. Just because the "but-for" test has been satisfied does not mean the defendant's action was the main cause of the plaintiff's injury. In addition to cause-in-fact, the proximate cause of the injury must be evaluated. Proximate cause is discussed later in this chapter. Both cause-in-fact and proximate cause are necessary to prove the defendant caused the injury to the plaintiff.

Examples of the But-For Test

■ Timothy is stopped at a four-way stop. Lee does not see the stop sign at the same intersection. Timothy proceeds into the intersection. Lee does not stop and plows into Timothy. But for Lee running the stop sign, Timothy would not have been injured.

■ Ernie is sitting in the law library, looking at a rare legal manuscript. He pulls out a can of cola he concealed in his backpack and brought into the library. He sips the cola while reviewing the document. When he goes to grab the open can of cola, he accidentally knocks it over, destroying the rare document. But for Ernie knocking over the can of soda, the document would not have been destroyed.

More than one defendant's actions might be the reason why the plaintiff is harmed. Two actions might be necessary for an accident to occur. The but-for test does not require there be only one action that brings about an injury. However, if there is more than one action, then each action must be a but-for cause (necessary cause) of the injury.

The more contributors to an injury and the more events necessary to cause an injury, the less helpful the but-for test is. The but-for test should not be used when there are two or more causes to an injury, either one of which, by itself, would have been enough to cause the injury. For this instance, the substantial factor test needs to be used. The but-for test will work in most instances. Notice the difference between the two tests:

But-for Test	Substantial Factor Test
But for the defendant's negligence, the plaintiff would not have suffered an injury.	Two or more events combine to cause an injury to the plaintiff and each is a substantial factor in causing the injury.

b.   Substantial Factor Test

Substantial factor test
test that asks was the defendant a big contributor in causing the injury to the plaintiff?

Concurrent causes
causes acting together to cause the injury, although each cause by itself would not have caused the injury.

The **substantial factor test** asks the following: was the defendant a substantial factor, or a big contributor, in causing the injury to the plaintiff? The defendant will be liable for the injuries to the plaintiff where the defendant was a substantial factor in causing the injury. The substantial factor test, unlike the but-for test, addresses the issue of concurrent causes. **Concurrent causes** are causes acting together to cause the injury, although each cause by itself would not have caused the injury. If two causes combine into one harm, one which cannot be cleanly divided, then each cause will be considered a substantial factor of the harm. For example, if two fires merge to cause an injury, the test to apply would be the substantial factor test, rather than the but-for test.

The following case is one of the foremost cases on concurrent causation. In *Summers v. Tice*, there were two hunters, who separately fired their guns at the same time in the direction of the plaintiff. The plaintiff was struck in the eye. Which defendant should be held liable for the injury? How can liability be determined? Is it not a fifty-fifty chance whether one defendant or the other shot the plaintiff? The court determined the plaintiff was not in the best position to determine which defendant was at fault. Therefore, the court ruled the burden of proof shifted to the defendants to show each of them was not liable. The burden of proof requires a party, in this case, the defendant, to prove a fact in dispute between the parties. The defendants could not prove which defendant was more liable, so both were found liable. The ruling prevented the defendants, who were both negligent, from avoiding responsibility for their negligence.

Warning

Note that *Summers v. Tice* is not the law in all states. A paralegal student needs to research whether his jurisdiction follows the *Summers* rule or the but-for test.

Charles Summers v. Harold Tice

Supreme Court of California
33 Cal. 2d 80; 199 P.2d 1 (1948)

Plaintiff's action was against both defendants for an injury to his right eye and face as the result of being struck by bird shot discharged from a shotgun. . . . [O]n November 20, 1945, plaintiff and the two defendants were hunting quail on the open range. Each of the defendants was armed with a 12 gauge shotgun loaded with shells containing 7 1/2 size shot. Prior to going hunting plaintiff discussed the hunting procedure with defendants, indicating that they were to exercise care when shooting and to "keep in line." In the course of hunting plaintiff proceeded up a hill, thus placing the hunters at the points of a triangle. The view of defendants with reference to plaintiff was unobstructed and they knew his location. Defendant Tice flushed a quail which rose in flight to a 10-foot elevation and flew between plaintiff and defendants. Both defendants shot at the quail, shooting in plaintiff's direction. At that time defendants were 75 yards from plaintiff. One shot struck plaintiff in his eye and another in his upper lip. . . .

It is argued by defendants that they are not joint tort feasors, and thus jointly and severally liable, as they were not acting in concert, and that there is not sufficient evidence to show which defendant was guilty of the negligence which caused the injuries — the shooting by Tice or that by Simonson. . . .

. . . [B]oth defendants were negligent and "That as a direct and proximate result of the shots fired by defendants, and each of them, a birdshot pellet was caused to and did lodge in plaintiff's right eye and that another birdshot pellet was caused to and did lodge in plaintiff's upper lip." . . . [T]he negligence of both defendants was the legal cause of the injury . . . both were responsible. . . . [T] court was unable to ascertain whether the shots were from the gun of one defendant or the other or one shot from each of them. The one shot that entered plaintiff's eye was the major factor in assessing damages and that shot could not have come from the gun of both defendants. It was from one or the other only.

It has been held that where a group of persons are on a hunting party, or otherwise engaged in the use of firearms, and two of them are negligent in firing in the direction of a third person who is injured thereby, both of those so firing are liable for the injury suffered by the third person, although the negligence of only one of them could have caused the injury. . . . It is said in the Restatement: "For harm resulting to a third person from the tortious conduct of another, a person is liable if he . . . (b) knows that the other's conduct constitutes a breach of duty and gives substantial assistance or encouragement to the other so to conduct himself, or (c) gives substantial assistance to the other in accomplishing a tortious result and his own conduct, separately considered, constitutes a breach of duty to the third person." . . . Under subsection (b) the example is given: "A and B are members of a hunting party. Each of them in the presence of the other shoots across a public road at an animal, this being negligent as to persons on the road. A hits the animal. B's bullet strikes C, a traveler on the road. A is liable to C." . . . An illustration given under subsection (c) is the same as above except the factor of both defendants shooting is missing and joint liability is not imposed. It is further said that: "If two forces are actively operating, one because of the actor's negligence, the other not because of any misconduct on his part, and each of itself is sufficient to bring about harm to another, the actor's negligence may be held by the jury to be a substantial factor in bringing it about. . . ."

When we consider the relative position of the parties and the results that would flow if plaintiff was required to pin the injury on one of the defendants only, a requirement that the burden of proof on that subject be shifted to defendants becomes manifest. They are both wrongdoers — both negligent toward plaintiff. They brought about a situation where the negligence of one of them injured the plaintiff, hence it should rest with them each to absolve himself if he can. The injured party has been placed by defendants in the unfair position of pointing to which defendant caused the harm. If one can escape the other may also and plaintiff is remediless. Ordinarily defendants are in a far better position to offer evidence to determine which one caused the injury. . . .

c. Joint and Several Liability

As discussed earlier, an injury can be caused by the negligence of one or more people. The defendants causing the same injury are dubbed joint tortfeasors. **Joint tortfeasors** are two or more defendants who all contributed through their actions to cause the injury to the plaintiff. **Joint and several liability** is two or more defendants being held responsible for the plaintiff's injury. Each defendant is responsible for paying the full amount (100%) of the damages to the plaintiff, even though the plaintiff cannot receive more than 100% of the award due.

Joint tortfeasors
two or more defendants who all contributed through their acts to cause the injury to the plaintiff.

Joint and several liability
two or more defendants being held responsible for the plaintiff's injury.

Example of Joint Tortfeasors

An example of joint tortfeasors is codefendants, defendant Todd and defendant Norma, who are jointly liable for a settlement. The plaintiff could sue each defendant separately or both defendants together. Thus, the plaintiff could sue defendant Todd and receive 100% of her settlement, $100,000, from Todd. The plaintiff could, in the alternative, sue defendant Norma and receive 100% of her settlement, $100,00, from Norma. Finally, the plaintiff could jointly sue Todd and Norma and receive 100% of her settlement, $100,000, altogether.

The plaintiff cannot obtain more than $100,000 no matter how she decides to sue Todd and/or Norma because this would allow the plaintiff to amass more than her fair share.

Joint and several liability gives the plaintiff a greater chance of being compensated, especially when one of the defendants is insolvent. Joint and several liability allows the injured plaintiff more likelihood of obtaining a full monetary settlement, but does not give her multiple settlements in excess of 100%.

d. Contribution

If the plaintiff decides to litigate against only one of several defendants, the one defendant would initially be responsible for 100% of the monetary award. **Contribution** is when the defendant who paid the plaintiff the entire settlement amount seeks at least partial reimbursement from the other defendants who also caused the injury. In short, contribution refers to reimbursement. The defendant who pays the entire settlement or judgment should be able to recuperate part of the money through contributions from the other tortfeasors.

Many states base their contributions laws upon the Uniform Contribution Among Tortfeasors Act.[2] The Act states:

> 1(a) . . . [W]here two or more persons become jointly and severally liable in tort for the same injury to person or property . . . , there is a right of contribution among them even though judgment has not been recovered against all or any of them.
>
>   (b) The right of contribution exists only in favor of a tortfeasor who has paid more than his pro rata [proportionate] share of the common liability, and his total recovery is limited to the amount paid by him in excess of his pro rata share. No tortfeasor is compelled to make contributions beyond his **pro rata** share of the entire liability. . . .[3]

In order for the defendant who paid to be able to seek contribution, the defendant must prove the other tortfeasors were also liable to the plaintiff. How does the defendant do this? If the plaintiff sued Defendant Todd, Todd could bring Defendant Norma into the lawsuit. If Todd did not bring Norma into the original lawsuit, then Todd would have to bring a separate suit (usually more costly) against Norma for contribution.

Sample Language in a Contribution Complaint

■ Defendant LaFuze was also negligent in following too closely to the Plaintiff's car. This negligence caused Defendant LaFuze to hit the plaintiff's car when bumped by Defendant Hillman's car. Ms. LaFuze's negligence was a proximate cause of the accident.

Contribution
when a defendant who paid the plaintiff the entire settlement amount seeks at least partial reimbursement from the other defendant who also caused the injury.

Pro rata
proportionate.

---

2. 12 U.L.A. 7 (1982).
3. *Id.*

■ As a result of Ms. LaFuze's negligence, Ms. LaFuze is a joint tortfeasor fully liable for the injury to the Plaintiff.

■ Defendant Hillman has satisfied the judgment in the underlying case in full. Hence, Defendant Hillman has paid more than his pro rata share and is entitled to contribution from Defendant LaFuze, in the amount of fifty percent of the judgment.

Example of Contribution

Plaintiff	Possible Defendants
Deborah Sorenson	Malcom Xing
	Cleveland Ostrom
	George Lusk
	Dana's Liquor & Snacks, Inc.

Using the parties in the table above as an example, Plaintiff Sorenson can decide to only sue Dana's Liquor & Snacks, Inc. Assume Plaintiff Sorenson wins the lawsuit for $1,000,000. The one defendant who pays the award then has the right to be reimbursed by any other defendant(s) the plaintiff did not litigate against. In our example, Dana's Liquor & Snacks, Inc. would pay the award of $1,000,000 and then receive two hundred and fifty thousand dollars each from Malcom Xing, Cleveland Ostrom, and George Lusk. This is assuming all four defendants were equally at fault. Some states divide a 100% total recovery by the number of defendants, and then the resulting amount is each defendant's share.

Comparative fault
a weighing of each defendant's negligence against the other defendant(s).

Other states look at the **comparative fault** among the defendants. If Dana's Liquor & Snacks had been found at trial to only have 10% liability, then Dana's Liquor & Snacks, Inc. will be able to recover $900,000, or 90%, from the other defendants.

4.3 Proximate Cause

It is not enough that a defendant's action is a cause of the plaintiff's injury; the action must also be the proximate cause of the plaintiff's injury. Proximate cause is also known as legal cause. If a tortfeasor's conduct is closely connected to the victim's injuries, then the tortfeasor will probably be found liable. A defendant cannot be negligent unless it is reasonable he should have known his actions might cause injury. Some consequences of an action, even though negligent, are so remote the defendant should not be held liable.

Example of Result of Defendant's Negligent Act That Defendant Will *Not* Be Held Liable For

Edwin is eating outside at lunch in the park and throwing crumbs to the birds. The birds defecate on the tables as the birds are picking up the breadcrumbs.

Jerome and his son Colby come by an hour later and sit at the table where Edwin was feeding the birds. Colby is two years old and starts pounding on the table with his fists where the birds defecated, demanding lunch. Jerome puts a peanut butter and jelly sandwich on a plate and gives it to Colby. Colby eats the sandwich with his hands. Colby contracts severe salmonella poisoning from the bird feces. Colby becomes severely dehydrated from related diarrhea and dies.

Just how wide a net should there be around the defendant's conduct? In the above example, Edwin will most likely not be found liable because his feeding the birds is too far removed from Colby's dying. While Edwin's behavior is a cause-in-fact of Colby's dying, the law holds that because Colby's dying is so extreme and unexpected a consequence of feeding the birds, Edwin will not be held liable for Colby's death.

Proximate cause
a cut-off of the defendant's liability when the defendant is only a remote cause of the injury.

A line must be drawn somewhere to prevent a person from being responsible for the most remote consequences of his actions. Proximate cause attempts to drawn the line. The concept of **proximate cause** cuts the defendant's liability off when the defendant is only a remote cause of the injury.

a.   Foreseeability and Unforeseeability

One test for determining proximate cause is to look at the defendant's action at the time of the action and determine whether the defendant could have foreseen the risk. Was the consequence the foreseeable result of the defendant's actions? The damage to the plaintiff must be a foreseeable result of the defendant's actions or inactions. If the risk was foreseeable and the defendant did not avoid the risk, he will be held liable. In the example of Edwin above, it was foreseeable that Edwin's feeding the birds would cause the birds to defecate on the picnic tables. It may even be foreseeable someone would get sick as a result. However, it was not foreseeable the spreading around of some crumbs would lead to Colby's death. Thus, a defendant is responsible for injuries reasonably foreseeable. If a plaintiff's injuries were an unforeseen consequence of the defendant's actions, then the law does not necessarily hold the defendant responsible.

The *Palsgraf v. The Long Island Railroad Company* case illustrates the concept of foreseeability. In *Palsgraf*, railroad workers were helping a passenger to get aboard a moving train. One of the workers hit a passenger's arm, and the passenger dropped his package. The worker was negligent when he hit the passenger's arm. The package contained fireworks. The fireworks exploded and caused scales further down the platform to fall. Ms. Palsgraf was injured from the scales. The court held the act of hitting the passenger's arm caused a foreseeable risk of harm to the passenger, but not to Ms. Palsgraf, who was located at the other end of the station platform. The railroad employees could not have foreseen she would have been injured. Therefore, the railroad worker was not liable for the injury to Ms. Palsgraf.

Palsgraf v. The Long Island Railroad Company

Court of Appeals of New York
248 N.Y. 339; 162 N.E. 99 (N.Y. 1928)

Plaintiff was standing on a platform of defendant's railroad after buying a ticket to go to Rockaway Beach. A train stopped at the station, bound for another place. Two men ran forward to catch it. One of the men reached the platform of the car without mishap, though the train was already moving. The other man, carrying a package, jumped aboard the car, but seemed unsteady as if about to fall. A guard on the car, who had held the door open, reached forward to help him in, and another guard on the platform pushed him from behind. In this act, the package was dislodged, and fell upon the rails. It was a package of small size, about fifteen inches long, and was covered by a newspaper. In fact it contained fireworks, but there was nothing in its appearance to give notice of its contents. The fireworks when they fell exploded. The shock of the explosion threw down some scales at the other end of the platform, many feet away. The scales struck the plaintiff, causing injuries for which she sues.

The conduct of the defendant's guard, if a wrong in its relation to the holder of the package, was not a wrong in its relation to the plaintiff, standing far away. Relatively to her it was not negligence at all. Nothing in the situation gave notice that the falling package had in it the potency of peril to persons thus removed. . . .

. . . What the plaintiff must show is "a wrong" to herself, i.e., a violation of her own right, and not merely a wrong to some one else. . . . We are told that one who drives at reckless speed through a crowded city street is guilty of a negligent act and, therefore, of a wrongful one irrespective of the consequences. . . . If the same act were to be committed on a speedway or a race course, it would lose its wrongful quality. The risk reasonably to be perceived defines the duty to be obeyed, and risk imports relation; it is risk to another or to others within the range of apprehension. . . . This does not mean, of course, that one who launches a destructive force is always relieved of liability if the force, though known to be destructive, pursues an unexpected path. . . . Some acts, such as shooting, are so imminently dangerous to any one who may come within reach of the missile, however unexpectedly, as to impose a duty of prevision not far from that of an insurer. . . . Here, by concession, there was nothing in the situation to suggest to the most cautious mind that the parcel wrapped in newspaper would spread wreckage through the station. If the guard had thrown it down knowingly and willfully, he would not have threatened the plaintiff's safety, so far as appearances could warn him. His conduct would not have involved, even then, an unreasonable probability of invasion of her bodily security. Liability can be no greater where the act is inadvertent.

Intervening cause
a cause occurring after the tortfeasor's negligent act that contributes to the victim's injury.

b.   Intervening Causes

An **intervening cause** is a cause occurring after the tortfeasor's negligent act that contributes to the victim's injury. If the intervening cause is big enough, it can

Superseding cause
an act of negligence occurring after the first defendant's negligent act, which overshadows the original act of negligence.

become a superseding cause. A **superseding cause** arises when a defendant was negligent, but a later act of negligence arises and overshadows the original act of negligence. The second act of negligence breaks the link between the first negligence and the injury.

If two defendants are negligent towards the plaintiff, but one defendant's negligence is much greater than the other, then the more negligent defendant's acts are a superseding cause and only that defendant is held liable to the plaintiff. Thus, a defendant's act can be a substantial factor in causing an injury to the plaintiff, but then an additional defendant's intervening act comes into pay and supersedes the original defendant's negligence. A superseding cause can negate the original tortfeasor's liability. The intervening act will not be a superseding cause if the intervening act was reasonably foreseeable.

Example of a Superseding Cause

A store employee knocks over a jar of juice in the store, thus spilling juice and broken glass on the floor. The employee leaves the mess while he goes to get a mop. There is no caution sign up. The defendant could be considered liable for leaving this mess in the middle of an aisle way. A couple comes down the row, doing their shopping. The man does not see the spill, and the woman accidentally shoves him into path of the spill, causing him to fall. The woman is the superseding cause that may keep the store employee from being liable for negligence.

c. Eggshell Plaintiff

Eggshell plaintiff theory
a defendant is liable for an injury caused to a particularly sensitive plaintiff, even if the injury would have been much less to a normal person.

A defendant must take a plaintiff as she finds the plaintiff. The **eggshell plaintiff theory** states that if a defendant strikes the head of a plaintiff with a thin skull with a blow that would not injure a normal person, but severely injures the plaintiff with a thin skull, then the defendant will still be responsible for the injury. In other words, a defendant is liable for an injury caused to a particularly sensitive plaintiff, even if the injury would be much less to a person with a normal skull. The theory carries over in to injuries to different body parts as well. Even though the severity of the injury might not have been reasonably foreseeable, the defendant will be liable for the injury.

4.4 Res Ipsa Loquitur

Res ipsa loquitur
a tort which would not have ordinarily occurred without negligence.

It can be difficult for a victim of a tort to prove a tortfeasor's negligence when the victim does not have easy access to information regarding the tortfeasor's conduct. Therefore, in those causes, res ipsa loquitur may apply. Translated from Latin, **res ipsa loquitur** means "the thing speaks for itself." The victim needs to show the tort was not one which would have ordinarily happened without negligence. (See Figure 4.1.) The instrument causing the injury to the victim must have been in the

Figure 4.1

Elements of Res Ipsa Loquitur

Elements of Res Ipsa Loquitur	Brief Discussion of Elements
• The event causing the plaintiff's injuries does not normally occur unless there has been negligence.	This element will not include every, or even most, negligence cases.
• The instrument causing the plaintiff's injury was under the defendant's exclusive control.	This element becomes an issue when a product leaves the defendant's control. However, the defendant may still be found negligent, so long as the conduct of the plaintiff and third parties were not the cause of the negligence.[4]
• The plaintiff did not cause his own injuries.	If the plaintiff was part of the cause of her own injuries, then comparative negligence will come into play.
• The defendant is in a better position to explain the cause of the plaintiff's injuries than the plaintiff.	

defendant's control. Finally, to prove res ipsa loquitur the victim must show she did not cause her own injuries.

Res ipsa loquitur allows a plaintiff to sue even when she cannot prove exactly what occurred to cause her injury. An example of a case where the plaintiff won under a theory of res ipsa loquitur is a plane crash. Even if the plaintiff cannot prove negligence, a plane does not normally fall out of the sky. There must have been some act of negligence that caused the plane to crash.

Other examples of res ipsa loquitur

■ Richard and Sheryl decide to add an outside deck to their second story bedroom. They hire Gerald to build the deck. Once the deck is completed, Richard and Sheryl go out onto the deck to see the finished product. As they are standing on the deck, the deck collapses. When an accident investigator looks at the crumpled deck, he is unable to determine the cause of the accident. However, decks do not normally collapse unless they were negligently built, so negligence can be inferred.

■ John parked his semi-truck with attached trailer in the loading area at a warehouse. While John was unrolling a canvas cover off of the trailer of his semi-truck, he was struck in his back from behind by a forklift. Juan did not see the

4. Restatement (Second) of Torts Section 328D.

forklift coming towards him and no one was driving the forklift. In addition, there were no witnesses. Forklifts, in the absence of negligence, do not move on their own and hit a person in the back.

In a res ipsa loquitur case, there is not a lot of direct evidence to prove negligence. However, there is indirect evidence. The jury must infer from all the circumstances that X happened. Without negligence, the accident could not have happened.

Byrne v. Boadle is an old, but still excellent, example of res ipsa loquitur. In fact, the *Byrne v. Boadle* case largely began the concept of res ipsa loquitur. Byrne was walking down the road when he was hit in the head by a barrel of flour. The barrel fell out of the window. The court held, absent negligence, barrels of flour do not normally fall out of upper-story windows.

Byrne v. Boadle

S.C. 33 L.J. Ex. 13; 12 W.R. 279 (1863)

. . . [T]he defendant, by his servants, so negligently and unskillfully managed and lowered certain barrels of flour by means of a certain jigger-hoist and machinery attached to the shop of the defendant, situated in a certain highway, along which the plaintiff was then passing, that by and through that negligence of the defendant, by his said servants, one of the said barrels of flour fell upon and struck against the plaintiff, whereby the plaintiff was thrown down, wounded, lamed, and permanently injured, and was prevented from attending to his business for a long time . . . , and incurred great expense for medical attendance, and suffered great pain and anguish. . . .

. . . A witness name Critchley said: "On the 18th July, I was in Scotland Road, on the right side going north, defendant's shop is on that side. When I was opposite to his shop, a barrel of flour fell from a window above in defendant's house and shop, and knocked the plaintiff down. He was carried into an adjoining shop. A horse and cart came opposite the defendant's door. Barrels of flour were in the cart. I do not think the barrel was being lowered by a rope. I cannot say: I did not see the barrel until it struck the plaintiff. It was swinging when it struck the plaintiff. It struck him on the shoulder and knocked him towards the shop. No one called out until after the accident." . . . It was admitted that the defendant was a dealer in flour. . . .

First, there was no evidence to connect the defendant or his servants with the occurrence. It is not suggested that the defendant himself was present. . . . [T]he declaration alleges that the defendant, by his servants, so negligently lowered the barrel of flour, that by and through the negligence of the defendant, by his said servants, it fell upon the plaintiff. That is tantamount to an allegation that the injury was caused by the defendant's negligence. . . . The plaintiff could not properly plead to this declaration that his servants were not guilty of negligence, or that the servants were not his servants. . . . [T]here was no evidence that the defendant, or any person for whose acts he would be responsible, was engaged in lowering the barrel of flour. It is consistent with the evidence that the purchaser of the flour was superintending the lowering of it by his servant, or it may be that a stranger was engaged to do it without the knowledge or authority of the defendant. . . .

Secondly, . . . these facts do not disclose any evidence for the jury of negligence. The plaintiff was bound to give affirmative proof of negligence. But there was not a scintilla of evidence, unless the occurrence is of itself evidence of negligence. . . .

Becoming a Paralegal for a Retirement Job
By Barbara Barmore, Paralegal

Life has often been described as a highway, a road traveled with twists and turns leading to a final destination. You start out as a shiny new vehicle, well equipped to handle the hills and valleys, the successes and failures. Then there comes a time to put on the brakes and pull into the garage of retirement.

The question remains as to whether the old clunker is up to the challenge of taking another spin. You would be on the road with models that are decades newer, brighter and more durable. Do you really want to run the risk of breaking down? Are you able to gear up to handle the rigors of the road?

Education and job training can prepare you to meet the challenges of competing against the newer editions. It can provide the skill and confidence to negotiate the unexplored terrain. Learning to drive again in the world of academia can present a unique challenge. Steering your way over the speed bumps of classes, dodging the exam potholes, motoring through reading assignments and term papers provides little time for pit stops. The fear of running out of gas, of failure and self-doubt, can be crippling. There's no GPS to guarantee success.

What gives you the strength and stamina? It is the relentless hope and dream of taking in a new horizon. It is the realization that life has no destination. You just have to have the courage to take the wheel and go the distance.

E T H I C S

Guideline 4: A lawyer is responsible for taking reasonable measures to ensure that clients, courts, and other lawyers are aware that a paralegal, whose services are utilized by the lawyer in performing legal services, is not licensed to practice law.[5]

The attorney is responsible for making clients, the courts, and other attorneys know the paralegal is not licensed to practice law. One of the ways the attorney can do so is to ask the paralegal to identify herself as a paralegal when talking to the client, the courts, or other attorneys. However, the ultimate responsibility for the client, the courts, and the other attorneys knowing the paralegal is not licensed to practice law is placed upon the attorney. The attorney could satisfy this obligation by writing a letter to the client.

---

5. ABA Model Guidelines for the Utilization of Paralegal Services, Guideline 4 (ABA 2004).

Chapter Summary

A defendant must have caused the injury in order to be negligent. The negligent acts must be directly linked to the injury, which is also known as cause-in-fact or actual cause. Actual cause is assessed by one of two tests: the but-for test or the substantial factor test. The but-for test is but for the defendant's negligence, the plaintiff would not have been injured. The defendant's act (or inaction) must have been necessary to the cause the plaintiff's injury.

The substantial factor test is the test to use when there are two or more events which combine to cause an injury to the plaintiff, and each is a substantial factor in causing the injury. The substantial factor test asks if the defendant was a substantial factor in causing the injury to the plaintiff.

Joint and several liability addresses the issue of two or more defendants being responsible for the plaintiff's injury. Each defendant will be responsible for paying the full amount of damages to the plaintiff, although the plaintiff cannot recover more than 100% of the award. If a defendant does pay for the total reward, but is not the sole contributor to the injury, he may seek reimbursement or contribution from the other defendants for their share.

In addition to actual cause, proximate cause is also necessary to prove causation. A defendant must have been able to reasonably foresee his actions might cause injury. If the consequences of the defendant's actions are remote, then the defendant will not be held liable.

Key Terms

- Actual cause
- But-for test
- Cause-in-fact
- Comparative fault
- Concurrent causes
- Contribution
- Eggshell plaintiff theory
- Foreseeability
- Intervening cause
- Joint and several liability
- Joint tortfeasors
- Pro rata
- Proximate cause
- Res ipsa loquitur
- Sine qua non
- Substantial factor test
- Superseding cause

Review Questions

- What are joint tortfeasors?
- How may damages be assigned between joint tortfeasors?
- Explain how foreseeability is important in personal injury cases.

Web Links

- http://www.hg.org. Heiros Gamos is a worldwide legal directory. The site not only has a torts guide, but it also has job listings. This site is a good starting point for just about any area of law (it currently has 70 practice areas listed).

- http://www.counsel.net/chatboards/torts/ is a torts chatboard.

- http://www.law.stetson.edu/courses/torts/fltorts/powerpoint/Causation.ppt. This website has a good PowerPoint Presentation on proximate cause.

- Take a mini torts quiz on causation at: http://home.ubalt.edu/ntlacbs/ T_F06_PCCIFandD_01.htm.

Exercises

- Mindy stops suddenly in the road to avoid hitting a squirrel. The sudden stop surprises Ryan, another driver, and he hits his brakes hard, narrowly avoiding hitting Mindy's car. Ryan's car stops. Tonya is also taken by surprise and is not able to avoid hitting Ryan, whose car is propelled into Mindy's. Who is liable to Mindy?

- Letty is a passenger on a train. Due to the carelessness of the train engineer, the train jumps the tracks and Letty injures her left leg in the resulting crash. Letty crawls away from the train because she is concerned about how precariously the train is balancing. However, this means she is unprotected against the elements, and she sits out in the rain, getting soaked, until rescue workers arrive. She contracts pneumonia as a result of sitting in the rain. Is the train company the proximate cause of the leg injury and pneumonia?

- Josh is driving through an intersection and negligently hits a pedestrian, Lou. While Lou is still lying on the asphalt, another person accidentally hits him, and Lou suffers additional injuries. The second driver does not stop. Josh stops his car and gets out to help Lou. Lou sues Josh for negligence and wins the lawsuit in the amount of $400,000. Will Josh have to pay all $400,000 to Lou?

- Yvette goes to a Mexican restaurant at lunch and orders a bean and cheese burrito. While eating the burrito, she bites down on a piece of metal and cracks a tooth. Will Yvette be able to prevail against the Mexican restaurant under the theory of res ipsa loquitur?

- Kevin has surgery on his right arm, performed by Dr. Lim. Kevin notices a loss of sensation in his arm after the surgery. Dr. Lim tells Kevin he should regain sensation in his right arm within six months of the surgery. Nine months later, Kevin still cannot feel much with his right arm. Can res ipsa loquitur be applied in this case? How?

Fourth Element of Negligence: Damages

"Lawsuit mania"... a continual craving to go to law against others, while considering themselves to be the injured party.[1]

Chapter Outline

Chapter Objectives

- Explain the three major types of damages: compensatory, punitive, and nominal
- Show the difference between special and general damages

---

1. Ceasre Lombroso, *The Man of Genius*, part 1, chapter 2 (1891).

- Discuss how damages are proven
- Illustrate present value
- Describe damages for pain and suffering
- Define the Collateral Source Rule
- Give the rule for mitigation of damages
- Compare wrongful death actions to survival actions

5.1 Introduction to Damages

Damage
a loss, frequently monetary.

Tort damages
the losses a plaintiff suffers due to the actions of the defendant.

The fourth element of negligence is damages. A **damage** is a loss, frequently monetary. **Tort damages** are the losses a plaintiff suffers due to the actions of the defendant. Damages can also be part of intentional torts as well, but this chapter is geared towards negligence damages. Damage awards are awarded by the courts to restore the plaintiff (as much as possible) to the condition he was in before he was harmed. The law is attempting to return the plaintiff to the same position he was in before the injury. This goal may not be possible, as a plaintiff might never return to his pre-injury physical health. However, the system of monetary damages can still help the plaintiff by paying for medical care and/or property damages. This chapter covers: 1) the types of compensatory damages, which are general and special; 2) punitive damages; and 3) nominal damages. However, punitive and nominal damages are usually not available for negligence actions.

Figure 5.1

Types of Damages

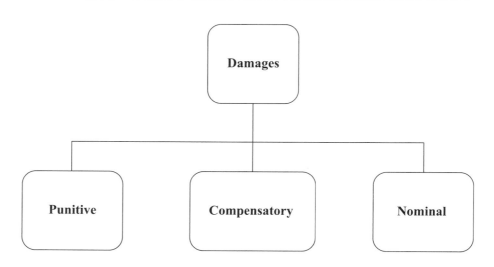

In addition, this chapter covers the plaintiff's duty to minimize the potential damages to her person. Collateral sources, such as insurance, are discussed. Wrongful death actions are mentioned in this chapter, because this is a type of damage.

However, the major issue with both wrongful death and survival actions is who can bring the action.

5.2 Compensatory Damages

Out-of-pocket expenses
those expenses the plaintiff already paid or is going to have to pay.

Compensatory damages compensate the plaintiff for his losses resulting from the injury. Compensatory damages are further divided into non-economic and economic damages. Non-economic damages are more difficult to prove than economic damages. Non-economic damages include pain and suffering, emotional distress, and loss of consortium. It is more difficult to assign a dollar amount to someone's pain and suffering than to out-of-pocket expenses. Economic damages are out-of-pocket damages. **Out-of-pocket expenses** are those expenses the plaintiff already paid or is going to have to pay. The medical damages worksheet in Figure 5.3 (see page 65) is an excellent way to keep track of out-of-pocket expenses. Economic damages include medical expenses, property damages, and loss of earnings. Compensatory damages are also divided into general and special damages.

Types of compensatory damages:

General/nonspecific (usually non-economic)
Special/specific (usually economic)

a. General Damages

General damages compensate for losses that are a natural consequence of the injury. General damages include pain and suffering, emotional distress, and loss of consortium — the non-economic damages discussed above.

1. Pain and Suffering

Pain and suffering does not lend itself easily to quantifying how much it is worth. The plaintiff first needs to prove he did indeed have pain and suffering. Pain and suffering includes one-time pain from an accident or on-going pain from an accident. If the accident causes a permanent injury, the plaintiff's permanent pain and suffering is covered. Pain and suffering also covers the pain the plaintiff feels as a result of having painful treatment (such as surgery) due to the injury.

To determine the monetary amount of pain and suffering, one tip is to examine the length of any hospital stays. The longer the hospital stay, the higher the monetary damages will be. Another tip in determining pain and suffering damages is to look up jury verdicts in similar cases. Lexis-Nexis and Westlaw (online legal research tools) have special sections on jury verdicts. The number and importance of surgeries also factor into pain and suffering damages. The plaintiff's medical records can provide indicators of how much pain the plaintiff was in. For review of medical records, see Chapter 8. It can be a valuable tool for the plaintiff to keep a pain diary for longer and more severe injuries. At the plaintiff's deposition, the defense attorney will ask the plaintiff about the pain and suffering he has endured as a result of the accident. The plaintiff can take the stand at trial and testify about his pain.

2.   Emotional Distress

Emotional distress damages
damages awarded for mental anguish.

Emotional distress damages are damages awarded for mental anguish. Mental anguish includes fright, anxiety, depression, embarrassment, humiliation, and inconvenience caused by the injury. A plaintiff's fear of the accident reoccurring would fall under the category of emotional distress. Emotional distress might arise from a physical disfigurement caused by the injury. If the plaintiff suffers humiliation from the disfigurement, the humiliation falls under emotional distress. Emotional damages are hard to prove because these damages are subjective. Emotional distress damages can be substantiated a therapist's testimony.

3.   Explanation of Loss of Consortium

Loss of consortium
the loss of benefits of the marital relationship because the injured spouse is not well enough to provide those benefits; examples of benefits include date nights, household help, and sex.

When a person is injured by a defendant, the spouse of the injured person can also be affected by the injury. The spouse can suffer damages, such as loss of consortium. **Loss of consortium** is the loss of the benefits of the marital relationship because the injured spouse is not well enough to provide those benefits. These benefits can include things such as date nights, the loss of the injured spouse's household help, and a decrease or loss of a sex life.

Example of Loss of Consortium

When William is injured, he is unable to mow the lawn, fix the family car, or drive the children to school. His wife Kay would thus have a claim for loss of consortium.

b.   Special Damages

Special or economic damages
actual monetary damages particular to the plaintiff.

Special damages are losses other than general damages. Special damages are actual monetary damages particular to the plaintiff. For example, Katie had back surgery, which cost $40,000. Not all plaintiffs will have back surgery, so the back surgery is special to Katie. A defendant would not assume the plaintiff had these damages unless the plaintiff gave notice of them in the complaint.

Special damages include many of the economic damages discussed previously: medical expenses, property damages, and loss of earnings. In addition, special damages can also include funeral costs, special equipment the plaintiff now needs, and nursing care. Special damages are more easily assigned monetary amounts than general damages.

1.   Lost Wages

Lost earnings are the plaintiff's past income losses due to the injury. These wages include lost wages up until the time of settlement or trial. However, what about the loss of future wages? How can future wages be determined unless the plaintiff sues for those wages after he loses the wages? The plaintiff should have only one trial—so at the one trial, future loss of income must be calculated. A calculation of future lost wages requires figuring out how long the plaintiff would have continued working had he not been injured. When determining future lost wages, employer benefits should also be taken into consideration. (See Figure 5.2.)

Figure 5.2

How to Determine Future Income Loss

- What is the most the plaintiff could have been paid had the accident not occurred?
- How many more years would the plaintiff have worked if the accident had not occurred?
- How does the plaintiff's injury affect this potential earning?
- Will the plaintiff need to be trained to perform a new job, consistent with his injuries?
- What is the highest salary the plaintiff can earn at his job after the injury?
- Add all of the above, except the highest salary the plaintiff can earn at his job after the injury, which is subtracted, to determine the total amount.
- Reduce the total amount to a present value.

To determine future income loss, it is helpful to obtain the plaintiff's employment description, salary, and benefits from his employer. Income can be verified through income tax returns and W-2s. Another way of determining future earning capacity is to have a vocational expert evaluate the plaintiff's future earning capacity.

2. Medical Bills

A plaintiff who wins at trial may receive compensation for all the medical costs of treating the injuries caused by the defendant. Medical bills are not routinely produced with the medical records. The bills must be specifically requested during discovery, often by the paralegal. Several examples of medical treatments are provided below. However, this is not an exhaustive list. In addition, nowadays many patients are undergoing more holistic treatments, such as acupuncture. **Holistic treatments** are treatments considered outside of traditional Western medicine. On the plaintiff's side, the law firm would argue for those treatments to be paid for by the defendant. On the defendant's side, the defense would argue those treatments are not reliably effective, and the plaintiff should try more conventional types of medicine.

Some examples of medical expenses are:

- x-rays,
- acupuncture (holistic),
- massage therapy (holistic),
- doctor visits (including orthopedists),
- hospital stays,

Holistic treatment
treatments considered outside of traditional Western medicine, such as acupuncture.

- nursing care,
- labs,
- tests,
- pharmaceuticals,
- medical aids (such as a cervical collar),
- dental work,
- physical therapy,
- chiropractic treatment,
- ambulance transportation,
- home health aids, and
- emergency room treatment.

The cost of regular transportation to and from medical appointments is also part of the medical expenses.

One of the ways in which a paralegal is most useful at a personal injury firm is by going through the medical bills in a systematic way and keeping track of the amount of the medical bills. Figure 5.3 is an example of a medical damages summary sheet used for keeping track of the amounts of each medical bill. The entries in this particular form are chronological, although the entries could be categorized by provider or type of medical bill. An up-to-date medical damages summary sheet aids the attorney in calculating a settlement figure. The actual bills need to be photocopied and attached as proof to the summary sheet.

This medical damages summary sheet is from a case where the plaintiff was injured while eating at a restaurant. The plaintiff was sitting in a chair at a table, eating. She was seated next to a moveable room divider (the room divider was on casters). The room divider (which just looked like a wall) was leaned against by another patron and fell on the plaintiff, knocking her out of her chair. The plaintiff hit the concrete floor hard, damaging a disc in her back. Some of her medical bills are shown in Figure 5.3.

When determining medical damages, a plaintiff's future medical treatment, if any, needs to be included in the final tally. A medical expert may be needed to testify as to the likely cost of future medical expenses. Damages for future expenses are typically reduced to present day dollars. Present day values are awarded because the plaintiff will receive the money in a lump sum after trial. The plaintiff can invest the money and earn interest. If the plaintiff received a settlement in future dollars, she could also invest the money and earn interest, which would result in a windfall to the plaintiff. Present day value is normally determined by an expert in present day value. However, the following table is a more basic example of present day value.

Present Value of One Dollar ($1.00)

In _____ Years:	At 10% Interest
1	Approx. 91 cents
5	Approx. 62 cents
10	Approx. 39 cents
20	Approx. 15 cents

Figure 5.3

Medical Damages Summary Sheet

Date	Provider	Description	Type of Expense	Out-of-Pocket Cost
6/24/05	Urgent Care	Medical Visit	Medical	$15.00
6/24-6/25/05	Memorial Hospital	Emergency Accident Drugs, X-rays, Room Service	Medical	$421.28
6/24-6/25-05	Emergency Medical Services	Emergency Accident Care	Medical	$16.11
6/24/05	Diagnostic Radiology	X-ray Services	Medical	$4.80
6/25/05	Diagnostic Radiology	X-ray Services	Medical	$5.06 $9.86
6/27/05	Medical Group	Emergency Accident Care	Medical	$15.00
6/27/05	Ace Parking	Parking for Medical Visit	Parking	$1.50
6/27/05	Orthopedic Associates	Consultation	Medical	$30.00
6/27/05	Ace Parking	Parking for Medical Visit	Parking	$4.00
7/2/05	Savon Drugs	Prescription for Hydrocodone & Meclizine	Prescription	$10.00
7/7/05	Yellow Cab	Taxi from Dr.'s office to home	Taxi	$17.50
7/8/05	Savon Drugs	Prescription for Tramadol	Prescription	$5.00
7/11/05	Ace Parking	Parking for Medical Visit	Parking	$2.25
7/13-10/28/05 & 11/21-1/05/06	Physical Therapy Associates	25 physical therapy sessions	Medical	$249.50
7/13/05	Yellow Cab	Taxi to physical therapy	Taxi	$19.40
7/13/05	Yellow Cab	Taxi from physical therapy	Taxi	$16.50
7/18/05	Yellow Cab	Taxi to physical therapy	Taxi	$16.50
7/18/05	Yellow Cab	Taxi from physical therapy	Taxi	$17.10

The table on page 64 indicates one dollar, in one year, is worth ninety-one cents today. One dollar, in five years, is worth sixty-two cents today, and so on.

Other factors in anticipating future medical costs are:

- rehabilitation therapy,
- counseling,
- surgeries,
- equipment,
- medications,
- transportation,
- housekeeping assistance.

Equipment could include a wheelchair, shower bars and chairs, and so on. Transportation may include outfitting a car to accommodate a wheelchair. Housekeeping assistance could include someone to help prepare meals, do laundry, shop for food, and assist in dressing. In addition, the home in which the plaintiff lives may need outfitting to accommodate a wheelchair, such as making a ramp to the front door where there were only steps before.

3.   Property Damages

If the plaintiff is in a car accident, the plaintiff will have damages to his car. Damages include damages to property, such as the car. If the car was completely destroyed, the plaintiff will be able to recover the fair market value of the car at the time of the accident. **Fair market value** is the value of a good on the open marketplace. Fair market value is not necessarily the manufacturer's suggested retail price.

If a piece of property is not completely destroyed, then the fair market value of the property both before and after the accident is evaluated. The plaintiff will receive the difference between the value of the property prior to the accident, less the value of the property after the accident. If the plaintiff cannot use her car while it is being repaired, then the plaintiff can also be compensated for the loss of use.

Fair market value
the value of a good on the open marketplace.

Damages Checklist

_____Obtain doctors records
_____Obtain hospital records
_____Obtain income tax returns
_____Verify any loss of income
_____Document/verify medical expenses (use the damages summary worksheet at Figure 5.3 to document medical expenses)
_____Document/verify any other bills
_____Determine whether or not there is insurance

5.3 Punitive Damages

Punitive damages

non-compensatory damages
that punish the defendant and
act to deter others from the
same or similar conduct.

Punitive damages are above and beyond the damages necessary to compensate the plaintiff. Punitive damages are usually awarded when there is outrageous behavior that devalues human life. This behavior is usually criminal or quasi-criminal. The defendant must have acted wrongfully. Punitive damages are intended to punish the defendant and to serve as a warning to other potential defendants against performing such risky behavior. In short, **punitive damages** are non-compensatory damages that punish the defendant and act to deter others from the same or similar conduct. Thus, punitive damages are often customized to the defendant's actions and his income to act as punishment. Punitive damages are not awarded in all states. To be awarded, there must have been some actual damages (for instance, the medical expenses discussed above). There is frequently a ratio between compensatory and punitive damages, such as one-to-three or so forth.

Example of Punitive Damages Ratio

Aaron and Ferdinand are in a bar fight. Both are throwing punches at the other. However, when Aaron throws one final punch, he hits Ferdinand in the jaw and Ferdinand loses consciousness. Ferdinand starts to fall to the ground, and on the way down, his head hits the bar stool, causing permanent brain damage. Ferdinand and his family sue Aaron for damages. Ferdinand has $200,000 in medical bills. The jury finds Aaron liable. The jury also determines Aaron should pay $1,000,000 in punitive damages. The ratio between punitive damages ($1,000,000) and compensatory damages ($200,000) here is then five to one. $200,000 multiplied by five is $1,000,000.

Because punitive damages are intended to act as a deterrent, the defendant's finances are often taken into consideration. Large corporations are not going to be deterred from certain behavior without sufficient punitive damages. However, some of the large awards against corporations have been the subject of much debate, as such awards may raise the costs of doing business. Number one on the list of most unfair jurisdictions in which to be sued was South Florida, which awarded $521 million against an accounting firm.[2] The cost for the United States tort system for 2003 (2003 is the most recent year for which data is available) was $845 per United States citizen.[3]

One specific area of tort reform is the medical malpractice arena, discussed in Chapter 8. The allegation regarding medical malpractice punitive damages is high damage awards increase the cost of medical professionals' insurance premiums and the public's cost of health care. Tort reform would limit the amount of punitive damages allowed or set a higher standard of proof for obtaining punitive damages. Another reform would be to decrease the statute of limitations a plaintiff has to bring a medical malpractice claim. Yet another type of tort reform is for states to require

2. ATRA, *Judicial Hellholes 2007,* http://www.atra.org/reports/hellholes/ (last accessed Dec. 22, 2007).
3. Tillinghast-Towers Perrin. *U.S. Tort Costs: 2004 Update,* (New York, New York, 2005).

Arbitration
a type of alternative dispute resolution where the parties go to a neutral third party who makes a binding decision on the case.

the plaintiff to arbitrate his claim before going to trial. **Arbitration** is a type of alternative (to trial) dispute resolution. The parties go to a neutral third party who decides the case. Arbitration is typically binding, meaning the parties cannot then have a trial. For instance, Kaiser Permanente requires patients to arbitrate their claims, which greatly reduces their costs.

In California, the state enacted the Medical Injury Compensation Reform Act ("MICRA"). This act puts restrictions on attorneys' fees and allows collateral sources, such as insurance payments, to come into evidence at trial. Non-economic damages in medical malpractice causes of action are limited to $250,000.[4]

However, on the other side of the general argument for tort reform is the argument corporations will not be deterred without high punitive damages. Read the following case summary. Do you think the punitive damages finally awarded were sufficient to deter McDonalds?

The Infamous McDonald's Hot Coffee Case

The McDonald's hot coffee case is touted by the media as the perfect example of why the United States' punitive damages system needs to be limited. The media presents the case as a woman bought coffee at a McDonald's drive-through, spilled coffee on herself and received almost $3 million in punitive damages. Summarized in this manner, the case does not seem reasonable. However, this summary is not the full story.

Stella Liebeck was almost eighty years old when she bought the coffee. She did place the coffee cup in between her legs while trying to remove the lid. The 170-degree coffee spilled and the coffee burned her private parts to the point of second- and third-degree burns. Stella Liebeck spent a week at the hospital and almost a month at home with her daughter helping her. The daughter lost time from work as a result. Afterward Ms. Liebeck still had to have skin grafts. She lost about one-fifth of her total body weight.

She tried to settle the case out-of-court; however, McDonald's offered less than $1,000 to settle. The case went to trial. At trial, evidence was presented as to the number of complaints McDonald's had received regarding the temperature of its coffee. In the ten years prior, McDonald's had received seven hundred complaints. The caution label on the coffee cup was very small. In addition, the jury learned if the coffee temperature was lowered, it would take almost six times as long for the coffee to burn someone. During the approximately twenty seconds it would take to burn a person, the person could remove the coffee. With Ms. Liebeck, the coffee burned her within 3-4 seconds, which did not give her enough time to react. The jury found for the plaintiff and did award $2.7 million in punitive damages. However, the trial judge reduced the amount of punitive damages to three times the compensatory damages, or around $600,000.

---

4. *See Hoffman v. U.S.*, 767 F.2d 1431 (9th Cir 1985).

5.4   Nominal Damages

Nominal damages
small amounts of money (frequently $1) awarded to the plaintiff when the defendant's actions have caused little to no harm.

Nominal damages are those damages the plaintiff might receive if the plaintiff is not able to prove any actual damages, although the plaintiff proved the remaining elements on her case. Nominal damages are small amounts of money (frequently $1) awarded to the plaintiff when the defendant's actions have caused little to no harm. The monetary award might then be pennies on the dollar. For instance, if a defendant trespasses on a property owner's land, what the property owner most wants is an injunction for the defendant to stop. The court might award a nominal amount of money along with the injunction.

5.5   Mitigation of Damages

Mitigation of damages
the obligation of plaintiffs to lessen their potential injuries through prompt medical treatment or other actions a reasonable person would have performed under similar circumstances.

Mitigation of damages is the obligation plaintiffs have to lessen their potential injuries through prompt medical treatment or other actions a reasonable person would have performed under similar circumstances. Plaintiffs are required to mitigate or reduce damages when reasonably possible. One way in which the plaintiff can mitigate damages is by seeking prompt medical care for an injury caused by the defendant. Seeking prompt medical treatment can prevent the injury from worsening. For instance, if the plaintiff suffers a deep leg wound from the defendant, the wound might become infected if not properly treated. However, if the plaintiff did get the wound properly and immediately treated, the treatment might reduce the risk of infection and cause less damage. Mitigation of damages helps limit the damages a defendant might potentially have to pay.

5.6   Collateral Source Rule

Collateral source rule
rule prohibiting the defendant from mentioning in court that the plaintiff has already had his medical treatment provided by his insurance company.

The **collateral source rule** does not allow a defendant to mention in court that the plaintiff has already had his medical treatment provided by his insurance company. If the defendant could do so, it might prevent the jury from awarding the plaintiff damages for the injury caused by the defendant.

Public policy holds a plaintiff should be able to immediately seek medical treatment through his insurance and still be able to later recover for the damages caused by the defendant. Insurance then may try to recover its payments from an award or settlement made to the plaintiff by the defendant. Most insurance policies state if an insured receives a monetary award as a result of a personal injury action, the insured must repay the insurance company for medical treatment provided to treat the related injury.

However, a plaintiff is not entitled to receive both a monetary award from the defendant and payment of his medical expenses from the insurance. There cannot be a double recovery.

Example

Erin is in a car accident. She goes to the emergency room and presents her personal insurance card. The treatment in the emergency room is paid for by her health

insurance company, in the amount of $10,000. Erin then files a lawsuit against the other driver and wins $100,000. Erin will have to reimburse her insurance company $10,000. Therefore, Erin will actually only receive $90,000 from the award.

Insurance companies frequently send out letters after reviewing claims to determine whether there might be a defendant who is responsible for the medical bills. Patients are expected to report such accidents.

The following is a sample of a letter an insurance company might send to a client after reviewing the medical bills. The medical bills or records might indicate the client, or insured, had an accident. The letter will be sent to the insured so the insurance company can determine whether there is another source of payment for the medical bills.

Example

Dear Valued Member:

This insurance company appreciates your cooperation in providing information that reduces our costs. Thus, we have enclosed a questionnaire to help us determine if payment for the treatment we covered may be the responsibility of someone else.

If you have received an award or settlement for injury-related medical expenses (including other health insurance, car insurance, and/or worker's compensation), we demand you repay us. This subrogation right is outlined further in your health plan booklet.

Sincerely,
Your Health Care Provider

Subrogation right
an insurance company's right to seek reimbursement for a claim it has already paid.

5.7 Wrongful Death

Wrongful death laws are statutory laws, which vary from state to state. Thus, paralegals need to research the laws of the state that they work in.

Elements of Wrongful Death:

The defendant injures the plaintiff
The plaintiff dies as a result of the injury.

Wrongful death action
a legal action for damages due to the death of another person.

A **wrongful death action** is a legal action for damages due to the death of another person. Wrongful death occurs when a victim dies because of the injury or tort that is the subject of the lawsuit. The wrongful death must have resulted due to a tort committed by the defendant. One example of wrongful death is medical malpractice causing the death of the patient. If the plaintiff had only been injured, not killed, then the plaintiff would have been able to sue the defendant himself.

Figure 5.4

Who May Bring a Wrongful Death Claim?

Spouse	All jurisdictions
Minor children	All jurisdictions
Parents	Many jurisdictions
Siblings	Some jurisdictions
Non-Adopted Stepchildren	Some jurisdictions
Domestic partners	Some jurisdictions
Divorced spouse	No jurisdictions

Many relatives can bring a wrongful death action against the tortfeasor. Some states allow only children, spouses, or people who financially relied on the victim to recover money. Children allowed to bring a wrongful death action include adopted children. However, a divorced spouse would not be able to recover. Other states allow the victim's parents or brothers and sisters to recover in a wrongful death suit. Still other states allow the domestic partner of the deceased to recover. No states allow a divorced spouse to bring a wrongful death action.

Figure 5.5

What Can a Qualifying Relative Recover?

Lost support	Almost all jurisdictions
Grief	Almost all jurisdictions
Value of services provided by deceased	Many jurisdictions
Loss of companionship	Some jurisdictions

Once a court has determined who is able to recover, the next major issue in wrongful death suits is what the qualifying relative will receive as compensation. Lost support is the most commonly provided benefit. The majority of jurisdictions allow the relative to recover for his grief over the deceased's death. In addition, a qualifying relative may receive compensation for the services the deceased used to provide. Some states also allow monetary damages for loss of companionship.

5.8   Survival Actions

If a plaintiff in a lawsuit dies for unrelated reasons, can the deceased plaintiff's estate represent the plaintiff? Yes. Here, unlike with wrongful death, it is an unrelated incident that causes the death of either party. A survival action is so-named because causes of action survive after the death of either party.

The damages obtained in a survival action belong to the estate of the deceased. In other words, if a person dies before his cause of action is litigated, then the cause of action can be continued by the estate of the deceased. The estate can include an executor to a will, a trustee, or a court-appointed representative. Then, the heirs of the deceased's estate will receive the money.

The estate's representative is suing regarding injuries to the deceased before the deceased died. If the deceased had lived, the deceased would have litigated the matter himself. If the tort was personal to the particular plaintiff, such as in a defamation case, then usually the plaintiff's estate will not be able to sue on the plaintiff's behalf. If the tort was against the personal property of a plaintiff, then the claim will survive the plaintiff's death and the plaintiff's estate will be able to sue on the plaintiff's behalf. If the tort was to the plaintiff's real property, then the cause of action will survive the death of the plaintiff.

5.9   Wrongful Birth

One of the newer tort claims is wrongful birth. With wrongful birth, the plaintiff is contending the child should have never been born. The plaintiff further argues the birth of the child is a compensable injury. This tort claim usually arises where a medical professional does not diagnosis a condition in the mother, leading to a birth defect in the child. The moral ethics of wrongful birth actions are contested.

Example

Kimberly is six weeks pregnant and goes to visit her obstetrician, Dr. Jarod. Dr. Jarod does not diagnosis Kimberly with AIDS at the same time. Kimberly's child is born with AIDS. Kimberly then sues Dr. Jarod, arguing she did not have the information she needed to decide whether or not to bear her child to term. Kimberly is not arguing she never wanted the child, as is the case in wrongful conception, below. Kimberly may be able to recover damages for the increased cost of raising a child with AIDS.

Another similar tort is wrongful conception. For instance, if a woman takes some antibiotics, without being warned the antibiotics cause a decrease in the effectiveness of birth control, she may become pregnant. The woman could then attempt to make a wrongful conception claim. This is a moral ethical hotbed like wrongful birth. The potential damages are strongly contested.

Legal Networking 101
By Annie Parrish, Director of the San Diego
Legal Secretaries Association

net·wor·king *noun* 1967 : the exchange of information or services among individuals, groups, or institutions; *specifically*: the cultivation of productive relationships for employment or business (Merriam Webster Dictionary, 10th ed.)

Networking is an essential tool in nearly every business and industry, but perhaps no more so than in the legal industry. Networking with your industry peers provides the ideal opportunity for the "exchange of information . . . among individuals." A perfect forum for this is a local, state, or national professional association.

Paralegal association objectives and purposes include joining paralegals together for further education and to cooperate with attorneys, judges and bar associations in stimulating a high order of professional standards and ethics among those performing duties in law offices. The group encourages friendship, cooperation and an exchange of ideas among members.

Paralegal Associations:

- http://www.nala.org. The National Association of Legal Assistants' website.
- www.paralegals.org. This website has information from the National Federation of Paralegals Association, which is made up of state and local paralegal associations in both the United States and Canada.
- http://www.nationalparalegal.org. The website for the National Paralegal Association, an international paralegal association. Paralegal students can join.

E T H I C S

Rent and watch the movie *A Civil Action*. While this movie is rife with legal issues, concentrate on the damages discussed in the movie. What types of plaintiffs does this movie state are the most "valuable"? Is this claim ethical? Research whether the claim made in the movie is true in your jurisdiction. In addition, pay particular attention to how much the case actually settled for, how much were the attorneys' fees, and the amount of the expenses. How much did the families each get in the end? Did this seem just?

Chapter Summary

Compensatory damages compensate the plaintiff for losses from the injury. Compensatory damages are further divided into two types: general and special damages. General damages are to compensate for losses that are a natural consequence of the injury. General damages are for pain and suffering, emotional distress, and loss of consortium. Emotional distress is mental anguish, including fright, anxiety, depression, embarrassment, humiliation, and inconvenience. Loss of consortium is the loss of the benefits of the martial relationship because the injured spouse is not well enough to provide those benefits. These benefits include household help and sex.

Special damages are for other losses, such as lost wages, medical bills, and property losses. Special damages compensate a plaintiff for losses particular to the plaintiff. For instance, not all plaintiffs will need back surgery, but this particular plaintiff does. Therefore, this plaintiff's back surgery is a special damage because it is particular to him.

Punitive damages are intended to punish the defendant and are usually awarded when there is outrageous behavior. However, punitive damages are currently coming under attack as being too excessive.

Nominal damages are those the plaintiff might receive if unable to prove any actual damages. Nominal damages are a minimal amount awarded to plaintiff, often in the amount of one dollar.

Plaintiffs are required to mitigate or reduce potential damages. The collateral source rule prohibits defendants from discussing a plaintiff's personal insurance coverage or payments at trial. Wrongful death is a death caused by the tort that is the subject of the lawsuit. Survival actions arise when a party dies, but not due to an injury that is the subject matter of the litigation.

Key Terms

- Arbitration
- Collateral source rule
- Compensatory damages
- Damage
- Emotional distress damages
- Fair market value
- Holistic treatment
- Loss of consortium
- Mitigation of damages
- Nominal damages
- Out-of-pocket expenses
- Pain and suffering
- Punitive damages
- Special and general damages
- Subrogation right
- Survival actions
- Tort damages
- Tort reform
- Wrongful death action

Review Questions

- Give some examples of special damages.
- Give some examples of general damages.
- What is the difference between special and general damages?
- Which is easier to prove: special damages or general damages? Why?
- What is loss of consortium and who receives damages for it?
- What effect on damages does present value have?
- When should nominal damages be awarded? Punitive?
- What is the issue with awarding damages for pain and suffering?
- How does a plaintiff prove lost future wages?
- What are the social goals behind punitive damages?
- Who might be eligible to take over the cause of action (legal case) of a deceased person?
- Who might be eligible to recover money in a wrongful death lawsuit?

Web Links

- The American Tort Reform Association has its website located at http://www.atra. org. This website raises awareness about the need for tort reform. Refer to the state and federal reforms to determine what reforms your jurisdiction has undergone. While at this website, check out the "looney lawsuits" section. This association is also responsible for publishing "judicial hellholes," which are the United States' most unfair jurisdictions in which to be sued.

- Know X is a resource for finding information on businesses, individuals and the assets of both. This information is complied form public record information, such as court filings. www.knowx.com/. It will provide some basic information for free, but is essentially a fee-based program.

- http://www.injuryboard.com/help-center/wrongful-death/. Go to the Injury Board website and click on the wrongful death section. Read the wrongful death section to learn more about this torts topic. Find out what the major sources of accidental death are.

Exercises

- Go to the American Tort Reform Association's website and see if your jurisdiction was included in the "judicial hellholes," otherwise known as the most unfair jurisdictions in which to be sued in the United States.

- If a person is injured by a defendant to the point the person is in a vegetative state, what are the damages available?

- Aaron is crossing the road at the crosswalk, but is still run over by a negligent driver. He unfortunately suffers the loss of his left leg as a result. What damages would Aaron seek?

- Assume Aaron is hit crossing the street by a negligent driver, but only suffers a concussion as a result. He is taken to the hospital via ambulance and placed under medical supervision for three days, during which he cannot work. What damages would Aaron seek in this instance?

- Is your jurisdiction one that allows domestic partners to recover in a wrongful death lawsuit?

- Is your jurisdiction one that allows qualifying relatives to recover damages for loss of companionship in a wrongful death lawsuit?

- Jimbo dies during an operation. He is survived by his parents, his ex-wife, and his ten-year-old son. Who will be able to recover damages?

Special Issues Related to Negligence

In no country perhaps in the world is law so general a study. . . . This study renders men acute, inquisitive, dexterous, prompt in attack, ready in defense, full of resources. . . .[1]

Chapter Outline

---

1. Edmund Burke, *Second Speech on Conciliation with America. The Thirteen Resolutions* (March 22, 1775).

Chapter Objectives

- Describe the theory of premises liability
- Draw distinctions between trespassers, licensees, and invitees
- Give an example of attractive nuisance
- Discuss how vicarious liability and respondeat superior work
- Cover negligent infliction of emotional distress

6.1   Introduction to Special Issues Related to Negligence

So far, this book has covered negligence. The first chapter was an introduction, and Chapters 2-5 each covered an element of negligence. This chapter discusses issues related in some way to negligence. First, there is premises liability, which is not altogether a negligence issue. However, we will look at the duties owed to different types of people and note the reasonableness requirement, which is similar to the reasonableness discussed in negligence.

Vicarious liability is discussed in this chapter because employers can be liable for the negligent acts of their employees under certain circumstances. The employer might not have been negligent himself, but he may still be found liable for his employee's acts. Finally, negligent infliction of emotional distress is discussed. Negligent infliction of emotional distress is a difficult concept in negligence law, in part because the standards regarding this tort change from state to state. While reading this section, remember to check the law of the jurisdiction you are in.

6.2   Premises Liability

Premises liability
law governing when a person in possession of land is responsible for injuries incurred by people on those premises.

Premises liability law dictates when a person in possession of land is responsible for injuries incurred by people on those premises. The person in possession of the land does not have to be the actual owner of the land. A possessor of land has a duty to visitors on his property. There are three types of visitors to real property: trespassers, licensees, and invitees. A different type of duty is owed to each type of visitor. The lowest duty is owed to a trespasser and the greatest duty is owed to an invitee.

Figure 6.1

Duty Owed to Types of Visitors

Type of Visitor:	Duty Owed:
Trespasser	Duty to avoid intentional injury.
Licensee	Duty of reasonable care to fix known dangerous conditions on land.
Invitee	Duty of reasonable care to discover and fix unknown dangerous conditions on land.

a.   Trespassers: No Duty of Care

Trespassing

entering another's land without permission and without having a legal privilege for being on the land.

Trespassing is entering another person's land without permission and without having a legal privilege for being on the land.[2] Trespassing implies interference with possession and occupation of land. The trespasser is on the premises of another for his own purpose, such as picking fruit from a tree for his personal consumption.

Trespassing is itself an intentional tort. If an injured party is a trespasser, the possessor of the property, in general, will not be found liable for the injury because a duty of care is not owed to trespassers. However, the possessor of the property may not commit an intentional tort against a trespasser. The following case is an example of an owner of a property preparing a mantrap for an expected trespasser. In this case, the possessor of the property was held responsible for the injury to the trespasser.

Katko v. Briney

183 N.W.2d 657 (1971)

The primary issue presented here is whether an owner may protect personal property in an unoccupied boarded-up farm house against trespassers and thieves by a spring gun capable of inflicting death or serious injury.

Infra

below.

We are not here concerned with a man's right to protect his home and members of his family. Defendants' home was several miles from the scene of the incident to which we refer **infra** [below].

Plaintiff's action is for damages resulting from serious injury caused by a shot from a 20-gauge spring shotgun set by defendants in a bedroom of an old farm house which had been uninhabited for several years. Plaintiff and his companion, Marvin McDonough, had broken and entered the house to find and steal old bottles and dated fruit jars which they considered antiques. . . .

Most of the facts are not disputed. In 1957 defendant Bertha L. Briney inherited her parents' farm land in Mahaska and Monroe Counties. Included was an 80-acre tract in southwest Mahaska County where her grandparents and parents had lived. No one occupied the house thereafter. Her husband, Edward, attempted to care for the land. He kept no farm machinery thereon. The outbuildings became dilapidated.

For about 10 years, 1957 to 1967, there occurred a series of trespassing and housebreaking events with loss of some household items, the breaking of windows and "messing up of the property in general." The latest occurred June 8, 1967, prior to the event on July 16, 1967 herein involved.

Defendants through the years boarded up the windows and doors in an attempt to stop the intrusions. They had posted "no trespass" signs on the land several years before 1967. The nearest one was 35 feet from the house. On June 11, 1967 defendants set "a shotgun trap" in the north bedroom. After Mr. Briney cleaned and oiled his 20-gauge shotgun, the power of which he was well aware, defendants took it to the old house where they secured it to an iron bed with the barrel pointed at the bedroom door. It was rigged with wire from the doorknob to the gun's trigger so

---

2. *Delgado v. S. Pac. Transp. Co.*, 763 F. Supp. 1509 (D. Ariz. 1991).

it would fire when the door was opened. Briney first pointed the gun so an intruder would be hit in the stomach but at Mrs. Briney's suggestion it was lowered to hit the legs. He admitted he did so "because I was mad and tired of being tormented" but "he did not intend to injure anyone." He gave no explanation of why he used a loaded shell and set it to hit a person already in the house. Tin was nailed over the bedroom window. The spring gun could not be seen from the outside. No warning of its presence was posted.

Plaintiff lived with his wife and worked regularly as a gasoline station attendant in Eddyville, seven miles from the old house. He had observed it for several years while hunting in the area and considered it as being abandoned. He knew it had long been uninhabited. In 1967 the area around the house was covered with high weeds. Prior to July 16, 1967 plaintiff and McDonough had been to the premises and found several old bottles and fruit jars which they took and added to their collection of antiques. On the latter date about 9:30 p.m. they made a second trip to the Briney property. They entered the old house by removing a board from a porch window which was without glass. While McDonough was looking around the kitchen area plaintiff went to another part of the house. As he started to open the north bedroom door the shotgun went off striking him in the right leg above the ankle bone. Much of his leg, including part of the tibia, was blown away. Only by McDonough's assistance was plaintiff able to get out of the house and after crawling some distance was put in his vehicle and rushed to a doctor and then to a hospital. He remained in the hospital 40 days.

Plaintiff's doctor testified he seriously considered amputation but eventually the healing process was successful. Some weeks after his release from the hospital plaintiff returned to work on crutches. He was required to keep the injured leg in a cast for approximately a year and wear a special brace for another year. He continued to suffer pain during this period.

There was undenied medical testimony plaintiff had a permanent deformity, a loss of tissue, and a shortening of the leg. . . .

The main thrust of defendants' defense . . . is that "the law permits use of a spring gun in a dwelling or warehouse for the purpose of preventing the unlawful entry of a burglar or thief". . . .

Prosser . . . states:

the law has always placed a higher value upon human safety than upon mere rights in property, it is the accepted rule that there is no privilege to use any force calculated to cause death or serious bodily injury to repel the threat to land or chattels, unless there is also such a threat to the defendant's personal safety as to justify self-defense . . . spring guns and other man-killing devices are not justifiable against a mere trespasser, or even a petty thief. They are privileged only against those upon whom the landowner, if he were present in person would be free to inflict injury of the same kind.

Restatement of Torts . . . states:

The value of human life and limb, not only to the individual concerned but also to society, so outweighs the interest of a possessor of land in excluding from it those whom he is not willing to admit thereto that a possessor of land has, as is stated in §79, no privilege to use force intended or likely to cause death or serious harm against another whom the possessor sees about to enter his premises or meddle with his chattel, unless the intrusion threatens death or serious bodily harm to the occupiers or users of the premises. . . . A possessor of land cannot do indirectly and by a mechanical device that which, were he present, he could not do immediately and in person. Therefore, he cannot gain a privilege to install, for the purpose of protecting his land from intrusions harmless to the lives and limbs of the occupiers or users of it, a mechanical device whose only purpose is to inflict death or serious harm upon such as may intrude, by giving notice of his intention to inflict, by mechanical means and indirectly, harm which he could not, even after request, inflict directly were he present.

In . . . Harper and James . . . this is found:

The possessor of land may not arrange his premises intentionally so as to cause death or serious bodily harm to a trespasser. The possessor may of course take some steps to repel a trespass. If he is present he may use force to do so, but only that amount which is reasonably necessary to effect the repulse. Moreover if the trespass threatens harm to property only — even a theft of property — the possessor would not be privileged to use deadly force, he may not arrange his premises so that such force will be inflicted by mechanical means. If he does, he will be liable even to a thief who is injured by such device. . . .

....

In *Katko*, the general rule regarding deadly force and property is laid out. A possessor of property is not legally allowed to protect just his property using deadly force. However, if the possessor of the property is at home at the time a burglar attempts to rob his house, the possessor of property could be justified in using deadly force because his own life might be at stake. A property owner is allowed to use reasonable force to prevent trespassers. For instance, a tiny electric shock, along with a warning, might be permissible to protect property, but an electric shock on the level of electrocution would not be.

1. General Rule for Adult Trespassers: No Duty

Known or discovered trespasser
a trespasser the possessor of the premises knows about.

The general rule is no duty of care is owed to an adult trespasser. However, there is an exception to this general rule for discovered trespassers. A **known or discovered trespasser** is a trespasser the possessor of the premises knows about. Known trespassers would be people who repeatedly use the land as a shortcut, and there have been so many of them they have left a worn path on the land. A discovered or known trespasser is owed a duty of reasonable care. The duty of reasonable care here does not require the occupier of the land to make the land safe for even the known trespasser. This duty of reasonable care requires the occupier to warn the known trespasser of dangerous artificial conditions the trespasser may not otherwise discover until it is too late. An **artificial condition** is one placed on the land by man, rather than a naturally occurring condition. A dangerous natural condition would be a

Artificial condition
a condition placed on the land by man, rather than a naturally occurring condition.

naturally occurring sinkhole. The occupier of land does not have to warn about dangerous natural conditions, only artificial ones.

2.   Exception to the General Rule: Child Trespassers and Attractive Nuisance Doctrine

Elements of Attractive Nuisance Doctrine:

The defendant knows or should have known there is a dangerous condition on her land and children will likely trespass on her land.

The defendant knows this condition poses an unreasonable risk of potential injury to a child.

The child, because of age and lack of maturity, does not appreciate the dangerous condition.

The cost of fixing the dangerous condition is small compared to the danger to the child.

The defendant failed to fix the dangerous condition.

Again, the general rule is a possessor of land does not owe a duty of care to trespassers. An exception to this rule is made for children who would find the property enticing. An **attractive nuisance** is a visible object enticing to and potentially harmful to children. A **child** is legally defined as a person who is too young to appreciate the dangers in a situation. The age, intellect, and experience of the child will be taken into consideration.

The presence of trespassing children has to be reasonably foreseeable. For instance, if the possessor of a premises lives in a singles community, with no children allowed, it might not be foreseeable children would trespass on the property.

Examples of Attractive Nuisance

A possessor of the premises leaves a backhoe in his unfenced yard with the key in the ignition. The backhoe, with the key in the ignition and no fence around it, poses an unreasonable risk of injury to a child. A child, due to her lack of experience, would not realize the danger of operating a backhoe by herself. The financial burden of erecting a fence or removing the key is small compared to a child potentially injuring herself.

Another example of an attractive nuisance would be a decaying barn. Children would be able to see the barn and want to play in the barn, which may pose a danger to them. Tearing the barn down would be cheaper than the potential injury to a child.

In both of the two above examples, the dangerous condition is an artificial one. Similar to adult trespassers, a possessor of the premises has a different duty regarding artificial conditions versus natural conditions. The trespasser does not have to exercise a duty of care regarding natural conditions on the land even when children are involved. A cave on the occupier's property would not be an

Attractive nuisance
a visible object enticing to children and potentially harmful to children.

Child
for legal purposes, a child is a person who is generally too young to appreciate the dangers in a situation.

attractive nuisance requiring the possessor of land to exercise a duty of care because the cave is a natural condition on the land.

b. Licensees: Duty of Reasonable Care

Licensee
a person on the land for her own purposes.

There are two types of persons who are invited onto a property, licensees and invitees. A **licensee** is on the land for her own purposes. The possessor of the property has given consent, whether implied or explicit, to have the licensee on his property. A possessor of the premises owes a duty of reasonable care to licensees. A licensee must be notified of dangerous conditions on the property. If a possessor of land knows of a dangerous condition, whether artificial or natural, on her property, then she is required to correct this dangerous condition. The duty of reasonable care, however, does not require the possessor correct unknown dangerous conditions.

Door-to-door salespeople are often categorized as licensees unless the possessor of the land has posted a sign stating salespeople are not welcome. Then, the door-to-door salesperson would be categorized as a trespasser. Public employees on the premises in order to perform their jobs are usually classified as licensees. This would include, for example, the water meter reader.

A licensee also includes a social guest. Even though Sally receives the most beautifully engraved invitation to a wedding in her friend's backyard, a social guest is only accorded the status of a licensee. Sally is presumed to be at the wedding for her own benefit, e.g., to drink champagne and eat cake. However, this classification of a social guest as a licensee is heavily criticized and will probably change. In the future, social guests will most likely be classified as invitees.

If a person comes onto the property, but then goes beyond the scope of the owner's permission, a licensee can become a trespasser. For instance, Joshua is invited to a party at his neighbor's house. The decorations and food are all inside the house, predominantly in the living room and kitchen. There is a detached garage off to the side of the house, but no lights are turned on out there and Joshua has not been invited out to the garage. However, Joshua decides to open the garage and go looking for tools he would like to borrow. Joshua has exceeded the permission the owner, or party thrower, gave Joshua in coming over to the house. Joshua had permission to be in the living room and kitchen, but Joshua did not have permission to be in the garage. Once Joshua entered the garage, he became a trespasser.

c. Invitees: The Highest Duty of Reasonable Care

Invitee
a person on the land for a business purpose or for a purpose for which the land is open to the public.

An **invitee** can be a customer of the possessor of the land. However, an invitee is more broadly defined as being on the land for a business purpose or for a purpose for which the land is open to the public. A business, for purposes of defining an invitee, includes not-for-profit businesses, such as a church. Thus, someone attending church would be an invitee. A customer (whether just browsing or buying) in a department store is an invitee. Someone using a public library is an invitee, though she does not pay to check out books.

With an invitee, the possessor of land impliedly or expressly invited the invitee onto the land by holding the land out for a specific business or purpose. Express invitation would be a shopkeeper saying "come on in." An implied invitation would be flipping the closed sign to "Open" and unlocking the doors for business.

For invitees, a possessor of land is required to use reasonable care to find and correct unknown dangerous conditions upon the land. Thus, a possessor of land must make an additional effort regarding invitees, greater than the duty owed to licensees. An example of this would be the wet clean-up announcement at the grocery store. A grocery store is required to periodically check its floors and clean up spills. The spills might cause a person to fall.

Some states have decided invitees and licensees should be treated the same, and that each are owed a duty of reasonable care.

d.   Vendor and Vendee

When land is sold, does the seller or vendor have a continuing duty to the buyer or vendee regarding dangerous conditions? Typically, once land is sold, the seller no longer has title or possession of the land. Therefore, the seller shifts all responsibility for the condition of land to the buyer.[3] A buyer of property is expected to inspect the land before buying the land.

However, if the seller of the land knew there was a hidden dangerous condition on the land, then the seller had a duty to warn the buyer of the condition or to fix the condition before selling the land to the buyer. If the seller does not disclose the condition, then the seller will be liable to the buyer. To be liable, the seller of the land has to know of the condition or should have known of the condition before selling the property.

If the dangerous condition arises after the sale of the land, the seller will not be liable for the dangerous condition. "A vendor of land is not subject to liability for physical harm caused to his vendee or others while upon the land by any dangerous condition, whether natural or artificial, which comes into existence after the vendee has taken possession."[4] To hold the seller responsible for dangerous conditions occurring after the seller's possession would not be reasonable.

e.   Lessor and Lessee

Lessor
landlord.

Lessee
renter.

A **lessor** is a landlord and a **lessee** is a renter. In general, "a lessor of land is not liable to his lessee or to others on the land for physical harm caused by any dangerous condition, whether natural or artificial, which existed when the lessee took possession."[5] When land is leased, the lease is considered the equivalent of selling the land for the lease period. The renter becomes liable — as the person in possession of the land — to those who come onto the land. A landlord needs to disclose or repair

---

3. *Prosser and Keeton on the Law of Torts*, Ch. 10, Owners and Occupiers of Land, §64, Vendor and Vendee (1984 West).
4. Restatement of the Law (Second) §351 (1965).
5. Restatement of the Law (Second) §356 (1965).

hidden dangerous conditions on the land before renting the land. Even after the land is rented, the landlord maintains responsibility for common areas such as communal laundry rooms.

6.3 Vicarious Liability

Vicarious liability
One person is held liable for another person's negligence

The term **vicarious liability** means one person is held liable for another person's negligence. Vicarious liability is liability for an injury actually caused by someone other than yourself. The person liable is known as the principal and the person who actually committed the wrongdoing is known as the agent.

a. Principal-Agent

Agent
a person who agrees to perform tasks for another

Principal
a person for whom the agent performs tasks.

Vicarious liability occurs when liability is imposed on a principal for the acts/omissions of the agent. An **agent** is a person who agrees to perform tasks for another. A **principal** is a person for whom the agent performs tasks. Thus, agents act on behalf of the principal. The principal can still be held liable for the agent's actions even if the principal properly supervised the agent.

Employers and employees fall under the principal and agent relationship. However, the concept of principal-agent is larger than the concept of employer-employee. For instance, the employer-employee relationship implies the employee is being paid for acting on behalf on the employer. However, payment is not necessary to find that vicarious liability will apply. An unpaid agent might be a daughter acting as a healthcare agent for her incapacitated mother. A real estate agent is another example of an agent and the principal would be the buyer or seller of the home. While a real estate agent is paid and working for the client, the real estate agent is not the employee of the client. In addition, an attorney is an agent for her client.

The central question in determining a principal-agent relationship is whether one person was acting on the behalf of another person. When one person acts on behalf of another person, this raises the issue of principal-agency and then vicarious liability.

b. Employer-Employee

Respondeat superior
the doctrine an employer is responsible for the harm the employee causes while working within the course and scope of her employment.

Respondeat superior is the doctrine that an employer is responsible for the harm the employee causes while working within the course and scope of her employment. The major reason why employers are held responsible is the employee is performing the work not for herself, but for the employer. The employee is working to benefit the employer. "He [the employer] who does a thing through another [employee] does it himself [the employer]."[6] The employee would not have undertaken the actions that were negligent unless she were working for the employer. In addition, employers usually have more money than their employees. If the plaintiff can hold

---

6. *Prosser and Keeton on the Law of Torts* 499 (1984).

the employer responsible for the employee's acts, then the plaintiff is more likely to receive a higher award than if the plaintiff were only able to hold the employee responsible. Yet another reason to apply respondeat superior is employers typically have insurance for their business, whereas employees typically do not have insurance for work. Under the doctrine of vicarious liability, negligence will be imputed or attributed to the employer.

c. Scope of Employment

Course and scope of employment
the behavior an employer expects of an employee as part of her job duties

For an employer to be found liable under the doctrine of vicarious liability, the employee must have been acting within the course and scope of his employment. **Course and scope of employment** is the behavior an employer expects of an employee as part of her job duties. Other questions to ask in determining whether an employee acted within the scope of employment are:

- Did the employer authorize the conduct?
- Was the conduct normal conduct for performing the job?
- Was the employee's conduct foreseeable to the employer?
- Did the employee's conduct occur during normal business hours?

Examples of Scope of Employment

- Bonnie is enjoying her weekend by shopping. As she is leaving the mall, an overzealous shopper hits her car when pulling into the parking space Bonnie just vacated. Is this accident within the course and scope of employment? No, because employees typically do not work weekends and typically are not paid for personal shopping.
- Using the same fact scenario as above, add these additional facts. Bonnie's boss, Josh, overhears Bonnie talking about her weekend plans on Friday. Josh is too busy at work to do his own shopping, and he is in dire need of a new suit for court on Monday. Josh asks Bonnie to find him a navy suit, appropriate for his work as an attorney, and he gives her $500 to buy the suit. Bonnie does go shopping for herself and her boss over the weekend, and then is hit in the parking lot when leaving the mall. Is this accident within the course and scope of employment? It is much more likely this accident will be considered within the course and scope of employment because Bonnie was performing a task for her employer, at his request. The task is also related to their legal work. Even though Bonnie did some of her own shopping in addition to shopping for her boss, this does not take the accident outside the course and scope of her employment.

Going and coming rule
an employer is not vicariously liable for accidents occurring to an employee on his way to and from work.

There is a major exception to scope of employment. This exception is dubbed the "going and coming" rule. Under the **going and coming rule**, an employer is not vicariously liable for accidents occurring to an employee on his way to and from work.

The reasoning behind the going and coming rule is the employee would have to travel to and from work no matter what job he held. Thus, an employee who has a car accident on the way to work will not usually be compensated for the accident by his employer. Only after the employee is at the employer's place of work will the doctrine of vicarious liability apply.

Another major exception to scope of employment is the **frolic and detour** exception. Once the employee is at work, the employee's behavior can so deviate from the employer's business purpose that the employer will not be found vicariously liable. An employer should not be held liable for an employee's negligence when the employee substantially deviated from his assigned tasks. For instance, if a paralegal is asked to meet her supervising attorney at a deposition two hours away from the law office, and the deposition starts at 1:00 p.m., the paralegal would be expected to be on the road by 11:00 a.m., at the latest. Because the paralegal's normal lunch hour has been disrupted, she would be entitled to stop for a quick bite to eat on her way to the deposition. Her employer would be responsible should anything happen to her when she made an exit off the freeway, en route, for a quick burger stop.

However, should the paralegal then decide to add a stop at Larry's Liquor, she has detoured from the employer's business purpose significantly. The employer should not be found vicariously liable should the employee cause an accident due to inebriation. There is simply no legitimate business purpose in stopping at Larry's Liquor on the way to a deposition.

Example of Frolic and Detour Exception

Plaintiff Pete and Defendant Ken were coworkers employed by a computer manufacturing company. Plaintiff Pete alleges Defendant Ken repeatedly pushed down on Plaintiff's shoulders, knowing Pete had under gone two previous bilateral rotator cuff surgeries. Pete further alleges Ken did these acts with the intent to cause an unprovoked physical act of aggression toward Ken. Lastly, Pete contends he was injured by Defendant Ken's actions. Make an argument, using the frolic and detour exception, stating the computer manufacturing company should not be responsible for Ken's actions.

d. Independent Contractor

The general rule is that a person hiring an independent contractor will not be vicariously liable for the independent contractors' negligence. An **independent contractor** is a person hired for a specific job, who has control over how the job is performed and is not an employee. An independent contractor operates independently from the principal and thus should be held responsible for her own actions. An independent contractor includes a person who enters into a contract to provide a specific service. The relationship between an employer and employee is generally continuous, while the relationship between a principal and an independent contractor is usually for a certain task. The means by which the independent contractor performs her task is up to her. In contrast, the means in which an employee performs her job is up to her employer.

Frolic and detour
when the employee's behavior so deviates from the employer's business purpose that the employer will not be found vicariously liable.

Independent contractor
a person hired for a specific job, who has control over how the job is performed, and is not an employee.

Figure 6.2

Other Factors in Determining Independent Contractor Status:[7]	Discussion of Factors:
Who has control over how the task is performed?	If the payor has more control, then it is more likely this is an employer-employee relationship.
Does the potential independent contractor have his own business?	If the answer is yes, it is more likely he is an independent contractor.
Who provides the tools necessary for the job?	If the answer is the payor, it is more likely this is an employee-employer relationship.
Who provides the work space or office for the job?	If the payor provides the work space, it is more likely this is an employer-employee relationship.
How long is the potential independent contractor employed?	If the potential independent contractor is employed years, rather than days, weeks, or months, then it is more likely he is an employee.
Is the potential independent contractor paid by the job or by the hour?	If he is paid a flat rate for a job, it is more likely he is an independent contractor.
What do the parties themselves think their relationship is?	

The independent contractor is her own boss, and, as her own boss, is responsible for her own negligence. Therefore, employers are usually not found liable for actions committed by independent contractors.

Example: Employee or Independent Contractor?

Louis hires Karen to clean his house. Louis provides Karen with dust rags, mops, and cleaning solutions. Louis is very particular about his home and he oversees how Karen makes his bed (sheets tucked in), dusts his knickknacks (the knickknacks must be replaced in a line, all facing forward), and sweeps (the floor must be wetted down first, and the broom must stay close to the ground at all times). Is Karen an employee or an independent contractor? Karen is an employee because Louis provides all the items she needs in which to perform her job and she does not have control over the manner in which she performs her job.

---

7. Restatement of Agency (Second) §220.

An owner of a business can hire someone as an independent contractor to avoid much of the liability the owner would potentially face for an employee's acts. There are some tasks, which if the employer gives to an independent contractor, the employer will still be held responsible. These tasks include inherently dangerous tasks.[8] An example of an inherently dangerous activity would be the use of explosives.

Example

Christy has a large number of boulders in her backyard. She wants to remove the boulders, level the ground, and plant a vegetable garden. However, the boulders are too big to remove from her backyard in one piece because her property line is so close to her neighbor's fence. She hires Ross to blow up the boulders into smaller bits and remove them. In the process of blasting the rock, a shard of rock is catapulted into the neighbor's yard and strikes the neighbor in the eye. Can Christy be held vicariously liable for the act of Ross? Yes, because blasting is an inherently dangerous activity and Christy cannot pass on all responsibility for the activity onto independent contractor Ross.

e.   Family Automobile/Purpose Doctrine

Elements of Family Automobile/Purpose Doctrine

The parents own the car involved in the accident;

The car is available to the child;

The driver of the car is the child of the owners;

The child was using the car for a family purpose; and

The child had express or implied permission to drive the car.

Family purpose doctrine
if a member of the family is driving a family car with permission from the head of the household, then the head of the family is vicariously liable for the driver's negligence.

The **family purpose doctrine** holds if a member of the family is driving a family car with permission from the head of the household, then the head of the family is vicariously liable for the driver's negligence. A plaintiff can sue the owners (typically the parents of the driver) of the car, even if the driver (the child) was the one who caused the injury and the owners were not even present. The family purpose doctrine is not the law in all states.

---

8. Restatement (Second) of Torts §416 (1965).

6.4 Negligent Infliction of Emotional Distress (NIED)

Elements of a claim for negligent infliction of emotional distress:	Discussion:
Conduct by defendant which he should have reasonably foreseen would cause . . .	The plaintiff must prove the defendant breached his duty of reasonable care to avoid causing such harm and the plaintiff was a reasonably foreseeable plaintiff.
. . . significant emotional injury to the plaintiff.	The emotional injury must be some sort of psychological injury such as anxiety, fear, grief, or embarrassment.

If a defendant intentionally causes a plaintiff's emotional distress, then a claim for intentional infliction of emotional distress may arise. However, if a defendant negligently causes a plaintiff's emotional distress, then there may be a cause of action for negligent infliction of emotional distress. **Negligent infliction of emotional distress** is a claim for the emotional trauma suffered when one person sees another person injured. Another way of explaining negligent infliction of emotional distress is the emotional trauma a bystander undergoes when witnessing a physical injury to another. The shorthand way of referring to negligent infliction of emotional distress is NIED.

Negligent infliction of emotional distress
a claim for the emotional trauma suffered when one person sees another person injured.

Examples of NIED

- A parent watching her child being hit by a car
- A wife of a comatose patient going to the hospital and seeing her husband has been horribly bitten by rats

The concern with negligent infliction of emotional distress is false claims may be made. Thus, a plaintiff is behooved to show the circumstances regarding the event are genuine. If there is a physical impact, then there is some guarantee of the genuineness of emotional distress occurring as a result of the impact. Thus, where there is a physical impact, it is much easier to make a claim for emotional distress. This is known as the **impact rule**.

Impact rule
there must be a physical impact to the bystander in order for the bystander to make a claim for negligent infliction of emotional distress.

There are three instances when NIED may occur:

1. The plaintiff does not have a physical injury in addition to the emotional distress (in general, the first type of NIED is not compensated under the law);
2. The plaintiff does have emotional distress which manifests itself as a physical injury (physical manifestations rule); or
3. The plaintiff suffers emotional distress from watching another person be injured, but does not have a physical injury herself (bystander NIED).

a. The Second Type of NIED: The Physical Manifestations Rule

The second type of NIED may be compensated under the law, especially if the plaintiff can show the emotional distress caused the physical injury. Under the **physical manifestations rule**, the plaintiff must show the emotional distress caused physical injury in order to recover under negligent infliction of emotional distress. The plaintiff can make a claim not only for the physical injuries but also for pain, suffering, anxiety, and fear. A plaintiff may be able to recover even if the physical injury was slight compared to the psychological impact. While a physical impact is not required under the physical manifestations rule, the plaintiff has to have physical symptoms due to the mental anguish caused by the defendant.

Physical manifestations rule
the plaintiff must show the emotional distress caused physical injury in order to recover under negligent infliction of emotional distress.

b. Zone of Danger Rule

Another way of barring recovery in NIED is through the zone of danger rule. The **zone of danger rule** holds that a bystander witnessing an injury to a third party must be immediately threatened by the negligent action of the defendant to recover damages. Therefore, the bystander is close enough to the victim to have almost become a victim herself. Bystanders of accidents who are within the zone of danger can recover for NIED. If a bystander reasonably feared for her own safety, then this would constitute being within the zone of danger. Using the example from above, where the mother watched her child being hit by a car, the zone of danger test would require the mother to have been walking alongside the child when the child was hit. If the mother had been immediately next to her child, then she too might have been a victim.

Zone of danger rule
a bystander witnessing an injury to a third party must be immediately threatened by the negligent action of the defendant to recover damages.

The reason for the zone of danger test is if a bystander was within a zone where she could have been harmed, then it is more likely any emotional trauma as a result of seeing the accident is real. A defendant owes the bystanders in the zone of danger a duty of care because injury to these bystanders is foreseeable.

c. The Third Type of NIED: Bystander

The zone of danger test would cut off recovery to a mother who watched from the window as her child was hit by a car. In response to the zone of danger test, the bystander test was implemented in several states, but by no means all states. Otherwise, if a bystander just witnessed the defendant's conduct, but did not suffer any physical harm and was not in the zone of danger, then the bystander will not be able to recover so long as the defendant's conduct was not intentional. Until now, bystander has been used as a term for witness. This section discusses bystander as a specific type of NIED.

Under the bystander type of NIED, if a person is closely related to the victim, the bystander may be able to recover. This is known as the **family relationship rule**. Under the family relationship rule, the bystander must be a family relative of the person injured by the defendant's negligence. The infliction of emotional distress in this case would be indirect. The bystander who suffered the emotional injury would

Family relationship rule
a rule allowing a bystander who is closely related to the victim to recover under negligent infliction of emotional distress

suffer the emotional injury indirectly from watching an injury occur to another person.

In *Dillon*,[9] a mother saw her child killed by the negligence of the defendant. While the mother was never in danger herself, she was still allowed to recover for her emotional trauma of watching her child be killed. *Dillon* also raises two more factors to be considered in bystander NIED. The second factor was whether the bystander was close to the scene of the accident. The third factor was whether the emotional distress occurred from the contemporaneous witnessing of the event. *Dillon* is not the law in all states.

Warning

Research the holding in *Dillon* to determine whether the holding is true for a particular jurisdiction. Jurisdiction is what allows a court to hear and decide a case. Jurisdiction may be based upon federal, state, or local (such as municipal) authority.

The holding in *Dillon* would prevent a relative who is not at an accident scene from recovering for emotional distress, even though once the relative learns of the injury, she might suffer emotional distress.

Dillon v. Legg

68 Cal. 2d 728, 441 P.2d 912, 69 Cal. Rptr. 72 (1968)

That the courts should allow recovery to a mother who suffers emotional trauma and physical injury from witnessing the infliction of death or injury to her child for which the tortfeasor is liable in negligence would appear to be a compelling proposition. . . .

In the instant case plaintiff's first cause of action alleged that on or about September 27, 1964, defendant drove his automobile in a southerly direction on Bluegrass Road near its intersection with Clover Lane in the County of Sacramento, and at that time plaintiff's infant daughter, Erin Lee Dillon, lawfully crossed Blue-grass Road. The complaint further alleged that defendant's negligent operation of his vehicle caused it to "collide with the deceased Erin Lee Dillon resulting in injuries to decedent which proximately resulted in her death. . . ." Plaintiff, as the mother of the decedent, brought an action for compensation for the loss.

Plaintiff's second cause of action alleged that she, Margery M. Dillon, "was in close proximity to the . . . collision and personally witnessed said collision." She further alleged that "because of the negligence of defendants . . . and as a proximate cause [*sic*] thereof plaintiff . . . sustained great emotional disturbance and shock and

---

9. *Dillon v. Legg*, 68 Cal. 2d 728, 441 P.2d 912, 69 Cal. Rptr. 72 (1968).

injury to her nervous system" which caused her great physical and mental pain and suffering.

Thus we have before us a case that dramatically illustrates the difference in result flowing from the alleged requirement that a plaintiff cannot recover for emotional trauma in witnessing the death of a child . . . unless she also feared for her own safety because she was actually within the zone of physical impact. . . .

In order to limit the otherwise potentially infinite liability which would follow every negligent act, the law of torts holds defendant amenable only for injuries to others which to defendant at the time were reasonably foreseeable. . . .

The obligation turns on whether "the offending conduct foreseeably involved unreasonably great risk of harm to the interests of someone other than the actor. . . . [The] obligation to refrain from . . . particular conduct is owed only to those who are foreseeably endangered by the conduct and only with respect to those risks or hazards whose likelihood made the conduct unreasonably dangerous. Duty, in other words, is measured by the scope of the risk which negligent conduct foreseeably entails. . . ."

This foreseeable risk may be of two types. The first class involves actual physical impact. A second type of risk applies to the instant situation. "In other cases, however, plaintiff is outside the zone of physical risk (or there is no risk of physical impact at all), but bodily injury or sickness is brought on by emotional disturbance which in turn is caused by defendant's conduct. Under general principles recovery should be had in such a case if defendant should foresee fright or shock severe enough to cause substantial injury in a person normally constituted. . . .

. . . [W]e deal here with a case in which plaintiff suffered a shock which resulted in physical injury and we confine our ruling to that case. In determining, in such a case, whether defendant should reasonably foresee the injury to plaintiff, or, in other terminology, whether defendant owes plaintiff a duty of due care, the courts will take into account such factors as the following:

(1) Whether plaintiff was located near the scene of the accident as contrasted with one who was a distance away from it.

(2) Whether the shock resulted from a direct emotional impact upon plaintiff from the sensory and contemporaneous observance of the accident, as contrasted with learning of the accident from others after its occurrence.

(3) Whether plaintiff and the victim were closely related, as contrasted with an absence of any relationship or the presence of only a distant relationship.

The evaluation of these factors will indicate the *degree* of the defendant's foreseeability: obviously defendant is more likely to foresee that a mother who observes an accident affecting her child will suffer harm than to foretell that a stranger witness will do so. Similarly, the degree of foreseeability of the third person's injury is far greater in the case of his contemporaneous observance of the accident than that in which he subsequently learns of it. The defendant is more likely to foresee that shock to the nearby, witnessing mother will cause physical harm than to anticipate that someone distant from the accident will suffer more than a temporary emotional reaction. . . .

In the instant case, the presence of all the above factors indicates that plaintiff has alleged a sufficient prima facie case. Surely the negligent driver who causes the death of a young child may reasonably expect that the mother will not be far distant and will upon witnessing the accident suffer emotional trauma. As Dean Prosser has stated: when a child is endangered, it is not beyond contemplation that its mother will be somewhere in the vicinity, and will suffer serious shock." . . .

Thus we see no good reason why the general rules of tort law, including the concepts of negligence, proximate cause, and foreseeability, long applied to all other types of injury, should not govern the case now before us. . . .

In short, the history of the cases does not show the development of a logical rule but rather a series of changes and abandonments. . . . [T]he cases have assumed a variety of postures. At first they insisted that there be no recovery for emotional trauma at all. . . . Retreating from this position, they gave relief for such trauma only if physical impact occurred. . . . They then abandoned the requirement for physical impact but insisted that the victim fear for her own safety . . . holding that a mother could recover for fear for her children's safety if she simultaneously entertained a personal fear for herself. . . . They stated that the mother need only be in the "zone of danger." . . . The final anomaly would be the instant case in which the sister, who observed the accident, would be granted recovery because she was in the "zone of danger," but the *mother*, not far distant, would be barred from recovery.

. . . The test that we have set forth will aid in the proper resolution of future cases. . . .

To deny recovery would be to chain this state to an outmoded rule of the 19th century which can claim no current credence. No good reason compels our captivity to an indefensible orthodoxy.

Being a Legal Secretary Versus a Paralegal
By Laura Glennon, Paralegal

Rather than leaping into law school without professional experience, a decision to attain a graduate level paralegal certificate was my first step into the legal arena. My studies within the paralegal program provided me with a breath of different areas of the law, the organization of the court system, how to perform proper legal research and writing, and an overview of the process of litigation. My expectation of a career and life as a paralegal stemmed from these studies. However, there is a difference between the designation of paralegal and legal secretary.

My position as a legal secretary within a civil litigation law firm, assisting two separate attorneys, has displayed to me the vast variety of law, the extreme importance of attention to detail, along with the stressful and deadline-driven culture of law. I have found that many of my duties as a legal secretary require intense organization, and less research than I expected. While I enjoy the work I do, there is a desire to perform more of the legal research I was taught within my paralegal program. The level of detail orientation needed to perform my position successfully was an expectation of mine. However, the amount of work placed upon me, a legal secretary with no prior law experience, along with two very busy and demanding attorneys, is combative with the amount of time one is expected to spend pouring over the details of every document. The combination of these factors creates a stressful environment. However, there is a support system among the legal secretaries, which is a welcomed benefit.

E T H I C S

Guideline 5: A lawyer may identify paralegals by name and title on the lawyer's letterhead and on business cards identifying the lawyer's firm.[10]

Most states allow paralegals to have their names on the firm's stationery, but there must also be an indication by the name that the paralegal is a paralegal. Paralegals can also have business cards, with the title of paralegal on the card.

Ethics Exercise: Determine whether your state is one of the states allowing paralegals to have their names on firm letterhead.

Chapter Summary

The duty a possessor of land owes to people who come onto her land depends upon whether those who come onto the land are trespassers, licensees, or invitees. In general, trespassers are not owed a duty. However, there are exceptions to this general rule for discovered trespassers and children. As to licensees, a possessor of land has the duty to warn licensees of known dangerous conditions the licensee will not reasonably discover on her own. A possessor of land has a duty to invitees to inspect the premises for hidden dangerous conditions. Sellers of land are not liable for dangerous conditions on property after the property is sold, unless the seller failed to disclose a dangerous condition of which she was or should have been aware.

Vicarious liability holds one person is liable for the torts of another if there is a special relationship between the two. An example of this special relationship is the relationship between employers and employees. The employer may be liable for the actions of the employee who is acting within the course and scope of his employment, but the employer will not be liable for the actions of an employee if the employee is on a frolic and detour. With regards to independent contractors, those who hire them are not usually vicariously liable for the independent contractor's torts. The family purpose doctrine states if a member of the automobile owner's household has permission to be driving the family car, then the owner of the automobile will be held liable for the driver's negligent acts.

NIED is when a defendant acts in a manner producing mental anguish in a foreseeable plaintiff. Typically, a plaintiff who never has a physical injury cannot recover under NIED. However, if the plaintiff was in the zone of danger, or related to the person injured, then the plaintiff may be able to recover.

Key Terms

■ Agent
■ Artificial condition on the land

■ Attractive nuisance
■ Business

---

10. ABA Model Guidelines for the Utilization of Paralegal Services, Guideline 5 (ABA 2004).

- Child
- Common area
- Consent
- Course and scope of employment
- Discovered trespasser
- Emotional distress
- Employer/employee relationship
- Express
- Family purpose doctrine
- Family relationship rule
- Frolic and detour rule
- Going and coming rule
- Impact rule
- Implied
- Imputed negligence
- Independent contractor
- Invitee
- Lessee
- Lessor

- Licensee
- Natural condition on the land
- Negligent infliction of emotional distress
- Omission
- Physical manifestation
- Premises liability
- Principal
- Principal-agent relationship
- Scope of employment
- Social guest
- Trespassing
- Trespasser
- Respondeat superior
- Vendee
- Vendor
- Vicarious liability
- Zone of danger

Review Questions

Premises Liability

- What duty of care is required towards a trespasser?
- Are there exceptions to the general duty of care owed to a trespasser?
- What is the duty owed to a discovered trespasser?
- What is the duty of care required towards a licensee?
- What is the duty of care required towards an invitee?
- Can a person lose his invitee status? How?
- Who does attractive nuisance apply to? Why is there a different duty of reasonable care in an attractive nuisance case?
- How is a person determined to be a child?
- What is an example of an attractive nuisance?
- What is a vendor's responsibility for dangerous conditions occurring after his possession of the land?
- What is a lessor's responsibility for common areas?

Vicarious Liability

- Who is an example of an agent?
- Explain respondeat superior.
- When will an employer be vicariously liable for the acts of an employee?
- How are independent contractors different from employees?

- Give an example of a frolic and detour.
- When will the employer of a paralegal be vicariously liable for the torts of his paralegal employees?
- What makes someone an independent contractor rather than an employee?
- What is the family purpose doctrine?

Negligent Infliction of Emotional Distress

- What are the elements of negligent infliction of emotional distress?
- Why can plaintiffs recover under a zone of danger theory?
- Why was the mother able to recover in *Dillon*, though she was never in any danger herself?

Web Links

- http://www.injuryboard.com/help-center/property-owners-liability/. Go to the Injury Board website and click on the property owners liability section. Read the article on what steps someone should take if he is injured on another's property. This information will help you when acting on behalf of someone who is injured on another's property.

- http://www.expertlaw.com/library/personal_injury/agency.html/. Go to this website by Expert Law and read more about principal-agency law.

Exercises

Premises liability

- Determine whether your state is one of the states that still classifies the duties owed under premises liability by trespasser, licensee, and invitee.

- On or about November 22, Margot was attending a conference by El Mundo Evangelism at the Marina Hotel. As Margot was leaving the Marina Hotel, she slipped and fell. Prior to the slip and fall, there had been heavy rain at the Marina Hotel. Plaintiff Margot was wearing shoes with very thin soles. There were yellow "caution" signs located in prominent places because of the dampness of the ground due to rain. The surface where the incident occurred was covered by indoor/outdoor carpeting. There were also Marina Hotel employees who were warning conference attendees to watch their step because it was wet. Plaintiff Margot was the only person out of 500 people who slipped and fell.
  - Did the Marina Hotel exercise its duty towards Margot?
  - In a lawsuit, who do you think will prevail: Margot or Marina Hotel?

- Under which category (trespasser, licensee, and/or invitee) do the following fall?
  - A cosmetic representative going door to door.

- ○ A customer who goes behind the store's counter to throw something away.
- ○ Children who build a tree house on a deserted lot. The landowner has seen the tree house, but does nothing to it.

Vicarious Liability

▪ Suzanne is a paralegal at a major law firm. She is asked to help at a deposition two hours away, and must drive to the deposition. The deposition is at one o'clock, and Suzanne leaves at 10:30 a.m. to allow plenty of time to arrive at the deposition. She normally receives a lunch break from noon to 1:00 p.m. However, she is driving to the deposition during this time. She decides to stop at a fireworks shop. It is almost the Fourth of July and her children would love it if she got them some fireworks. She looks at her watch and sees that she is very early for the deposition. She takes the freeway exit and follows the signs until she gets deeper and deeper into a rural area. When she gets to the fireworks stand, she starts picking up the merchandise. She picks up one sack of fireworks. She drops the bag onto another customer's foot, causing injury to the customer. If the customer sues the employer under the theory of respondeat superior, will the customer recover from the law firm?

▪ Instead of purchasing fireworks, Suzanne decides to hit the dry cleaners and pick up some suits for work. The dry cleaners is only five minutes off the route to the deposition, and going to the dry cleaners on the way to the deposition will save her time. At the dry cleaners, she does not find anyone at the front counter. In an effort to get an employee, she ventures into the back, calling as she goes. The floor is uneven and she trips and twists her ankle. If Suzanne attempts to sue her employer under the theory of respondeat superior, will she win the lawsuit?

▪ Is the family purpose doctrine the law in your state?

▪ The Davis family has only one car, which is used by Mr. Davis to drive to and from work, and to run family errands on the weekends. Mr. and Mrs. Davis decide to go on a tenth-anniversary trip, leaving the car and the children at home with a grandmother to babysit the children. One of the family's children becomes sick, and the grandmother takes the child to emergency room. While granny is racing to the ER, she sideswipes another car. The owner of the car sues Mr. Davis for negligence. Will the family purpose automobile doctrine apply?

Negligent infliction of emotional distress

▪ Look up whether your jurisdiction is one that follows the holding in *Dillon.*

▪ Cindy and Larry, spouses, go to the state fair together. Larry invites Cindy onto the giant Ferris Wheel. Cindy, thinking it will be romantic, agrees. However, when the two get to the front of the line, the ride operator states they cannot ride together because of the weight restrictions, and then proceeds to pair Cindy up with an unknown child and put Larry into a seat by himself. Cindy is disappointed but keeps smiling and waving to Larry who is below her on the Ferris Wheel. Cindy is startled when one of the bright light bulbs bursts and falls to the ground.

She looks down at Larry and sees not only has the light bulb burst, his entire chair has come loose and is only hanging onto the Ferris Wheel on one side. She screams at Larry to hang on, but Larry falls about fifty feet to the ground. Larry's legs stick out at horrible angles. Cindy brings a lawsuit against the owners and operators of the Ferris Wheel.

○ What will the result be if Cindy sues in a state with the impact rule?

○ What will the result be if Cindy sues in a state with the zone of danger rule?

○ What will the result be if Cindy sues in a state with the *Dillon* rule?

▧ Using the fact scenario above, now assume Cindy is on the Ferris Wheel and the accident happens to her girlfriend, Fanny.

○ What will the result be if Cindy sues in a state with the impact rule?

○ What will the result be if Cindy sues in a state with the zone of danger rule?

○ What will the result be if Cindy sues in a state with the *Dillon* rule?

The Defenses to Negligence

When a man points a finger a someone else, he should remember that four of his fingers are pointing at himself."[1]

Chapter Outline

Chapter Objectives

- Describe contributory and comparative negligence, along with the differences between the two
- Explain the doctrine of last clear chance
- Point out the exceptions to contributory negligence
- Discuss how defenses to negligence are used
- Explain assumption of the risk
- Illustrate the statute of limitations

---

1. Louis Nizer.

7.1   Introduction to Defenses to Negligence

Defenses are those allegations the defendant makes in response to the allegations in the complaint. Defenses state why the plaintiff should not win. Just as the plaintiff must prove every element of his cause of action, the defendant must prove every element of his defense. The major defenses to negligence are contributory negligence, comparative negligence, assumption of the risk, and statutes of limitations. If the defendant is able to prove each element of a defense, then this is the outcome:

Contributory Negligence	Bars plaintiff from recovering.
Comparative Negligence	Reduces plaintiff's recovery.
Assumption of risk	Bars plaintiff from recovering or reduces plaintiff's recovery.
Statutes of limitations	Bars plaintiff from recovering.

7.2   Contributory Negligence

Elements of Contributory Negligence:

The plaintiff breaches the duty to protect himself from injury.
The plaintiff's acts concur with the negligent acts of the defendant.
The plaintiff's acts contribute to his injuries and are a proximate cause of his injuries.

Affirmative defense
even if what is alleged in the complaint is true, this defense (such as contributory negligence) is a defense to the complaint.

Contributory negligence
the plaintiff must not have played a role in causing the injury to himself, if the plaintiff is to recover damages.

Contributory and comparative negligence, along with assumption of the risk, are all affirmative defenses that must be proven by the defendant. **Affirmative defenses** state even if what is alleged in the complaint is true, this defense (such as contributory negligence) is a defense to the complaint. The burden is placed upon the defendant to show the plaintiff was contributorily negligent. The defendant will typically bring contributory negligence up as an affirmative defense in the defendant's answer. Contributory negligence is not a defense to an intentional tort, strict liability, or products liability.

Contributory negligence is the idea the plaintiff must not have played a role in causing the injury to himself, if the plaintiff is to recover damages. The plaintiff has a duty of care to himself. This duty of care requires the plaintiff to exercise reasonable care to protect himself. The plaintiff may have to bear the entire cost of the injury if he is at all negligent, even if the defendant also committed negligence. Under contributory negligence, the defendant would not have to pay at all for her portion of the negligence because the plaintiff also contributed to his own injury. Contributory negligence is an all-or-nothing approach. The plaintiff must not be at all at fault for his injury in order to recover damages in a contributory negligence state. The burden is on the defendant to prove the contributory negligence of the plaintiff.

Example of Contributory Negligence

Fanny and Francis are on opposite sides of a swinging door. Francis is in a hurry and bursts through the door, hitting and knocking Fanny down. Fanny breaks her

hip from the fall and incurs $50,000 in medical bills. Fanny was hit in part because she was standing too close to the door. Fanny, the plaintiff, is 10% at fault for her injuries, and Francis, the defendant, is 90% at fault for Fanny's injuries. However, Fanny and Francis live in a contributory negligence jurisdiction. Thus, Fanny cannot recover any of her $50,000 in medical bills from Francis because Fanny was partially responsible (10%) for her own injury.

There are very few states left with a system of contributory negligence. (See Figure 7.1.)

Figure 7.1

States with Contributory Negligence (List is subject to change)

Alabama	Maryland
North Carolina	Virginia
Washington, D.C.	

The majority of jurisdictions determined that contributory negligence is inequitable to the plaintiff. Contributory negligence holds that so long as the plaintiff had something to do with his own accident, then no matter how badly he is injured, he cannot recover from the defendant. In contrast to contributory negligence, comparative negligence still allows the plaintiff to recover from the defendant, even when the plaintiff is partially responsible for his own injuries. The plaintiff's role in his own injury will merely lessen the plaintiff's recovery from the defendant.

a. Exceptions to Contributory Negligence: Last Clear Chance
Elements of Last Clear Chance:

Defendant knew of the peril to plaintiff.
Defendant had the opportunity to prevent the peril.
Defendant failed to take precautions to prevent the peril.
A reasonable person would have taken precautions.
The plaintiff is injured.

Last clear chance
if a defendant could have avoided the harm at the last minute, but did not, then the defendant will be found liable to the plaintiff even though the plaintiff contributed to his own injury.

One method of reducing the harshness of contributory negligence to the plaintiff is the last clear chance rule. The doctrine of **last clear chance** is only available to a plaintiff in a contributory negligence situation. If a defendant could have avoided the harm at the last minute, but did not, then the defendant will be found liable to the plaintiff even though the plaintiff contributed to his own injury. The burden is on the plaintiff to prove last clear chance. If the plaintiff fails to see a stop sign and goes through the stop sign, the plaintiff has acted negligently. If the defendant sees the plaintiff has run the stop sign and is able to stop, but does not and plows into the plaintiff, then the defendant did not take the last clear chance to prevent the injury.

Therefore, the defendant will be liable under the doctrine of last clear chance, even though the plaintiff contributed to his own injury.

Example of Last Clear Chance

Using the earlier example of Fanny and Francis, Fanny is still standing too close to the swinging door. However, right before Francis is about to burst through the door, he hears someone on the other side of the door. If Francis still goes bursting through the door, even though he heard someone right on the other side of the door, then Francis would be liable to Fanny under the doctrine of last clear chance.

b. Exceptions to Contributory Negligence: Sudden Emergency

Elements of Sudden Emergency

There was a sudden emergency.
The plaintiff's reaction to the emergency was a reasonable one.
The emergency could not have been anticipated.
The emergency was caused by the defendant.
The plaintiff was placed into danger.

Sudden emergency is an exception under contributory negligence. If the plaintiff can prove the above elements, then a plaintiff may be able to recover damages, even in a contributory negligence state. In other words, even if the plaintiff was negligent in causing his injury, he might be excused from his contributory negligence if he was in a sudden emergency. If there is a sudden emergency, then a plaintiff is not held to the same standard he would be held to under normal circumstances. Very few people are able to act at their optimal performance level under a state of emergency. Thus, the law has stepped in to reduce the standard of care a plaintiff must utilize in an emergency.

7.3 Comparative Negligence

Comparative negligence allows the plaintiff to obtain a recovery from the defendant even if the plaintiff is partially responsible for his injury; plaintiff's recovery will be reduced by the percentage of his own negligence.

Comparative negligence was enacted by many states to avoid the all-or-nothing consequences of contributory negligence. **Comparative negligence** does not keep the plaintiff from obtaining a recovery if the plaintiff is partially responsible for his injury. Comparative negligence reduces the plaintiff's recovery by the percentage of his own negligence. The plaintiff's negligence will be weighed against the defendant's negligence. While the plaintiff cannot obtain a settlement of 100%, because he is also at fault, this does not prevent him from obtaining a settlement at all.

Types of Comparative Negligence:

Pure
Modified

In *Li v. Yellow Cab*, the Supreme Court of California ruled contributory negligence was inequitable because contributory negligence leaves the plaintiff with all or nothing. The court ruled comparative negligence would be the law in California. In making this ruling, the court looked at 25 other states that already had comparative negligence law. The court was persuaded by how many states had already changed to comparative negligence. Under comparative negligence, the plaintiff can recover even if the plaintiff is negligent. The court adopted pure comparative negligence, under which the plaintiff could recover 100%, less the percent the plaintiff was held liable.

Li v. Yellow Cab Co. of California

13 Cal 3d 804; 532 P.2d 1226, 119 Cal. Rptr. 858 (1975)

In this case we address the grave and recurrent question whether we should judicially declare no longer applicable in California courts the doctrine of contributory negligence, which bars all recovery when the plaintiff's negligent conduct has contributed as a legal cause in any degree to the harm suffered by him, and hold that it must give way to a system of comparative negligence, which assesses liability in direct proportion to fault. As we explain in detail infra, we conclude that we should. In the course of reaching our ultimate decision we conclude that:

(1) The doctrine of comparative negligence is preferable to the "all-or-nothing" doctrine of contributory negligence from the point of view of logic, practical experience, and fundamental justice. . . .

(4) The doctrine of comparative negligence should be applied in this state in its so-called "pure" form under which the assessment of liability in proportion to fault proceeds in spite of the fact that the plaintiff is equally at fault as or more at fault than the defendant. . . .

The accident here in question occurred near the intersection of Alvarado Street and Third Street in Los Angeles. At this intersection Third Street runs in a generally east-west direction along the crest of a hill, and Alvarado Street, running generally north and south, rises gently to the crest from either direction. At approximately 9 p.m. on November 21, 1968, plaintiff Nga Li was proceeding northbound on Alvarado in her 1967 Oldsmobile. She was in the inside lane, and about 70 feet before she reached the Third Street intersection she stopped and then began a left turn across the three southbound lanes of Alvarado, intending to enter the driveway of a service station. At this time defendant Robert Phillips, an employee of defendant Yellow Cab Company, was driving a company-owned taxicab southbound in the middle lane on Alvarado. He came over the crest of the hill, passed through the intersection, and collided with the right rear portion of plaintiff's automobile, resulting in personal injuries to plaintiff as well as considerable damage to the automobile.

. . . [D]efendant Phillips was traveling at approximately 30 miles per hour when he entered the intersection, that such speed was unsafe at that time and place, and that the traffic light controlling southbound traffic at the intersection was yellow when defendant Phillips drove into the intersection. It also found, however, that plaintiff's left turn across the southbound lanes of Alvarado "was made at a time when a vehicle was approaching from the opposite direction so close as to constitute an immediate hazard." The dispositive conclusion of law was as follows: "That the driving of Nga Li was negligent, that such negligence was a proximate cause of the collision, and that she is barred from recovery by reason of such contributory negligence." . . .

"Contributory negligence is conduct on the part of the plaintiff which falls below the standard to which he should conform for his own protection, and which is a legally contributing cause cooperating with the negligence of the defendant in bringing about the plaintiff's harm." . . . "Except where the defendant has the last clear chance, the plaintiff's contributory negligence bars recovery against a defendant whose negligent conduct would otherwise make him liable to the plaintiff for the harm sustained by him. . . ."

This rule, rooted in the long-standing principle that one should not recover from another for damages brought upon oneself . . . has been the law of this state from its beginning. . . . [T]he "all-or-nothing" rule of contributory negligence can be and ought to be superseded by a rule which assesses liability in proportion to fault.

It is unnecessary for us to catalogue the enormous amount of critical comment that has been directed over the years against the "all-or-nothing" approach of the doctrine of contributory negligence. The essence of that criticism has been constant and clear: the doctrine is inequitable in its operation because it fails to distribute responsibility in proportion to fault. . . .

It is in view of these theoretical and practical considerations that to this date 25 states have abrogated the "all-or-nothing" rule of contributory negligence and have enacted in its place general apportionment *statutes* calculated in one manner or another to assess liability in proportion to fault. . . . We are likewise persuaded that logic, practical experience, and fundamental justice counsel against the retention of the doctrine rendering contributory negligence a complete bar to recovery — and that it should be replaced in this state by a system under which liability for damage will be borne by those whose negligence caused it in direct proportion to their respective fault. . . .

. . . It remains to identify the precise form of comparative negligence which we now adopt for application in this state. Although there are many variants, only the two basic forms need be considered here. The first of these, the so-called "pure" form of comparative negligence, apportions liability in direct proportion to fault in all cases. . . . The second basic form of comparative negligence, of which there are several variants, applies apportionment based on fault up to the point at which the plaintiff's negligence is equal to or greater than that of the defendant — when that point is reached, plaintiff is barred from recovery. . . . The principal argument advanced in its favor is moral in nature: that it is not morally right to permit one more at fault in an accident to recover from one less at fault. Other arguments assert the probability of increased insurance, administrative, and judicial costs if a "pure" rather than a "50 percent" system is adopted, but this has been seriously questioned. . . .

We have concluded that the "pure" form of comparative negligence is that which should be adopted in this state. In our view the "50 percent" system simply shifts the lottery aspect of the contributory negligence rule to a different ground. As Dean Prosser has noted, under such a system "[it] is obvious that a slight difference in the proportionate fault may permit a recovery; and there has been much justified criticism of a rule under which a plaintiff who is charged with 49 percent of the total negligence recovers 51 percent of his damages, while one who is charged with 50 percent recovers nothing at all. . . ."

For all of the foregoing reasons we conclude that the "all-or-nothing" rule of contributory negligence as it presently exists in this state should be and is herewith superseded by a system of "pure" comparative negligence, the fundamental purpose of which shall be to assign responsibility and liability for damage in direct proportion to the amount of negligence of each of the parties. Therefore, in all actions for negligence resulting in injury to person or property, the contributory negligence of the person injured in person or property shall not bar recovery, but the damages awarded shall be diminished in proportion to the amount of negligence attributable to the person recovering. . . .

a. Pure Comparative Negligence

Elements of Pure Comparative Negligence:

The plaintiff was negligent and contributed to his injury.
100% plaintiff's negligence.

Pure comparative negligence
no matter how great the plaintiff's degree of fault, he is allowed a recovery so long as he is 99% or less at fault.

Pure comparative negligence is where the amount of the plaintiff's recovery is reduced by the amount of the plaintiff's negligence. No matter how great the plaintiff's degree of fault, he is allowed a recovery so long as he is 99% or less at fault. The plaintiff's award is limited to the percentage of the injury attributed to the defendant. If a plaintiff has $25,000 in damages and is 10% at fault, then the plaintiff would get 90% of $25,000. The plaintiff would get a $22,500 award from the defendant.

Example of Pure Comparative Negligence

Again, Fanny and Francis are on opposite sides of a swinging door. Francis is in a hurry and bursts through the door, hitting and knocking Fanny down. Fanny breaks her hip from the fall and incurs $50,000 in medical bills. Fanny was hit in part because she was standing too close to the door. Fanny, the plaintiff, is 10% at fault for her injuries, and Francis, the defendant, is 90% at fault for Fanny's injuries. Fanny and Francis live in a pure comparative negligence state. Fanny can recover from Francis 100% minus Fanny's 10% contribution to the injury. Fanny can recover 90% of the $50,000 from Francis, which is $45,000.

Figure 7.2

States with Pure Comparative Negligence (List is subject to change)

Alaska	Arizona
California	Florida
Kentucky	Louisiana
Mississippi	Missouri
New Mexico	New York
Rhode Island	South Dakota
Washington	

b. Modified Comparative Negligence

Modified comparative negligence
if a plaintiff has equal or greater than an amount of negligence as compared to the defendant, then the plaintiff cannot recover.

Modified comparative negligence is when a plaintiff has equal or greater than an amount of negligence as compared to the defendant. In these situations the plaintiff cannot recover. If a plaintiff is 50% or 51% responsible for his injury, then the plaintiff cannot recover an award against the defendant. However, if plaintiff was 49% at fault, the plaintiff would still recover damages from the defendant. In other words, if the plaintiff was 49% at fault, he could recover 51% of his damages under modified comparative negligence.

Example of Modified Comparative Negligence

Fanny and Francis are standing on opposite sides of a swinging door. Both try to open the door at the same time, but Francis tries with more force and knocks Fanny down. Fanny, the plaintiff, breaks her hip from the fall and incurs $50,000 in medical bills. Fanny is determined to be 49% at fault for her own injury. Fanny and Francis live in a modified comparative negligence state. Fanny can still recover 51% from Francis, the defendant. Fanny could recover 51% of $50,000, that is, $25,500.

Figure 7.3

States with Modified Comparative Negligence (List is subject to change)

Arkansas	Colorado
Connecticut	Delaware
Georgia	Hawaii
Idaho	Illinois
Indiana	Iowa
Kansas	Maine
Massachusetts	Michigan
Minnesota	Montana
Nebraska	Nevada

New Hampshire	New Jersey
North Dakota	Ohio
Oklahoma	Oregon
Pennsylvania	South Carolina
Tennessee	Texas
Utah	Vermont
West Virginia	Wisconsin
Wyoming	

7.4 Assumption of the Risk

Elements of Assumption of the Risk:

Plaintiff voluntary assumption of known risk (remember this is a subjective standard).
Plaintiff has a full understanding of the dangers.

Assumption of the risk
when a plaintiff knowingly takes a chance he will be injured, the plaintiff takes responsibility for the consequences of his actions.

Assumption of the risk is when a plaintiff knowingly takes a chance he will be injured. When a plaintiff knowingly takes a chance he will be injured, the plaintiff takes responsibility for the consequences of his actions. Assumption of the risk is based upon the belief individuals have the right to make their own risky decisions, but if an individual is injured as a result of his choice, he must bear the responsibility of the choice. The major difference between assumption of the risk and contributory negligence is the degree in which the plaintiff realizes there is a danger. In assumption of the risk, the plaintiff must realize there is a danger and voluntarily take on the danger. The realization of the danger is a subjective standard, rather than an objective one. Previously, the standards discussed were based upon what would a reasonable person do under similar circumstances. Which is an objective standard. With assumption of the risk, the importance is placed upon what the particular plaintiff believed. Did this particular plaintiff realize he assumed the risk of the tortfeasor's conduct? Did the plaintiff realize there was a safety risk to himself, but go ahead and take the risk anyway?

a. Voluntary Assumption of Known Risk: Express Assumption of the Risk

Express assumption of the risk
the plaintiff signs a written waiver of the risk or verbally states he accepts the risk.

Express assumption of the risk occurs when the plaintiff either signs a written waiver of the risk or verbally states he accepts the risk. An example of an express assumption of the risk would be when a plaintiff signs a release of all liability. A plaintiff can agree ahead of time to waive the defendant's liability for potentially negligent conduct. If the plaintiff does so expressly, the waiver is bargained for, and if the waiver is not against the public interest, then a court will probably up hold the waiver.

For instance, if a person decides to go white-water rafting, he is asked by the rafting company to sign a waiver of all liability on behalf of the rafting company for any of the plaintiff's injuries or potential death. The plaintiff, in signing the release, must know he is signing a release. If the release of liability is in tiny print, buried within a long contract, the release will not suffice to relieve the defendant of liability. If the release is a valid release, a defendant can then be dissolved of a duty to prevent an injury from happening to the plaintiff because plaintiff assumed the risk of injury to himself. In this instance, the plaintiff assumed the risks of white-water rafting, such as drowning.

b. Voluntary Assumption of Known Risk: Implied Assumption of the Risk

Implied assumption of the risk

when a plaintiff shows by his conduct he has accepted a risk.

An **implied assumption of the risk** is where by his conduct, a plaintiff shows he has accepted the risk. If a person goes to Yosemite to rock-climb, by his conduct of climbing the rock, he has assumed the risk he may fall and injure himself. If a person goes hang gliding off a cliff, she assumes the risk the glider may crash and injure her. These risks are part and parcel of the activity. Neither one of these people were forced to perform the activities. They chose to perform the activities. In order for the plaintiff to assume the risk, the plaintiff must have appreciated the danger he was going to be subjected to.

7.5 Statutes of Limitations

Statute of limitations

a time limit in which the plaintiff must file a lawsuit; the time limit changes based on the type of lawsuit and the jurisdiction.

Statutes of limitations are a defense to negligence. A statute of limitations puts a limit on the amount of time in which a plaintiff must file a lawsuit. If a plaintiff did not file within the time limits, then the defendant would argue the plaintiff is barred from bringing a personal injury action.

Figure 7.4

Differences in Personal Injury Statutes of Limitations by State

States with one-year personal injury statutes of limitations

Kentucky[2]	Tennessee[4]
Louisiana[3]	

States with two-year personal injury statutes of limitations

Alabama[5]	California[8]
Alaska[6]	Colorado (three for a car accident)[9]
Arizona[7]	Connecticut[10]

2. Ky. Rev. Stat. Ann. §413.140 (West 2006).
3. La. Civ. Code Ann. Art. 3492 (2004).
4. Tenn. Code Ann. §28-4-104 (West 2002).
5. Ala. Code §6-2-38 (1993).
6. Alaska Stat. §09.10.070 (Michie 2000).
7. Ariz. Rev. Stat. Ann. §12-542 (West 2003).
8. Cal. Code Of Civ. Proc. §335.1 (West 2007).
9. Colo. Rev. Stat. §§12-80-102, 13-80-101 (West 1997).
10. Conn. Gen. Stat. Ann. §54-584 (West 1991).

States with two-year personal injury statutes of limitations

Delaware[11]
Georgia[12]
Hawaii[13]
Idaho[14]
Illinois[15]
Indiana[16]
Iowa[17]
Kansas[18]
Minnesota[19]

New Jersey[20]
Ohio[21]
Oklahoma[22]
Oregon[23]
Pennsylvania[24]
Texas[25]
Virginia[26]
West Virginia[27]

States with three-year personal injury statutes of limitations

Arkansas[28]
Maryland[29]
Massachusetts[30]
Michigan[31]
Montana[32]
New Hampshire[33]
New Mexico[34]
New York[35]

North Carolina[36]
Rhode Island[37]
South Carolina[38]
South Dakota[39]
Vermont[40]
Washington[41]
Washington, D.C.[42]
Wisconsin[43]

11. Del. Code Ann. tit. 10, §§8107, 8119 (Michie 1999).
12. Ga. Code Ann. §9-3-33 (1982).
13. Haw. Rev. Stat. §657-7 (1993).
14. Idaho Code §5-219 (Michie 1998).
15. Ill. Ann. Stat. ch. 5, §13-202 (West 2005).
16. Ind. Code Ann. §34-11-2-4 (West 1999).
17. Iowa Code Ann. §614.1 (West 1999).
18. Kan. Stat. Ann. §60-513 (1999).
19. Minn. Stat. Ann. §541.07 (West 2000).
20. N.J. Stat. Ann. §2A-14-2 (West 2000).
21. Ohio Rev. Code Ann. §2305.10 (West 2004).
22. Okla. Stat. Ann., tit. 12 §95 (West 2000).
23. Or. Rev. Stat. §12.110(1) (1999).
24. 42 Pa. Consd. Stat. Ann. §5524 (West 2004).
25. Tex. Civ. Prac. & Rem. Code. tit. 2 §16.003 (West 2006).
26. Va. Code Ann. §8.01-243 (Michie 2000).
27. W. Va. Code §55-2-12 (2000).
28. Ark. Code Ann. §16-56-105 (Michie Supp. 1999).
29. Md. Ct. & Jud. Proc. Code Ann. §5-101(2002).
30. Mass. Gen. Laws Ann., ch. 260, §2A, 4 (West 2004).
31. Mich. Comp. Laws §600.5805 (2000).
32. Mont. Code Ann. §27-2-204 (1999).
33. N.H. Rev. Stat. Ann. §508.4 (West 1997).
34. N.M. Stat. Ann. §37-1-8 (West 2003).
35. N.Y. Civ. Pract. L. & R. §214 (West 2006).
36. N.C. Gen. Stat. Ann. §1-52 (Lexis 2003).
37. R.I. Gen. Laws §9-1-14 (1999).
38. S.C. Code Ann. §15-3-530 (2005).
39. S.D. Codified Laws §§15.2.12.2, 15.2.14 (2001).
40. Vt. Stat. Ann., tit. 12, §512 (2000).
41. Wash. Rev. Code §4.16.080 (2000).
42. D.C. Code Ann. §12-301 (Lexis).
43. Wis. Stat. Ann. §893.54 (West).

States with more than three-year statutes of limitations:	Years:
Florida[44]	4 years
Maine[45]	6 years
Missouri[46]	5 years
Nebraska[47]	4 years
North Dakota[48]	6 years
Utah[49]	4 years
Wyoming[50]	4 years

Life as a New Paralegal
By Olga Gonzalez, Paralegal

As I look at the pile of files on my desk, I take a deep breath and begin my day. Almost every day starts at 9:00 a.m. and ends at 3:00 p.m. I work part time. Although it may seem as if I don't work as hard as others—because of my short hours—it feels like I work twice as hard because I am trying to cram eight hours of work into a six-hour work day. As a result, I am ALWAYS busy, but fortunately I enjoy my job.

I like working with an attorney even though there are times I feel overwhelmed. Sometimes he leaves the office without letting me know, or he forgets to tell me that he has already met with a client privately, thus immediately changing what I need to do for a file. Despite these little annoyances, working with an attorney is intellectually stimulating and every day is different.

I work for an attorney who expects me to be flexible with my hours. Client meetings often dictate both of our schedules. I can't tell you how many times people get confused about when their appointments are, which is why I have to continuously remind the client and the attorney. As his paralegal, I must know how to manage my time and his time. I am in charge of his calendar and all the clients' files.

I would say my client interaction is very personal, simply because I am dealing with their personal information and often meet with them when the attorney does. There are times when we have to go to their homes. My job is challenging in many different aspects, but I enjoy every moment of it. Life as a new paralegal is good.

44. Fla. Stat. Ann. §95.11(4) (2002).
45. Me. Rev. Stat. Ann. tit. 14, ch. 205, §752 (West 2003).
46. Mo. Rev. Stat. tit. 35, §516.120 (West 2001).
47. Neb. Rev. Stat. §25-207 (1995).
48. N.D. Cent. Code Ann. §28-01-16 (1991).
49. Utah Code Ann. §78-12-25(3) (West 2004).
50. Wyo. Stat. Ann. §1-3-105 (Michie 2000).

E T H I C S

Model Rules of Professional Conduct Client-Lawyer Relationship

Rule 1.6 Confidentiality of Information
(a) A lawyer shall not reveal information relating to the representation of a client unless the client gives informed consent, the disclosure is impliedly authorized in order to carry out the representation or the disclosure is permitted by paragraph (b).
(b) A lawyer may reveal information relating to the representation of a client to the extent the lawyer reasonably believes necessary:
    (1) to prevent reasonably certain death or substantial bodily harm;
    (2) to prevent the client from committing a crime or fraud that is reasonably certain to result in substantial injury to the financial interests or property of another and in furtherance of which the client has used or is using the lawyer's services;
    (3) to prevent, mitigate or rectify substantial injury to the financial interests or property of another that is reasonably certain to result or has resulted from the client's commission of a crime or fraud in furtherance of which the client has used the lawyer's services;

(4) to secure legal advice about the lawyer's compliance with these Rules;
(5) to establish a claim or defense on behalf of the lawyer in a controversy between the lawyer and the client, to establish a defense to a criminal charge or civil claim against the lawyer based upon conduct in which the client was involved, or to respond to allegations in any proceeding concerning the lawyer's representation of the client; or
(6) to comply with other law or a court order.[51]

The attorney should ensure the paralegal keeps client information confidential. The attorney therefore is required to instruct the paralegal on how to keep the client's information confidential. An attorney or a paralegal cannot reveal information relating to the representation of the client. The client needs to feel she can discuss the case freely with her attorney and paralegal. This rule helps the client to feel safe in providing the information the attorney needs to represent the client. This rule not only includes the information the client provides, but any information relating to the representation, no matter how the attorney learned the information.

Ethics Exercise: Watch the movie *The Client*. Pay particular attention to the discussions of client confidentiality.

Chapter Summary

Defenses are the defendant's response to the allegations the plaintiff made in the complaint. The major defenses to negligence are contributory negligence, comparative negligence, assumption of the risk, and statutes of limitations. If the plaintiff is in a contributory negligence state, any negligence on her part in causing her injury will prevent her from recovering from a defendant who was also negligent. Since this is inequitable to plaintiffs, there are some exceptions to this general rule. The exceptions include last clear chance and sudden emergency. Even if the plaintiff

51. Model R. Prof. Conduct 1.6 (ABA 2004).

was negligent, if the defendant could have avoided the harm at the last minute, but did not do so, then the defendant can be found liable. If there is a sudden emergency, and the plaintiff acts negligent as a result of the sudden emergency, then the plaintiff may still be able to recover from the defendant.

Comparative negligence was instituted to avoid the harsh consequences of contributory negligence. Comparative negligence does not prevent the plaintiff from recovering if the plaintiff is partially responsible for causing his own injury. There are two types of comparative negligence: pure and modified. Under pure comparative negligence, the plaintiff's recovery is 100% minus whatever percentage of the injury was the plaintiff's fault. Even if the plaintiff was 99% at fault, the plaintiff can still recover one percent from the defendant. With modified comparative negligence, the plaintiff must be 50% or less at fault to recover damages from the defendant.

Assumption of the risk is the next major defense to negligence a defendant can raise. If the plaintiff knowingly took a chance he would be injured, then the plaintiff should be responsible for the consequences of his action. The plaintiff can either expressly or impliedly assume the risk. An express assumption would be a written release or a verbal statement by the plaintiff stating he knows he is undertaking a risk. An assumption of the risk can also be made through conduct, which is known as implied assumption of the risk.

The last major defense to negligence is a statute of limitations defense. Under a statute of limitations defense, a defendant is alleging the plaintiff did not file the lawsuit within the allowed time period. Each type of lawsuit and each state has a different statute of limitations, which could be one year, two years, and so on.

Key Terms

- Affirmative defense
- Assumption of risk
- Comparative negligence
- Contributory negligence
- Express assumption of the risk
- Implied assumption of the risk
- Last clear chance
- Modified comparative negligence
- Pure comparative negligence
- Statute of limitations

Review Questions

- Do you think the concept of contributory negligence is a fair way of dividing responsibility for damages in a lawsuit? Why?
- Do you think the concept of comparative negligence is a fair way of dividing responsibility for damages in a lawsuit? Why?
- If someone signs a waiver how does it affect his legal rights if he is injured?
- What is the statute of limitations? How can it differ?

Web Links

- http://www.findlaw.com/. Findlaw is a stand-in for many law firms who do not have an account with Lexis-Nexis or WestLaw. The professional section of Findlaw relates more information than the consumer section. If you are interested in torts, you can perform a search for jobs in the personal injury field of law.

- http://www.expertlaw.com/library/personal_injury/negligence.html/. This website run by Expert Law has an excellent state-by-state overview of statutes of limitations. You have been provided the general statute of limitations for negligence actions in this chapter. However, different types of torts, such as libel and defamation, have different statutes of limitations. Go to this website and look up the applicable statutes of limitations in your state.

Exercises

- Contributory negligence is the law in the following hypothetical. Linda is a mother with a part-time job at the corner liquor store. She works at night, after her husband comes home from work to take care of the kids. The liquor store has been held up in the past on multiple occasions. The liquor store has a video camera, but no alarm system or security, other than iron bars on the windows. Linda is held up at gunpoint. She has frequent, intense anxiety after the incident. She sues the liquor store for failing to have adequate safeguards in place. Could the liquor store successfully assert assumption of the risk?

- On Halloween, a child wearing a dark costume decides to cross a busy street, but does not use the crosswalk. Unable to see him at night, a driver hits the child. Did the child assume the risk of being hit?

- William is a high school student who has cut across his neighbor's yard every day he walks to school. The neighbors, tired of having their grass trampled on, erect a fence and put up a big sign stating: "Warning, vicious guard dog on duty." William sees the fence, and realizes he can scale it and still make it to class on time even though he is running late. Once William lands inside the neighbors' yard, he is bitten by a dog. If William sues the neighbors, will the neighbors be able to successful argue an assumption of the risk defense?

- Michael goes to a monster truck rally. Before going to the rally, he does not read the back of his ticket, which states: "Monster truck rallies are extremely noisy. Ear protection is highly recommended. By purchasing this ticket, the bearer of the ticket has expressly assumed any and all risk of ear injury associated with attending this event." Michael, not having read the back of the ticket, does not bring earplugs or other protective ear equipment to the rally. After the rally, he has constant ringing in his ears and cannot hear people talk to him. Did Michael expressly assume the risk of ear injury? What about impliedly?

Medical Malpractice

Operate? Yes, operate — only do a good job.[1]

Chapter Outline

Chapter Objectives

- Provide a definition of medical malpractice, indicating it is negligence
- Discuss the standard of care for medical professionals
- Describe informed consent and its implications
- Give exceptions to informed consent
- Outline defenses to medical malpractice

---

1. *Bad Medicine* (Twentieth Century Fox 1985) (motion picture).

8.1   Introduction to Medical Malpractice

Medical malpractice
the failure of a medical
professional to act as a
reasonable medical
professional would to comply
with the applicable standards
of care under the
circumstances.

Medical malpractice is negligence. The only modification is the standard of reasonable care. Medical malpractice is frequently handled at personal injury law firms which also handle general tort claims. Legal malpractice is another type of negligence as well. However, legal malpractice is typically handled by specialists in legal malpractice, who do not necessarily practice general tort law. Thus, medical malpractice is discussed in this book because it is more likely a paralegal will work with medical malpractice claims.

Medical malpractice is not a separate tort, but rather a type of negligence. Since there are many issues specific to medical malpractice, it has its own chapter. However, be sure to remember that medical malpractice is *not* a separate tort.

Medical malpractice is the failure of a medical professional to act as a reasonable medical professional would to comply with the applicable standards of care under the circumstances. A medical professional may commit malpractice and still not injure the patient. But damages, or an injury to the plaintiff, is an element of the cause of action for medical malpractice. This chapter explains the elements of malpractice and the standards of reasonable care, as well as informed consent.

8.2   Elements of Medical Malpractice

As discussed above, medical malpractice is not a separate tort, but rather the tort of negligence. Therefore, the elements of medical malpractice are the same as negligence: duty, breach, causation, and damages. These elements of negligence are often dressed up in medical terminology, but are the same as the four elements of negligence. As the elements are the same, proving a medical malpractice case is similar to proving negligence. The burden of proof is on the plaintiff to prove all of these elements of medical malpractice.

a.   Standard of Care for Medical Professionals

One of the main issues arising in medical malpractice is medical professionals are held to a higher standard of care than the ordinarily prudent person. The standard of care outlines what is acceptable behavior under the circumstances. Medical professionals are held to the standard of care of a reasonable medical professional under similar circumstances. Medical malpractice occurs when a medical provider does not practice to the standard of care of a reasonable medical professional under the circumstances. If a competent health care provider would have utilized the particular procedure or treatment in question under similar circumstances, then malpractice normally will not be found. Medical specialists are held to a higher standard than regular medical practitioners. Specialists must use the same standard of care as another specialist in the field would under similar circumstances. Specific examples of medical malpractice would be diagnostic errors, treatment issues, problems in communication, medication errors, and falls. If a medical professional does not properly diagnosis the plaintiff's condition, then the medical professional could be found to have breached the standard of care she owed to the plaintiff.

Example of Medical Malpractice

Dana died on January 2. Dr. Brennan, an employee of the University Hospital, examined the Dana prior to her death at the University Clinic. Dr. Brennan saw Dana on only one occasion, the day before her death, when Dana presented with symptoms consistent with viral gastroenteritis and a mild exacerbation of Chronic Obstructive Pulmonary Disease ("COPD"). On the patient intake sheet, Dana stated she had been homeless for a year and she had smoked a pack of cigarettes per day for twenty years. On the day of Dana's death and immediately prior to 5:00 p.m., when the clinic closed, a friend of Dana's called the clinic. The friend told the clinic's receptionist Dana was worsening and asked if Dana could be brought back to the clinic. The receptionist advised the friend to take Dana to seek treatment at the emergency room.

Dana's autopsy showed Dana died from acute bronchopneumonia. Dana's family alleged the care rendered by the University Clinic failed to comply with the standard of care and the clinic failed to provide the appropriate access to care, leading to the negligent, wrongful death of Dana.

- Look up viral gastroenteritis and COPD. Compare the systems of these with the symptoms of bronchopneumonia, from which Dana died. Is bronchopneumonia related to viral gastroenteritis and COPD? Bronchopneumonia has many of the same symptoms of COPD.
- Do you think the University Clinic failed to comply with the standard of care? If a reasonable doctor would have diagnosed Dana with bronchopneumonia, it probably would not have changed her treatment since the symptoms for both COPD and bronchopneumonia are similar. However, we would still need medical expert testimony to verify this. If the medical expert testified the treatment would not have been different even if Dr. Brennan had diagnosed Dana with bronchopneumonia, the question is no longer whether Dr. Brennan acted as a reasonable medical professional under the circumstances. To determine this, we would again need medical expert testimony.
- Do you think the University Clinic failed to comply with the standard of care?
- Do you think the clinic failed to provide appropriate access to care? The clinic probably provided appropriate access to care. The clinic was not set up for emergency medical treatment, so referring Dana to an emergency room was probably the best course of action.

The standard of care for medical professionals is determined, in part, by reference to statutes and regulations, state practice guidelines, facility policy and procedures, equipment manuals, job descriptions, medical literature, and court cases. A medical provider must have the proper licensing; if the provider does not, this may be prima facie evidence the provider was negligent. Another way in which the standard of care can be established is through medical expert's testimony.

1. Establishing the Standard of Care through Medical Expert Witnesses

To determine whether the standard of care has been met, medical expert testimony usually is needed. The average person, who does not have medical knowledge, would not be able to testify as to whether the standard of care was met. Medical expert witnesses testify regarding what the proper standard of care was, and whether the standard was breached. When searching for a medical expert in a malpractice case, a medical expert with similar training and education to the training and education of the defendant is often chosen. Medical experts can testify whether a procedure was proper under the circumstances, what would be the common resulting complications, whether there should have been a referral to a specialist, and what is most likely the cause of the patient's injuries.

In addition, experts comment on proximate cause and damages. One of the jobs of a paralegal is to find expert witnesses. How do you, as the paralegal, find expert witnesses? There are several references for finding experts at the end of the chapter, in the web links. If your client is an insurance carrier, frequently the insurance carrier will have a list of expert witnesses it prefers to use. Your law firm may be a member of an association with recommendations for experts, such as the Association of Trial Lawyers of American (pro-plaintiff) or the Defense Research Institute for defense attorneys. There are also referral agencies, such as the Technical Advisory Service for Attorneys ("TASA"). Another good source for experts is a professional, technical, or trade organization.

The paralegal should verify the medical expert witness has:

■ a current license to practice, without any disciplinary procedures;
■ training in the medical specialty at issue; and
■ recent clinical experience in the same area as the defendant.

To determine whether a doctor has a current license and no disciplinary actions, one should check the state's medical board website.

Before the medical expert testifies, the expert should become familiar with the case and the medical standard at issue in the case. Part of the paralegal's job is to send to the expert documents to review in order to testify. Since medical experts can be costly, the law firm may have a policy of providing the doctor with summaries of the records (discussed in Chapter 15) rather than the entire records. For instance, summaries of depositions are sent to the expert rather than having her review the whole deposition transcript at a high hourly rate. See Chapter 16.

The client may have two different types of experts on the case. The first expert may review the file and help the attorney prepare for trial and the second may testify at trial. The first expert is known as a **consulting expert** and the second is known as a **testifying expert**. These two experts can be the same.

Consulting expert
expert who reviews the file and helps the attorney prepare for trial.

Testifying expert
expert who testifies at trial.

2.   National vs. Local Standards of Care

Originally, the standard of care a doctor was required to follow was limited by locality. A medical professional only had to utilize the level of care ordinarily used by similar medical professionals in the locality where she practiced. However, in part because it was so difficult to find doctors within a limited area to testify against one another, this rule started going by the wayside. In a small community, a doctor usually does not want to be seen as testifying against another. In addition, now public policy is to require all medical practitioners to reach a certain threshold level of care.

b.   Duty of Medical Provider

There must be a duty owed to the patient by the medical provider. This duty arises after the medical provider agrees to treat and care for the patient. If a health care provider has not undertaken this obligation to provide treatment, then, usually, the health care provider will not owe a duty. The health care provider owes the treatment obligation to the patient, not to the person who is paying the patient's bills.

In emergency medical situations, the health care provider may not have the opportunity to decline treatment. In general, an emergency room with a patient in critical care will have to service the patient. This is a matter of public policy. If, however, the emergency room is unable to handle the particular type of problem presented by the patient, then the hospital might be required to stabilize the patient and then transfer the patient. In addition, even if the medical treatment is undergone at decreased or no cost, the standard of care still applies.

c.   Breach

The central issue with breach of duty in a medical malpractice case is the following: did the medical professional uphold the standard of care required of him while treating the patient?

d.   Proximate Cause

There must a connection between the breach of this duty and the harm the plaintiff suffers. Just as in regular negligence cases, there must be both actual cause and proximate cause.

e.   Damages

Medical malpractice damages closely follow damages in a general negligence case. The medical record review (discussed in more detail in Chapter 15) is especially invaluable in calculating damages in a medical malpractice case. You, as the paralegal, will need to gather the information about the plaintiff's injuries and personal medical history, including the plaintiff's family medical history. If you are working for a plaintiff's law firm, you will obtain this information directly from the client. If you are working for a defense law firm, you will obtain this information from the medical records and depositions. If a plaintiff was in poor health before an incident of medical malpractice, this may change the value of her claim. A family history of ill health is a potential argument on the defense's side that the plaintiff was predisposed to a certain ailment.

The paralegal should take a detailed accounting of the medications the patient has been on, both currently and previously. The paralegal should get the dosage and the dates the client took the medications. The paralegal will also want to obtain all the names of the medical providers the plaintiff has seen for this condition in order to request records from those providers. (See Figure 8.1.)

Figure 8.1

Medical History Form

Client's Name: _____

Age: _____   **Height:** _____   **Weight:** _____

Under treatment now? _____

Have or Have Had	Condition	Yes	No
	Diabetes		
	High blood pressure/Hypertension		
	Heart problems, such as a murmur, angina, or a heart attack		
	Kidney problems		
	Mental health issues		
	Any history of seizures or epilepsy		
	Liver problems, such as hepatitis and cirrhosis		
	Thyroid problems		
	Immune deficiency, such as HIV or AIDS		
	Tuberculosis		
	Asthma, including allergy problems		
	Cancer or tumors		
	Prior accidents		
	Arthritis		
	High cholesterol		
	Stomach ulcer or colon disease		
	Stroke		

Medication List

Medication	For what condition?	Adverse side effects?	Dosage

Hospitalizations/Operations

Year	Reason for Hospitalization/Operation

Family Medical History

Did any of the following family members have the following conditions? If so, please check the appropriate box.

Condition	Mother	Father	Sibling	Child
Cancer				
Diabetes				
Heart attack				
High blood pressure				
Stroke				
Mental illness				

Lifestyle

Have you ever used the following:

Cigarettes, Pipes, or Cigars	Chew Tobacco	Illicit Drugs	Alcohol Use	Marijuana Use
Date Quit _____ *or* Cigarettes per day How many years: _____	Date Quit _____ *or* How much per day How many years: _____	Check whether you have used: ___ Cocaine ___Ampheta-mines ___ IV drug use ___ Other (list) _____	Check how many drinks you normally have: ___ 4+ a day ___ 1-3 a day ___ 2-3 a week ___ 1-3 a month ___ Never	Was this use medicinal? Date Quit _____ How many years: _____

In awarding damages in a medical malpractice case, a jury may look at:

- How permanent the injury to the plaintiff is;
- How disfiguring the injury is;
- If the injury causes the plaintiff to not be able to earn as much money;
- If the injury caused the plaintiff's life expectancy to be reduced; and
- Future medical costs.

8.3   Arbitration

Arbitration
when a case is taken in front of a neutral third party, often a retired judge, for a final and binding decision.

One way in which defendants can reduce the costs of lawsuits is to arbitrate. In many jurisdictions, **arbitration** is a prerequisite to a medical malpractice lawsuit (in those jurisdictions, arbitration may not be a final decision). Arbitration takes the case in front of a neutral third party, often a retired judge, for a final and binding decision. In binding arbitration, once the arbitrator makes her decision, the decision is binding in a court of law.

Both parties decide on the arbitrator. The arbitration process is less formal than litigation and will often take place at the arbitrator's office. Arbitration is also faster than handling a lawsuit through the courts. Many arbitrations can be finished within a few months. There is less discovery in arbitration than trial, which also makes it more cost effective.

8.4   Informed Consent

Informed consent
a patient understanding and making a decision based upon the information provided by a health care provider who discloses material information.

Lack of informed consent is one of the specific types of claims a plaintiff can bring against a medical provider. Informed consent involves a health care provider disclosing material information to a patient who is able to understand the information

Material information
information essential to the patient's determination of whether to undergo treatment.

and make a decision based upon the information. **Material information** is information essential to the patient's determination of whether to undergo treatment. The medical professional is required to disclose the risks a reasonable patient would want to know. Some of the material information a patient has the right to know are:

- the potential pain of a treatment,
- the side effects of a treatment,
- alternatives to treatment,
- the risks of those other treatments,
- the risks of not being treated,
- how long the patient is expected to live, and
- whether the doctor has a financial interest in the treatment.

A patient, such as a terminal cancer patient, also has the right to decide whether the risks of a new treatment outweigh death. A patient could have a health care directive allowing a designated person to make this decision if the patient is unable to do so.

Examples of when consent might need to be obtained are for surgery, anesthesia, chemotherapy, or immunization. The consent should be in writing. Medical professionals need to be careful to provide informed consent and document the informed consent. There are both general and specific consent forms. A **general consent form** allows the patient to consent to medical care. A **specific consent form** is for a specific procedure, such as a hysterectomy. The forms should be signed by the patient and should be witnessed. If a patient does not speak English, then a translator's signature needs to be obtained as well. Consents should include the following:

General consent form
a consent to medical care.

Specific consent form
a consent to a specific procedure.

- The name of the patient,
- The date and time the consent was given,
- The condition the patient is being treated for,
- A description of the medical treatment to be provided,
- The name of the medical care provider who is obtaining the consent,
- A statement regarding the risks of the procedure,
- Viable alternatives to the procedure being proposed,
- A statement that the undergoing of such procedure is not a guarantee of the success of the procedure,
- A statement of consent by the patient to the procedure and to deviations from the procedure should it become medically necessary during the procedure,
- A statement by the patient that she has had the opportunity to ask any questions she may have, and
- The signature of the patient or her guardian.

In general, a medical professional is required to obtain informed consent prior to performing a procedure. There can be two types of informed consent cases:

1. where the extent of the consent was exceeded or
2. where consent was not obtained at all.

Even if a treatment is experimental, the medical professionals must give fair warning of known risks.[2] However, the medical professionals are not required to warn of an unknown risk.

a.   Care Can Be Provided Without Consent Under the Emergency Treatment Exception

Emergency treatment exception if a person is unconscious and unable to given consent in an emergency, then consent does not need to be obtained.

Under the **emergency treatment exception**, if a person is not conscious and is unable to give consent in an emergency, then consent does not need to be obtained. The emergency treatment exception prevents patients from dying before consent can be obtained. Consent when the person is unconscious is also known as implied consent. It is assumed a reasonable person, in an emergency, who was unconscious would want treatment. Thus, the patient is said to have impliedly consented to the treatment. Medical emergencies, under this exception, include when a patient's life is in danger and when the patient might suffer a permanent impairment if not treated.

b.   Care Can Be Provided Without Consent Under the Therapeutic Exception

Therapeutic exception a doctor does not have to provide information when he believes the information would be harmful to the patient or prevent the patient from healing.

The **therapeutic exception** is not a widely used exception because it only applies in rare circumstances. Under the therapeutic exception, a doctor does not have to provide information when he believes the information would be harmful to the patient or prevent the patient from healing. If it is reasonable to assume the patient might harm himself, such as a psychiatric patient, then the doctor can withhold such information and provide care without consent.

c.   Consent for Minors and the Mentally Incompetent

Minor a person under the age of 18.

Mentally incompetent people and children under 18 are not able to consent on behalf of themselves. Another person can act on behalf of the mentally incompetent person or minor. A court-appointed guardian will normally provide consent for a mentally incompetent person. A **minor** is a person under the age of 18. Therefore, parents or a legal guardian must give consent for their children under the age of 18. However, there are situations, often governed by statute, where a minor can consent to procedures without a parent's approval.

8.5   Defenses to Medical Malpractice

Since medical malpractice is a type of negligence, the defenses to negligence will normally apply to medical malpractice as well. The defendant has the defenses of the plaintiff's contributory negligence, assumption of the risk, and the plaintiff's duty to mitigate the damages. In addition, if the medical professional never agreed to treat

---

2. *Goodman v. U.S.*, 298 F.3d 1048, 1057 (9th Cir. 2002).

the patient, then normally the medical professional will not be found negligent for failing to provide treatment.

8.6 Statutes of Limitations

The purpose of a statute of limitations is to curtail the time in which a plaintiff has to bring an action against the defendant. There is usually a separate statute of limitations for medical malpractice from the statute of limitations for general negligence, which varies from state to state. The statute of limitations may be different for minors (usually longer) and severely disabled people than it is for adults.

Paralegal Program Proves Helpful for Getting into Law
By Brian Decerda, Law Student

The director of admissions at the law school kept asking me about the paralegal program and firm I had been working at. It seems the paralegal program and work experience were really big factors in their decision to accept me. I would tell any paralegal student that everything you learn in the paralegal program will be beneficial in some way if you are applying to law school. So far, I feel comfortable in my classes since I recognize the terminology and points

they are trying to convey as a result of my previous experience with the paralegal program. It was a blessing in disguise to attend the program because it really does give you a head start. Even though I'm learning a lot of theory now, the paralegal program was definitely able to ground that theory into practical applications, which is helpful in understanding my classes.

E T H I C S

Model Rules of Professional Conduct
Information about Legal Services

Rule 7.3 Direct Contact with Prospective Clients
(a) A lawyer shall not by in-person, live telephone or real-time electronic contact solicit professional employment from a prospective client when a significant motive for the lawyer's doing so is the lawyer's pecuniary gain, unless the person contacted:
  (1) is a lawyer; or
  (2) has a family, close personal, or prior professional relationship with the lawyer.
(b) A lawyer shall not solicit professional employment from a prospective client by written, recorded or electronic communication or by in-person, telephone or real-time electronic contact even when not otherwise prohibited by paragraph (a), if:
  (1) the prospective client has made known to the lawyer a desire not to be solicited by the lawyer; or
  (2) the solicitation involves coercion, duress or harassment.[3]

Ethics exercise: Rent and watch the movie *The Verdict.* The attorney's client in the film is rendered brain dead after a medical procedure goes wrong. Pay attention to the scenes involving the expert witness. There are also a number of ethics violations in the movie; see how many you can spot. While the solicitation at funerals is certainly callous, does the location alone make the solicitation wrong?

3. Model R. Prof. Conduct 7.3 (ABA 2004).

Chapter Summary

Medical malpractice is negligence and the elements of a medical malpractice case are the same as the elements to a negligence case. However, because there are issues specific to medical malpractice, such as the standard of care, medical malpractice deserves its own chapter. Medical malpractice is the failure of a medical professional to act as a reasonable medical professional would under similar circumstances. People without medical training usually cannot determine whether a medical professional acted as a reasonable medical professional should have. Therefore, the testimony of medical expert witnesses, who do have medical training, is needed to determine whether the defendant met her duty of care.

Informed consent is a special issue in medical malpractice. A medical professional must obtain informed consent from a patient before performing a procedure. To have a proper consent, the plaintiff must have been given the information essential or material to make a decision. One example of material information is an explanation of the risk of treatment. There are two exceptions to the requirement that a doctor obtain informed consent: the emergency treatment exception and the therapeutic exception. If a person is not conscious and is unable to give consent in an emergency situation, then the consent does not need to be obtained under the emergency treatment exception. If information would be harmful to a patient, then under the therapeutic exception, a doctor does not have to provide the patient with the information.

Lastly, the defenses to medical malpractice were discussed in brief, because the defenses to malpractice are the same as the defenses to negligence. Statutes of limitations were also discussed specifically because the statute of limitations for medical malpractice cases usually differs from the statutes of limitations for negligence cases.

Key Terms

- Arbitration
- Consulting expert
- Emergency treatment exception
- General consent form
- Informed consent
- Material information
- Minor
- Proximate cause
- Specific consent form
- Standard of care
- Testifying expert
- Therapeutic exception

Review Questions

- How does the duty of a medical provider change in an emergency as opposed to an elective treatment? How might the rules of informed consent vary?
- How is the standard of care different for a specialist?
- What is the purpose of informed consent?

Web Links

- The United States Department of Health & Human Services runs the www.healthfinder.gov website. Of particular help on the web page is the "drug interaction checker and the drug library, which will allow you to look up the different uses and interaction of medications. The drug library includes potential side effects of the drugs as well.

- www.tasanet.com/. TASA was discussed in the chapter as a resource for finding experts.

- If you need to find an expert, another resource is www.expertpages.com. The website divides experts by categories.

- Use www.depoconnect.com to research the expert's past testimony.

- www.ama-assn.org/. Verify a doctor's credentials by using the American Medical Association's doctor finder, which has over 690,000 doctors listed.

- www.lectlaw.com is the "The 'Lectronic Law Library." The website has a good section on medical malpractice.

Exercises

- Log onto the healthfinder.gov website run by the U.S. Department of Health & Human Services. Click on the drug interaction checker. Look up whether the herbal supplement, valerian, may interact with alcohol.

- On the same website, look up the prescription drug Remeron. What is Remeron used for?

- Dr. Leonard is a spinal surgeon. While performing surgery on Renee, he accidentally nicks Renee's spinal cord. As a result, Renee suffers a loss of mobility in her leg. Renee sues Dr. Leonard for negligence. What could Dr. Leonard potentially raise as a defense? How would the standard of care be determined in this case?

- Review the following radiology report. Look up the medical language and then write a brief summary on your findings.

Amy McDonald   DOB: 4/30/1957

Radiology Report

XRAY T-SPINE, AP/LAT

CLINICAL HISTORY

Vomiting, seizures, pain.

REFERENCE FILMS

No previous studies are available for comparison.

CERVICAL SPINE FINDINGS:

The odontoid view is suboptimal. No odontoid fracture is seen. Vertebral heights and alignment appear satisfactory. The prevertebral soft tissues are normal. No acute bone or joint injury is seen.

IMPRESSION:

Limited odontoid view but no acute injury is seen. Clinical correlation as to need for follow-up study is recommended.

LUMBAR SPINE FINDINGS:

Vertebral heights and alignment are normal. No acute bone or joint injury is seen. The pelvic ring and hips are normal.

THORACIC SPINE FINDINGS:

The lateral view is limited. Vertebral heights and alignment appear satisfactory on the AP view. If clinical symptoms persist, a repeat lateral view is recommended.

IMPRESSION:

No acute bone or joint injury is seen with a limited lateral thoracic spine study.

End of Report

■ You, the paralegal, receive a medical bill on the plaintiff after you have requested the medical records and bills. The following tests were run on the plaintiff. Look up the medical terminology and write a short summary explaining the tests in plain English.

STATEMENT

Bill to:
Judy Toledo
1235 Manhasset Street
Washington, D.C.

Remit to:
Pathologists Medical
P. O. Box 884591
Washington, D.C.

DATE	PROVIDER EXPLANATION OF ACTIVITY	CHARGES
2/5/08	Bilirubn, total	$7.68
2/5/08	Alkaline Phosphatase	$7.88
2/5/08	Lipase	$10.50
2/5/08	Preg Screen, Blood	$11.48
2/5/08	CBC	$11.88
2/5/08	Urinalysis Reflex cult	$4.83
2/6/08	Metabolic Panel, Comp	$49.15
2/6/08	Metabolic Panel	$13.88
2/6/08	Urinalysis, Macro only	$3.43

CHAPTER

Intentional Torts to Persons

An unconditional right to say what one pleases about public affairs is what I consider to be the minimum guarantee of the First Amendment.[1]

Chapter Outline

---

1. *New York Times Company v. Sullivan*, 376 U.S. 254 (1964).

Chapter Objectives

- Provide and explain the elements of intentional torts
- Discuss the difference between negligence and intentional torts
- Outline the elements of assault
- Define and provide the elements of battery
- List the elements of false imprisonment
- Discuss intentional infliction of emotional distress
- Define fraud and misrepresentation, along with the elements of each
- Explain defamation, how it applies in the real world, and emphasize the importance of publication
- Illustrate defamatory statements
- Emphasize the defamation requirement of the falseness of a statement
- Point out the differences between libel and slander
- Discuss the concepts of libel per se and slander per se
- Stress invasion of privacy is four torts: intrusion, appropriation, public disclosure of private facts, and false light
- Explain the elements of malicious prosecution

9.1   Introduction to Intentional Torts to Persons

Intentional torts are divided into two different chapters. Intentional torts to persons are the subject of this chapter. Intentional torts to property are the subject of the next chapter. The reason for this separation is to make the intentional torts easier to learn.

An intentional tort, in comparison to negligence, is nonaccidental behavior. A person has 1) an intent to commit an act and 2) an intent for a result to occur. What is intent, though? **Intent** consists of what a person wants to happen as a result of his actions or what a person believes will likely happen as a result of his actions.[2]

Intent
want or purpose for a result to happen or knowing to a substantial certainty that a result will happen.

Intent Is One of Two Things:

1. The want or purpose for a result to happen, or
2. Knowing to a substantial certainty a result will happen.

Act
a voluntary movement.

An **act** is a voluntary movement. In short, the defendant acted with a purpose. In negligence, the issues were a lack of care and what a reasonable person would do. With intent, the issue is something more than carelessness; the defendant acted with a purpose to cause or was substantially certain his actions would cause consequences. Often, civil assaults and batteries rise to the level of criminal assaults and batteries.

---

2. Restatement (Second) of Torts §8A (1965).

Example of a Civil Assault and Battery Giving Rise to Criminal Assault and Battery Charge

Amy Winger was assaulted and battered on a train. She called the police and the police eventually arrested Devin Charles, who was found guilty at the criminal trial for the assault and battery. Ms. Winger also brought her own civil suit against Mr. Charles for civil damages for emotional distress claim and lost wages caused by the same assault and battery.

Example of Battery Being Tried Both Civilly and Criminally

Perhaps the most famous case of battery being tried both civilly and criminally is the O.J. Simpson case. O.J. had two trials, one was the criminal trial and one was the families of Nicole Brown and Ron Goldman suing O.J. for battery and wrongful death. Wrongful death was discussed in more detail in Chapter 5. The criminal jury found O.J. did not commit the crime of murder. However, the civil jury did find O.J. committed the tort of wrongful death.

9.2 Elements of All the Intentional Torts to Persons

Causes of action
legally acceptable reasons for bringing about a lawsuit.

Element
an element is part of a rule making up a cause of action.

Intentional torts are **causes of action**, or legally acceptable reasons for bringing about a lawsuit. Each intentional tort cause of action is made up of elements that must be proven. An **element** is just a part of a rule. The entire rule would be a cause of action. The intentional tort causes of action are listed below and are broken up by elements. Each element must be supported factually to be proven.

The elements of all the intentional torts to people are placed here in one central location for easier reference and each intentional torts element will also be placed by the discussion of each intentional tort. (See Figure 9.1.)

Figure 9.1

Elements of Intentional Torts

Tort	Elements
Assault	• Intent • Fear • Of Harmful/Offensive Contact
Battery	• Intent • Act • Harmful/Offensive Contact
False Imprisonment and False Arrest	• Intent • Confinement

	• Unlawful Restraint
	• Appreciable Amount of Time
	• No Reasonable Escape
Infliction of Emotional Distress	• Intent
	• Outrageous Conduct
	• Conduct Causes Mental Anguish
Fraud	• Intent
	• False Statements
	• Defendant Knows Statement Is False
	• Purpose Is to Obtain Item of Value from Victim
	• Victim Is Injured by Giving Up Item
Misrepresentation	• Intent
	• False Statements
	• Defendant Knows Statement Is False
	• Victim Is Injured
Defamation	• Intent
	• Defamatory Language Regarding Plaintiff
	• Publicized and False
	• Injury
Malicious Prosecution	• Intent
	• Criminal Charge Brought by Defendant
	• Plaintiff Wins
	• Defendant Acted with Malice in Bringing Charge

9.3 Battery

Elements to Battery

- Intent
- Act
- Harmful/Offensive Contact

Battery
a harmful or offensive contact with a person, caused by the defendant's intent to cause the harmful or offensive contact.

    Battery is a harmful or offensive contact with a person, caused by the defendant's intent to cause the harmful or offensive contact. A battery is not every unsolicited or unwanted touch. A battery must be harmful or offensive in some way. A battery can also give rise to a criminal action in addition to a civil cause of action as seen in the example above. Criminal battery is prosecuted by the people on behalf of the state.

a. First Element of Battery: There Has to Be an Act

The defendant must harm the plaintiff by an act, which is a voluntary movement of the body. If the defendant is having a seizure and hits the plaintiff during the seizure, the defendant is not guilty of battery. The defendant did not have control over his body at this time; rather his body was acting involuntarily. Therefore, a sense of fairness prohibits the law from holding the defendant liable for this involuntary act.

b. The Second Element of Battery: The Defendant Must Have Acted with Intent

The defendant must have acted with the intent to make contact with the plaintiff. If, for instance, passengers on a crowded subway accidentally bump into each other due to the movement of the train, the passengers did not act with the intent to make contact.

The defendant's intent must have been to cause an imminent harmful or offensive contact. By imminent, the law means an immediate harmful or offensive contact. See the discussion on assault for more on imminent contact.

The battery cannot be justified or subject to a privilege (such as self-defense, which we will learn about more in Chapter 11); in either of those two cases, the contact will not constitute battery. However, it is not a defense to argue the person the defendant hit is not the person he intended to hit. If the defendant intended to act and intended for the result to occur, just not to the person he did hit, then the intent to hit one person will be transferred to the person the defendant actually did hit.

c. The Third Element of Battery: The Contact Must Be Harmful or Offensive

Harmful contact
a contact causing physical damage or pain.

Offensive contact
a contact that would offend the dignity of a reasonable person.

The third element of battery is the contact must be harmful or offensive. A **harmful contact** is a contact causing physical damage or pain. Hitting someone and causing a bruise would satisfy the harmful requirement. An **offensive contact** is a contact, which would offend the dignity of a reasonable person. Not every contact is a battery. For instance, if Tara grabs Donald's arm to stop him from stepping in front of a car, this contact is not a battery. This contact is not harmful, as it was beneficial to Donald.

Example

Tim and Mary are taking a hike in the forest. Tim notes Mary is standing right under a boulder that looks like it could fall and hit her. Tim shoves Mary out of the path of the falling boulder, and in the process, causes Mary to fall forward, breaking her forearm. If Mary sues Tim for battery, what will be the result? Mary will not win because the contact was not offensive, but rather, the contact was beneficial to Mary and kept her from being crushed by a boulder.

Whether a contact is harmful or offensive is judged by the reasonable person standard. However, the question is not the same question asked in negligence, i.e., would a reasonable person have committed the battery? Rather the question is would a reasonable person be offended by this contact? Socially unacceptable contact can also be a battery. If a person was on a crowded subway and intentionally groped the rear end of the woman (whom he did not know) in front of him, then this could be considered battery. This contact on the subway is not necessarily physically harmful to the woman, but it is an offensive contact, so it will still constitute a battery. Even though this particular woman may have enjoyed having her rear end groped, a reasonable woman would probably not, and so the groping is still considered a battery.

One's person
a body and items so closely attached or associated with one's body as to be identified with one's body.

The contact requirement of battery can be made through the use of weapons or other objects. **One's person** is a body, but can also include items attached to one's body or so closely associated with one's body as to be identified with one's body. Thus, pulling on a girl's dress sash would constitute contact with her body. Knocking a beer out of a man's hand at a bar would also constitute contact with his body. This is contact with the body even if contact was not made with the hand holding the beer, but just the beer can itself.

If addition, contact can be made through weapons. If the defendant used pepper spray, even though his body never touched the plaintiff, using pepper spray is so closely associated with one's body as to be identified with one's body.

Usually there is some physical contact. This contact can be directly against the victim or with an object in close contact with the victim, such as a backpack, purse, or umbrella.

d.   Issues of Consent and Privilege in the Context of Battery

Consent
an agreement to allow an event to occur or not occur.

If a person consents to a harmful contact, then there is no battery. Consent is a complete defense to the intentional tort of battery. **Consent** is an agreement to allow an event to occur or not occur. If, for example, both adults legally consented to a boxing match, then there is not a battery.

Other Examples of Consent to Battery

- If you are playing sports and are injured, it is usually not considered a battery because you have consented to the physical contact normally associated with the game.
- If you ride the subway during rush hours, you have impliedly given consent to be jostled. The moving vehicle and number of passengers virtually make it impossible for jostling not to occur.

But a defendant can exceed the scope of the consent he was initially given. For instance, a group of fraternity brothers agree to play a game of flag football with each other. Normally in flag football, there is minimal contact. However, Gregg, one of the fraternity brothers, is tackled and then all of his teammates pile on top of him. Gregg consented to the minimal contact of flag football. He did not consent to have several men tackle him and pile on top of him.

Defenses to battery include not only consent, but also self-defense or defense of others, which will be discussed in Chapter 11.

Damages sought by the plaintiff for battery could include:

■ compensatory damages,
■ pain and suffering,
■ medical costs, and
■ lost wages.

Punitive damages might be awarded if the plaintiff could show the defendant acted with hate or malice in committing a battery.

Sample Cause of Action from a Complaint: Battery

■ On or about June 18, Brenda cut in the line ahead of Thomas, who was waiting for the trolley at the station.
■ Defendant Thomas took both hands and shoved Brenda.
■ In shoving Brenda, Defendant Thomas acted with the intent to make a contact with Brenda's person.
■ At no time did Brenda consent to Defendant Thomas' shoving her.
■ As a proximate result of the shoving, Brenda suffered injuries necessitating her to have a cervical dissectomy and fusion.

Can you identify each of the elements of battery in the cause of action above?

9.4 Assault

Elements of Assault:
Intent
Fear
Of Harmful/Offensive Contact

In most instances, where there is a battery there will be an assault. A battery would be a person hitting another. Most battery victims see the fist coming towards them, which would be an assault. The big difference between battery and assault is contact. Battery usually involves contact, whereas assault does not.

Assault
an act committed with intent to harmfully or offensively touch another person, which causes the person to be apprehensive he is about to be harmfully or offensively touched.

An **assault** is an act committed with intent to harmfully or offensively touch another person, which causes the person to be apprehensive he is about to be harmfully or offensively touched. While assault does not require an actual contact, an assault usually requires more than just words. If a mother, exasperated with her son, states "I'm going to kill you," then this alone is not enough to constitute an assault. However, if the mother stated, "I'm going to kill you," and then proceeds to lunge at her son with both hands outstretched, this would constitute an assault.

Assault allows a plaintiff to recover for an emotional injury alone and does not require showing the defendant made physical contact with the plaintiff. If a defendant strikes a plaintiff from behind, but the plaintiff did not see the defendant was about to hit him, then the plaintiff will not have a cause of action for assault.[3] The plaintiff would still have a cause of action for battery because he was hit.[4]

a.   The First Element of Assault: The Defendant's Actions Were Intentional

The first element of assault, as for all intentional torts, is intent. The intent in assault is to act with the purpose to cause fear or apprehension of a harmful or offensive touch, or to act with substantial certainty another person will be made fearful or apprehensive of a harmful or offensive touch. Often, when an assault is committed, the defendant actually meant to commit a battery, which did not result in contact. The mental fear, rather than bodily injury the plaintiff does not suffer, is still actionable.

b.   The Second Element of Assault: The Action(s) of Defendant Put the Plaintiff in Fear or Apprehension

Apprehension
an anticipation or awareness of something.

The second element of assault is the act of the defendant must have placed the plaintiff in fear or apprehension. **Apprehension** is an anticipation or awareness of something. Used in terms of an assault, apprehension is the anticipation of harmful or offensive contact. The apprehension must be a reasonable apprehension. If a 120-pound woman tells a 250-pound man she is going to strangle him, the man is not necessarily reasonable in fearing she will strangle him. There needs to be a combination of words and conduct causing the plaintiff to think he is about to be hit.[5]

Example

Stephanie is five foot, four inches tall, and weighs 120 pounds. She becomes angry with her boyfriend, Mark, who is six feet, two inches tall, and weighs 235 pounds. She swings her purse at Mark, but he steps back, missing the blow. He laughs at her attempt to strike him. Has Stephanie committed a tort? If so, which one(s)? Stephanie is probably not going to be found to have committed the tort of assault. Mark laughed at her attempt to hit him, and did not appear to be in apprehension of an imminent offensive or harmful contact.

c.   The Third Element of Assault: The Plaintiff Must Be in Fear or Apprehension of an Imminent Harmful or Offensive Contact

The third element of assault is the plaintiff must have a fear of imminent harmful contact. The key is the harmful or offensive contact must be imminent. In the

---

3. *See McCraney v. Flanagan*, 47 N.C.App. 498 (1980).
4. *Id.*
5. *Webbier v. Thoroughbred Racing Protective Bureau, Inc.*, 105 R.I. 605, 614, 254 A.2d 285, 290 (1969).

context of an assault, imminent means the defendant has immediate and easy access to the plaintiff. If the defendant calls the plaintiff on the phone and states he is planning to beat the plaintiff up, this is not an imminent threat. The defendant is not in the plaintiff's face, threatening to beat her up at the moment. She still has the opportunity to flee. Typically, verbal threats, without any further conduct will not be sufficient to satisfy this element. The defendant has to have the apparent present ability to carry out whatever threat he is making in order to satisfy this element.

Sample Cause of Action from a Complaint: Assault

- On or about June 18, Defendant Thomas came towards Plaintiff Brenda with both hands outstretched.
- In doing the acts alleged, Defendant Thomas intended to cause or to place Brenda in apprehension of a harmful contact with Brenda's person.
- As a result of Defendant Thomas' acts, Brenda, in fact, was placed in great apprehension of a harmful contact with her person.

Can you identify each of the elements of assault in this cause of action?

d.   The Issue of Transferred Intent in the Context of Assault

Transferred intent
a defendant's intent to injure one plaintiff may be transferred to the plaintiff who was actually injured; a defendant's intent to commit one tort may be transferred to the tort the defendant actually committed.

Transferred intent allows a defendant's intent to injure one plaintiff to transfer to the plaintiff the defendant actually injured. In addition, transferred intent also allows the intent from the tort the defendant intended to commit to be transferred to the tort the defendant actually committed. Even if the defendant's intended victim is not the one affected by the assault, the defendant's intent to commit the assault can be transferred to the actual victim (this is also true for battery, false imprisonment, trespass to land, and trespass to chattels).

Figure 9.2

Transferred Intent

Intent Transferred to an Unintended Plaintiff	Intent Transferred to an Unintended Tort
Defendant intends to commit an assault, battery, false imprisonment, trespass to land, or trespass to chattel.[6]	Defendant intends to commit an assault, battery, false imprisonment, trespass to land, or trespass to chattel. For instance, the defendant intended to commit an assault.
Defendant commits an assault, battery, false imprisonment, trespass to land, or trespass to chattel, but to a plaintiff other than the one he intended.	Defendant commits an assault, battery, false imprisonment, trespass to land, or trespass to chattel, but this is not the tort he intended to commit. For instance, instead of committing an assault, the defendant commits a battery.

6. Trespass to land and trespass to chattel are discussed in Chapter 10.

Intent Transferred to an Unintended Plaintiff	Intent Transferred to an Unintended Tort
Defendant did not mean to injure this particular person. Result: the defendant's intent will transfer from the plaintiff he intended to injure to the plaintiff he did in fact injure.	Defendant did not mean to commit this particular tort (i.e., battery). Result: the defendant's intention will transfer from the tort he intended to commit (assault) to the tort he did in fact commit (battery).

Example

Bruno throws a pencil at Rosa, intending to hit Rosa in the eye. However, the pencil actually hits Petra, instead of Rosa. Bruno will still be held liable for hitting Petra, though he did not intend to hit her. Bruno did intend to hit Rosa, so his intent to hit Rosa will be transferred to the person he actually did hit, who is Petra.

The other instance in which transferred intent applies is when a defendant intends to commit one tort but actually commits another tort. The intent to commit tort A will be transferred to tort B, the tort actually committed.

Example

Bruno throws a pencil at Rosa, intending to hit Rosa in the eye. However, the pencil flies right by Rosa's eye and never hits her. Bruno intended to commit a battery against Rosa. However, he actually committed assault (as the pencil did not hit Rosa). Therefore, Bruno's intent to commit a battery will be transferred to the assault. Bruno will be liable for assault.

9.5   False Imprisonment and False Arrest

Elements of False Imprisonment and False Arrest:

Intent

Confinement

Unlawful Restraint

Appreciable Amount of Time

No Reasonable Escape

False Imprisonment
a person is confined through physical or emotional restraints, such as threatening to harm another.

For a **false imprisonment** to occur, a person has to be confined through physical or emotional restraints (such as threatening to harm another).

a.   The First Element of False Imprisonment: The Plaintiff Must Be Confined

The first element of false imprisonment is the plaintiff must be confined. Confinement requires the plaintiff must have no way of leaving the place where she is being confined. Being in a moving vehicle would satisfy the confinement requirement. The choice of staying in the vehicle versus sustaining bodily injury satisfies the confinement element.

Example of Physical Confinement

An example of physical confinement is locking someone in a room. The confined person must be aware he is confined and he has to be injured as a result of the confinement. If, for instance, a child is locked in a room with a bunch of toys and does not even notice he is confined, there has not been a false imprisonment. Note, however, that parents will probably be able to lock their own children in a room, for a reasonable amount of time, without it being considered false imprisonment. This is because there is some infra-family immunity of torts. See Chapter 11.

b. The Second Element of False Imprisonment: The Defendant Had the Intent to Restrain

The defendant must have intended to restrain the plaintiff. The intent is to detain the plaintiff or restrict his movement without his consent. Again, a threat of force is enough. However, if someone accidentally locks someone in, this behavior will not be considered a false imprisonment.

c. The Third Element of False Imprisonment: The Restraint Used Against the Plaintiff Must Be Unlawful

The next element of false imprisonment is the restraint used must be an unlawful restraint. If a retail store has a reasonable belief a person on their property has stolen store property, then the store may have a right to detain the alleged shoplifter. This is an example of a lawful restraint. The shoplifting detention cannot be unreasonably long or abusive, such as a public accusation against the detainee. The key to whether the store can detain this person is did the store have a reasonable belief? Videotape footage of the theft would be indicative of a reasonable belief.

The restraint in false imprisonment can be achieved through verbal threats or threatening conduct.

d. The Fourth Element of False Imprisonment: The Imprisonment Must Be for an Appreciable Amount of Time

Appreciable amount of time an unreasonable amount of time.

To be actionable, a false imprisonment must be for an appreciable amount of time. An **appreciable amount of time** means an unreasonable amount of time. For instance, it would not be reasonable to hold someone for eight hours on suspicion of shoplifting. However, it would be permissible to hold the suspected shoplifter for an hour, while waiting for the police to arrive.

False arrest
false imprisonment committed by a person who appears to have the authority to confine the victim.

False arrest is false imprisonment committed by a person who appears to have the authority to confine the victim. False arrest often arises in shoplifting situations. The security guard at the store appears to have authority to confine the victim. Most retail stores are extremely careful to have a strong case of shoplifting before detaining a customer for the arrival of the police. If the store does not have the appropriate documentation of a shoplifting, frequently the store will not pursue the incident. The lawsuits regarding false arrest and the monetary awards against retailers brought about this caution.

e. The Fifth Requirement of False Imprisonment: There Is No Reasonable Means of Escape

The last requirement of false imprisonment is there must not be reasonable means of escape. If a person has the option to leave the situation, then there has not been a false imprisonment.

If all of these elements of false imprisonment are met, then a plaintiff will not have to prove up damages.

Sometimes holding personal property hostage is enough to constitute false imprisonment. For instance, holding someone's clothing hostage so the person cannot leave a situation without going naked is sufficient to constitute confinement for purposes of false imprisonment.

9.6 Intentional Infliction of Emotional Distress

Elements of Infliction of Emotional Distress:

Intent

Outrageous Conduct

Conduct Causes Mental Anguish

Intentional infliction of emotional distress
when a defendant's extreme and outrageous conduct disturbs the plaintiff's peace of mind.

Outrageous behavior
behavior so outside normal behavior, it is actionable.

The **infliction of emotional distress** can be negligent or intentional. Negligent infliction of emotional distress was covered in Chapter 5, and is not the law in all states. This section discusses intentional infliction of emotional distress. Intentional infliction of emotional distress ("IIED") occurs when a defendant's behavior intentionally disturbs the plaintiff's peace of mind. When a defendant's actions are extreme and outrageous and cause emotional distress, this can be a separate tort.

Extreme and outrageous or reckless behavior is frequently categorized as intentional infliction of emotional distress. **Outrageous behavior** is so outside normal behavior, it is actionable.

If the emotional distress was negligent, then the plaintiff will usually also have to prove physical damages. If the emotional distress was intentional, then the plaintiff will usually not have to prove physical damages. With IIED, the plaintiff suffers a psychological damage because of the defendant's outrageous actions.

a. The First Element of IIED: The Defendant's Actions Must Be Outrageous

With IIED, the defendant's action must be outrageous. The conduct must be greatly beyond the conduct acceptable in the course of normal behavior. Rude behavior does not usually rise to the level of extreme and outrageous behavior. Submitting someone to ridicule also does not usually rise to the level of extreme and outrageous. However, this may change in light of school bullying and related shootings. Certain levels of bullying can rise to the level of extreme and outrageous. Pulling a teenage boy's pants and underwear down in the high school cafeteria at lunchtime may be extreme and outrageous. IIED is one theory under which a bullied person might recover damages, if he were to pursue the issue in a court of law.

b. The Second Element of IIED: There Is Intentional or Reckless Conduct Intended to Cause Severe Mental Anguish to the Plaintiff

The next element of IIED is the defendant must have intentionally or recklessly acted, to cause the plaintiff severe mental anguish. Intent can be proven either by showing the defendant acted with the purpose to commit an intentional conduct or the defendant knew it was highly likely the conduct was going to occur. Note the difference between intentional and reckless conduct. With reckless conduct, a person is acting in such a manner that the result is almost certain to happen.

c. The Third Element of IIED: The Plaintiff Suffers Severe Mental Anguish as a Result of the Defendant's Intent to Cause Severe Mental Anguish

To recover under a IIED claim, a plaintiff must show he suffered severe mental anguish as a result. Bringing an action in emotional distress was not intended to result in a windfall for plaintiffs. Rather, it was invented to prevent severe interference with a plaintiff's mind. To verify the truthfulness of an emotional distress claim, judges frequently want to see a physical manifestation of the emotional distress through sleeplessness, loss or gain of weight, and other stress-induced illnesses.

Sample Cause of Action for Intentional Infliction of Emotional Distress

- Defendant has engaged in a course of outrageous conduct because Defendant knows Plaintiffs are susceptible to injuries through mental distress and/or is acting intentionally and/or unreasonably with the recognition the acts are likely to result in illness through mental distress.
- Defendant has acted with the intent to inflict injury and/or the realization that the injury was substantially certain to result from his conduct.
- Defendant's actions were directed at Plaintiffs and/or occurred in the presence of Plaintiffs with Defendant's awareness of that presence.

■ Plaintiffs have suffered serious and/or severe mental distress as the result of Defendant's actions.
■ Plaintiffs' emotional distress was actually caused by Defendant's action.
■ Wherefore, Plaintiffs pray for judgments against Defendant for the described injuries and losses.

9.7   Fraud

Elements of Fraud:

Intent

False Statements

Defendant Knows Statement Is False

Purpose Is to Obtain Item of Value from Victim

Victim Is Injured by Giving Up Item

Fraud and misrepresentation are very similar. Fraud, however, has the added element of the defendant's intent to gain something of value from the plaintiff.

a.   Fraud and Deceit

Fraud
any act or omission hiding the breach of a duty or material fact.

Material fact
a fact important to an event or transaction, usually between the parties.

Fraud and deceit are synonymous. The only difference between the two words is some states use the term fraud, and other states use the term deceit. Fraud is any act or omission hiding the breach of a duty or material fact. A **material fact** is a fact important to an event or transaction, usually between the parties. This act or omission must cause injury the plaintiff.

b.   The First Element of Fraud: There Are False Statements Made by the Defendant, Which Are Intended to Deceive

To commit fraud, the defendant must make false statement with the intent to deceive. If Joseph tells Joan he can invest Joan's money for her and achieve a high rate of return, and Joseph knows he knows nothing about investments, then Joseph has made a false statement to deceive Joan. However, if Joseph does have some knowledge about financial investments and was merely exaggerating his abilities, the exaggeration does not rise to the level of fraud.

c.   The Second Element of Fraud: The Defendant Has Knowledge of the Falsity of Those Statements

The defendant has to have knowledge the statements he is making are false. Using the example above, if Joseph reasonably believed he had some talent at financial investing, his belief negates this element.

d.   The Third Element of Fraud: The Statements Are Designed to Get the Victim to Surrender Something of Value

The defendant must make the statement attempting to have the plaintiff give him something of value. If Joseph told Joan he could invest her money for the purpose of getting his hands on Joan's money, then Joseph's statement was designed to get Joan to surrender something of value (her money).

e.   The Fourth Element of Fraud: The Plaintiff Does, in Fact, Suffer an Injury

The plaintiff must suffer an injury in order to recover under a fraud claim. For instance, Joan must show she lost her money by giving it to Joseph to "invest."

f.   Silence

Special relationship
a relationship where the parties are in a position of trust with one another.

Under the common law, remaining silent about a material fact was not considered fraud. However, with more modern statues, this is changing. In particular, if there is a **special relationship**, then a more stringent requirement to disclose may come into play. Special relationships were discussed in Chapter 6, and can include an employer-employee relationship or a family relationship. In general, special relationships are relationships where the parties are in a position of trust with one another, such as an attorney-client relationship.

Real property is not a type of property where silence is acceptable. While many types of property retain the proviso "let the buyer beware," homeowners are not to remain silent about material problems with their real property. If a homeowner knows he has asbestos, mold, or termites, nowadays he is usually required to disclose this information when selling his house.

Example

The plaintiffs entered into a written agreement to purchase the property from defendants Charlotte and Rick Leonard. The escrow closed.

At some time prior to the execution of the Residential Purchase Agreement, and continuing through the escrow period, the defendants became aware of certain defects in the property, such as structural cracks in the plaster of the pool surface. Defendants failed to disclose to plaintiffs the existence of these defects with the intent to induce Plaintiffs to buy the property. Defendants took actions to insure that Plaintiffs would not discover the defects: defendants arranged to have all cracks in the pool plastered and painted over.

What about other disclosures regarding homes? Should sellers of their homes be expected to disclose whether there was a crime, such as murder, committed in their home? How recent must the murder have been in order for the seller to have to disclose it? What if the house had a ghost? Should a seller have to disclose ghosts as well?

There are two ways a plaintiff can be made whole when she has been a victim of fraud. The plaintiff could be returned to the state she was in before the fraud. In the alternative, she could be placed where she would have been had the fraud been truthful.

9.8 Misrepresentation

Elements of Misrepresentation:

Intent

False Statements

Defendant Knows Statement Is False

Victim Is Injured

Misrepresentation requires the plaintiff rely upon the misrepresentation to recover for this tort. The tort of misrepresentation is a subset of fraud.

a. The First Element of Misrepresentation: The Defendant Makes False Statements with the Intent to Deceive

The first element of misrepresentation is the defendant must make a false statement with the intent to deceive. If a homeowner states to a potential buyer that the house has never had termites, when in fact the house is infested with termites, then this is a false statement made with the intent to deceive the potential buyer.

b. The Second Element of Misrepresentation: The Defendant Has Knowledge of the Falsity of Those Statements

The defendant must make the statements with the knowledge his statements are false. The defendant needs to believe the statement he is making is not truthful. Simply deciding not to verify facts will not satisfy this element.

c. The Third Element of Misrepresentation: The Plaintiff Does, in Fact, Suffer an Injury

To recover damages in misrepresentation, the plaintiff must show he suffered an injury. One possible remedy to misrepresentation is to reform an inaccurate document into a document reflecting the actual agreement the parties made. Another remedy would be to allow the plaintiff to rescind (cancel) the agreement. The plaintiff also has the option of recovering monetary damages. Lastly, the plaintiff may be able to recover the financial gain the defendant made using the plaintiff's money.

9.9 Invasion of Privacy

Invasion of privacy torts are based on the belief a citizen has a right to privacy. Invasion of privacy addresses an individual's privacy wrongly being subjected to

Invasion of privacy
when a defendant places the
plaintiff's private life into the
public in an intrusive manner.

Public figure
a person with power or whose
reputation is known in the
community.

Appropriation
the use of someone's name or
likeness (a photograph, a
drawing, or a cartoon) without
his permission and usually for
commercial advertising.

public scrutiny. **Invasion of privacy** is when a defendant places the plaintiff's private life into the public in an intrusive manner. The plaintiff's private interests are publicized to a third party. There are four types of invasion of privacy torts: appropriation, false light in the public eye, unreasonable intrusion, and public disclosure of private facts.

There are also several degrees to invasion of privacy, depending upon how public a figure a citizen is. In general, a **public figure** is a person with power or whose reputation is known in the community. Public figures do not receive as much protection of their privacy as private figures do. The definition of a public figure is becoming more of a grey area with the prevalence of reality television shows and the widespread use of the Internet. Agreeing to go onto a reality television show (along with signing legal waivers) would negate a claim a person might have for invasion of privacy. However, if a person placed a video on the Internet showing a video of his pet, using a site such as YouTube, should he lose his right to file an invasion of privacy claim if his love life subsequently becomes the subject of someone else's video? No.

a. Appropriation

Appropriation is the use of someone's name or likeness (such as a photograph, a drawing, or a cartoon) without his permission and usually for commercial advertising. The defendant usually benefits from using the plaintiff's name, likeness, or personality. Therefore, the plaintiff's name, likeness, or personality must have some commercial value. For instance, if an actor's image is used to promote a product without his permission, then people may be more likely to buy the product. The actor's image has some commercial value, i.e., trustworthiness that encourages people to buy the product. The person using the image has benefited from using the image because of increased sales of the product.

b. False Light in the Public Eye

Elements to False Light in the Public Eye:

The defendant publicized a matter to the public,

The matter put the plaintiff into a false light,

The false light is offensive to a reasonable person, and

The defendant either knew the matter was false or acted with a reckless disregard as to whether the matter was false.

False light in the public eye
occurs when a defendant
publicly attributes offensive
statements or actions to the
plaintiff.

When a person is portrayed in an unsavory manner in front of the public, the portrayal gives rise to a cause of action, if the defendant purposefully or recklessly caused this to occur. **False light in the public eye** occurs when a defendant publicly attributes offensive statements or actions to the plaintiff. The tort of false light differs from the tort of defamation, mainly due to the intensity of the publicity and the consequences the plaintiff suffers.

c. Unreasonable Intrusion

Unreasonable intrusion
a tort action for a high level of offensive intrusion into the privacy of another.

A high-level of offensive intrusion into the privacy of another is considered unreasonable and is an actionable tort. The **unreasonable intrusion** must be so offensive it would be considered unreasonable to a reasonable person. The intrusion must also be excessive. Peeping Toms can fall under this category. Another example of unreasonable intrusion would be the wiretapping of someone's phone.

Sample Cause of Action for Intrusion

- People have the right to be free from intrusion into their private affairs.
- Defendant has intended to intrude into the private affairs of Plaintiffs by mounting picture-recording devices (including a moving picture camera as well as still picture cameras), which are pointed towards Plaintiffs' residence.
- Plaintiffs have the right to be left alone.
- Defendant's intrusion on Plaintiffs' private affairs is highly offensive to reasonable persons because a reasonable person would expect to move around on their private property without being taped and photographed.
- Therefore, Plaintiffs pray for judgments against Defendant for the above-described injuries and losses.

d. Public Disclosure of Private Facts

Elements to Public Disclosure of Private Facts:

Publicity,

concerning the private life of the plaintiff, and

this publicity is highly offensive to a reasonable person.

Public disclosure of private facts
a defendant's communication of private information about the plaintiff to the public, without the plaintiff's permission, which a reasonable person would find offensive.

Public disclosure of private facts occurs when a defendant communicates private information about the plaintiff to the public without the plaintiff's permission. A reasonable person must find this disclosure to be offensive, or the plaintiff cannot recover under this theory. The truth of the facts is not a defense the defendant can use. The publication of public records is not covered under public disclosure of private facts. Public records would include criminal and civil court records. If a person is convicted of a driving under the influence charge, and the record is not sealed, then the information may be publicized as far as this tort is concerned. If the record were sealed, then the information may not be publicized. If it is publicized, this would be a public disclosure of a private fact.

9.10 Defamation

Elements of Defamation:

Defamatory language regarding Plaintiff

Publicized and false

Injury

Defamation
a spoken or written falsehood about another, which causes injury to the person's character or reputation.

Defamation involves an injury to the plaintiff's reputation caused by an oral or written false statement about the plaintiff. To defame another is to speak or write a falsehood about another, which causes injury to the person's character or reputation. In other words, defamation is A's untrue communication to C, which harms B. To constitute defamation, a third party must hear or see the untrue statement.

Types of Defamation:	Definition:
Libel	Libel is written defamation.
Slander	Slander is verbal defamation.

a. The First Element of Defamation: The Defendant Must Use Defamatory Language

Defamatory language
statements causing a plaintiff to be hated, treated with contempt, or subjected to ridicule.

The first element of defamation is the defendant must use defamatory language. **Defamatory language** includes any statements causing a plaintiff to be hated, treated with contempt, or subjected to ridicule. Statements causing a person to be shamed or disgraced can also be defamatory. If an oral or written statement is true, then the statement is not defamatory. Truth is a defense to an allegation of defamation.

b. The Second Element of Defamation: The Defamatory Statement Refers to the Plaintiff

The defamatory statement must refer to the plaintiff. There can only be defamation when a third party reasonably believes the statement refers to the plaintiff. If a defamatory statement is made about someone with a common name, then it may not be reasonable to assume the statement was made about the plaintiff. In *New York Times v. Sullivan* (discussed later in this chapter), the public official was not reasonable in believing third parties would think the potentially defamatory comments were about him. However, if a defamatory statement provides enough information to identify the plaintiff even though the plaintiff is not specifically named, then a defendant will be found to have defamed the plaintiff.

c. The Third Element of Defamation: The Defamatory Statement Is Publicized and Is a False Statement

Publication
the communication of the information to a third party.

The defamatory statement must be publicized to a third party. If a person just makes a defamatory statement to the person the statement is about, then there has not been defamation. **Publication** is the communication of the information to a third party. Publication can be made through a written or oral statement. An oral publication can be by radio, television, telephone, or movies. A written publication can be made by a letter, newspaper, or email. Again, if the statement is made to or read by the plaintiff alone, then there is not a cause of action for defamation. A third party must be involved for the statement to qualify as defamation. If the statement is only publicized to one person other than the plaintiff, then this is sufficient to satisfy the publication requirement. The statement must also be false. Truth is a defense to defamation.

d. The Fourth Element of Defamation: The Plaintiff's Reputation Is Injured

The plaintiff's reputation must be injured in order for the defamation to be actionable. It is harder to injure a public figure's reputation than a private individual's reputation. Public figures do not have as much protection from defamation as private individuals do. This is because the public figure, by being out in the public, has made his life subject to scrutiny. For instance, *New York Times v. Sullivan* discusses how the public's right to criticize our public officials is of much greater importance than the public official's right not to be criticized.

In determining what amount of damages to award, the jury can look at the statement to see how outrageous the statement is. The jury can also take into consideration how many people heard or read the statement. The jury can look at how the statement effected the plaintiff's reputation and the amount of humiliation the plaintiff suffered.

Sample Cause of Action for Defamation

- On January 29, 2008, the defendant came to the plaintiff's place of work, and in the presence and hearing of the plaintiff's employer and fellow co-workers, accused the plaintiff of failing to pay child support. In addition, the defendant stated the plaintiff was a "lying, no-good, cheating ex-husband who didn't deserve to see his children."
- Defendant's statements were false.
- As a result of the defendant's publication of these defamatory statements, the plaintiff lost his job, has been injured in his reputation, and suffered great pain and mental anguish, in the sum of $_____.
- Therefore, plaintiff demands judgment against defendant in the amount of $_____; and plaintiff prays for such other and further relief as is just and proper.

e. Libel

Elements of Libel:

A written defamatory statement made by the defendant;

The statement was of and concerning the plaintiff;

The statement was publicized.

Libel
written defamation.

Libel per se
written statements, which by their very nature are considered libel.

Libel is written defamation. Some statements, by their very nature, are almost automatically considered libel if untrue and are called **libel per se**. For instance, a written statement that Jane is a convicted felon or has a sexually transmitted disease, is a libel per se statement. For an accusation of a crime to be held as libel per se, the crime must be one of moral turpitude. Moral turpitude crimes have an adverse effect on a person's character. For instance, the crime of forgery adversely reflects on a person's ability to tell the truth. If Jane is falsely accused of forgery, Jane may be able to recover special damages.

f. Slander

Elements of Slander:

Speaking

Defamatory language

Language exposes the plaintiff to public hatred or ridicule

Slander
oral defamation.

Slander per se
oral statements, which by their very nature are considered slander.

Slander involves oral defamation. **Slander per se** is based upon the same concept as libel per se. Some statements are so inflammatory, if the statements are spoken, the statements will almost automatically be considered slander if untrue. Such statements include smearing someone's business, or accusations of a crime of moral turpitude (a crime related to the plaintiff's ability to tell the truth), a sexually transmitted disease, and sexual misconduct.

Example of a Complaint for Libel and Slander

- On March _____, 2007, the defendant came to the plaintiff's work, and in hearing of the plaintiff's co-workers, stated in effect the plaintiff was a "dead-beat" dad who refused to "make good on his child support obligations." [slander]
- On March _____, 2007 the defendant published similar words in a letter to the plaintiff's mother. [libel]
- Defendant's statements were false.
- As a result of the defendant's publication of these defamatory statements, the plaintiff lost his job and suffered great pain and anguish.

g. Privileges to Defamation

If a person has been defamed, he has a qualified privileged to respond to the defamation, meaning the plaintiff will receive some protection from liability in responding to the defamation. A qualified privilege is not an absolute, without caveats attached, privilege. Therefore, the plaintiff's response to the defamatory statements should be commensurate with the original defamation.

Absolute privilege
provides complete protection from liability.

An **absolute privilege** is not qualified, meaning a person who makes a defamatory comment is completely protected from liability in making the defamatory statement. Some of the main absolute privileges to defamation are:

- court proceedings,
- government proceedings,
- publications that have been consented to, and
- publications between married persons.

Statements made during trial, made by lawyers, witnesses, the plaintiff, the defendant, or judges, are privileged. This privilege protects judges from defamation suits, when a judge makes a statement in the course and scope of performing her job duties. This same rule will also protect the lawyers, the parties to the lawsuits, whatever witnesses testify, and the jurors. Congress people have an absolute privilege against defamation while speaking on the congressional floor. This privilege would also apply to witnesses speaking at the House of Representatives or Senate.

Actual malice (in defamation)
making a statement with knowledge of its falsity or with reckless disregard of whether it was true or false.

New York Times Company v. Sullivan illustrates public figures, in their official capacity, must prove a different standard of defamation than private persons. A public official cannot be awarded damages for defamation relating to his official conduct "unless he proves '**actual malice**' — that the statement was made with knowledge of its falsity or with reckless disregard of whether it was true or false."[7]

New York Times Co. v. Sullivan

376 U.S. 254 (1964)

. . . Held: A State cannot under the First and Fourteenth Amendments award damages to a public official for defamatory falsehood relating to his official conduct unless he proves "actual malice" — that the statement was made with knowledge of its falsity or with reckless disregard of whether it was true or false.

. . . Respondent L. B. Sullivan is one of the three elected Commissioners of the City of Montgomery, Alabama. He testified that he was "Commissioner of Public Affairs and the duties are supervision of the Police Department, Fire Department, Department of Cemetery and Department of Scales." He brought this civil libel action against the four individual petitioners, who are Negroes and Alabama clergymen, and against petitioner the New York Times Company, a New York corporation which publishes the New York Times, a daily newspaper. . . .

Respondent's complaint alleged that he had been libeled by statements in a full-page advertisement that was carried in the New York Times on March 29, 1960. Entitled "Heed Their Rising Voices," the advertisement began by stating that "As the whole world knows by now, thousands of Southern Negro students are engaged in widespread non-violent demonstrations in positive affirmation of the right to live in human dignity as guaranteed by the U.S. Constitution and the Bill of Rights." It went on to charge that "in their efforts to uphold these guarantees, they are being met by an unprecedented wave of terror by those who would deny and negate that document which the whole world looks upon as setting the pattern for modern freedom. . . ."

Of the 10 paragraphs of text in the advertisement, the third and a portion of the sixth were the basis of respondent's claim of libel. They read as follows:

Third paragraph:

In Montgomery, Alabama, after students sang 'My Country, 'Tis of Thee' on the State Capitol steps, their leaders were expelled from school, and truckloads of police armed with

---

7. *New York Times Co. V. Sullivan*, 376 U.S. 254 (1964).

shotguns and tear-gas ringed the Alabama State College Campus. When the entire student body protested to state authorities by refusing to re-register, their dining hall was padlocked in an attempt to starve them into submission.

Sixth paragraph:

Again and again the Southern violators have answered Dr. King's peaceful protests with intimidation and violence. They have bombed his home almost killing his wife and child. They have assaulted his person. They have arrested him seven times—for "speeding," "loitering" and similar "offenses." And now they have charged him with "perjury"—a felony under which they could imprison him for ten years. . . ."

Although neither of these statements mentions respondent by name, he contended that the word "police" in the third paragraph referred to him as the Montgomery Commissioner who supervised the Police Department, so that he was being accused of "ringing" the campus with police. He further claimed that the paragraph would be read as imputing to the police, and hence to him, the padlocking of the dining hall in order to starve the students into submission. As to the sixth paragraph, he contended that since arrests are ordinarily made by the police, the statement "They have arrested [Dr. King] seven times" would be read as referring to him; he further contended that the "They" who did the arresting would be equated with the "They" who committed the other described acts and with the "Southern violators." Thus, he argued, the paragraph would be read as accusing the Montgomery police, and hence him, of answering Dr. King's protests with "intimidation and violence," bombing his home, assaulting his person, and charging him with perjury. . . .

It is uncontroverted that some of the statements contained in the paragraphs were not accurate descriptions of events which occurred in Montgomery. . . .

Under Alabama law as applied in this case, a publication is "libelous per se" if the words "tend to injure a person . . . in his reputation" or to "bring [him] into public contempt"; the trial court stated that the standard was met if the words are such as to "injure him in his public office, or impute misconduct to him in his office, or want of official integrity, or want of fidelity to a public trust. . . ." The jury must find that the words were published "of and concerning" the plaintiff, but where the plaintiff is a public official his place in the governmental hierarchy is sufficient evidence to support a finding that his reputation has been affected by statements that reflect upon the agency of which he is in charge. Once "libel per se" has been established, the defendant has no defense as to stated facts unless he can persuade the jury that they were true in all their particulars. . . . His privilege of "fair comment" for expressions of opinion depends on the truth of the facts upon which the comment is based. . . . Unless he can discharge the burden of proving truth, general damages are presumed, and may be awarded without proof of pecuniary injury. A showing of actual malice is apparently a prerequisite to recovery of punitive damages, and the defendant may in any event forestall a punitive award by a retraction meeting the statutory requirements. Good motives and belief in truth do not negate an inference of malice, but are relevant only in mitigation of punitive damages if the jury chooses to accord them weight. . . .

The question before us is whether this rule of liability, as applied to an action brought by a public official against critics of his official conduct, abridges the freedom of speech and of the press that is guaranteed by the First and Fourteenth Amendments. . . .

The general proposition that freedom of expression upon public questions is secured by the First Amendment has long been settled by our decisions. . . .

Thus we consider this case against the background of a profound national commitment to the principle that debate on public issues should be uninhibited, robust, and wide-open, and that it may well include vehement, caustic, and sometimes unpleasantly sharp attacks on government and public officials. . . . The present advertisement, as an expression of grievance and protest on one of the major public issues of our time, would seem clearly to qualify for the constitutional protection. The question is whether it forfeits that protection by the falsity of some of its factual statements and by its alleged defamation of respondent.

Authoritative interpretations of the First Amendment guarantees have consistently refused to recognize an exception for any test of truth — whether administered by judges, juries, or administrative officials — and especially one that puts the burden of proving truth on the speaker. . . . The constitutional protection does not turn upon "the truth, popularity, or social utility" of the ideas and beliefs which are offered.

Injury to official reputation affords no more warrant for repressing speech that would otherwise be free than does factual error. Where judicial officers are involved, this Court has held that concern for the dignity and reputation of the courts does not justify the punishment as criminal contempt of criticism of the judge or his decision. . . . This is true even though the utterance contains "half-truths" and "misinformation." . . . If judges are to be treated as "men of fortitude, able to thrive in a hardy climate," . . . surely the same must be true of other government officials, such as elected city commissioners. Criticism of their official conduct does not lose its constitutional protection merely because it is effective criticism and hence diminishes their official reputations. . . .

A rule compelling the critic of official conduct to guarantee the truth of all his factual assertions — and to do so on pain of libel judgments virtually unlimited in amount — leads to a comparable "self-censorship." . . . [W]ould-be critics of official conduct may be deterred from voicing their criticism, even though it is believed to be true and even though it is in fact true, because of doubt whether it can be proved in court or fear of the expense of having to do so. . . . [This would dampen] the vigor and limits the variety of public debate. . . .

The constitutional guarantees require, we think, a federal rule that prohibits a public official from recovering damages for a defamatory falsehood relating to his official conduct unless he proves that the statement was made with "actual malice" — that is, with knowledge that it was false or with reckless disregard of whether it was false or not. . . .

[W]e consider that the proof presented to show actual malice lacks the convincing clarity which the constitutional standard demands, and hence that it would not constitutionally sustain the judgment for respondent under the proper rule of law. The case of the individual petitioners requires little discussion. . . . [T]here was no evidence whatever that they were aware of any erroneous statements or were in any way reckless in that regard. The judgment against them is thus without constitutional support. . . .

We also think the evidence was constitutionally defective in another respect: it was incapable of supporting the jury's finding that the allegedly libelous statements were made "of and concerning" respondent. . . .

9.11 Malicious Prosecution

Elements of Malicious Prosecution:

Intent

Criminal charge brought by defendant

Plaintiff wins

Defendant acted with malice in bringing charge

No probable cause for the charge

Malicious prosecution
a cause of action for malicious prosecution arises when the defendant misuses the court system unjustly to retaliate against the plaintiff.

Malicious prosecution is brought as a civil suit. A malicious prosecution case arises when the defendant uses the court system unjustly to retaliate against the plaintiff. Therefore, in a malicious prosecution case, there is an underlying case. The plaintiff, who was unjustly prosecuted in criminal court, can sue the person responsible for having the plaintiff prosecuted. To win a malicious prosecution case, a plaintiff must show he suffered damages. If the plaintiff incurred legal fees in defending himself in criminal court, then the fees are evidence he sustained damages.

a. The First Element of Malicious Prosecution: The Defendant Brings or Continues to Bring a Criminal Charge Against the Plaintiff

The defendant must bring a criminal charge against the plaintiff and the criminal charge must be groundless. One of the unfortunate areas where malicious prosecution is rife is during ugly and contested divorces. A spouse may be angry with her husband and want custody of the children. To bolster her case, the wife may make allegations of spousal and child abuse, and the husband may be tried in criminal court on those allegations.

b. The Second Element of Malicious Prosecution: The Plaintiff "Wins" the Criminal Case

The second element required for winning a malicious prosecution case is the person who was prosecuted (the defendant in the underlying criminal case, but the plaintiff in the civil case for malicious prosecution) wins the criminal case. Winning the underlying case substantiates the criminal charge being groundless. If the person prosecuted in the underlying case does not win, then he cannot bring a cause of action for malicious prosecution. Using the example from above, if the husband was found guilty for spousal and child abuse, he could not bring a civil case against the wife for malicious prosecution.

c. The Third Element of Malicious Prosecution: The Defendant Acted with Malice, in Bringing the Charge Against the Plaintiff

Malice in malicious prosecution
the defendant brought the charge against the plaintiff with the knowledge the charge was false.

The next element of **malicious prosecution** is the defendant acted with malice in bringing the charge against the plaintiff. Malice, in this context, means the defendant brought the charge against the plaintiff with the knowledge the charge was false. In the example of the wife bringing spousal and child abuse allegations against the husband, the wife knew the allegations were not true and thus acted with malice in bringing the allegations.

d. The Fourth Element of Malicious Prosecution: There Was No Probable Cause for the Charge

The last element of malicious prosecution is there must not have been probable cause for the charge. Still using the same example, if the wife saw bruises on her children's arms and asked her husband about the bruises, to which he replied: "I played with them a little rough." The wife might have probable cause in bringing allegations of child abuse.

The Temporary Restraining Order Process[8]
By Christy Monahan, Paralegal

The first step in obtaining a Restraining Order was to obtain a Temporary Restraining Order, referred to as a TRO. Being unfamiliar with the process I went to my state website's Self-Help link to find step-by-step information. There was a very helpful information sheet, entitled "Can a Civil Harassment Restraining Order Help Me?" The information consists of frequently asked questions and how to get started.

A simple call to the Court let me know what I needed to bring, where to go, and when to arrive for the pre-hearing. The two forms I needed to bring were a Request for Orders to Stop Harassment and a Notice of Hearing and Temporary Restraining Order [the form names vary from state to state]. Along with

these forms, I went through all of the back-up documentation to determine what would be most pertinent to support the claim. I was glad that the client had started documenting everything as soon as the situation had begun to grow out of control and I believe that this step strengthened her claim.

Next all the paperwork had to filed and entered into the court's system and calendared. Be prepared to stand in line and wait. Here, the clerk assigned the case number along with the place, date (that same day), and time (that afternoon) of the initial hearing. The clerk returned several sets of documents. Each set had a helpful notation on what to do with that particular group of documents.

8. If a client has been assaulted and/or battered, in addition to filing a civil suit, the law office may need to file a temporary restraining order ("TRO") against the defendant in order to protect the plaintiff. The following essay discusses how to obtain a temporary restraining order.

For the initial hearing it is important [for the client] to be on time, bring all of the documentation, and be prepared to wait. Along with the case, there were a number of other cases all assigned to the same initial hearing date and time. We were not allowed to enter the courtroom and sat in the hallway. The bailiff came out to check-in each party. The judge would ask questions while reviewing the documentation. The judge made his decision that the TRO was granted. The bailiff returned more papers and the hearing date along with the official TRO. The court required that the client must keep the TRO with her at all times. The TRO indicated that X was not allowed to contact the client and specified the distance that must be maintained.

Anyone, with the exception of the client, can serve the TRO, but the court recommends that the Sheriff's Office perform this task. The next stop was the Sheriff's Office, which was in the same building. The defendant had the right to know all of the charges brought forward and to defense at the hearing. Therefore, part of the documents that were served included copies of the back-up documentation and the declaration. The

other forms to be served were an Answer to Request for Orders to Stop Harassment, Proof of Firearms Turned In or Sold, and How I Can Answer a Request for Orders to Stop Harassment. Whoever served the TRO must file a Proof of Service or POS with the court. The POS must be filed by the date indicated by the court. Since the defendant, who lived in another state, had left the area, service was not completed. I contacted the local Police where the defendant lived to discuss how the TRO could be served. Immediately thereafter I send the necessary documents to the local Police where the defendant lived. They were able to achieve service, complete the POS, and return the POS to me. I filed the POS with the Court within the time allotted.

For the hearing, remember to bring all required papers, arrive early, and be prepared to wait. Also be prepared for the client to see the defendant. Again, several cases were assigned the same date and time as ours for a hearing. Most importantly, when applying for a TRO remember that nothing is certain until sanctioned by the judge and be prepared to wait.

E T H I C S

Guideline 8: A lawyer may include a charge for the work performed by a paralegal in setting a charge and/or billing for legal services.[9]

A lawyer can charge the client the going rate for paralegal services, instead of the actual cost of the

paralegal services to the lawyer. Frequently, paralegals are used to cut costs, as the rates for paralegals are typically less than the rate for attorneys. Usually, the paralegal must have been performing legal, rather than clerical, work in order to charge the client for the paralegal's services.

Chapter Summary

Intentional torts require both the intent to commit the act and the consequence. Intent is what a person wants to happen as a result of his actions or what a person knows is likely to happen as a result of his actions. Intentional torts are different from negligence, which is accidental behavior. If the defendant intended to cause a tort to

---

9. ABA Model Guidelines for the Utilization of Paralegal Services, Guideline 8 (ABA 2004).

plaintiff A, but actually injures plaintiff B, then the defendant's intent to injure A can be transferred to B. This allows B to sue the defendant for the injury. In addition, if the defendant meant to batter the plaintiff, but actually assaulted the plaintiff, then the defendant's intent to batter can be transferred to the assault. This allows the plaintiff to sue for the assault.

Battery is a harmful or offensive contact with another, caused by the defendant's intention to cause the harmful or offensive contact. Assault is a separate tort from battery, and the major difference between the two torts is that assault does not require physical contact. An offensive contact is a contact that would offend the dignity of a reasonable person. If a battery is consented to, then there is no battery. For example, people playing football consent to being tackled; there is no battery then when a player is tackled.

While assault does not require contact, it does require the plaintiff to be in fear or apprehension of an imminent harmful or offensive contact. Apprehension is the anticipation of something. The plaintiff must anticipate the imminent contact. Imminent means the defendant has immediate quick and easy access to the plaintiff. If the defendant calls the plaintiff and states he will injure the plaintiff tomorrow, this does not satisfy the imminent requirement.

A false imprisonment is a confinement through physical or emotional restraints. The confinement must be unlawful, and for an unreasonable amount of time. In addition, the plaintiff must have no means of escape from the confinement. If the plaintiff could merely walk around the defendant to escape, then this does not constitute confinement.

In Chapter 5, negligent infliction of emotional distress was discussed. This chapter discusses intentional infliction of emotional distress. Intentional infliction is when a defendant's behavior intentionally disturbs the plaintiff's peace of mind. The defendant's behavior must be extreme and outrageous. Intentional infliction of emotional distress is easier to prove damages on than negligent infliction of emotional distress because with IIED, a plaintiff does not normally have to show physical damages.

Fraud is the use of false statements, intended to deceive, made with the knowledge of the untruthfulness of the statements, and designed to obtain something of value from the plaintiff. The plaintiff must actually lose something of value. If the defendant is merely silent about something important to a transaction, depending on the jurisdiction, this may or may not constitute fraud. Misrepresentation is a subset of fraud.

Invasion of privacy torts are based upon the belief that individuals have a right to privacy. Invasion of privacy torts allow an individual to sue for different wrongful subjections to public scrutiny. There are four invasion of privacy torts: appropriation, false light in the public eye, unreasonable intrusion, and public disclosure of private facts. Appropriation involves the use of someone's name or likeness, without his permission, and usually for financial gain. False light in the public eye is portraying a person in an unsavory manner in the public. This tort is mainly different from defamation by degree, defamation usually being worse. Unreasonable intrusion is a high-level of offensive intrusion into the privacy of another. The final invasion of privacy tort is public disclosure of private facts, which is publicizing private information about the plaintiff. The publication must be highly offensive to a reasonable person.

Defamation is an injury to the plaintiff's reputation caused by oral or written false statement about the plaintiff. Libel is written defamation and slander is oral defamation. Defamatory language is a statement about the plaintiff that subjects the plaintiff to hatred, contempt, or ridicule. The statement must be made to a third party, meaning the statement must be made to someone other than the plaintiff and the defendant. Some people are privileged, or protected from lawsuits, if they make defamatory comments. These people include judges in a court proceeding and senators speaking on the Senate floor.

A malicious prosecution claim arises when a person uses the court system unjustly to retaliate against another. The person retaliated against has a cause of action for malicious prosecution, and would be the plaintiff in the malicious prosecution case (whereas he was the defendant in the underlying criminal case). The allegations in the underlying criminal case must be groundless and the defendant in the malicious prosecution case must have maliciously started the underlying case. Malicious in this context means the defendant knew the allegations were false when she made the allegations.

Key Terms

- Absolute privilege
- Act
- Appreciable amount of time
- Apprehension
- Appropriation
- Assault
- Battery
- Cause of action
- Consent
- Defamation
- Defamatory language
- Element
- False arrest
- False imprisonment
- False light in the public eye
- Fraud
- Harmful contact
- Imminent
- Intentional infliction of emotional distress

- Intent
- Invasion of privacy
- Libel
- Libel per se
- Material fact
- Misrepresentation
- Malicious prosecution
- Offensive contact
- One's person
- Outrageous behavior
- Privilege
- Public disclosure of private facts
- Public figure
- Slander
- Slander per se
- Special relationship
- Transferred intent
- Unreasonable intrusion

Review Questions

- How are intentional torts different from negligence? Are we concerned about the reasonable person standard in intentional torts?
- How are intentional torts different than prosecuting the defendant for crimes in criminal court?
- Identify two intentional torts and the elements for those two torts.
- What does a defendant have to intend in order to be liable for an intentional tort?
- What is the difference between assault and battery?
- What is transferred intent?
- What would be an example of a lawful restraint?
- How does consent negate battery?
- What is the common element of every tort in this chapter?
- Explain how false imprisonment becomes an issue if a store owner holds a suspected shoplifter.

Web Links

- www.freeadvice.com/all_topics.htm/. The foremost legal subject on this website is accidents or personal injury law. In addition, this website has resources to legal forms. The site will give you a free preview to the form and then require payment to see the whole form. Look up libel and slander on the website. The website discusses specific instances of libel and slander, such as a negative employment reference.
- For a good article on defamation and slander, go to: http://theinjuryguide.com/ pdefamation-libel-and-slander.html.

Exercises

- A posse of White supremacist skinheads stands on the sidewalk in front of a Hispanic man's house for an hour, staring into the living room window of the house. The man is frightened. Have the skinheads assaulted this man?
- Holly is cut off in traffic by Bruce. She is very angry about being cut off. She sees Bruce about to turn the wrong way onto a one-way street. She cheers, but does nothing to warn him, such as honking her horn. Bruce is hit by oncoming traffic. Has Holly committed a battery?
- Lorraine is European and grew up with a custom of kissing people hello. Elaine is a United States citizen and does not believe women should kiss each other.

The two end up as roommates at a college in the United States. When Lorraine meets Elaine, she tries to kiss her on both cheeks. Has Lorraine committed a tort? What if Elaine, seeing Lorraine try to kiss her, hits Lorraine?

- A prisoner is inside an enclosed bulletproof glass cage within a courtroom, awaiting arraignment. The prisoner rams his handcuffed hands against the bulletproof glass, startling his attorney who is talking to him through holes in the glass. Has a battery been committed? Why or why not? What if the prisoner was actually able to crack the class? Was another tort committed?

- Below is a statement of facts from one of the cases the author has worked on, though the names have been changed. See how many intentional torts to people you can identify. Use the chart below the fact pattern. What intentional torts were committed on Lee? Was Lee assaulted if she did not see who attacked her? What other claim, discussed in a previous chapter, might Lee have for watching her sister being hit and kicked? What intentional torts were committed on Jane? Was Lee justified in taking her knife out and swinging it?

Statement of Facts

On March 29, 2008, Lee attended a party at the Ice Factory located on Union Street. Lee's sister, Jane, was rushed and hit in the face. Lee was also hit, but Lee did not see who hit her. Lee saw her sister being hit and kicked. Jane fell to the ground. Lee got around the man that was pushing everyone back from Jane and picked Jane up. Jane was bleeding. Lee grabbed her purse, took her knife out, and started swinging it. Jane was cut by a straight blade.

Tina was in the group that was hitting and kicking Jane. Harriet was also in the group. Lee did not see Tina or Harriet with any objects in their hands. Lee never saw Tina or Harriet with any kind of sharp object that night.

When Lee was swinging the knife, she does not know if Tina or Harriet were still in the group.

What torts were committed? Were any crimes committed as well?

Plaintiff	Defendant	Intentional Tort	Crimes
Lee			
	Lee		
Jane			
	Tina		
	Harriet		

- Ted Doth is a photographer. He is scoping out the UCLA medical center, waiting to see if any celebrities emerge. He spots a famous actress leaving the hospital with one arm in a cast, the other arm holding onto her boyfriend, who has documented violent tendencies. The actress and boyfriend get into the boyfriend's car and drive off. Ted revs up his car and speeds after the couple. He manages to pull ahead of the couple by crossing the center divider of a two-lane road. He then proceeds to swoop and squat. Not wanting to cause an accident or violate traffic laws, the celebrity couple stops. Ted starts flash photographing the couple through the car window. Due to the bright lights, the couple are unable to safely drive away until Ted stops snapping photos twenty minutes later. Can the couple successfully sue for false imprisonment?

■ Sherry comes home from work to find her apartment has been burglarized. Sherry calls the police and "volunteers" she is certain her ex-husband is behind the crime. The police investigate, but based upon the evidence, the district attorney's office is unsure whether or not to prosecute the ex-husband. Sherry throws a fit, she repeatedly calls up the D.A.'s office and demands the D.A. prosecute the case against her ex-husband. The D.A. refuses. If the ex-husband sues Sherry for malicious prosecution, what will the result be?

■ Determine whether your jurisdiction requires a plaintiff to show some physical harm in order to recover for intentional infliction of emotional distress.

■ Larry is riding go-carts at Family Fun Center on a Saturday afternoon. There are several other patrons of the fun center also racing go-carts. Aaron is another one of the go-cart riders. Due to the gross negligence of the fun center in failing to properly maintain its go-carts, Aaron's go-cart catches on fire and he is horribly disfigured. Larry did not actually see the go-cart on fire as Aaron was behind him on the racecourse. Larry turned around once he heard Aaron's terrible screams. He stopped his go-cart and rushed back to Aaron's car to try to help him. He gasped in horror when he saw Aaron had suffered severe burns. Larry froze and felt sick to his stomach. He has been unable to sleep because he repeatedly sees Aaron's burnt face in his sleep. Larry sues Family Fun Center for negligent infliction of emotional distress. Will Larry be able to recover under this theory? What about under IIED?

■ Each of the following statements is publicized to a third party or third parties. Which of the following statements are defamatory, if any
  ○ Chandler calls Ira a terrorist. Ira is not a terrorist.
  ○ An abortion protester carries a sign outside of Dr. Ying's office that reads: "Dr. Ying murders babies." Dr. Ying does not perform abortions.
  ○ "The jury must have been bribed to let the defendant off."
  ○ "Used car salesmen are crooks."

■ Homer takes a photograph of Charlotte picking her noise in her car. Has an invasion of privacy occurred?

■ Bud and Abigail have been married for fifty years and are celebrating their wedding anniversary in a hotel ballroom with family and friends. Other guests mill about just outside the ballroom. Early in their marriage, Abigail had a torrid love affair with the postal carrier. Abigail's sister, who has always resented her, announces loudly at the party: "Abigail had an affair." Does Abigail have a cause of action against her sister?

CHAPTER

Intentional Torts to Property

Ownership does not always mean absolute dominion.[1]

Chapter Outline

---

1. Justice Hugo Black.

b. The Second Element of Conversion: Deprive of Possession
c. The Third Element of Conversion: Extent of Deprivation
d. The Fourth Element of Conversion: Lack of Consent
e. Remedies for Conversion

Chapter Objectives

- Differentiate between intentional torts to persons and intentional torts to property
- Define and discuss the elements of trespass to land, trespass to chattel, and conversion
- Clarify the differences between trespass to chattel and conversion
- Discuss the damages available for intentional torts to property

10.1 Introduction

Chattel
personal property.

In intentional torts to property, the defendant is interfering with the plaintiff's right to possession of property. Intentional torts to property involve the defendant interfering with real property (land and everything attached to it) or personal property (also known as "**chattel**"). You might view personal property as any type of property that could be carried by Hercules, the mythical strongest man in the world. Therefore, a huge sports utility vehicle would be personal property.

Trespass to chattels and conversion, while two separate torts, overlap. The major difference between the two torts is the degree of the interference with the personal property. Trespass to chattels requires damage to the property. Conversion occurs when the damage to the chattel is so great, or the chattel was sold to a third party, so that the person who damaged the chattel should have to buy the chattel.

10.2 Trespass to Land

Comparison between:

Trespass to Land	Trespass to Chattel
Unauthorized entry onto another person's real property	Unauthorized possession or interference with another person's personal property
Intent to enter without consent	Intent to possess or interfere
Interference with the real property owner's exclusive right to possess his land without permission	The defendant damages the chattel

Trespass to land
occurs when a person enters a landowner's real property without consent.

In Chapter 6, a landowner's duty to a trespasser was discussed. In this chapter, the tort of trespassing is discussed. A **trespass to land** occurs when a person enters a landowner's or renter's real property without consent. The plaintiff in a trespass to land case could be the owner of the real property or a renter of the real property, because the renter has the exclusive right to possess the land. Thus, it is not necessary that a plaintiff actually own the land to maintain a trespass to land cause of action. The key to trespass to land is people have exclusive rights to possess their real property. Trespass to land interferes with the possessor's exclusive right to possess his real property.

a.   The First Element to Trespass to Land: The Entry onto the Land Was Unauthorized

The unprivileged element of trespass to land simply means the person who committed the trespass did not have the consent of the owner or possessor of the land to be upon the land. Typically, utility companies have an easement to property so their employees, such as meter readers, can enter upon the property and read the meter without becoming trespassers. A meter reader would then be considered privileged to be on the land.

b.   The Second Element to Trespass to Land: The Defendant Acted with Intent

The second key element to trespass to land is that the trespass is intentional. There must be the intent to enter upon the land. However, the trespasser does not have to have intent to cause harm to the property or to interfere with the plaintiff's possession of property. So long as the defendant intentionally entered upon the land, it does not matter even if the defendant mistakenly thought the land was hers!

c.   The Third Element to Trespass to Land: There Was an Entry onto the Plaintiff's Property Which Interfered with Exclusive Right

To constitute an entry onto the plaintiff's property, the defendant does not have to personally enter upon the plaintiff's land. Instead, the defendant could throw something onto the plaintiff's property and it would still constitute a trespass. The entry onto the real property must be an interference with the real property owner's exclusive right to possess the land. This could constitute going onto the land, staying on the land, or traveling to a prohibited part of the land.

d.   The Fourth Element of Trespass to Land: Without Permission

The defendant has to make an unauthorized entry onto the real property to satisfy the element of "without permission." The defendant must intend to enter onto the land without the real property owner's consent. Intent is shown by an actual intention to enter the land or by knowledge with substantial certainty an entry onto the land will occur. It is not a defense for the defendant to show she was reasonable in entering the plaintiff's land. The only intent necessary is the defendant intended to make physical contact with the land. The plaintiff does not need to show the defendant intended to cause harm to the real property.

Examples

■ Cal is a door-to-door salesperson. Jerry, a landowner, has a welcome mat at his front door. Cal comes to the front door and rings the doorbell. Has Cal committed a trespass? No, unless a landowner has signs up stating he does not want solicitors, Cal has not committed a trespass. In fact, rather than having a sign up, warning people off his land, Jerry has a welcome mat out. Therefore, Cal has not committed a trespass to land.

■ Timmy's land is fenced and has signs stating, "Beware of Dog." John enters the land anyway. Having a sign out stating "Beware of Dog" is much less welcoming than the welcome mat Jerry had out at his front door. Timmy also has a fence. Timmy is trying to avoid people coming onto his land. John will probably be considered a trespasser. However, what if John were a meter reader? Meter readers are usually privileged to be on the land, so John would not be a trespasser.

A trespass to land may also occur if a person exceeds the permission he has been given to be on the land. Using the example from above, Cal rings Jerry's doorbell. Jerry comes to the door and Cal asks Jerry if he can mow Jerry's lawn. Jerry says yes. Cal has permission to be upon Jerry's land to mow his lawn, but Cal can still be found a trespasser if he exceeds the permission to just mow the lawn. Cal mows Jerry's lawn from 2:00 p.m. to 5:00 p.m. on Saturday. Cal sees Jerry leave the property around 5:00 p.m. Cal calls his friends and asks them to come over and bring beer with them. Cal and his friends have a little party on Jerry's land and leave beer cans all over the freshly mowed lawn. Cal had permission or consent to be on Jerry's land for the limited purpose of mowing the lawn. Cal did not have permission to be upon the land to drink and leave refuse on the land. Therefore, Cal can still be found to be a trespasser although he originally did have permission to be on Jerry's land to mow his lawn.

e.   The Fifth Element of Trespass to Land: Damages

The rule regarding damages in trespass to land is there does not have to be actual harm to the land for the plaintiff to prove damages. It is enough that the defendant interfered with the real property owner's use of his land. If there is not actual harm to the land, however, the damages awarded will most likely be nominal damages. Children cutting across someone's land on their way to school would technically be trespassers. However, a court is not likely to award more than nominal damages in such a case: what damages to the land have the trespassers caused by merely walking across the land? None. If there are actual damages, then the plaintiff may recover compensatory damages such as the actual cost of the damage to the land or the cost of repair to the land. For instance, the trespassing children cut across the plaintiff's vegetable garden, upon which the owner relies on for food and entering her vegetables in the state fair. The vegetable garden is trampled and useless. The children's parents might have to pay for the land to be tilled again and seeded. If a trespass is egregious, then the trespasser may even have to pay punitive damages.

One of the more common remedies awarded to plaintiffs in a trespass case are injunctions. Typically, injunctions are awarded for continuing trespasses rather than one-time trespasses. If the trespass only occurred once, the plaintiff does not normally need an injunction against future trespasses. A property owner could ask the judge for an injunction against the children who cut across her lawn, whether or not the children damaged her lawn.

Issues also arise when trespassers make use of what appears to be abandoned property. For instance, if a home is deserted-looking, a trespasser might move in. If the trespasser was living on the land, then the trespasser could also potentially owe the plaintiff rent. If a field was deserted-looking, a trespasser might plant crops on the land. If the trespasser is using the land for her own use, such as growing corn and selling the corn, then the trespasser may have to pay to the plaintiff the profits made from selling the corn.

10.3   Trespass to Chattels

Comparison between:

Trespass to Chattel	Conversion
Intention to Deprive or Interfere	Intent to Deprive and Convert to One's Own Use
Defendant Damages Chattel or Defendant Deprives Possessor of the Chattel's Use	Extent of Deprivation Is so Great, the Owner Cannot Use the Personal Property at All
Lack of Consent	Lack of Consent
Damages	Damages

Trespass to chattels and conversion are very similar torts. However, conversion is more extreme and is discussed in more detail following trespass to chattel. Chattel is personal property, other than land or things attached to land. A mobile home would be chattel, whereas a house would not. This is because the mobile home is capable of being picked up and moved, whereas the house is not.

Trespass to chattels
when a person harms or interferes with the plaintiff's use of chattel.

Trespass to chattels occurs when a defendant possesses the plaintiff's personal property without consent and causes harm to the plaintiff. The trespasser to the chattel either harms the chattel or interferes with the plaintiff's use of the chattel. A modern day example of trespass to chattel might be someone intentionally sending you a computer virus via email. The sender intended to harm your computer without your consent, and now your computer does not work.

With trespass to land, the plaintiff does not need to show actual harm to the land in order to obtain an injunction or nominal damages. In order for a plaintiff to recover damages in a trespass to chattel situation, the plaintiff has to show actual damage to the chattel. Thus, a difference between trespass to land and trespass to chattel is the damages the plaintiff must prove.

Damages in trespass to chattels are normally limited to the harm caused to the chattel. The plaintiff would receive as compensation repair costs. Another type of damages the plaintiff could potentially receive is the costs of renting a replacement for the chattel until the chattel is recovered.

a.   The First Element to Trespass to Chattels: Intent to Deprive or Interfere

Trespass to chattels is an intentional tort. The trespasser must have intended to harm or interfere with the property owner's possession of the personal property. If the trespasser accidentally injures the chattel, then he might be negligent, but he does not have the intent necessary to have committed a trespass to the chattel.

b.   The Second Element to Trespass to Chattels: The Defendant Damages Chattel

A minor damage to the chattel gives rise to a trespass to chattels action, not conversion.

1.   *An Alternate Second Element to Trespass to Chattels: Defendant Deprives Possessor of the Chattel's Use for a Substantial Amount of Time*

An alternate second element to trespass to chattels is when the defendant deprives the plaintiff of the personal property for a substantial period of time. With trespass to land, once the trespasser steps onto the land, a trespass has been committed. The same is not true for trespass to chattel. If a trespasser merely touches Rebecca's iPod for a moment, this will not constitute a trespass to chattel. If a trespasser takes Rebecca's iPod and uses it for a month, this could constitute trespass to chattel.

2.   *An Alternate Second Element to Trespass to Chattels: Defendant Dispossesses the Possessor of the Chattel*

Dispossess
to take away.

Another alternative to the second element of trespass to chattels is when the defendant **dispossess** the plaintiff of the personal property. Dispossess means to take away. This element is very similar to conversion in that both in conversion and trespass to chattels the defendant has to dispossess the owner of the chattel. However, the reason for two separate torts is a matter of the degree of dispossession and whether the defendant used the chattel herself. In trespass to chattel, the defendant does not need to have used the chattel herself.

10.4 Conversion

Conversion
when a defendant deprives the personal property owner of her chattel, without consent, and then puts the property to his own use so the property owner is completely unable to use her property.

Conversion is when a defendant deprives the personal property owner of her chattel, without consent, and then puts the property to his own use so the property owner is completely unable to use her property.

The Restatement (Second) of Torts defines conversion as:

> An intentional exercise of domination and control over chattel, which so seriously interferes with the right of another to control it that the actor may justly be required to pay the other the full value of the chattel.[2]

In conversion, the defendant puts the personal property to his own use. Sally brought a mouthwatering lunch to work on Tuesday. Sally daydreamed about eating the lunch all Tuesday morning. When Sally went to eat her lunch, she found her co-worker Tom licking the last bits of the crumbs of her lunch from his lips. Tom converted Sally's lunch to his own use, to the point Sally would not eat her lunch.

Trespass to chattels differs from conversion because trespass to chattels does not require the defendant convert the property to his own use, just that the defendant deprive the personal property owner of the use of her personal property.

a. The First Element of Conversion: Intent to Deprive and Convert to One's Own Use

To prove conversion, the plaintiff must show the defendant intended to convert. The intent that must be shown is the defendant intended to take the item and use it as his own.

b. The Second Element of Conversion: Deprive of Possession

The "deprive of possession" element requires the defendant's use of the plaintiff's personal property to completely deprive the plaintiff from using her personal property. Essentially, the defendant is using the personal property, or chattel, as if it is his.

c. The Third Element of Conversion: Extent of Deprivation

"Extent of deprivation" is the element most distinguishable between conversion and trespass to chattels. With conversion, the extent of deprivation is much greater than with trespass to chattels. The deprivation must be substantial in conversion. Did the defendant so substantially deprive the plaintiff of her right to her chattel so that the defendant should have to pay the plaintiff for the chattel? For instance, if the defendant purposefully destroyed the chattel, this would rise to the level of conversion.

---

2. Restatement (Second) of Torts §222A (1965).

Example

Rosalie had her car taken and then found it days later, three blocks away from where it had been taken. The battery was the only thing missing when she recovered the vehicle and she was able to replace the battery for less than $100. Put aside the criminal issues presented by this example. Has the person who took Rosalie's car so converted the car that he should have to pay Rosalie for the total value of her car? Has the person who took Rosalie's car so converted the battery, he should have to pay her for the value of the battery? The taker should have to pay the cost of replacing the battery, and any rental car costs Rosalie incurred while her car was gone for a few days, but will not be responsible for paying the total value of the car. If the car were only gone for a few days, this would probably be considered a trespass to chattel. However, if the car was taken and never returned, then the theft would also be a conversion.

d. Fourth Element of Conversion: Lack of Consent

The property must have been taken without consent in order for the conversion to take place. Consent would be a defense to the plaintiff's claim the defendant wrongfully converted her property. Using the example above, if Rosalie lent her car to Fred, then he had her permission to drive the car.

A limited amount of consent could be provided but then exceeded and still constitute conversion. Rosalie agreed to let Fred drive her car, but did not agree Fred could abscond with the car's battery. Thus, Fred should have to pay Rosalie for the battery he took without her consent, plus the cost of repair, and a rental car.

e. Remedies for Conversion

Damages for conversion are typically the fair market value of the personal property at the time of the conversion. The damages are greater with conversion than with trespass to chattels because the defendant's interference with the plaintiff's property has been so substantial, the plaintiff should be paid the full value of the property. In essence, the defendant is forced to buy the property he has been using as his own.

Another remedy available to the plaintiff is to have the personal property returned to the plaintiff. For instance, in the example above, a court could order the sheriff's department to seize the property, the car, back from the defendant.

The plaintiff can also potentially obtain the gain the defendant made on any sale of the personal property. This is the preferred remedy if the value of the personal property has gone up since the plaintiff had possession of it and the defendant was able to sell the personal property for more money. For example, Jane bought gold coins for $200 and placed the coins in her safe. The next day, David converts Jane's gold coins to his use by taking the coins from Jane's safe in her house. David sells the coins to a coin dealer a year later for $300. Jane would prefer and can get the $300 that David sold the coins for rather than the $200, as she would receive $100 more.

If a plaintiff has to rent a replacement for the personal property, then the defendant may have to pay for the rental of a replacement.

Paralegal Experience Before Law School
By Josh Davis, Law Student

People talk about the first year of law school as a grueling experience in which no one sleeps, eats, or has any social life. However, with a little planning it's not hard to do all three and excel. While law school utilizes a method different than most university classes, it teaches students to think out of the box and on their toes. The law is written in English, but operates as a totally different language and the only way to successfully understand and apply the law is through practice. Without prior knowledge of the law, comprehending the usefulness of "Westlaw" and "Lexis" and figuring out what a "tort" is would boggle anyone's mind. Luckily, I knew what a tort was before I started law school, which I thought to be somewhat important being that an entire year's class was devoted to "Torts." It's true that anyone could look up a legal definition, but understanding the basics behind some of the essential first year classes such as torts, property, civil procedure, legal writing, and contracts makes the transition to law school considerably smoother.

To learn these basics I became a paralegal first. The paralegal program slowly guides students and familiarizes them with the law without the intense pressure and competition that parallels the life of a first year law student. Receiving a paralegal degree not only enables a person to immediately enter the workplace in a law related field, but also provides the grease that makes the shift into law school easier. When I stepped into my first day of orientation in law school I already knew how to IRAC (Issue, Rule, Analysis, and Conclusion) cases and pull out relevant information. I knew how to research and find information quickly on Westlaw and Lexis and while other people were trying to figure out what a tort even entailed, I already had it engrained and processed in my head.

The paralegal program and law school are quite different in that most of law school involves reading cases. However, becoming a paralegal not only provides the framework to shine in law school, but also offers the tools to achieve the ultimate result of becoming a successful and ethical lawyer.

E T H I C S

Rule 5.4 Professional Independence of a Lawyer

    (a) A lawyer or law firm shall not share legal fees with a nonlawyer. . . .[3]

    The attorney cannot split legal fees with a paralegal. The attorney cannot pay the paralegal for referring

business to the attorney. In addition, the attorney is not supposed to split fees with a doctor or a chiropractor.

Ethics Exercise: Watch the movie *The Rainmaker*. There is a scene in the movie where a lawyer and nonlawyer decide to split fees between the two of them. Based upon the Model Rule of Professional Conduct above, is this ethical?

---

3. Model R. Prof. Conduct 5.4 (ABA 2004).

Chapter Summary

There are three intentional torts to property: trespass to land, trespass to chattels, and conversion. Trespass to land occurs when a defendant enters the real property owner or possessor's land without permission from the property owner or possessor. This entry interferes with the real property owner's or possessor's right to possess his land. Trespass to land is an intentional tort, so the defendant must have intended to enter the real property without consent. The big difference between trespass to land and trespass to chattels (other than the type of property involved) is the plaintiff in a trespass to land case does not have to have actual damages to the land, caused by the trespass. It is simply enough that the defendant trespassed on the defendant's land. Even though the plaintiff in a trespass to land case can win without showing actual damages, the damages would most likely be nominal.

Trespass to chattels occurs when a defendant interferes with the use of another's personal property without consent to do so, and some harm is caused. Chattel is another term for personal property. Personal property is anything not so attached to land it cannot be moved. Trespass to chattels is different from conversion; the defendant does not need to use the chattel for his own use in order to constitute trespass to chattels. In conversion, the defendant needs to convert the personal property to his own use. In trespass to chattels, there must be some harm caused by the defendant interfering with the possessor's right to his chattel. The chattel must be damaged, the possessor must be without the chattel for a substantial period of time, or the chattel must be taken from the possessor for good. Actual damages need to be shown in order for the plaintiff to recover in a trespass to chattels cause of action.

Conversion is when a defendant deprives another person of her possession of personal property and converts the personal property to his own use. Conversion is considered a more serious interference than trespass to chattels, but there is a lot of overlap between conversion and trespass to chattels. Conversion is considered more severe because the extent of the deprivation is much greater than with trespass to chattels. The usual damages for conversion are the fair market value of the personal property at the time of the conversion.

Key Terms

- Actual damages
- Chattel
- Consent
- Conversion
- Fair market value
- Injunction
- Nominal damages
- Personal property
- Real property
- Trespass
- Trespass to land
- Trespass to chattels

Review Questions

- How are intentional torts to property different from intentional torts to persons?
- What is a chattel?
- In order to win a cause of action for trespass to land, does the plaintiff have to prove actual damage?
- What is the difference between trespass to chattels and conversion?

Web Links

- http://www.gleim.com/accounting/professors/outlines/buslaw/lce-ch07.php? GHP_SESSION_www_gleim_com=30d9587e2a775acf6a18c55c16363966/. This site has a good outline on torts. Read the section on intentional torts to property to reiterate what you learned in this chapter.

Exercises

- Determine when conversion constitutes a crime in your state.

- Robert and Jill are boyfriend and girlfriend. During a heated debate, Robert takes Jill's purse and leaves. Jill's car keys were in her purse. She is unable to drive her car. Has Robert converted the car?

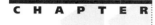

CHAPTER 11

The Defenses to Intentional Torts and Immunities

I don't even call it violence when it's in self-defense; I call it intelligence.[1]

Chapter Outline

---

1. Malcolm X.

Chapter Objectives

- Introduce defenses
- Explain how a defense acts as a justification of intentional misconduct
- Determine when a defense arises
- Explain how consent is a defense to all intentional torts
- Show how privileges act as a defense against intentional torts
- Compare circumstances under which self-defense is an available defense
- Discuss defense of property, and how this is not as paramount as a defense of person
- Describe how the necessity defense argues the harm the defendant causes thwarts a greater harm
- Distinguish immunities from privileges
- Explain sovereign immunity
- Discuss public official immunity
- Discuss family and charitable immunity

11.1 Introduction to Defenses to Intentional Torts

An intentional tort may be legally justified. In a lawsuit for an intentional tort, the plaintiff will draft a complaint stating what intentional torts the defendant allegedly committed. In response to the complaint, the defendant can draft an answer and raise defenses to those intentional torts in the answer.

There are two ways in which a defendant defends himself in a lawsuit. First, the defendant could prove one of the elements of the tort was not met. For instance, with assault, if the defendant proved the plaintiff was not in fear or apprehension, then the plaintiff will not be able to win. The second way a defendant defends himself is by affirmative defenses. Even if the plaintiff can successfully raise all the elements of a cause of action, an **affirmative defense** or additional information means the defendant is not liable. An affirmative defense can protect a defendant from liability. In other words, an affirmative defense can either mitigate the defendant's damages or completely prevent the defendant from being liable. The defendant has the burden of proof to prove the affirmative defense.

An **immunity** provides protection to someone who did commit an intentional tort. Immunity will prevent the plaintiff from suing the defendant. The main difference between a defense and an immunity is a defense relies upon the plaintiff's behavior. An immunity relies on a defendant's status. Due to the defendant's status, the defendant should be protected, even though the defendant did in fact commit the tort. For example, governmental immunity may prevent a plaintiff from suing the government even though an official of the government did commit the tort.

Affirmative defense
additional information, which if proven by defendant, will protect a defendant from liability even if the plaintiff can successfully raise all the elements of a cause of action.

Immunity
the protection from liability provided to the defendant based upon the defendant's status.

Figure 11.1

Defenses to Intentional Torts

Possible Defense to:	Defense:	Requirements for Defense:
All intentional torts	Consent	Plaintiff must have capacity to consent, and the consent must be voluntary.
Assault, battery, false imprisonment, trespass to land, trespass to chattel, conversion	Privilege	
Assault, battery, false imprisonment	Defense of self	Force must be reasonable, and the harm must be imminent.
Assault, battery, false imprisonment	Defense of others	
Assault, battery	Defense of property	Force must be reasonable, and defendant may not use deadly force to protect property.
Trespass to chattel, conversion, assault, battery	Recapture of chattel	Force must be reasonable, and the property owner should be in hot pursuit. Further, the chattel must have been wrongfully taken.
Conversion, trespass to land	Necessity	

11.2 Consent

Issues with Consent:

Does the plaintiff have the legal capacity to consent?

Did the plaintiff show an express or implied willingness to undergo defendant's conduct?

Was the consent voluntary?

Did the Plaintiff fully understand the consequences of the defendant's conduct?

Did the defendant exceed the consent?

Consent
a voluntary agreement to a tort or a willingness to undergo a tort made with a full understanding of the consequences.

Consent is a defense to each and every intentional tort. Consent is a voluntary agreement to the intentional tort or willingness to undergo an intentional tort. Consent consists of two elements. The first element is the consent is voluntary. The plaintiff must voluntarily accept the defendant committing an intentional tort upon her person. If a victim is coerced into providing consent, then the consent will not be valid or voluntary. The first requirement of consent is that the consent be voluntary. A threat of injury, for instance, will render the consent invalid as the consent would not be voluntary. The second element of consent is the plaintiff gives consent with a full understanding of the consequences. If a plaintiff consents to an intentional tort, then the defendant is not responsible for an injury resulting from the intentional tort.

Consent Examples

Chris has been working out for months and has lost a lot of weight. He is especially proud of his new "six pack" or washboard stomach. He picks Nancy up for a date and tells her how many "reps" of sit-ups he can do. When she acts impressed, he tells her to hit him in the stomach so she can see how "rock solid" he is. Nancy protests, but Chris keeps insisting. Nancy hits him lightly in the stomach, but Chris tells her to hit him again, with all her strength. Nancy complies, and Chris is knocked to the ground. Did Chris consent to the hitting? Yes, Chris consented (even begged) to be hit. Thus, Chris would not be able to win if he were to sue Nancy for hitting him.

Issues to consent arise when a person does not have the capacity to legally consent. A drunk may be incapable of providing consent. Some children are not legally capable of providing consent. For instance, if a mother takes a child of seven years to see the doctor and the doctor states the child needs his appendix out, who signs the medical authorization, the child or the mother? The mother signs because the child does not have the legal capability to provide consent. Those persons who have been adjudged mentally incompetent are also incapable of providing consent, and a legal guardian will have to provide consent on their behalf.

Express consent:
consent verbally stated or written.

Implied consent:
nonverbal consent, inferred from conduct.

Consent can be express or implied. **Express consent** is verbally stated or written down. **Implied consent** is nonverbal consent and can be inferred from conduct. One example of implied consent to an intentional tort is participating in a boxing match. Participating in a boxing match implies the boxers consented to being hit. The issue in implied consent is whether a reasonable person in the defendant's position would have believed the plaintiff consented to the intentional tort. For instance, in the case of *O'Brien v. Cunard* the plaintiff had a vaccination before coming into the United States. The plaintiff alleged the vaccinator committed an intentional tort by vaccinating her. The plaintiff stated she did not want to receive the vaccination, but she only made this statement after she received the vaccination. She waited in line for the vaccination. She saw people ahead of her receiving vaccinations. The court held her behavior of waiting in line, after seeing others ahead of her being vaccinated, constituted implied consent. The issue was what a reasonable person in the vaccinator's position would have believed. In this case, a reasonable person would have believed the plaintiff consented to the vaccination.

Mary E. O'Brien v. Cunard Steamship Company

154 Mass. 272; 28 N.E. 266 (1891)

This case presents two questions: first, whether there was any evidence to warrant the jury in finding that the defendant, by any of its servants or agents, committed an assault on the plaintiff. . . . [T]he surgeon who was employed by the defendant vaccinated her on shipboard, while she was on her passage from Queenstown to Boston. On this branch of the case the question is whether there was any evidence that the surgeon used force upon the plaintiff against her will. In determining whether the act was lawful or unlawful, the surgeon's conduct must be considered in connection with the circumstances. If the plaintiff's behavior was such as to indicate consent on her part, he was justified in his act, whatever her unexpressed feelings may have been. In determining whether she consented, he could be guided only by her overt acts and the manifestations of her feelings. . . . It is undisputed that at Boston there are strict quarantine regulations in regard to the examination of immigrants, to see that they are protected from small-pox by vaccination, and that only those persons who hold a certificate from the medical officer of the steamship, stating that they are so protected, are permitted to land without detention in quarantine or vaccination by the port physician. It appears that the defendant is accustomed to have its surgeons vaccinate all immigrants who desire it, and who are not protected by previous vaccination, and give them a certificate which is accepted at quarantine as evidence of their protection. Notices of the regulations at quarantine, and of the willingness of the ship's medical officer to vaccinate such as needed vaccination, were posted about the ship, in various languages, and on the day when the operation was performed the surgeon had a right to presume that she and the other women who were vaccinated understood the importance and purpose of vaccination for those who bore no marks to show that they were protected. By the plaintiff's testimony, which in this particular is undisputed, it appears that about two hundred women passengers were assembled below, and she understood from conversation with them that they were to be vaccinated; that she stood about fifteen feet from the surgeon, and saw them form in a line and pass in turn before him; that he "examined their arms, and, passing some of them by, proceeded to vaccinate those that had no mark"; that she did not hear him say anything to any of them; that upon being passed by they each received a card and went on deck; that when her turn came she showed him her arm, and he looked at it and said there was no mark, and that she should be vaccinated; that she told him she had been vaccinated before and it left no mark; "that he then said nothing, that he should vaccinate her again"; that she held up her arm to be vaccinated; that no one touched her; that she did not tell him that she did not want to be vaccinated; and that she took the ticket which he gave her certifying that he had vaccinated her, and used it at quarantine. She was one of a large number of women who were vaccinated on that occasion, without, so far as appears, a word of objection from any of them. They all indicated by their conduct that they desired to avail themselves of the provisions made for their benefit. There was nothing in the conduct of the plaintiff to indicate to the surgeon that she did not wish to obtain a card which would save her from detention at quarantine, and to be vaccinated, if necessary, for that purpose. Viewing his conduct in the light of the circumstances, it was lawful; and there was no evidence tending to show that it was not.

11.3 Privilege

Elements of Privilege:

The defendant's reason for committing the intentional tort are greater than the injury to plaintiff or plaintiff's property.

The defendant was justified in committing the intentional tort. This justification is a socially acceptable justification.

There was not an alternative available that would have caused less injury.

Privilege
allows a person to act in a way adverse to another person's right without being subjected to tort liability.

A privilege provides a justification for an intentional tort. "One who otherwise would be liable for a tort is not liable if he acts in pursuance of and within the limits of a privilege of his own or of a privilege of another that was properly delegated to him."[2] Thus, a **privilege** allows a person to act in a way adverse to another person's rights without being subjected to tort liability. The defendant is given the "privilege" of committing a tort in order to protect himself or others from a tort. The privilege is given to accomplish a valued societal goal. The following are considered privileges:

- Self-defense
- Defense of others
- Necessity
- Defense of property
- Recapture of chattels

11.4 Defense of Self

Elements of Self-Defense:

Reasonable force

Used to counter an attack or offensive contact

Use of reasonable force is necessary to prevent injury, offensive contact, or confinement

---

2. Restatement (Second) of Torts §890 (1979).

Self-defense
the privilege to use force to protect one's self against unprivileged acts a person reasonably believes will physically harm him.

With **self-defense**, the defendant is admitting he assaulted, battered, or falsely imprisoned the plaintiff, but that he was justified in doing so. Self-defense involves using reasonable force to stop an attack upon one's person. Self-defense is the right or privilege to use force to protect one's self against unprivileged acts a person reasonably believes will physically harm him. The act of self-defense must be necessary to prevent injury or unlawful confinement to one's self. The attack should be imminent, meaning the attack should be about to occur. If a person is being threatened by another person in another state, the threat is not imminent.

Self-defense does not allow retaliation for past harms. If a woman was assaulted on Tuesday, she cannot go the following Thursday and pepper spray the person who assaulted her. The more appropriate and lawful remedy available to the woman is a criminal and/or civil case.

Self-Defense Examples

- Theresa calls Julia an ugly name, and Julia slaps Theresa in response. Does Julia have the defense of self-defense? No, because Julia was not physically threatened by Theresa.
- After Julia slaps Theresa, Julia starts to walk away. Theresa shoves Julia in the back. Was Theresa privileged, under the doctrine of self-defense, to shove Julia? No, because Julia was no longer posed a physical threat to Theresa. Julia had turned her back and started to leave.

a. The Response in Self-Defense Must Be Equal to the Threat

Reasonable use of force
the force necessary to stop an attack.

In self-defense, the force used to prevent the threat must be a **reasonable use of force**. In other words, the force used cannot be greater than necessary to stop the attack. If the response is excessive, then the defense of self-defense is not available. In fact, if a person uses excessive force, he may be liable for the excessive force, less the force he was privileged in using.

When a person uses deadly force, the deadly force is only reasonable if the threat against him is deadly. In addition, the Restatement of Torts states the deadly self-defense must be an "immediate use" of deadly force in order for deadly self-defense to be privileged.[3] A person is not privileged to use deadly force against nondeadly force.

b. Limitations on Self-Defense

For nondeadly force, a person does not have an obligation to retreat. For deadly force, some jurisdictions require a person to retreat if retreat is safely available. The retreat requirement is a minority viewpoint.

Aggressor:
the person who starts a fight.

Self-defense may be used against **aggressors**. Aggressors, or fight-starters, are not usually able to claim self-defense. However, if an aggressor starts a fight but then later

---

3. Restatement (Second) of Torts §65 (1965).

voluntarily stops fighting, then the original aggressor may be allowed to claim self-defense.

11.5 Defense of Others

Comparison between:

Defense of Persons	Defense of Property
Use of reasonable force	Use of reasonable force
To protect third party from injury	To protect property from injury
Third party is threatened	Property is threatened

People are privileged to defend others. The people being defended can be family, friends, or even strangers. The rules regarding defense of others are similar to the rules regarding defense of self. The use of force to prevent the attack upon another must be reasonable. As with self-defense, the threat must be imminent. If a would-be attacker states: "As soon as I get my cast off my right arm, I'm going to punch you," then this threat is not considered an imminent threat of attack.

Defense of others is an affirmative defense, which must be asserted and proven by the defendant. When defending another, a person is privileged to use the same amount of force the other person could have used to protect himself.

11.6 Defense of Property

Defense of property
a limited right to defend one's property from damage or possession by another.

People have a limited right to defend their property from damage or possession by another, which is **defense of property**. Defense of property includes both real and personal property. However, a person will probably be able to use more force if protecting real property, in particular one's home. For instance, if Jim is asleep in his bed and he hears someone break into his house, he may be able to use deadly force because not only is his real property in danger, but also Jim's life may be in danger.

However, deadly force is not permissible to protect property by itself. This is because of our societal belief that human life is more valuable than property. One of the ways in which force is used to protect property is by using a fence. There may be barbed wire on top of the fence. While this barbed wire would likely cause an injury if someone crossed it, the barbed wire would not be the use of deadly force to protect the real property. This force may reasonably be used to prevent a trespass to land. However, a spring gun, which could case death, is not reasonable to protect property. See the *Katko v. Briney* case in Chapter 6.[4] In *Katko*, the court held the use of a spring gun (a gun that goes off when the door is opened) was not acceptable to use to protect unoccupied property.

---

4. 183 N.W.2d 657 (1971).

11.7 Recapture of Chattel

Recapture of chattel
owners of personal property
have a limited right or
privilege to repossess their
property.

Owners of personal property have a limited right to repossess their property, which is the **recapture of chattel**. The right is primarily limited to when an owner is in hot pursuit of the person who took his property. Recapture of chattel can also occur once the original tort, of taking the chattel, has already taken place. However, the law provides much greater leniency when preventing a tort from being committed. When recapturing the chattel, the rightful owner must use reasonable force (which must be less than deadly force) to regain his personal property that was wrongfully taken from him. If the property owner cannot stop the taking of his chattel, then the efforts to recapture the chattel must be made as soon as possible after the property was taken. A reasonable step to regain personal property might be to enter upon the real property of the person who took the property. The rightful owner of the personal property then would have a defense to trespass to land.

11.8 Necessity

Elements of Necessity:

An intentional tort used to thwart a more serious injury.

The threat of more serious injury comes from a third party.

The defendant's actions were reasonably necessary to thwart the more serious harm.

Necessity
the privilege of using an
innocent person's property to
prevent greater harm.

Public necessity
an absolute privilege allowing
a defendant a complete defense
to injure private property to
protect the community.

Private necessity
a qualified privilege, which
allows a defendant to damage
the plaintiff's property to
prevent a greater harm to his
own property, but still requires
the defendant to pay the
plaintiff for the harm caused to
the plaintiff's property.

Necessity allows the use of an innocent person's property to prevent greater harm. The defendant claims the defense of necessity to assert the defendant was justified in committing one type of harm to avoid a greater harm. With necessity, there is a weighing between which of two potential outcomes will be worse. The rationale behind this defense is the overall loss will be lessened and a more substantial harm is thwarted. There are two major types of necessity: public and private.

    Public necessity occurs when a defendant injures private property to protect the community. For public necessity, there must be a large number of people to be protected involved. For instance, in Southern California, some homes during the wildfires are allowed to burn to prevent the fires from moving into areas that are more populous. As the interest in public necessity is greater than in a private necessity case (community versus individuals), public necessity provides a complete defense, or absolute privilege, to a tort.

    Private necessity is a qualified privilege, which is not a complete defense to a tort. With private necessity, the defendant may have been privileged to damage another's property to prevent greater harm, but the defendant will still have to pay for the harm. Private necessity occurs when a defendant injures plaintiff's property to avoid greater damage to his own property. The damage being caused to the defendant's property is not caused by the plaintiff; rather, the plaintiff is innocent. Therefore, the

Emergency
a situation threatening life or property, which requires an immediate response.

defendant does not have a complete defense to ruining the plaintiff's property to protect his own property because the plaintiff has nothing to do with the damage to the defendant's property. Necessity arises in an emergency situation and there must have been a reasonable invasion of property rights in response to the emergency. As legally defined, an **emergency** is a situation threatening life or property, which requires an immediate response.

11.9 Duress

Duress
a defendant's defense to committing an intentional tort based on his own physical safety being threatened.

The defense of **duress** allows a defendant to commit an intentional tort because his physical safety is threatened. The duress is usually accomplished through threats of harm. For example, "Steal that money or I'll shoot you." Peer pressure is not sufficient to constitute duress. The threat must be for bodily injury. However, another type of duress is economic duress.

Example of Economic Duress

Charles is starving to death. He does not have any money to buy food and his situation is becoming more and more dire. If he does not eat soon, he will die. He breaks into a quickie mart and crams junk food into his mouth. If the quickie mart sues him, what defense could Charles use? Charles could use the defense of economic duress. However, he would still have to pay for the food and for any losses caused by his break-in.

11.10 Statute of Limitations

Statute of limitations was also a defense to negligence. Lawsuits for intentional torts must be filed within certain time limits or the lawsuits will be barred from being brought. Statutes of limitations were devised to provide an end to potential liability to defendants. In addition, statute of limitations encourage plaintiffs to bring lawsuits closer to the time in which events actually occurred, which in turn provides some safeguards on the "freshness" of evidence.

11.11 Intoxication

Involuntary intoxication
a defense to intentional torts, which occurs when a person becomes intoxicated without knowing it or intending to become intoxicated.

The defense of intoxication occurs when the defendant, due to alcohol or another substance, was not acting in his right mind. **Involuntary intoxication** occurs when a person becomes intoxicated without knowing it or intending to become intoxicated. Involuntary intoxication is a defense to intentional torts. Intoxication includes liquor, drugs, or other intoxicating substances. Involuntary intoxication includes situations where a person is tricked into taking an intoxicating substance, or a person is ignorant of the intoxicating character of a substance.

If intoxication results from a medication being taken as it was prescribed, this situation is generally considered involuntary intoxication because a patient is entitled to assume a doctor would not prescribe an intoxicating dose.[5] However, if there is a warning label on the medication bottle stating the prescription might cause drowsiness, or should not be taken prior to driving a vehicle, then a person will not be able to claim ignorance of the drug's intoxicating effect.

In contrast to involuntary intoxication is voluntary intoxication. With voluntary intoxication, the allegation is the alcohol prevented the defendant from forming the intent necessary to commit an intentional tort. However, voluntary intoxication is not a legitimate defense if the defendant voluntarily became intoxicated before committing the intentional tort. Otherwise, a defendant could avoid liability for a tort simply because he drank before committing the tort. In this case, an intoxicated person is still going to be held to the same standard a reasonable, sober person would be held to.

11.12   Immunities

An immunity is given to particular groups or people. The public policy is to protect these particular groups or people, even when the protection comes at the cost of allowing these particular groups or people to commit torts without being held liable. These particular groups or people have included families, charities, governments, and public officials.

11.13   Intra-Family Immunity

Intra-family tort
when a family member commits a tort against another family member.

Intra-family torts occur when a family member commits a tort against another family member. Traditionally, family members could not sue each other for intentional torts to persons. Thus, under common law spouses had immunity from lawsuits brought by their spouses or their non-adult children.

Nowadays the tendency is to allow family members, such as a husband and wife, to sue each other for intentional torts. It is still difficult to sue family members for negligence causing injury to another family member. It is a commonly accepted practice for family members to be able to sue each other for intentional or negligent injuries to property. For instance, spouses are allowed to sue each other if one wrecks the family automobile because car insurance should cover such an injury.

11.14   Charitable Immunity

Under the common law, charities were provided immunity. The theory was even though an injury was caused by negligence, the injury occurred while the defendant

---

5. *Perkins v. United States,* 228 F. 408, 415 (4th Cir. 1915).

was trying to be charitable or kind. Thus, to encourage the work charities did, charities were given immunity. In addition, those people donating money to a charity did not want the money they donated to be used to pay lawsuits. Thus, if a charity fed the homeless but accidentally gave them food poisoning, the charity was not liable. This is no longer the case. The majority of states now allow charities to be sued, in large part because charities can insure themselves against many torts.

11.15 Governmental Immunity

Sovereign immunity
a governmental right preventing suit against the government without the government's consent.

Federal Tort Claims Act
law providing immunity to the federal government from certain types of lawsuits.

The concept of governmental immunity is that the government cannot be sued without its consent. This is known as **sovereign immunity**. There are several complex exceptions to this immunity. Certain plaintiffs can sue the federal government. Federal governmental immunity is in part governed by the **Federal Tort Claims Act** ("FTCA").[6] The FTCA gives federal district courts jurisdiction over lawsuits against the United States of America. The FCTA gives immunity to intentional torts to people and to discretionary functions. In following chart, note the exceptions to immunity made for intentional torts to property and invasion of privacy torts.

Figure 11.2

Torts Excluded and Included Under the Federal Torts Claims Act

Torts the government cannot be sued for under the FTCA:	Torts the government can be sued for under the FTCA:
Assault	Trespass to land
Battery	Trespass to chattels
False imprisonment	Conversion
Malicious prosecution	Invasion of privacy
Libel	
Slander	
Misrepresentation	

The FTCA states monetary damages can be recovered from the United States government for injury, loss of property, personal injury, or death.[7] The injury or loss must be caused by the negligent or wrongful act or omission of a United States employee who is acting within the course and scope of his

---

6. The relevant portions of the FTCA can be found at 28 U.S.C.A. §§1346, 1402, 1504, 2210, 2401, 2411-2412, 2671-2680 (West 2004).
7. 28 U.S.C. §1346(B) (2000).

Discretionary functions
policy-making decisions.

Ministerial functions
functions which carry out
policy decisions; the
government is not given
immunity for ministerial
functions.

employment.[8] In addition, the federal government can only be sued in a situation where if the United States were a private individual, it could be liable to the plaintiff.[9] This is another exception to governmental immunity.

However, the United States' government will not normally be liable for intentional torts unless those torts are committed by federal law enforcement. Intentional torts are excluded under the FTCA, meaning the United States will not be held liable for the intentional torts of its agents or employees.

In addition, the federal government makes a distinction between discretionary functions and ministerial functions. This distinction is used to determine whether the federal government may be sued or not. Liability will not exist when a federal employee is exercising a discretionary function, even if the federal employee abuses the discretionary function.[10] **Discretionary functions** are policy-making decisions. The law holds the best way to deal with improper discretionary functions is through elections, rather than lawsuits. **Ministerial functions** are when the government carries out those policy decisions. The government is not given immunity for ministerial functions. Thus, ministerial functions are an exception to governmental immunity. The United States is also not liable under strict liability for torts.

Other types of governmental immunities include state government immunity, local government immunity, and public official immunity. Most states started with the concept of their own sovereign immunity. Over the years, it has become easier to sue states. Many states now have tort claims acts, similar to the Federal Tort Claims Act. A state may still limit the amount of a plaintiff's recovery, even if the state allows its citizens to sue it.

a.   Common Law — Full Immunity

Under the common law, federal and state government had full immunity against being sued. This general rule covered the all departments of the state and federal government. Even though the federal and state government had full immunity against being sued under the common law, they could go ahead and consent to being sued.

b.   11th Amendment

The 11th Amendment to the constitution provides states with immunity from suit in federal court. However, a state can still be sued in state court. In addition, state officers are not protected under the 11th Amendment.

---

8. *Id.*
9. *Id.*
10. 28 U.S.C. 2680(A).

The general rule that the federal and state governments had full immunity from being sued did not cover the officers and employees of the federal and state governments. The officers and employees of the state and federal government were frequently left to fend for themselves.

Today, many federal and state officers and employees have at least a qualified immunity from being sued. Employees and officers of public entities often have immunity for the harm caused by them while carrying out their job. Otherwise, how would some officials effectively carry out their jobs? Government employees, such as judges, are frequently given immunity. By the very nature of the job, a judge is likely to injure another. For instance, if a judge could be sued for finding an innocent man guilty (and there was no malfeasance on the judge's part), then a judge would not be able to perform his job. So long as the judge is legitimately acting within the course and scope of his job, he will not be held legally responsible for committing an intentional tort.

c. Today

Proprietary function
a function performed by the government that could have been performed by a private corporation, which is provided immunity.

Local government, for purposes of immunity, includes police, fire fighters, schools, and public hospitals. The issue arising with local government immunity is whether the function performed was a governmental or a proprietary function. A **proprietary function** is a function performed by the government that could have been performed by a private corporation. If for instance, the local government, such as a city water department, is issuing and collecting bills, then the issuing and collecting of bills is considered a proprietary function because it could have been performed by a private corporation. A private corporation could have issued and collected the bills. In contrast, police departments do not typically charge for their services, and those services are therefore considered governmental functions. Governmental functions are provided immunity. Proprietary functions are not provided immunity.

11.16   Minors and Incompetents

Common law holds children may be immune from tort liability, especially for intentional torts. For instance, children under seven are typically considered immune from tort liability. The argument for providing children under seven with immunity is that children under this age do not have the mental development to fully appreciate the significance of their actions. Therefore, the child did not have the intent necessary to commit an intentional tort. Older children can be charged as adults in criminal situations, but typically in civil tort situations children are not held liable. An exception for civil torts would be if a child were participating in an adult activity, then the child might be held civilly liable.

In addition, if a mentally incompetent person is incapable of forming intent, then the person cannot be held responsible for an intentional tort.

Taming the Bar
By Rami Nicola Haddad, Attorney at Law

The following essay is for those students interested in becoming attorneys.

I took the July 2007 Bar Examination for the first and thankfully only time. It is an exam I like to call the beast because it is nothing short thereof and nothing you did in law school will prepare you for it. In fact they will tell you to forget everything you learned in law school and begin to learn "bar-law." Amidst all the rumors and the scary stories of preparing for the bar and actually taking it, one must remember that at the end of the day it is an exam that can be passed with the right amount of preparation. I will address essays and the multistate bar examination of the bar, as well as how to prepare for each, and some tips to keep in mind. All states have the MBE section of the bar. Most states have essays. Only a few states have performance tests, so they are not discussed. This review is also helpful advice in how to study the law in general.

The Essays

The only way to prepare for the essays is to practice writing them. Merely reading the essays and the model answers (example answers) will not cut it. In addition, you need to actually practice doing the essays in a simulated exam format. This means you should get a timer and set it for the applicable time and practice writing the essay for that time. Then you should stop when the time is up, no matter what, and then compare your answer to the model answer. By comparing your answer to the model one you not only learn the law as you go along but you also learn how to answer the question in the proper format.

There are some important tips that you should keep in mind with the essays. First and foremost, always outline your answer before you start writing. The majority of points are awarded on how many issues you spot thus you should spend the first several minutes at least to issue spot and outline your answer. Second, you should use all the facts given to you in the fact pattern. There is no such thing as useless facts on the exam. The more facts you use in your analysis of an issue the more points you get. Third, the format of your answer is crucial and, no matter what format your bar preparation course suggests, always underline your issues. The graders spend a mere two to three minutes grading each essay, so if they have to dig to find your issue statement then you are off to a bad start. Fourth, do not look for issues that are not there. One of the worst mistakes you can do is spot a non-issue, not because they take points off, but because you would waste precious time. Last but not least, always write a conclusion to each issue and to the final essay in its entirety.

The MBE

The Multistate Bar Examination [MBE] portion of the exam is in multiple-choice format. There are 200 total questions with the first half of the questions administered in the morning session of the exam and the second half in the afternoon session.

This part of the exam covers only six subjects or as bar studiers call them the "Big 6" and they are:

(1) Contracts
(2) Torts
(3) Evidence
(4) Constitutional Law
(5) Real Property
(6) Criminal Law and Procedure

Once again, the only way to prepare for the MBE is to do hundreds upon hundreds of practice questions. By the time I took the actual bar, I had completed at least two thousand practice MBE questions. The more questions you do, the more you will be prepared for the MBE because there are only so many ways they can ask the questions. With the right amount of exposure to the different types of question formats on the MBE, you will not be caught off-guard on the actual exam. Even if you are taking a bar preparation course, you should consider taking another course just for the MBE because it would certainly better your chances of doing well. Courses aside, however, the only way to do well on these questions is to do as many of them as you can. Merely doing the questions and then just checking to see if you got the correct answers will not cut it. The most important step in practicing the MBE questions is to carefully read the explanations of the answers whether or not you got the right answer.

E T H I C S

Rule 1.1 Competence

A lawyer shall provide competent representation to a client. Competent representation requires the legal knowledge, skill, thoroughness and preparation reasonably necessary for the representation.[11]

The attorney should encourage the paralegal to maintain her competence and attend continuing education classes. As a paralegal, you need to keep current on the areas of law you are working in. One way in which to stay current in those areas of law is to attend legal education classes in those areas of law. Often, the firm you are working for will reimburse you for these continuing legal education classes, so you should keep records of the costs of such classes. If you are responsible for paying for the continuing legal education classes, and you are a member of a paralegal association, the association will usually have a few continuing legal education classes included in the cost of membership. Another good source of pertinent, low-cost continuing legal education credits is through the alumni program at the paralegal school you attended.

Chapter Summary

Sometimes committing an intentional tort is legally justified by a defense to the intentional tort. Possible defenses include: consent, defense of self, defense of others, defense of property, recapture of chattel, and necessity.

Consent is a defense that can be applied to each intentional tort. Consent involves a voluntary agreement to the intentional tort. This consent must be an informed consent, meaning it was made with an understanding of the consequences of the intentional tort. If the consent is valid, then the defendant will not be held liable for the injury that occurred as a result of the intentional tort.

Defense of self must involve reasonable force to prevent an attack upon one's self or to prevent false imprisonment. The force to prevent the attack must be equal to or less than the attack. Defense of others requires the use of reasonable force, to protect a third party from an attack. Defense of property may not also involves the use of reasonable force, but this reasonable force rise to the level of deadly force. This is because society places a higher value on human life than on property.

Recapture of chattel allows the rightful owner to trespass on the land of the person who took the chattel in order to recapture the chattel. The recapture of the chattel needs to take place as soon as possible after the chattel is taken.

Necessity weighs which is the worst of two possible outcomes. If the defendant commits a tort to prevent a worse tort to himself, the defendant may be partially justified in doing so. This is private necessity and the defendant will still have to pay for the damage done. With public necessity, the defendant commits a tort to protect the community.

---

11. Model R. Prof. Conduct 1.1 (ABA 2004).

Immunities provide protection to people who committed an intentional tort. An immunity is based upon the defendant's status. If the defendant is a family member, a charity, the government, a minor, or an incompetent, then there may be an immunity preventing the plaintiff from suing the defendant.

Traditionally, family members could not sue each other. Today, much of this tradition has evaporated, although children may still find it difficult to sue their parents for reasonable discipline. Traditionally, charities were able to claim an immunity, in part to encourage people and entities to be charitable. However, with the progressively easier means in which to obtain insurance, much of this immunity has also evaporated.

Governmental immunity depends upon what level of government is involved. If the federal government is involved, then the Federal Torts Claims Act will come into play. The FTCA still provides immunity for intentional torts and discretionary functions. Discretionary functions are public policy-making decisions.

Many state governments also have their own torts claims acts now. With regard to the immunity of local government, the determining factor is whether the function performed by the local government was a governmental or a proprietary function. A proprietary function is one that could be performed by a private company, and is not given immunity. A governmental function is, for example, a fire fighter saving a community member's house without charge. Governmental functions are given immunity.

Key Terms

- Affirmative defense
- Aggressor
- Charitable immunity
- Chattels
- Consent
- Course and scope of employment
- Defense
- Defense of others
- Defense of property
- Defense of self
- Discretionary function
- Duress
- 11th Amendment
- Emergency
- Express consent
- Federal Tort Claims Act
- Governmental function
- Governmental immunity
- Imminent

- Immunity
- Implied consent
- Incompetent
- Intra-family
- Intentional tort
- Involuntary intoxication
- Ministerial function
- Minor
- Necessity
- Private necessity
- Privilege
- Proprietary function
- Public necessity
- Public policy
- Reasonable force
- Recapture of chattel
- Self-defense
- Sovereign immunity
- Statute of limitations

Review Questions

- What must a defendant show in order to prove a plaintiff consented?
- How would you describe the reasonable force allowed in defense of self and defense of others?
- How does this reasonable force differ when discussing defense of property or recapture of chattel?
- How can a defendant lose the defense of self-defense?
- When will the federal government be liable for the torts committed on its behalf?
- Which torts are specifically excluded from liability for the federal government?
- When will a state government be liable for the torts committed on its behalf?
- When will a local government be liable for the torts committed on its behalf?

Web Links

- www.legalassistanttoday.com is a legal assistant's magazine. One of the nicest features of the website is that it has sample letters and documents you can use in personal injury cases. There are also job listings on this website.
- To learn more about lawsuits against the government, go to: http://www.access.gpo.gov/nara/cfr/waisidx_99/45cfr35_99.html/. This contains Title 45 of the Code of Federal Regulations, which is on Public Welfare. Under Subtitle A, Department of Health and Human Services is Part 35, Tort Claims against the Government.

Exercises

- Look up the statute of limitations for intentional torts in your state.
- Determine whether your state follows the minority view regarding retreat from deadly force.
- Peter and Lucy have sex. Lucy contracts a sexually transmitted disease from Peter and sues Peter for battery. Does Peter have a defense of consent? What if Peter was a prostitute Lucy hired?

■ James is walking down a dark alley, when a homeless person lunges at him with a knife. The homeless person does not actually cut James. Can James grab his gun and lawfully shoot the homeless person?

■ Review the *Katko v. Briney* case from Chapter 6 in the context of defense of property. Why is there not a privilege to use deadly force to protect property? If a property owner does use deadly force, will the property owner be liable?

CHAPTER

Strict Liability and Products Liability

[The Law] is a jealous mistress, and requires a long and constant courtship. It is not to be won by trifling favors, but by lavish homage.[1]

Chapter Outline

---

1. Joseph Story, *The Value and Importance of Legal Studies* (1829).

Chapter Objectives

- Show the difference between strict liability and negligence
- Appreciate the significance of *Rylands v. Fletcher*
- Describe absolute liability for abnormally dangerous activities
- Explain a wild animal owner's absolute liability
- Make a distinction between wild and domesticated animals
- Introduce the parties in products liability cases
- Discuss the elements of a products liability case
- Describe the three theories under which a plaintiff can bring a products liability case
- Describe the categories of defects
- Explain the defenses to products liability

12.1 Introduction to Strict Liability and Products Liability

Public policy holds individuals should be protected from abnormally dangerous activities. Some activities are so dangerous that liability will be imposed whether or not there was negligence. Fault is irrelevant in strict liability. Strict liability imposes a much greater duty upon defendants than negligence. For strict liability, a breach of duty does not need to be proven, unlike with negligence. In strict liability, it is assumed the defendant's actions caused the plaintiff's injury. Also, strict liability is very different than intentional torts. The concern in intentional torts is what the defendant intended. With strict liability, even if the defendant intended for the consequence not to occur, the defendant can still be found strictly liable.

In strict liability, it does not matter how much care the defendant exercises. Rather, so long as the defendant commits the abnormally dangerous activity, he will be held responsible.

Damages for strict liability consist of compensatory damages, as well as possibly punitive damages, if the defendant was malicious or reckless in causing the injury to occur.

Strict liability is further subdivided into three main areas:

- Strict liability for abnormally dangerous activities
- Strict liability for damages caused by animals owned or possessed by the defendant
- Strict products liability

Products liability law
law involving cases against manufacturers or sellers of items that injure people.

Products liability law involves cases against manufacturers or sellers of an item that injures a person. The public policy argument for products liability laws is that corporations need to be discouraged from producing defective products that can injure consumers. A manufacturer of a product can be held liable for making a defective product even when the manufacturer used all safety precautions. The concept behind products liability is the burden of a defective product is better absorbed as a cost of doing business for the manufacturer than as a burden placed upon the consumer.

12.2 Strict Liability Caused by Abnormally Dangerous Activities

Strict liability
abnormally dangerous activities for which a defendant has liability, without regard to the defendant's negligence.

Abnormally dangerous activities for which a defendant has liability, without regard to the negligence of the defendant, is **strict liability**. A defendant who undertakes an abnormally dangerous activity should be held responsible for the harm caused to a person or the person's property, whether or not the defendant exercised caution. The policy behind strict liability is well expressed in *Indiana Harbor Belt Railroad v. American Cyanamid Co.*:

> . . . By making the actor strictly liable . . . we give him an incentive, missing in the negligence regime, to experiment with methods of preventing accidents that involve not greater exertions of care, assumed to be futile, but instead relocating, changing or reducing (perhaps to the vanishing point) the activity giving rise to the accident.[2]

2. *Indiana Harbor Belt Railroad v. American Cyanamid Co.*, 916 F.2d 1174 (1990).

No amount of care can make abnormally dangerous activities safe. Rather, the only way to potentially make the activity safe is for the activity to stop or be relocated away from humans.

One of the most important cases in strict liability for abnormally dangerous activity is the *Rylands v. Fletcher*[3] case. In *Rylands*, the defendants owned a mill and had a water reservoir on their property. The plaintiff was the property owner of land abutting the defendants. Due to negligence on the part of the constructor of the reservoir, water from the reservoir entered upon and damaged the plaintiff's property. The court held "the person who for his own purposes brings on his lands and collects and keeps there anything likely to do mischief if it escapes, must keep it at his peril and if he does not do so, is . . . answerable for all the damage which is the natural consequence of its escape."[4] The *Rylands* decision indicates that strict liability must be imposed upon persons who cause great and unusual risks on others.

Rylands v. Fletcher

13 Hurl & C. 774 (1865);
L.R. 1 Ex. 265 (1866),
L.R. 3 H.L. 330 (1868)

. . . [I] this case the Plaintiff . . . is the occupier of a mine and works under a close of land. The Defendants are the owners of a mill in his neighbourhood, and they proposed to make a reservoir for the purpose of keeping and storing water to be used about their mill upon another close of land, which . . . may be taken as being adjoining to the close of the Plaintiff. . . . Underneath the close of land of the Defendants on which they proposed to construct their reservoir there were certain old and disused mining passages and works. There were five vertical shafts, and some horizontal shafts communicating with them. The vertical shafts had been filled up with soil and rubbish, and it does not appear that any person was aware of the existence either of the vertical shafts or of the horizontal works communicating with them. In the course of the working by the Plaintiff of his mine, he had gradually worked through the seams of coal underneath the close, and had come into contact with the old and disused works underneath the close of the Defendants.

In that state of things the reservoir of the Defendants was constructed. It was constructed by them through the agency and inspection of an engineer and contractor. Personally, the Defendants appear to have taken no part in the works, or to have been aware of any want of security connected with them. As regards the engineer and the contractor, we must take it from the case that they did not exercise, as far as they were concerned, that reasonable care and caution which they might have exercised, taking notice, as they appear to have taken notice, of the vertical shafts filled up in the manner which I have mentioned. However, . . . when the reservoir was constructed, and filled, or partly filled, with water, the weight of the water bearing upon the disused and imperfectly filled-up vertical shafts, broke through those shafts. The water passed down them and into the horizontal workings,

---

3. 13 Hurl & C. 774(1865); L.R. 1 Ex. 265 (1866), L.R. 3 H.L. 330 (1868).
4. *Id.*

and from the horizontal workings under the close of the Defendants it passed on into the workings under the close of the Plaintiff, and flooded his mine, causing considerable damage, for which this action was brought. . . .

. . . [T] principles on which this case must be determined appear to me to be extremely simple. The Defendants, treating them as the owners or occupiers of the close on which the reservoir was constructed, might lawfully have used that close for any purpose for which it might in the ordinary course of the enjoyment of land be used; and if . . . there had been any accumulation of water, either on the surface or underground, and if, by the operation of the laws of nature, that accumulation of water had passed off into the close occupied by the Plaintiff, the Plaintiff could not have complained that that result had taken place. If he had desired to guard himself against it, it would have lain upon him to have done so, by leaving, or by interposing, some barrier between his close and the close of the Defendants in order to have prevented that operation of the laws of nature. . . .

On the other hand if the Defendants, not stopping at the natural use of their close, had desired to use it for any purpose which I may term a non-natural use, for the purpose of introducing into the close that which in its natural condition was not in or upon it, for the purpose of introducing water either above or below ground in quantities and in a manner not the result of any work or operation on or under the land — and if in consequence of their doing so, or in consequence of any imperfection in the mode of their doing so, the water came to escape and to pass off into the close of the Plaintiff, then it appears to me that that which the Defendants were doing they were doing at their own peril; and, if in the course of their doing it . . . the escape of the water and its passing away to the close of the Plaintiff and injuring the Plaintiff, then for the consequence of that, in my opinion, the Defendants would be liable. . . .

We think that the true rule of law is, that the person who, for his own purposes, brings on his land and collects and keeps there anything likely to do mischief if it escapes, must keep it in at his peril; and if he does not do so, is prima facie answerable for all the damage which is the natural consequence of its escape. He can excuse himself by shewing that the escape was owing to the Plaintiff's default; or, perhaps, that the escape was the consequence . . . the act of God; but as nothing of this sort exists here, it is unnecessary to inquire what excuse would be sufficient. The general rule, as above stated, seems on principle just. The person whose grass or corn is eaten down by the escaping cattle of his neighbour, or whose mine is flooded by the water from his neighbour's reservoir, or whose cellar is invaded by the filth of his neighbour's privy, or whose habitation is made unhealthy by the fumes and noisome vapours of his neighbour's alkali works, is damnified without any fault of his own; and it seems but reasonable and just that the neighbour who has brought something on his own property (which was not naturally there), harmless to others so long as it is confined to his own property, but which he knows will be mischievous if it gets on his neighbour's, should be obliged to make good the damage which ensues if he does not succeed in confining it to his own property. But for his act in bringing it there no mischief could have accrued, and it seems but just that he should at his peril keep it there, so that no mischief may accrue, or answer for the natural and anticipated consequence. And upon authority this we think is established to be the law, whether the things so brought be beasts, or water, or filth, or stenches.

12.3   The Rule of Strict Liability for Abnormally Dangerous Activities

Dangerous activity
an activity with a substantial degree of likelihood of causing injury to people or property, and this likelihood cannot be eliminated with due care.

Strict liability will be imposed for abnormally **dangerous activities** that created a high risk of substantive injury to a person or property. A dangerous activity is an activity with a substantial degree of likelihood of causing injury to people or property, and this likelihood cannot be eliminated with due care.

The next step is to determine whether the dangerous activity is also an abnormally dangerous activity. We now examine the six factors a court will take into consideration in determining whether an activity is abnormally dangerous.

a.   The First Factor of Abnormally Dangerous Activities: There Is a High Degree of Risk

The higher the degree of risk, the more likely the dangerous activity is an abnormally dangerous one.

b.   The Second Factor of Abnormally Dangerous Activities: There Is a Risk of Serious Harm

The second factor of abnormally dangerous activities is the risk of serious harm. If the harm will be widespread or severe, it is more likely the dangerous activity is an abnormally dangerous one.

c.   The Third Factor of Abnormally Dangerous Activities: The Risk Cannot Be Eliminated by Reasonable Care

The third factor of abnormally dangerous activities is the risk cannot be eliminated by reasonable care. If a defendant can reduce or eliminate the risk through reasonable care, then the activity is not considered abnormally dangerous.

d.   The Fourth Factor of Abnormally Dangerous Activities: The Activity Is Not Common

The fourth factor of abnormally dangerous activities is the activity is not common. Abnormally dangerous activities do not occur on a daily basis. A common activity would include driving a car or riding an airplane. An abnormal activity is one unusual or unnatural for the locale. For instance, it would not be abnormally dangerous to have defective plumbing installed in your house, though it might be highly inconvenient. Injuries associated with your household use of gas, water, or electricity are also not likely to rise to the level of abnormally dangerous either because use of gas, water, or electricity is a common activity.

e. The Fifth Factor of Abnormally Dangerous Activities: The Activity Should Not Have Taken Place Where the Victim Was Harmed

The fifth factor of abnormally dangerous activities is the activity should not have taken place where the victim was harmed. This element is about the appropriateness of an activity taking place where it did. For instance, usually a dangerous activity is considered much more appropriate if it occurs in a sparsely populated, rather than a densely populated, area. For instance, nuclear power plants should not be located in highly populous areas.

f. The Sixth Factor of Abnormally Dangerous Activities: The Hazards of the Activity Outweigh the Benefits[5]

The last factor of abnormally dangerous activities is the hazards of the activity outweigh the benefits of the activity. This element requires a weighing of the benefit to the community of the activity versus the downsides of the activity to the community. If an activity is extremely valuable to a community, even though it is highly dangerous, the activity may not be considered abnormally dangerous.

Each one of these six factors should be considered in determining whether an activity is abnormally dangerous.[6] Usually, one factor by itself will not be enough to show an abnormally dangerous activity.[7] In general, several factors must be satisfied to show abnormally dangerous activity.[8]

Examples of abnormally dangerous activities include:

■ Crop dusting by airplanes
■ Storing large amounts of flammable liquids in a residential or metropolitan area,
■ Manufacturing or use of explosives,
■ Releasing poisonous gases from a factory,
■ Operating nuclear power plants, and
■ Fumigation.

12.4 Strict Liability Applied to Owners of Animals

Wild animals	Domesticated Animals
The owner is strictly liable for any injuries caused by his wild animals.	The owner is strictly liable for injuries caused by his domesticated animals if the animal previously displayed any vicious tendencies, or if liability is set by a local ordinance

5. Restatement (Second) of Torts, Section 519 (1965).
6. Restatement (Second) of Torts, Section 520 (1965).
7. *Id.*
8. *Id.*

Domesticated animals
animals conditioned to live
among humans.

Domesticated animals are animals conditioned to live among humans. The Restatement (Second) of Torts Section 506 states a domesticated animal is an animal "devoted to the service of mankind." A cat or dog is an example of a domesticated animal. Other examples include birds kept as pets, cattle, horses, goats, sheep, and pigs. If a domesticated animal causes injury, the law will look at whether the owner was negligent. However, the owner may be held strictly liable if the owner of the animal knew or should have known the animal had vicious tendencies. If the animal had vicious tendencies, the owner will be strictly liable for the harm caused by the animal, no matter how much care the owner took to cage his animal and prevent an injury. Dog bites are among the most common types of animal-caused injuries to humans.

Wild animals provide an even greater potential risk to humans than domesticated animals. Thus, if a defendant owns a wild animal, the owner will be strictly liable for the injuries caused by the animal. The Restatement (Second) of Torts states: "A possessor a wild animal is subject to liability to another for harm done by the animal to the other . . . although the possessor has exercised the utmost care to confine the animal. . . ."[9] Examples of wild animals include squirrels, buffalo, bears, reptiles such as snakes, wolves, eagles, and exotic animals such as leopards. Even if the owner patiently trains the wild animal or takes steps to keep the animal away from humans, the owner will still be held strictly liable for the injuries caused by the animal. The policy reason behind this rationale is there is not a lot of social utility in keeping a wild animal, especially when compared to how potentially dangerous keeping the wild animal may be.

12.5   Defenses to Strict Liability

a.   Causation as a Defense to Strict Liability

As a defense to strict liability, a defendant can raise lack of proximate cause. The defendant would argue the damages were not as a result of the same type of risk that made the activity abnormally dangerous. For there to be causation in strict liability, the plaintiff needs to show the harm was one that was reasonably foreseeable. The plaintiff must also be a person within the foreseeable risk posed by the activity.

b.   Assumption of the Risk as a Defense to Strict Liability

Another defense to strict liability is assumption of the risk. To validly assume the risk, a plaintiff has to understand the risk and voluntarily subject herself to the danger. For instance, a plaintiff sticking her finger into a jaguar's cage at the zoo, despite all the signs stating "WARNING: THESE ANIMALS BITE," would be assumption of the risk of the jaguar biting her. In order for the defendant to prove assuming the risk as a defense, the plaintiff must have fully appreciated the danger involved.

---

9. Restatement (Second) of Torts Section 507.

12.6   Origin of Products Liability

Caveat emptor
let the buyer be aware.

Originally, buyers bought goods under the theory of "**caveat emptor**," or "let the buyer be aware." However, products liability is rapidly evolving into strict liability for defective products. There are three theories of products liability:

- Negligence,
- Breach of warranty, and
- Strict liability.

However, the Restatement (Third) of Torts states products liability should be based upon the type of product defect, i.e., whether the defect was a manufacturing defect, a design defect, or a warning defect.

12.7   The Parties in Products Liability

a.   Manufacturers

Manufacturer
maker of the product that caused injury to the consumer.

A **manufacturer** makes the product that causes the injury to the consumer. A manufacturer's duty is to inspect its products for manufacturing defects.

b.   Sellers

Seller
the party who makes defective products available to the public.

The **sellers** are the parties who make defective products available to the public.

c.   The Ultimate User

Ultimate user
the party who ends up using the product, who may not be the person who originally bought the defective product

The **ultimate user** of the product is the party who ends up using the product and may not be the person who originally buys a defective product. The buyer of the product may be buying the product as a gift. Then, the recipient of the gift would be the ultimate user.

12.8   Theories of Recovery

The majority of products liability cases are brought due to some sort of defect in the product. The major ways in which a product can be defective are through

- a design defect,
- a manufacturing defect, or
- a defect in the warning.

These defects can arise as a result of negligence, strict liability, or breach of warranty.

If the products liability case is brought under a negligence theory, then the plaintiff will need to prove the defendant had a duty to the plaintiff, the defendant breached the duty, the breach was the proximate cause of the injury, and there were damages. A risk-benefit test is applied — Judge Hand's formula — discussed in Chapter 3. Perhaps the most infamous case illustrating this risk-benefit analysis is the Ford Pinto case. Ford was selling automobiles with gas tanks susceptible to exploding during a vehicle collision. In determining there was sufficient evidence to support a finding of malice, the court weighed the likelihood of a car being hit from behind and the severity of an injury occurring if the gas tank exploded (serious bodily injury and/or death) and measured it against the cost of fixing the problem in the car (which was small).

Richard Grimshaw v. Ford Motor Company

119 Cal. App. 3d 757; 174 Cal. Rptr. 348 (1981)

. . . In November 1971, the Grays purchased a new 1972 Pinto hatchback manufactured by Ford in October 1971. The Grays had trouble with the car from the outset. . . . Their car problems included excessive gas and oil consumption, down shifting of the automatic transmission, lack of power, and occasional stalling. It was later learned that the stalling and excessive fuel consumption were caused by a heavy carburetor float.

On May 28, 1972, Mrs. Gray, accompanied by 13-year-old Richard Grimshaw, set out in the Pinto from Anaheim for Barstow to meet Mr. Gray. The Pinto was then 6 months old and had been driven approximately 3,000 miles. Mrs. Gray stopped in San Bernardino for gasoline, got back onto the freeway (Interstate 15) and proceeded toward her destination at 60-65 miles per hour. As she approached the Route 30 off-ramp where traffic was congested, she moved from the outer fast lane to the middle lane of the freeway. Shortly after this lane change, the Pinto suddenly stalled and coasted to a halt in the middle lane. It was later established that the carburetor float had become so saturated with gasoline that it suddenly sank, opening the float chamber and causing the engine to flood and stall. A car traveling immediately behind the Pinto was able to swerve and pass it but the driver of a 1962 Ford Galaxie was unable to avoid colliding with the Pinto. The Galaxie had been traveling from 50 to 55 miles per hour but before the impact had been braked to a speed of from 28 to 37 miles per hour.

At the moment of impact, the Pinto caught fire and its interior was engulfed in flames. According to plaintiffs' expert, the impact of the Galaxie had driven the Pinto's gas tank forward and caused it to be punctured by the flange or one of the bolts on the differential housing so that fuel sprayed from the punctured tank and entered the passenger compartment through gaps resulting from the separation of the rear wheel well sections from the floor pan. By the time the Pinto came to rest after the collision, both occupants had sustained serious burns. When they emerged from the vehicle, their clothing was almost completely burned off. Mrs. Gray died a few days later of congestive heart failure as a result of the burns. Grimshaw managed to survive but only through heroic medical measures. . . .

DESIGN OF THE PINTO FUEL SYSTEM

In 1968, Ford began designing a new subcompact automobile which ultimately became the Pinto. Mr. Iacocca, then a Ford vice president, conceived the project and was its moving force. Ford's objective was to build a car at or below 2,000 pounds to sell for no more than $2,000.

Ordinarily marketing surveys and preliminary engineering studies precede the styling of a new automobile line. Pinto, however, was a rush project, so that styling preceded engineering and dictated engineering design to a greater degree than usual. Among the engineering decisions dictated by styling was the placement of the fuel tank. . . . The Pinto's styling . . . required the tank to be placed behind the rear axle leaving only 9 or 10 inches of "crush space" — far less than in any other American automobile. . . . In addition, the Pinto was designed so that its bumper was little more than a chrome strip. . . . The Pinto's rear structure also lacked reinforcing members. . . . The absence of the reinforcing members rendered the Pinto less crush resistant than other vehicles. Finally, the differential housing selected for the Pinto had an exposed flange and a line of exposed bolt heads. These protrusions were sufficient to puncture a gas tank driven forward against the differential upon rear impact.

CRASH TESTS

During the development of the Pinto, prototypes were built and tested. . . . These prototypes as well as two production Pintos were crash tested by Ford to determine, among other things, the integrity of the fuel system in rear-end accidents. Ford also conducted the tests to see if the Pinto as designed would meet a proposed federal regulation requiring all automobiles manufactured in 1972 to be able to withstand a 20-mile-per-hour fixed barrier impact without significant fuel spillage. . . .

The crash tests revealed that the Pinto's fuel system as designed could not meet the 20-mile-per-hour proposed standard. . . .

THE COST TO REMEDY DESIGN DEFICIENCIES

When a prototype failed the fuel system integrity test, the standard of care for engineers in the industry was to redesign and retest it. The vulnerability of the production Pinto's fuel tank at speeds of 20 and 30-miles-per-hour fixed barrier tests could have been remedied by inexpensive "fixes," but Ford produced and sold the Pinto to the public without doing anything to remedy the defects. Design changes that would have enhanced the integrity of the fuel tank system at relatively little cost per car included the following: Longitudinal side members and cross members at $2.40 and $1.80, respectively. . . . Equipping the car with a reinforced rear structure, smooth axle, improved bumper and additional crush space at a total cost of $15.30 would have made the fuel tank safe in a 34 to 38-mile-per-hour rear-end collision by a vehicle the size of the Ford Galaxie. . . .

MANAGEMENT'S DECISION TO GO FORWARD WITH KNOWLEDGE OF DEFECTS

The idea for the Pinto . . . was conceived by Mr. Iacocca, then executive vice president of Ford. The feasibility study was conducted under the supervision of Mr. Robert Alexander, vice president of car engineering. Ford's Product Planning Committee, whose members included Mr. Iacocca, Mr. Robert Alexander, and Mr. Harold MacDonald, Ford's group vice president of car engineering, approved the Pinto's concept and made the decision to go forward with the project. During the course of the project, regular product review meetings were held which were chaired by Mr. MacDonald and attended by Mr. Alexander. As the project approached actual production, the engineers responsible for the components of the project "signed off" to their immediate supervisors who in turn "signed off" to their superiors and so on up the chain of command until the entire project was approved for public release by Vice Presidents Alexander and MacDonald and ultimately by Mr. Iacocca. The Pinto crash tests results had been forwarded up the chain of command to the ultimate decision-makers and were known to the Ford officials who decided to go forward with production. . . .

. . . On the issue of punitive damages, Ford contends . . . the punitive award was statutorily unauthorized and constitutionally invalid and . . . that the evidence was insufficient to support a finding of malice or corporate responsibility for malice. . . .

. . . [W]e have concluded that Ford has failed to demonstrate that any errors or irregularities occurred during the trial which resulted in a miscarriage of justice requiring reversal. . . .

(1) Design Defects

Some two weeks before this case went to the jury, the Supreme Court in *Barker* v. *Lull Engineering Co* . . . formulated the following "two-pronged" definition of design defect, embodying the "consumer expectation" standard and "risk-benefit" test:

> First, a product may be found defective in design if the plaintiff establishes that the product failed to perform as safely as an ordinary consumer would expect when used in an intended or reasonably foreseeable manner.
>
> Second, a product may alternatively be found defective in design if the plaintiff demonstrates that the product's design proximately caused his injury and the defendant fails to establish, in light of the relevant factors, that, on balance, the benefits of the challenged design outweigh the risk of danger inherent in such design.

. . . The "relevant factors" which a jury may consider in applying the *Barker* "risk-benefit" standard include

- "the gravity of the danger posed by the challenged design,
- the likelihood such danger would occur,
- the mechanical feasibility of a safer alternative design,
- the financial cost of an improved design, and
- the adverse consequences to the product and to the consumer that would result from an alternative design."

PUNITIVE DAMAGES . . .

(1) "Malice" Under Civil Code Section 3294

. . . In an action for the breach of an obligation not arising from contract, where the defendant has been guilty of oppression, fraud, or malice, express or implied, the plaintiff, in addition to the actual damages, may recover damages for the sake of example and by way of punishing the defendant.

. . . As this court recently noted, numerous California cases after *Davis* v. *Hearst, supra,* have interpreted the term "malice" as used in section 3294 to include, not only a malicious intention to injure the specific person harmed, but conduct evincing "a conscious disregard of the probability that the actor's conduct will result in injury to others." . . .

. . . [T]he availability of punitive damages has not been limited to cases in which there is an actual intent to harm plaintiff or others. . . . [C]onscious disregard of the safety of others is an appropriate description of the *animus malus* required by Civil Code section 3294, adding: "In order to justify an award of punitive damages on this basis, the plaintiff must establish that the defendant was aware of the probable dangerous consequences of his conduct, and that he wilfully and deliberately failed to avoid those consequences . . .".

The interpretation of the word "malice" as used in section 3294 to encompass conduct evincing callous and conscious disregard of public safety by those who manufacture and market mass produced articles is consonant with and furthers the objectives of punitive damages. The primary purposes of punitive damages are punishment and deterrence of like conduct by the wrongdoer and others. . . . In the traditional noncommercial intentional tort, compensatory damages alone may serve as an effective deterrent against future wrongful conduct but in commerce-related torts, the manufacturer may find it more profitable to treat compensatory damages as a part of the cost of doing business rather than to remedy the defect. . . . Deterrence of such "objectionable corporate policies" serves one of the principal purposes of Civil Code section 3294. . . . Governmental safety standards and the criminal law have failed to provide adequate consumer protection against the manufacture and distribution of defective products. . . . Punitive damages thus remain as the most effective remedy for consumer protection against defectively designed mass produced articles. They provide a motive for private individuals to enforce rules of law and enable them to recoup the expenses of doing so which can be considerable and not otherwise recoverable.

(3) Sufficiency of the Evidence to Support the Finding of Malice and Corporate Responsibility . . .

There was ample evidence to support a finding of malice and Ford's responsibility for malice.

Through the results of the crash tests Ford knew that the Pinto's fuel tank and rear structure would expose consumers to serious injury or death in a 20- to 30-mile-per-hour collision. There was evidence that Ford could have corrected the hazardous design defects at minimal cost but decided to defer correction of the shortcomings by engaging in a cost-benefit analysis balancing human lives and limbs against corporate profits. Ford's institutional mentality was shown to be one of callous indifference to public safety. There was substantial evidence that Ford's conduct constituted "conscious disregard" of the probability of injury to members of the consuming public. . . .

There is substantial evidence that management was aware of the crash tests showing the vulnerability of the Pinto's fuel tank to rupture at low speed rear impacts with consequent significant risk of injury or death of the occupants by fire. . . .

Proving products liability under a negligence theory proved difficult because the plaintiff had to be able to show when in the manufacturing or selling process the defendant's care fell below due care. Thus, the law morphed to allow plaintiffs to bring products liability cases without having to show fault. This is strict products liability. We now examine the five elements of a traditional products liability case, under strict liability theory.

a. The First Element of Products Liability Under Strict Liability Theory: The Defect Makes the Product Unreasonably Unsafe

The first element of products liability under a strict liability theory is the defect in the product makes the product unreasonably unsafe. The emphasis in strict products liability is on the defective item, and not on the conduct of the manufacturer or seller.

b. The Second Element of Products Liability Under Strict Liability Theory: The Seller or Manufacturer of the Product Has to Be the Business of Selling These Products

The second element of products liability under a strict liability theory is the seller or manufacturer of the product must be in the business of selling these products. If the sale is an isolated transaction, then this requirement is not met.

c. The Third Element of Products Liability Under Strict Liability Theory: The Product Should Not Have Been Substantially Changed Between the Time It Left the Seller or Manufacturer and the Time It Reached the End User

The third element of a strict liability theory case is the product should not have been substantially changed between the time the product left the seller or manufacturer and the time the product reached the ultimate user. If the product was changed between those two times, then the law does not hold the seller or manufacturer liable.

Example

Teddy ordered computer parts online. En route to Teddy's home, the box containing the parts was dropped by the postal carrier. The drop caused the parts to become defective. The manufacturer or seller of the parts would not be held liable for this defect because the drop caused the product to change in between the time the product left the manufacturer/seller and the time it reached Teddy.

d. The Fourth Element of Products Liability Under Strict Liability Theory: The Defect in the Product Must Be the Proximate Cause of the Injuries to the Plaintiff

The next element is the defect in the product must be the proximate cause of the injuries to the plaintiff. If the plaintiff did not have to prove the defect in the product is what caused injury to her, then the defendant would essentially be an insurer of the product. The plaintiff must prove the defect in the product is what actually caused her injuries, or she cannot recover damages under strict products liability.

e. The Fifth Element of Products Liability Under Strict Liability Theory: The Product Must Have Been Used Properly by the Plaintiff

The final element is the product must have been used properly by the plaintiff. If the product causes an injury to the plaintiff because of the plaintiff's misuse of the product, then the manufacturer or seller of the product may be able to avoid liability. A manufacturer or seller is not responsible for the plaintiff's misuse of the product.

Example

Cameron is trimming his hedges when he looks down at his fingernails and notices how long his fingernails are. He thinks to himself, "I really should trim my nails, but I'm too lazy to go into the house and get nail trimmers." Instead, Cameron decides to use the hedge trimmer to trim his nails. In doing so Cameron accidentally cuts off his thumb. The manufacturer or seller of the hedge trimmer will not be responsible for Cameron cutting off his thumb because Cameron misused the product.

12.9 Breach of Warranty

Breach of warranty
a theory under which a plaintiff can sue in products liability; combines tort and contract law to provide a remedy for a plaintiff.

Breach of warranty is yet another theory under which a plaintiff can sue in products liability. **Breach of warranty** combines tort and contract law to provide a remedy for

Uniform Commercial Code
a statute governing sales.

a plaintiff. Warranties are covered in the **Uniform Commercial Code** ("UCC"). The UCC is a statute governing sales. If the manufacturer/seller has breached a warranty, the liability is strict liability, not negligence.

a. Implied Warranties

Implied warranties are given by the seller when an item is offered for sale. There are two implied warranties: the warranty of merchantability and the warranty of fitness of the product for a limited purpose.

1. Warranty of Merchantability

Warranty of merchantability
an item must be fit and safe for its ordinary purpose.

The **warranty of merchantability** requires an item be fit and safe for its ordinary purpose. The product should work in a normal and safe way for the purpose for which it was intended. If the product does not work in a normal and safe way for its intended purpose, then the user of the product may be able to recover under the warranty of merchantability. Merchantability does not mean the product has to be completely perfect in every way.

Example

Christy bought a pair of blue jeans. Christy wore the blue jeans for two years, and then the zipper broke. The product worked in a normal and safe way for its intended purpose, which was to be worn. Just because the jeans broke after two years does not mean the jeans did not meet the warranty of merchantability. So long as the jeans conformed to the ordinary standards of the jeans (being wearable) and were of average quality, the warranty of merchantability has been met.

However, what if the jeans were sewn shut at the bottom of the legs? The jeans would not conform to the ordinary standards of jeans being wearable, and the warranty of merchantability would not have been satisfied.

The warranty of merchantability applies to all sold goods, whether or not the goods came with any other warranties. However, for the warranty of merchantability to apply, the seller of the item must be a merchant who is in the regular business of selling those kinds of items. Therefore, if Rodney sold an isolated item on eBay, the item Rodney sold would not have a warranty of merchantability attached to it.

2. Warranty of Fitness for Limited Purpose

Warranty of fitness for a limited purpose
a seller telling the buyer a product can be used for a purpose other than the purpose the item is normally used for.

The **warranty of fitness for a limited purpose** arises when a customer needs to use an item for a purpose the item is not normally used for. If the seller tells the buyer the product can be used in that manner, then the product is impliedly warranted for use for that particular purpose. The major difference between the warranty of merchantability and the warranty of fitness for a limited purpose is the buyer's communication with the seller occurring in the warranty for fitness. The seller steers the buyer toward a certain product.

Example

Jody goes to her local gardening store. She tells one of the salespeople she is looking for drought-resistant grass to put in her front lawn. The salesperson steers her towards a Fescue grass, which requires a lot of water. Jody spends money and invests time into putting in her Fescue grass. During the first summer, when there is not much rain, the grass dies. The grass was not fit for the purpose as the salesperson promised.

The Uniform Commercial Code, Section 2-315 defines the warranty of fitness for a limited purpose as follows:

> Where the seller at the time of contracting has reason to know any particular purpose for which the goods are required and that the buyer is relying on the seller's skill or judgment to select or furnish suitable goods, there is unless excluded or modified under the next section an implied warranty that the good shall be fit for such purpose.

The UCC definition requires two things:

- The seller's knowledge of the particular purpose that the buyer is going to use the product for, and
- The buyer's reliance on the seller's knowledge.

b. Express Warranties

When a seller makes representations to the buyer about the product, the seller is making an express warranty. Express warranties can occur in one of three ways. The first way in which an express warranty can occur is when a seller of the good makes an assertion about the product. The seller must make an assertion, not state an opinion. An example of an assertion is when the waiter at a restaurant tells John: "There are no nuts or nut byproducts in our carrot cake." An opinion would be the waiter telling John: "I don't think there are any nuts in the carrot cake, but I've never had it."

The second way in which in an express warranty can occur is when the seller describes the product. For instance, the seller could describe his product in a newspaper ad. The third way in which an express warranty can be made is when the seller uses a sample of the goods to demonstrate the product to consumers. The seller is representing that the product has certain qualities or performs in a certain way. Express warranties must occur before or during the sale of the product.

Sample of Warranty Cause of Action in Products Liability

- Defendant Cuts Saw Manufacturers expressly and impliedly warranted that the electric saw was fit for its intended use, was safe, and was of merchantable quality.
- The plaintiff relied upon the warranties of Cuts Saw Manufacturers.

- Defendant Cuts Saw Manufacturers breached its warranties in that the electric saw was unsafe and not suited for its intended purpose, and was not of merchantable quality.
- As a result of this breach, the plaintiff has been injured.

12.10   Restatement (Third) of Torts Approach to Products Liability

The Restatements of Torts, as discussed in more detail in Chapter 1, are not statutes. However, many judges do rely on the Restatements when deciding cases. Therefore, looking at the Restatements is of value. The Restatement (Third) of Torts concentrates on products liability. Many courts are moving towards an approach to products liability that follows the Restatement (Third) of Torts, which looks at products liability from three ways:

- design defect,
- manufacturing defect, and
- warning defect.

a.   Design Defect

Design defect
a product is not safe for its intended or reasonably foreseeable use; all products in a line have a design feature making them unreasonably unsafe.

In **design defect**, the problem with the product arises at the design level. Thus, all the products are defective because all the products have a feature making them unreasonably unsafe. Another way of stating this is a product is not safe for its intended or reasonably foreseeable use. The Restatement (Third) of Torts clarifies what a plaintiff must prove to win a design defect case. The plaintiff has to show the risk of the product's defective design was greater than the benefit of the product's defective design. In addition, the plaintiff has to show there was a reasonable alternative to the defective design.

b.   Manufacturing Defect

Manufacturing defect
a product which does not conform to the rest of the products in a line due to something occurring in the manufacturing process which damages the product.

With a **manufacturing defect**, the design of the product is not defective. However, something occurred in the manufacturing process, causing one of the products not to conform to the rest of the products. The nonconformity is unreasonably unsafe and injures the plaintiff. The Restatement (Third) of Torts states a manufacturing defect occurs when: "the product departs from its intended design even though all possible care was exercised in the preparation and marketing of the product."[10]

Sample Design or Manufacturing Defect Cause of Action

- Cuts Saw Manufacturers was and is engaged in the manufacture of electric saws.
- On or about February 4, 2008, plaintiff bought an electric saw from Cuts Saw Manufacturers at its retail store, located in _____(city), _____(state).

---

10. Restatement (Third) of Torts: Products Liability, Section 2(b).

■ On or about February 5, 2008, while plaintiff was operating said electric saw in accord with the instructions, plaintiff suffered a personal injury.
■ The defendant, Cuts Saw Manufacturers was negligent in the design, manufacture, and sale of the electric saw to the plaintiff.
■ The injury was caused by the defendant's negligence.
■ Plaintiff has been damaged.

c.   Defective Warning: There Are Not Proper Warnings or Directions

Some products are dangerous if the products do not have sufficient warnings or instructions for their use. A product should have instructions on how to use the product and should have reasonable warnings about non-obvious dangers. **Instructions** discuss how to safely and effectively use the product. A **warning** discusses dangers. The warning may be proper, but the instructions defective, and vice versa.

The product's warning must be large enough — in language or symbols — to convey to a reasonably prudent user what the particular danger of the product is. If a person reads the back of a bottle of bleach, for example, she should also see on the bleach label a discussion of foreseeable misuses of the product and counteractive measures to those misuses.

Instructions
a discussion on how to safely and effectively use a product.

Warning
a discussion of dangers.

Funny Warning Labels

■ Do not use iron while clothes are on the body.
■ The camera will only work when film is inside.
■ No purchase necessary. Details inside package.
■ For best results, open package.
■ Cook raw meat before eating.
■ This iron supplement contains iron.

The item must conform to any assertions made upon the label or container. If a child's life preserver states the life preserver is adequate for children from 20-40 pounds, then the life preserver should maintain children 20-40 pounds afloat.

12.11   Consumer Product Safety Act

Consumer products are regulated under the Consumer Products Safety Act ("the Act"). The Act established the United States Consumer Products Safety Commission. When there is an unreasonable risk of injury in a consumer product, the act directs the

Consumer Product Safety Commission ("CPSC") to develop a standard that will lessen or extinguish the risk. The Act also gives the CPSC the ability to ban products if the products cannot be made safe. However, there are many products that are not covered by the Consumer Product Safety Commission, including hazardous household substances. Similar to the Act, but for hazardous household substances, is the Federal Hazardous Substances Act ("FHSA"). The FHSA makes labels for such substances mandatory.

12.12   Defenses to Products Liability

Potential defenses to products liability include:

- assumption of the risk,
- product misuse,
- acts of a third person, and
- statute of limitations.

Contributory negligence is not considered a defense in products liability cases.

For an assumption of the risk defense, the plaintiff must voluntarily assume the risk with a full appreciation of what the consequences of the risk are. If the end user of a product notes a product is defective prior to use but uses the product anyway, then the end user has assumed the risk of injury. If the end user does not properly maintain the product, which then causes a defect, then the end user has assumed the risk of injury. If the end user does not read the instructions or warnings, then the end user has assumed the risk of injury.

Another defense to products liability is product misuse. If the end user of a product misuses the product, then she cannot recover under the theory of products liability. The misuse must be substantial and not an easily foreseen misuse of the product.

In addition, an act of a third person may work as a defense. There may not be a sufficient connection between the manufacturer or seller's breach of duty and the plaintiff's injury if there was a third person involved. This third party might have abused the product or ignored the warnings prior to the plaintiff obtaining the product. If the third party significantly abused the product, and this abuse was more substantial than the original defect of the product, then the manufacturer or seller of the product might be relieved of liability. Note the product was defective originally, but in comparison to the abuse the product received after it left the manufacturer or seller, the original defect is small.

Finally, the statute of limitations is a defense to products liability. If a plaintiff brings a products liability claim after the statute of limitations has run, then the products liability claim is barred. The defendant needs to affirmatively raise this defense.

Construction Defect
By Don Garcia, Paralegal

Homebuyers have an expectation that their home is built according to applicable codes and statutes, is safe, inhabitable, and that it is reasonably free of construction defects. When a construction defect is discovered the homeowner notifies the builder. The builder then evaluates the complaint and determines a plan of action. In most cases the defect is repaired or replaced at the builder's expense. In some cases the builder will offer monetary compensation. If the builder and homeowner cannot come to an agreement, the homeowner may bring an action against the builder. Generally speaking, the court maintains that construction defect litigation is more appropriate under the laws of contract and warranty. Tort law requires evidence of personal injury or property damage. The courts emphasize that under tort a plaintiff has the burden to provide the facts in support of the alleged claim of injury or damage. If plaintiff can provide this evidence, an action can be pursued against the builder in tort for strict liability.

Homebuyers rely on the expertise of a builder to ensure that their house is safe and built to the current industry standard. The defendant is in a better position to protect against unreasonable risks of harm.

Strict liability does not require the plaintiff to prove negligence. The courts have recognized builders who mass produce homes for sale as manufacturers and a

home as a product. These builder/vendors are susceptible to product liability laws akin to those of automobile manufacturers. Under the doctrine of strict liability, the plaintiff has the burden of proving that the product (home) was actually defective to the extent that it was unreasonably dangerous, the defect existed when the home was purchased, the defect was the proximate cause of the physical injury and/or property damage, and finally, the injury was reasonably foreseeable. Assigning liability to the builder-vendor as a manufacturer is based on the premise that the builder-vendor is in a better position than the homeowner to determine foreseeable risk. The builder has control and directs the work to build a fit and workman-like structure. When new ideas and products are available the builder-vendor can assess the risk and spread the cost of the risk across the product line.

The average homebuyer relies on the skill of the developer and implied representation that the house will be erected in a reasonably workman-like manner and will be reasonably fit for habitation. He has no architect or professional adviser of his own, and his inspection of the property is superficial. In regards to a latent construction defect, the issue to be determined is whether the defect was known to the builder or in the exercise of ordinary care would have been known to him.

E T H I C S

Rent and watch the movie *Class Action*. The movie dramatizes the Ford Pinto products liability case. While watching the movie also pay attention to ethical issues, such as the duty of confidentiality. Is it ethical to bury important evidence in voluminous discovery materials?

Chapter Summary

Strict liability applies with abnormally dangerous activities, dangerous animals, and products liability. The major difference between strict liability and negligence is a plaintiff does not have to prove fault with strict liability. Some activities are just so inherently dangerous that people who engage in those activities will be responsible for the resulting injuries, even if precautions were taken. Thus, negligence does not affect whether a defendant is strictly liable.

An abnormally dangerous activity is one with a high degree of serious harm that cannot be alleviated with reasonable care. Examples of abnormally dangerous activities include the use of:

- explosive devices,
- highly flammable materials, and
- poisonous gases.

Other factors in determining whether an activity is abnormally dangerous include whether the activity is common, whether the activity was appropriate for the location or usual for the area, and whether the activity's benefit outweighs the hazard to the community.

Products liability is extremely complex and has many different theories. Each theory involves manufacturers, sellers, and the ultimate user of the product.

One of the most traditional theories of products liability is the products liability case brought under strict liability. The elements to a strict products liability case are

- the product is defective;
- the defect makes the product unreasonably unsafe;
- the manufacturer or seller of the product has to be the business of selling those types of products;
- the product cannot have substantially changed between the time it left the manufacturer or seller and the time it reached the ultimate user;
- proximate cause; and
- the product must have been used properly.

Another theory under which a products liability cause might be brought is breach of warranty. Breach of warranty claims also involve contract law, through the Uniform Commercial Code. There are two types of implied warranties: the warranty of merchantability and the warranty of fitness for a limited purpose. The warranty of merchantability is the product has to be safe for the ordinary purpose for which the product is used. The warranty of fitness for limited purpose indicates that if the seller tells the buyer the product can be used for a purpose for which the product is not normally used, then the product must be safe for the additional purpose.

The Restatement (Third) of Torts looks at products liability from a defects viewpoint: design, manufacturing, and warning defects. A design defect occurs at the design level, and thus all the products made will have the same defect making the product unsafe. In a manufacturing defect, the design is fine. However, at some point in the manufacturing process, one or more of the products did not conform to the way in which the rest of the products were made. The nonconformity makes the product unsafe. A warning defect occurs if there are not proper warnings or instructions for a product's use.

Key Terms

- Abnormally dangerous activity
- Assumption of the risk
- Breach of warranty
- Caveat emptor
- Dangerous activity
- Defective warning
- Design defect
- Domestic animals
- Express warranty
- Foreseeable use
- Implied warranty
- Instructions
- Manufacturer
- Manufacturing defect
- Products liability
- Seller
- Strict liability
- Strict liability in tort
- Ultimate or end user
- Uniform Commercial Code
- Unreasonably dangerous
- Warning
- Warning defect
- Warranty
- Warranty of fitness for a particular purpose
- Warranty of merchantability
- Wild animals

Review Questions

- Explain the major difference between strict liability and negligence.
- What are the factors a court will take into consideration in determining whether an activity is abnormally dangerous?
- What is an example of an abnormally dangerous activity?
- Does reasonable care play a role in strict liability?
- What is the difference, legally, between wild and domesticated animals?
- What are some defenses a defendant could raise to a strict liability lawsuit?
- What is the public policy argument behind products liability?
- How is assumption of the risk a defense to products liability?

Web Links

- Dog bite law is a specialty of tort law. www.dogbitelaw.com contains strategy for firms representing dog bite victims. Even if your firm defends the dog owners' side, this is still a valuable site to help you understand the opposing strategy.

▪ For more discussion on the difference between negligence and strict liability read the article located at http://plato.stanford.edu/entries/tort-theories/#2.

▪ www.cpsc.gov/. The Consumer Product Safety Commission is a federal governmental agency with the mission of protecting the public from death and injury caused by everyday products. The Commission issues government standards for different products, which can be a basis for determining whether or not there has been products liability. This website also alerts the public to product recalls. In addition, the product safety standards, discussed above, are posted on this site.

▪ The American Association for Justice, formerly the Association of Trial Lawyers of America, is still located at www.atla.org. This is a good resource for products liability and medical malpractice issues. In addition, this is a useful site for finding continuing legal education seminars and books, and for networking.

Exercises

▪ Watch the movie *Erin Brockovich*. In the movie, Pacific Gas & Electric is alleged to have polluted the water, causing cancer. How does this film relate to torts? Pay attention to the statute of limitations issue. In addition, what do you think about the attorney taking forty percent of the clients' recovery? Does the way in which Erin explains the reason for it make ethical sense to you? Did Erin properly solicit the clients' business? In addition, is Erin's two million dollar bonus, at the end of the movie, ethical? Review the ethics section on split fees.

▪ Research whether the city or county you live in has a leash law.

▪ Kill Termites Now Pest Control, Inc. tents the Andrews' house. However, it does not put up any signs regarding the dangerousness of the chemicals it used in fumigating. The company also does not secure the site very well. Vanessa decides to steal from the Andrews' home, since the family is obviously away from the house. However, she enters into the home, starts to feel disoriented from the chemicals, and is unable to find her way out of the home. Vanessa dies from the poisonous gases. Is Kill Termites Now Pest Control, Inc. responsible for Vanessa's death?

▪ Go to the Consumer Products Safety Commission's website. What are the general requirements for a matchbook?

▪ Widget Company makes a revolutionary lawnmower that mows lawns without a human operator. The lawnmower starts flying off the shelves at the local Park Hardware store. Harry owns and runs the Park Hardware store. The lawnmower has a design defect because while it does mow lawns by itself, it also mows indiscriminately over small objects, including household pets. Customers start returning the lawnmower to Harry, telling him horror stories of how the lawnmower ran over their animals' tails. Harry's response is to tell the customers to take their concerns to Widget Company, and Harry does not remove the lawnmower from his shelves. This time, a customer buys the lawnmower, and the lawnmower runs over the customer's foot as he is laying back enjoying he lawn being mowed without his help. From whom can the customer successfully receive compensation for his injury?

▪ Does "this automobile is a great buy" constitute an assertion for the purpose of an express warranty?

▪ Try to identify unintended uses, but foreseeable uses, for the following products:
  ○ horse shampoo,
  ○ a flat screwdriver, and
  ○ a vacuum.

▪ Read the U.S. Consumer Product Safety Commission Requirements for pacifiers on the following page. Why were these requirements adopted? How much force does the pacifier have to be able to withstand? Why do pacifiers have to have two holes? Why can pacifiers not be tied around a baby's neck?

U.S. CONSUMER PRODUCT SAFETY COMMISSION

Office of Compliance

Requirements[1] for Pacifiers, 16 C.F.R. Part 1511

What is the purpose of the pacifier rule?

This rule keeps babies from choking or suffocating on pacifiers.

Where can I find the requirements for pacifiers?

The ban is published in the Code of Federal Regulations in Title 16, Part 1511

What is a pacifier?

A pacifier is an article with a nipple intended for a young child to suck on, but that is not designed to help a baby obtain fluid. A pacifier usually has a guard or shield at the base of the nipple that keeps the pacifier from being sucked completely into a child's mouth. It also has a handle or ring, usually on the other side of the guard or shield from the nipple that is used to hold or grasp the pacifier.

What does the pacifier rule require?

The rule requires that

(1) the shield not be so small or flexible that it can be sucked into a child's mouth;

(2) the a pacifier have no handles or other protrusions, that are long enough to force the pacifier into the child's mouth if the child falls or lies on its face;

(3) pacifiers are labeled to warn caregivers not to tie the pacifier around the child's neck.

(4) a pacifier not produce small parts when tested.

How do you test a pacifier's guard or shield to make sure it can't suffocate a child?

Center the nipple in opening in the pacifier test fixture (Figure 1). Pull on the nipple gradually until you reach a force of 2 lbs. Hold the 2-lb. force for 10 seconds. If the shield pulls completely through the fixture, the pacifier fails.

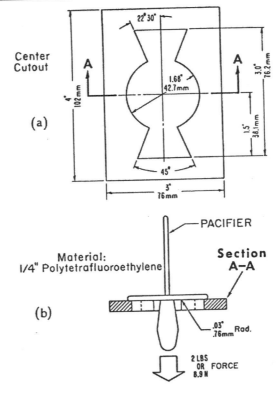

Figure 1 - Pacifier Test Fixture

Are there other requirements for shields and guards?

The pacifier guard or shield must have at least two holes, one on either side of the nipple. Each hole must be at least 0.2 inches wide and cannot be closer than 0.2 inch from the outside edge of the shield or guard. These holes allow a child to continue breathing even if the child sucks the pacifier guard into his or her mouth.

---

[1] This document is a general summary of the pacifier requirement and does not replace or supercede the requirements published in 16 C.F.R. 1511. This summary does not include all of the details included in those requirements. Please refer to the regulation for those details.

What does the standard say about protrusions?

Parts cannot stick out more than 0.63 inches from the face of the guard or shield on the side opposite the nipple. To test for a protrusion, clamp the pacifier by its nipple so that it will not move. Place an object with flat surface, such as a piece of wood or hard plastic, directly on any handle, ring, or other part that protrudes from the shield or guard on the other side of the nipple. Gradually push the object toward the nipple, allowing the protrusion you are testing to bend or, if it is a hinged handle or ring, to move. Make sure that you apply the force in the direction that follows the length of the nipple. Once you reach a force of two pounds, measure the distance between guard or shield and the surface of the test object.

Are there other requirements for pacifier strength?

Yes. There is a pull test. The pacifier must not come apart if you hold the handle or guard and gradually pull on the nipple in any possible direction for 5 seconds until you reach 10 pounds. Hold that force for 10 more

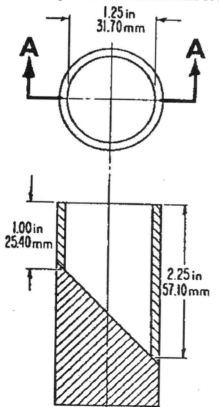

Figure 2 - Small Parts Test Cylinder

seconds. The handle or ring must pass the same test. Both the nipple and the handle or ring must also pass these same tests after the pacifier has been boiled and cooled six times. Boiling the pacifier simulates how parents sterilize pacifiers in the home.

If any pieces come off during the pull tests, test the parts to see if they fit entirely into the "small parts" test cylinder (Figure 2). The cylinder approximates the size of a child's throat. If any part fits, the pacifier is banned because a child could choke on the part.

Are there any other requirements for pacifiers?

Yes. To prevent a child from strangling, a pacifier cannot be sold or distributed with any ribbon, string, cord, chain, twine, leather, yarn or similar attachment. In addition, pacifier packages must be clearly labeled on the front "Warning- Do Not Tie Pacifier Around Child's Neck as it Presents a Strangulation Danger."

Does CPSC have any other requirements that apply to pacifiers?

Yes. Pacifiers may not have sharp points or edges or be painted with paint that contains more than 0.06% lead. (See 16 C.F.R. 1500.48, 16 C.F.R. 1500.49, and 16 C.F.R. 1303)

Are there any standards for chemical hazards?

The Commission has no mandatory standards addressing chemical hazards. ASTM F963, the Standard Consumer Safety Specification on Toy Safety, Pacifiers, Section 4.22 addresses cancer risks in rubber nipples by providing that these nipples shall not contain more than 20 ppb. total nitrosamines. See ASTM F1313 for more detail on nitrosamine testing.

Where can I find additional Information?

You can obtain the Requirements for Pacifiers, 16 C.F.R. Part 1511, from the Commission's Web Site at: http://www.cpsc.gov. For more information on the requirements for pacifiers contact the Consumer Product Safety Commission, Office of Compliance, Washington, D.C. 20207, telephone: (301) 504-7913, e-mail: sect15@cpsc.gov.

For copies of the Standard Consumer Safety Specification on Toy Safety (ASTM F 963) and Volatile *n*-Nitrosamine Levels in Rubber Nipples on Pacifiers (ASTM F1313) contact the American Society for Testing and Materials (ASTM), 100 Barr Harbor Drive, West Conshohocken, PA 19428-2959, telephone: (610)-832-9585, Fax (610)-832-9555, or visit http://www.astm.org.

Nuisance

The Liberty of the individual must be thus far limited; he must not make himself a nuisance to other people.[1]

Chapter Outline

Chapter Objectives

- Define public and private nuisance
- Explain the differences between public and private nuisance
- Discuss remedies to nuisance, including damages and injunctions

13.1 Introduction to and the Elements of Private Nuisance

Nuisance
the unreasonable or unlawful use of real property so as to interfere with the plaintiff's interest in the real property.

Nuisance is a rather loosely defined type of tort. A nuisance involves the use of real property so as to interfere with the plaintiff's interest in the real property. This use of real property is an unreasonable or unlawful use of the property. There are two types of nuisance, private and public nuisance. Private nuisance involves an unreasonable

---

1. John Stuart Mill, *On Liberty*.

interference with the use of private land and public nuisance involves an unreasonable interference with a public right. Nuisance has its own separate chapter as it can occur as a result of negligence, strict liability, intent, or due to a violation of statute.

Elements of Private Nuisance:

Interference with use and enjoyment of land.

The interference is unreasonable and substantial.

The defendant's activity must also proximately cause the plaintiff's injuries.

---

a. The First Element of Private Nuisance: Interference with Use and Enjoyment of Land

Private nuisance
an invasion of another's interest in his private use and enjoyment of land through means other than a physical entry onto the real property.

The first element of a private nuisance is there must be an interference with the use and enjoyment of the land. A **private nuisance** is an invasion of another's interest in his private use and enjoyment of land. The plaintiff does not have to own the property to make a private nuisance claim. The plaintiff can simply be the legal occupant of the land. This interference with land is not a trespass. Trespass is different from private nuisance because trespass interferes with a plaintiff's right to possess his property. When someone physically enters onto real property it is considered a trespass, whereas when something such as a smell or light enters onto the land it is considered a nuisance. Other examples of potential private nuisances are constant vibrations from explosions and sewage spilling across property lines.

b. The Second Element of Private Nuisance: The Interference Is Unreasonable and Substantial

The second element of private nuisance is the interference must be unreasonable and substantial. Whether the use of real property is unreasonable and substantial is assessed by how offensive the use of the real property is. The level of offensiveness is assessed using a reasonable person standard. If a reasonable person would find the use of real property offensive, then this element is met.

c. The Third Element of Private Nuisance: The Defendant's Activity Must Also Proximately Cause the Plaintiff's Injuries

The third element of private nuisance is the defendant's activity must proximately cause the plaintiff's injuries. This is the same proximate cause that was discussed in negligence and in strict liability.

Proving the severity of a nuisance injury is easier if the physical value of the land has been diminished. The value of the plaintiff's and defendant's use of the land is based upon whether the land is used for a home, business, or recreation. If the plaintiff's land is unoccupied, for instance, the plaintiff is going to have a much harder time proving that the interference with his unoccupied land is unreasonable.

An example of private nuisance can be seen in the case of *Barras v. Hebert.*[2] The plaintiff's neighbors operated an alligator farm. The foul and noxious odors that emanating from the farm could be smelled by the plaintiffs and were held to be a private nuisance. However, the remedy was not to shut down the alligator farm, so long as the odors could be contained in some other manner, such as through an airlock system.

Barras v. Hebert

602 So. 2d 186 (1992)

This is a nuisance case concerning a commercial alligator farm. The main issue is whether the odor that emits from the alligator "containing building" is so foul and noxious as to amount to a nuisance. Over 30 named plaintiffs filed suit seeking to enjoin the defendants' farming operation.

The plaintiffs . . . [are] seeking the complete shut-down of the alligator farm. . . .

The defendants, Tim Hebert and his wife Kathleen, started a commercial alligator farming operation in 1989. The farm is located on 4.2 acres of land in a residential area just outside of the corporate limits of St. Martinville in St. Martin Parish. The Heberts' home is on the same 4.2 acre tract of land. There was no evidence that the farming operation violated any state or local zoning, health, or other regulations or prohibitions, and no evidence of the existence of any subdivision restrictions.

The plaintiffs' respective homes are all located in close proximity to the Heberts' farm. The plaintiffs' petition alleged that the stench from the farm was so unbearable that it made the plaintiffs' homes nearly uninhabitable. The plaintiffs also claimed that the farm's presence devalued their respective properties.

A. NUISANCE

The obligations of vicinage are found in L.S.A.-C.C. arts. 667-669. These Articles state:

> *Art. 667. Limitations on use of property*
> Although a proprietor may do with his estate whatever he pleases, still he can not make any work on it, which may deprive his neighbor of the liberty of enjoying his own, or which may be the cause of any damage to him.

> *Art. 668. Inconvenience to neighbor*
> Although one be not at liberty to make any work by which his neighbor's buildings may be damaged, yet every one has the liberty of doing on his own ground whatsoever he pleases, although it should occasion some inconvenience to his neighbor.
> Thus he who is not subject to any servitude originating from a particular agreement in that respect, may raise his house as high as he pleases, although by such elevation he should

---

2. 602 So. 2d 186 (La. Ct. App. 1992).

darken the lights of his neighbor's [neighbor's] house, because this act occasions only an inconvenience, but not a real damage.

Art. 669. Regulation of inconvenience

If the works or materials for any manufactory or other operation, cause an inconvenience to those in the same or in the neighboring houses, by diffusing smoke or nauseous smell, and there be no servitude established by which they are regulated, their sufferance must be determined by the rules of the police, or the customs of the place. . . .

These obligations of vicinage are legal servitudes imposed on the owner of property. These provisions embody a balancing of rights and obligations associated with the ownership of immovables. As a general rule, the landowner is free to exercise his rights of ownership in any manner he sees fit. He may even use his property in ways which ". . . occasion some inconvenience to his neighbor." However, his extensive rights do not allow him to do "real damage" to his neighbor.

We sometimes use the term "nuisance" in describing the type of conduct which violates the pronouncements embodied in La. C.C. arts. 667-669. . . . At issue in this case is whether the smell from the Heberts' alligator operation has caused a mere "inconvenience" or "real damage" to their neighbors and their right to enjoy their own premises. . . .

. . . [In] the Louisiana Supreme Court case of *Robichaux v. Huppenbauer* . . . [t]here the court found a horse stable in a residential area in New Orleans to be a nuisance. In deciding whether to enjoin the entire operation of the stable, the court stated:

> The record also supports the conclusion that the stable is a nuisance because of the manner in which it is operated. However, we have not been shown that it is impossible to maintain this horse lot and stable in such a manner as to free it from the complaints which the plaintiffs make, therefore we will not abate the business entirely. . . . Instead we will permit defendant to continue his operations under the following mandates, restrictions and injunctions:
>
> - Spray ground and premises generally and thoroughly with a disinfectant and deodorizer, approved by the local health authorities, at such intervals as may be prescribed by those authorities.
> - Dispense rat poison at strategic locations about stables, sheds and bins and renew weekly.
> - Feed bins should be covered and so constructed as to deny rodents access to feed.
> - Remove all manure and other waste daily.
> - Limit the number of horses using the lot and stables to ten.
> - Keep the premises properly drained to prevent water from standing there. . . .

In other words, the court would not shut down the stable if the problem that it caused could be cured by less restrictive means. *Robichaux* is just one example in our jurisprudence wherein trial courts, when faced with corrective measures that would be greatly disproportionate in cost to the actual damage caused, have been ordered to fashion reasonable alternative remedies. . . .

Sample Cause of Action for Private Nuisance

■ The noise from Defendant's power tools and Defendant's actions towards Plainitffs has created a private nuisance as defined in Civil Code Section 3481.

■ Defendant's acts are injurious to the health of Plaintiffs, offensive to their senses, and/or an obstruction to the free use of their property so as to interfere with the comfortable enjoyment of their lives and/or property.

■ Defendant's acts have substantially and unreasonably interfered with the interests of Plaintiffs. Defendant harasses Plaintiffs whenever Cross-Complainants come outside of their residence or open the windows located on the front of their residence. There is no legal justification for Defendant's actions.

■ Therefore, Plaintiffs pray for judgments against Defendant for the above-described injuries and losses.

13.2   Public Nuisance

Elements of Public Nuisance:

An act unreasonably and substantially interfering with the use and enjoyment of public rights.

The plaintiff is governmental agency charged with protecting the public right.

The governmental agency has the authority to litigate this right.

Public nuisance
an unreasonable interference with a right common to the general public.

Public nuisance is a condition caused by the defendant, harming the general public. The Restatement (Second) of Torts classifies a public nuisance as "an unreasonable interference with a right common to the general public."[3] A right common to the general public includes issues regarding

■ the health,
■ safety, and
■ welfare of the public.

Usually, public nuisance arises when a property is not properly maintained or when activities conducted on a property are dangerous to the public. Originally, public nuisance law was designed to protect rights such as:

■ "the right to safely walk along public highways,
■ to breathe unpolluted air,

---

3. §821B(1) (1965).

- to be undisturbed by large gatherings of disorderly people and
- to be free from the spreading of infectious diseases."[4]

Modern day examples of public nuisance include

- blocking streets,
- storing dangerous fireworks within city limits, or
- running a "massage" parlor that is really a front for prostitution.

A public nuisance is different from a private nuisance. The defendant's conduct must have interfered with public health or safety. The conduct must have had a significant effect and been unreasonable under the circumstances. If the defendant violated a statute, then it will be easier to establish unreasonableness.

A public nuisance could also be a crime, punishable by law. In these instances, usually a public official will step in and litigate the matter. A public official can obtain an injunction. The purpose of public nuisance law is to halt quasi-criminal acts unreasonable to the general public.

Government can define activities as public nuisances in public ordinances. Below is an example of a public nuisance ordinance.

The Code of the City of Santa Clara, Chapter 22A, Public Nuisances, Public Nuisance Ordinance, Ordinance No. 1663

Section 22A-3 Property maintenance-public nuisances.
It is hereby declared to be a public nuisance for any owner or other person in control of said property or premises to keep or maintain property, premises or rights-of-way in such a manner that any of the following conditions are found to exist:

(b) Discarded putrescibles, garbage, rubbish, refuse, or recyclable items which have not been recycled within thirty (30) days of being deposited on the property which are determined by an Enforcement Officer to constitute a fire hazard or to be detrimental to human life, health or safety;

(c) Oil, grease, paint, other petroleum products, hazardous materials, volatile chemicals, pesticides, herbicides, fungicides or waste (solid, liquid or gaseous) which is determined by an Enforcement Officer to constitute a fire or environmental hazard, or to be detrimental to human life, health or safety;

---

4. Joseph W. Cleary, *Municipalities Versus Gun Manufacturers: Why Public Nuisance Claims Just Do Not Work*, 31 U. Balt. L. Rev. 273, 277 (2002).

(f) Swimming pool, pond, spa, other body of water, or excavation which is abandoned, unattended, unsanitary, empty, which is not securely fenced, or which is determined by the Enforcement Officer to be detrimental to life, health or safety. . . .

Sometimes a private plaintiff can sue a defendant under public nuisance. Private individuals who have suffered a harm different from that suffered by other members of the public may file a claim for public nuisance.[5] A private plaintiff has to prove there is a substantial interference with a public right and that he has undergone a harm different from the harm suffered by other members of the public.

When the Exxon oil spill occurred off the Alaskan coast, private plaintiffs attempted to recover monetary damages under the doctrine of public nuisance.[6] The private plaintiffs in *Alaska Native Class v. Exxon Corp.* tried to show their individual lives were affected by the oil spill, which made it so the plaintiffs could not fish in the area anymore. Fishing was a major way in which these Native Alaskan plaintiffs fed themselves. However, the court held those individual Alaskans did not suffer a more severe injury than the other members of the public who also could not fish. Thus, the Native Alaskans could not recover damages under public nuisance.

13.3 Remedies to Nuisance

The plaintiff in a private nuisance action has the option of seeking damages and/or an injunction. The injunction would be a court ordering the conduct causing the nuisance to stop. In a public nuisance case, a public official might seek fines or imprisonment.

Equitable Remedies	Monetary Remedies
Abatement	Monetary damages
Temporary injunction	
Permanent injunction	

a. Damages for Nuisance

Permanent nuisance
a nuisance where one act causes a lasting injury and the damages can be assessed once and for all; a nuisance that cannot be discontinued.

Nuisance can be divided into permanent nuisances and continuing nuisances. This distinction affects how damages are calculated. **Permanent nuisances** are nuisances where one act causes a lasting injury and the damages can be assessed finally. A permanent nuisance is one that cannot be discontinued. If the nuisance is permanent,

---

5. Restatement (Second) of Torts §821C (1965).
6. *Alaska Native Class v. Exxon Corp.*, 104 F.3d 1196 (9th Cir. 1997).

then damages can be calculated by determining how much the nuisance decreased the fair market value of the property.

If a nuisance is one that can be discontinued at any time, then it is a **continuing nuisance**. A plaintiff must bring successive actions for damages until the continuing nuisance is abated or stopped. The damages would be limited to the injury occurring prior to the lawsuit. If the nuisance is continuing, the better remedy might be an injunction.

With public nuisance, the government can issue an injunction to stop the behavior. A private plaintiff, in a public nuisance action, can seek monetary damages.

Continuing nuisance
a nuisance that can be discontinued at any time.

b.   Injunctions as a Remedy to Nuisance

Injunctions typically are sought when a monetary award will not make the plaintiff whole. However, most courts will also weigh whether the benefit to the plaintiff of an injunction outweighs the burden to the defendant. If a defendant's burden outweighs the benefit to the plaintiff, and monetary damages can compensate the plaintiff adequately, then an injunction may not be appropriate.

Court Personnel
By Robert Moore, Paralegal

Court personnel each have their own personalities and it is important for paralegals to learn how to deal with them as individuals. If you do not know the court personnel personally, one of your coworkers may be able to tell you their particular likes, dislikes, and quirks. If you cannot find out about the specific person that you will be dealing with, use the following information as a guide.

Judge: The judge rules the courtroom and demands the utmost respect. Judges continually deal with conflict between others and they have little tolerance for conflict directed toward them. Most judges are very particular about punctuality and are intolerant of cell phones, gum, tobacco, snacks, and beverages. Judges are always addressed as "Your Honor" and they must never be interrupted when they speak. In a courtroom, judges seldom speak to, or hear from, paralegals. That's the lawyers' job.

Lawyer: Lawyers expect their paralegals to support their preparation for cases, no matter which side they represent. Partners are the lawyers who own the law firm. Their main roles include bringing in the business,

deciding which cases to take. Associates are lawyers who have been hired by the partners, and usually do the grunt work. Ultimately, everyone at a law firm works for the partners, at their discretion.

Opposing Law Firm: In some court cases the lawyer from your firm seems to be presenting the truth, while the opposing lawyer does not, but that is often a matter of perspective. Both sides in court have the right to zealous representation so both lawyers are doing their jobs. In most real-world cases opposing law firms compare each other's evidence and discovery before a trial and settle out of court. They usually come up with a settlement in a professional manner, no matter how much personal animosity exists between the sides they represent. Paralegals and attorneys come and go from law firms, so opponents one day may be your coworkers or boss on the next.

Bailiff: The Bailiff provides physical protection for the courtroom under the direction of the judge.

Clerks: Clerks are the court personnel that paralegals interact with most and will be discussed in detail in the next chapter.

E T H I C S

Rule 6.1 Voluntary Pro Bono Publico Service [Free Public Service]

Every lawyer has a professional responsibility to provide legal services to those unable to pay. A lawyer should aspire to render at least (50) hours of pro bono publico legal services per year. In fulfilling this responsibility, the lawyer should:
- (a) provide a substantial majority of the (50) hours of legal services without fee or expectation of fee to:
  - (1) persons of limited means or
  - (2) charitable, religious, civic, community, governmental and educational organizations in matters that are designed primarily to address the needs of persons of limited means; and
- (b) provide any additional services through:
  - (1) delivery of legal services at no fee or substantially reduced fee to individuals, groups or organizations seeking to secure or protect civil rights, civil liberties or public rights, or charitable, religious, civic, community, governmental and educational organiza-

tions in matters in furtherance of their organizational purposes, where the payment of standard legal fees would significantly deplete the organization's economic resources or would be otherwise inappropriate;
- (2) delivery of legal services at a substantially reduced fee to persons of limited means; or
- (3) participation in activities for improving the law, the legal system or the legal profession.[7]

Possibly the most under-stressed ethical obligation listed under the Model Rules of Professional Conduct is to provide free or low-cost legal services to those who could not otherwise afford legal services. Hopefully, you will work for an attorney or a law firm with its own pro bono cases, which you will be able to work as part of your compensated job with the firm.

If the firm does not do pro bono work and should you still wish to volunteer, many low-cost legal agencies accept volunteer paralegals. For instance, many domestic violence clinics rely upon their paralegal volunteers.

Chapter Summary

A private nuisance is an unreasonable interference with the plaintiff's right to use and enjoy her land. The plaintiff's use has to be substantially interfered with. The interference will be considered unreasonable and substantial depending upon the level of offensiveness. If a reasonable person in the community would be offended, then the nuisance is substantial and unreasonable. The plaintiff can seek damages and/or an injunction for private nuisance.

A public nuisance is an interference with a right common to the general public. Usually a governmental agency will litigate the issue on behalf of the public. If a private plaintiff is to recover under public nuisance, then the plaintiff has to show the harm suffered by him was one specific to him and not common to the general public. The plaintiff in a public nuisance action will also have to show the harm was a substantial one.

---

7. Model R. Prof. Conduct 6.1 (ABA 2004).

Key Terms

- Continuing nuisance
- Damages
- Injunction
- Nuisance

- Permanent nuisance
- Private nuisance
- Public nuisance
- Remedy

Review Questions

- What is the difference between private nuisance and trespass?
- What is a private nuisance?
- What are some examples of private nuisance?
- When will an interference be deemed substantial?
- What is a public nuisance?
- What are some examples of public nuisance?
- How are the plaintiffs different between a private and a public nuisance?
- What are the remedies available to plaintiffs in nuisance cases?

Web Links

- www.lawnewsnetwork.com/. Torts are one of the practice areas available on this website, which also has job listings. If you were to select torts as a practice area, the website would provide you with current news, decisions, and practice papers all on torts.

Exercises

- For new developments in nuisance law read the following article: http://www.paint.org/pubs/ib_6-07.pdf.

Workers' Compensation

And so do as adversaries do in law, Strive mightily, but eat and drink as friends.[1]

Chapter Outline

Chapter Objectives

- Discuss how workers' compensation is different than negligence
- Cover when an injury fails under workers' compensation
- Outline the benefits available under workers' compensation
- Review filing a claim under workers' compensation

---

1. William Shakespeare.

14.1   Introduction to Workers' Compensation

Because workers' compensation is based upon a variety of statutes enacted and managed at the state level, it is more difficult to provide a complete picture of workers' compensation than other areas of law based upon common law. The workers' compensation programs vary by state regarding which injuries are compensable and what level of benefits will be provided. Despite these differences, most programs are funded by the employers. States dictate private employers shall have some form of workers' compensation coverage, or insurance. Workers' compensation insurance is available through private insurance companies and state-sponsored insurance funds. The workers' compensation benefits are usually paid out by the employer's insurance company. To be self-insured, the employer has to demonstrate it is financially capable of paying workers' compensation claims out of its own pocket. Either way, the employer is the responsible party.

Example

Sea World is self-insured, in part, because most insurance companies are not willing to cover the risks associated with killer whale injuries. In addition, if Sea World were to obtain insurance, the insurance would be very costly.

A large number of on-the-job injuries occur each year. Workers' compensation is an alternative to a negligence lawsuit. Workers' compensation statutes allow the employee to receive compensation for an on-the-job injury without having to prove negligence on behalf of the employer. Workers' compensation is a no-fault system, and in this way, similar to strict liability. This means even if the employer did nothing wrong, the employer will still have to pay for the injury. Defenses to negligence, such as contributory or comparative negligence and assumption of the risk, are not defenses to workers' compensation.

In workers' compensation, workers injured on the job receive a fixed monetary award. Employees generally receive workers' compensation whether or not the employee was negligent in causing his own injury. Employees like workers' compensation for this reason and because payment under workers' compensation can be faster through a regular court case. Employers usually prefer this system because the compensation the employee receives under workers' compensation is typically less than what the employee might recover in a negligence suit against the employer. However, workers' compensation insurance premiums are high, which is a detriment to employers.

14.2   Whether an Injury Is Covered by Workers' Compensation

a.   The Act Occurred Within the Employer/Employee Relationship

The test for determining whether an employee can sue in civil court or is limited to workers' compensation is whether the injury is within the employer/employee relationship. Examples of acts not considered within the normal employer/employee relationship are

- the employer intentionally caused injury to the employee;
- the employer knowingly employed someone in an illegal activity; and
- the employer violated the Occupational Safety and Health Act ("OSHA").

In these incidences, the employee will be able to sue the employer in civil court, and will not be limited to workers' compensation.

b. There Was an Employment Contract

To establish whether someone is an employee, and thus covered by workers' compensation, the worker must be a person in the service of an employer with any express or implied, contract to work for the employer. An employer may be a

- person,
- company,
- state,
- county,
- city,
- district, or
- public agency.

c. The Employer Has the Right to Control How the Job Is Done

There is a legal presumption that a worker is an employee. The principal test to conclusively determine whether there is an employee/employer relationship is whether the person to whom service is rendered has the right to control the way in which the desired outcome is reached. Employees are different from independent contractors. An independent contractor has control over the details of how the work is performed. Independent contractors are not covered by workers' compensation. Rather, an independent contractor must assume the risk of injury when she has the primary power over her own work safety, is in the best situation to distribute the risk and cost of an injury as one of the expenses of doing business, and has chosen to be self-employed.

d. There Was a Compensable Injury

When a finding has been made of an employee/employer relationship, the next step in determining whether workers' compensation benefits will be provided is establishing whether there is a compensable injury. In general, a compensable injury causes a disability or a need for medical treatment. There are four types of compensable injuries:

- a specific injury occurring as a result of one incident, and the employee immediately feels the effects of the injury;
- a specific injury occurring as a result of one incident, but the employee feels the effects of the injury at a later time;
- an injury occurring as a result of a number of minor injuries over a period of time; or
- or an injury occurring from continual exposure to harmful substances.

In some incidences, there will be more than one type of injury.

Example

A security guard, while on patrol, sees and apprehends someone who is robbing a store. The security guard is injured in the altercation, and has both an injured back and psychological stress as a result. The security guard has two injuries: the injured back and the psychological stress.

e. There Must Be Proximate Cause

Although workers' compensation does not require a finding of negligence, it does require proximate cause. There needs to be a connection between the conditions under which the work must be performed and the subsequently occurring injury. Proving a causal connection between work and injury becomes more difficult when discussing psychiatric injury cases. Some states require that the employment be the predominant cause (and not just a minor cause) of the psychiatric injury to prove the work was the cause of the psychiatric injury.

f. Course and Scope of Employment

Next, the injury must have also occurred in the course of employment — meaning at the time, place, and circumstances of the injury — that the employee was working. In contrast, an employee injured while performing tasks outside of the employment agreement, is injured outside the course of employment.

Example

The employee is an auto mechanic and an amateur racecar driver on the side. If the auto mechanic is injured while racing, this injury is not covered under workers' compensation. The employment was for the employee to act as an auto mechanic, not as a racecar driver. Even though car racing is related to the employment as auto mechanic, it was not part of the employment contract and the employer will not be liable under workers' compensation for a racecar accident.

14.3 Exclusions to Workers' Compensation

An employer may not be liable where

- an employee is injured while intoxicated,
- where the employee intentionally self-inflicts the injury, or
- where an employee is injured while committing a felony.

Certain categories of workers are excluded from workers' compensation, such as domestic workers and independent contractors. Different issues arise when the employee is injured

- going to or coming from work,
- during horseplay, or
- while conducting acts for the employee's own personal comfort.

Going-and-coming rule
if the employee is injured either going or coming to work, the injury is typically not covered by workers' compensation.

Most states have what is known as the **going-and-coming rule**. If the employee is injured either going or coming to work, the injury is typically not covered. If an employee is engaging in horseplay at work and is injured, then those injuries are not usually covered by workers' compensation. When the employee is taking a break, such as going to the restroom (which is considered for the employee's personal comfort), and injured, the injury is typically covered by workers' compensation. If an employee is performing an act of personal comfort, the legal assumption is this act makes the employee a better employee and thus the act should be covered by workers' compensation. Short breaks are normally covered under personal comfort, while longer breaks, such as lunch, are not usually covered.

14.4 The Specific Benefits Provided Under Workers' Compensation

The benefits available to injured workers under workers' compensation can include the following:

- medical treatment and related costs (as long as it is both reasonable and necessary),
- temporary disability payments,
- permanent disability payments,
- vocational rehabilitation benefits, and
- death benefits (if there is a fatality, the employee's dependents receive benefits).

The disability benefits can be further divided into

- permanent total disability,
- temporary total disability ("TTD"),
- permanent partial disability ("PPD"), and
- temporary partial disability.

Workers' compensation benefits are tax-free, so the value of these benefits in terms of purchasing power is more than it appears at first glance. In addition, an employee may be able to receive benefits outside of the workers' compensation system, through

- state disability,
- Social Security,
- a lawsuit if the injury was caused partially by a third party, or
- a lawsuit based on discrimination.

a.   Medical Treatment

Once it has been determined there is a compensable workers' compensation injury, employers should provide for medical treatment. The medical care should be provided immediately. This treatment is to be provided to the employees without cost to them. Treatment can include the following:

- services and supplies from doctors,
- chiropractors,
- hospitals,
- nurses, and
- physical therapists.

Prescriptions are covered, and many pharmacies have signs stating the pharmacy is happy to accept workers' compensation prescriptions. An employer will have to pay reasonable expenses of transportation to and from medical treatment. First aid is another form of treatment allowed under worker's compensation. An employer might also be liable for household services, especially if those household services (such as cleaning services) are recommended by a physician. However, medical treatment will usually not cover religious healers, hypnotists, or herbalists because these services are not technically deemed treatment.

In general, the employer is entitled to have the employee submit to medical exams conducted by a doctor selected by the employer. This is one way for the employer to verify the medical treatment the employee is receiving is reasonable and necessary. If the employee is unwilling to undergo these exams, her right to collect compensation may be suspended.

b.   Permanent Disability Benefits

Permanent disability
the disability left after a worker has reached her maximum medical improvement.

If the injury has lasting consequences after the employee heals, then permanent disability may be paid. **Permanent disability** is the disability left after a worker has reached her maximum medical improvement. The permanent disability could be 0%. Permanent disability can be measured in many ways. The methods for calculating what permanent disability benefits an employee is entitled to are complex and differ from state to state.

One way of measuring permanent disability is to base the measurement upon the disability and how the disability affects the employee's ability to earn money in the future. This formula anticipates the difficulty a worker may have in competing in the open labor market due to a mental or physical condition.

Example

The employee is a machinist and loses the ability to use his right hand. An injury to the right hand is more likely to receive greater compensation than if the machinist developed a stomach ailment related to the job. This is because the machinist needs his hand to complete his job, and most likely any job he might be rehabilitated into would require the use of his hand as well. The stomach, however, is not required to function perfectly in order for the machinist to perform his job.

The type of injury and how permanent the injury is affects the value of the employee's case. Medical testimony is needed to substantiate the employee's claims of permanent disability. A medical professional may have his deposition taken or may write a medical report with his findings.

Most benefits are limited to a specific duration or cap out at a certain dollar limit. However, an employee's permanent disability cannot be evaluated until her medical condition has reached a plateau. The plateau is the maximum medical improvement that can be expected, given the employee's injury.

Permanent disability benefits are usually computed based on some percentage of the employee's average weekly earnings and then multiplied by a series of weeks.

c. Temporary Disability Benefits

Temporary disability
an impairment that should be cured or greatly improved with the proper medical care.

Temporary disability is an impairment that should be cured or greatly improved with the proper medical care. Temporary disability benefits are a substitute for the wages the employee loses due to an inability to work because of the injury. These benefits should begin approximately three to seven days after the injury. However, these benefits are usually not equal to the money the employee was earning while working. A majority of states use a wage-replacement formula equal to two-thirds the gross earnings of the employee. Part of the reason the employee is not paid as much on temporary disability is because there are no taxes on workers' compensation payments.

When the employee has been restored to her original health as much as the injury will allow, then the employee's disability ceases to be considered temporary. Temporary disability benefits will terminate and permanent disability or vocational rehabilitation will take over (some states have terminated vocational rehabilitation benefits).

When a disability only partially prevents an injured worker from working, the injured worker will receive a combination of partial temporary disability and wages. This is known as temporary partial disability benefits. The injured worker is entitled to temporary partial disability for a longer period than temporary total disability.

d. Vocational Rehabilitation Benefits

If an employee is unable to return to her former job because of physical or mental limitations caused by the injury, some states provide for assistance in finding another type of employment, taking into consideration the employee's limitations. Often, another prerequisite for obtaining these benefits is the employer is unable to offer suitable employment to the employee within her new work restrictions. **Vocational rehabilitation** is a program providing retraining, academic instruction, and job placement assistance. The goal of vocational rehabilitation is to get the worker back to suitable, gainful employment as fast as possible.

Usually, the worker is given an allowance while she is re-training. Typically, there is a cap on the total amount of benefits (the allowance and the cost of re-training) that can be provided. The worker is also provided some living expenses necessitated by the vocational rehabilitation, such as transportation, childcare, and new clothes for interviewing.

Vocational rehabilitation benefits

assistance in finding another type of employment, taking into consideration the employee's work limitations.

14.5   Exclusive Remedy

Workers' compensation is different from the other areas of negligence-based law because it is a "no fault system." As a general rule, if an employee has an on-the-job injury, the employer will be responsible for providing compensation. The employee does not have to prove the employer caused the injury. The benefit to the employer is the employee gives up the right to sue the employer in court. As a result, the employee will usually receive much less in compensation than if the employee been able to sue in court. If a claim is compensable under workers' compensation, then the employee is usually limited to workers' compensation as the exclusive remedy. Workers' compensation has a separate system of "courts" (which are usually called workers compensation appeals boards) where the rules of evidence and discovery are much more relaxed than in civil court. A few cases will still be allowed to opt out of the workers' compensation system and go to civil court.

14.6   How to File a Workers' Compensation Claim

Usually to start a workers' compensation claim, no matter in what state the injured worker is located, the employee should notify the employer of the injury at the first opportunity. If the injury is a medical emergency, the first opportunity would be after the injured worker has been medically stabilized. To avoid the employer later stating the employee did not supply notification, it is always best to provide *written* notification and for the injured worker to keep a copy of the written notification.

Next, the worker gets medical treatment. In some states, the injured worker may choose the doctor she wishes to go to. Other states have industrial injury medical centers to which the employee can be referred. In California, to reduce medical costs, many employers have begun selecting medical provider networks for the treatment of injured workers. The state of Minnesota has something similar and calls these networks "certified managed care plans."

Frequently, a medical case-manager will be assigned to injured workers within the network. No matter what state system the injured worker is in, it is imperative if the worker has a life-threatening emergency that she is taken to the closest and best medical facility for the injury. However, if the employee needs to go undergo surgery or hospitalization in the future, the employee should notify the employer prior to entering the hospital.

The employer, in almost every state, is required to complete a form such as the "First Report of Injury" form. (See Figure 14.1.)

The employer then has a set amount of time, usually around ten days, in which the employer must report a claim resulting in time lost from work to the employer's insurance company. Most employers (or insurers) will provide the employee with an informational pamphlet on how to handle a workers' compensation claim.

After having had some initial medical treatment for stabilization, the employee should go to her state workers' compensation board and fill out a claim form and, if there is one, an application for adjudication of the claim. These forms will start the employee's claim with the Workers' Compensation Appeals Board. Most boards are extremely helpful to injured workers, providing informational clinics on how to handle workers' compensation claims or having an office at the board maintained by employees whose job it is to answer injured workers' questions.

The employee may have to undergo an independent medical examination ("IME") to help prove her case. In an IME, the doctor is chosen by the employer or the employer's insurance company. The employer or insurance company may also conduct surveillance on the employee to verify the employee is injured.

Depending upon the amount of time off work, the employee will be paid compensation in lieu of her salary. Most states hold that during the first few days of a workers' compensation injury (usually a week), the employee will not be compensated with workers' compensation for lost salary. Medical expenses are paid beginning from the time of the first treatment. Compensation for lost salary is based upon the employee's average monthly wage. This is determined from the last year's income.

If there is a dispute about benefits, then the agency responsible for each state's workers' compensation program is involved. A workers' compensation claim is filed at the workers' compensation board, not civil court. The workers' compensation board is considered an administrative hearing board.

A hearing is held on the disputed issues. The hearings are usually less formal than at the courthouse. Attorneys do not necessarily need to present the case; rather, a hearing representative or paralegal can present the case. The hearing board makes a decision. If the employee or employer does not like the decision, either party can appeal the decision to a court of law.

Figure 14.1

First Report of Injury Form

Minnesota Department of Labor and Industry
Workers' Compensation Division
443 Lafayette Road North
St. Paul, MN 55155-4305
(651) 284-5030

First Report of Injury

See Instructions on Reverse Side
PRINT or TYPE your responses.
Enter dates in MM/DD/YYYY format.

DO NOT USE THIS SPACE

1. EMPLOYEE SOCIAL SECURITY #	2. OSHA Case #

3. DATE OF CLAIMED INJURY	4. Time of injury	☐ am ☐ pm	5. Time employee began work on date of injury	☐ am ☐ pm

6. EMPLOYEE Name (last, first, middle)	7. Gender ☐ M ☐ F	8. Marital Status ☐ Married ☐ Unmarried

9. Home Address	10. Home phone #	11. Date of birth

City State Zip Code	12. Occupation	13. Regular department	14. Date hired

15. Average weekly wage	16. Rate per hour	17. Hours per day	18. Days per week	19. Employment Status	☐ Full time ☐ Part time ☐ Seasonal ☐ Volunteer

20. Weekly value of:	Meals	Lodging	2nd Income	21. Apprentice ☐ Yes ☐ No

22. **Tell us how the injury occurred and what the employee was doing before the incident (give details).** *Examples: "Worker was driving lift truck with a pallet of boxes when the truck tipped, pinning worker's left leg under drive shaft." "Worker developed soreness in left wrist over time from daily computer key entry."*

23. **What was the injury or illness (include the part(s) of body)?** *Examples: chemical burn left hand, broken left leg, carpal tunnel syndrome in left wrist.*	24. **What tools, equipment, machines, objects, or substances were involved?** *Examples: chlorine, hand sprayer, pallet lift truck, computer keyboard.*

25. Did injury occur on employer's premises? ☐ Yes ☐ No If no, indicate name and address of place of occurrence	26. Date of first day of any lost time	27. Employer paid for lost time on day of injury (DOI) ☐ Yes ☐ No ☐ No lost time on DOI
	28. Date employer notified of injury	29. Date employer notified of lost time
	30. Return to work date	31. Date of death

32. TREATING PHYSICIAN (name, address, and phone)	33. HOSPITAL/CLINIC (name and address) (if any)	34. Emergency Room Visit ☐ Yes ☐ No
		35. Overnight in-patient ☐ Yes ☐ No

36. **EMPLOYER** Legal name	37. EMPLOYER DBA name (if different)

38. **Mailing** address	39. Employer FEIN	40. Unemployment ID#

City State Zip Code	41. Employer's contact name and phone #

42. **Physical** address (if different)	43. Witness (name and phone)

City State Zip Code	44. NAICS code	45. Date form completed

46. **INSURER** name	51. **CLAIMS ADMIN COMPANY** (CA) name (check one) ☐ Insurer ☐ TPA
47. Insured legal name	52. CA address
48. Policy # or self-insured certificate #	City State Zip Code

49. Insurer FEIN	50. Date insurer received notice	53. CA FEIN	54. Claim #

MN FR01 (02/06)

Copies to: Insurer, Employer, Employee, and Workers' Compensation Division (if no insurer)

GENERAL INSTRUCTIONS TO THE EMPLOYER

Filing this form is not an admission of liability. You must report a claim to your insurer whenever anyone believes that a work-related injury or illness that requires medical care or lost time from work has occurred. If the claimed injury wholly or partially incapacitates the employee for more than **three** calendar days, the claim must be made on this form and reported to your insurer within **ten** days. Your insurer may require you to file it sooner. Failure to file within the **ten** days may result in penalties. Self-insured employers have 14 days to file this form with the Department of Labor and Industry (Department). It is important to file this form quickly to allow your insurer time to investigate the claim. **Your insurer will forward a copy of this form** to the Department, if necessary.

If the claim involves death or serious injury (including injuries that later result in death), you must notify the Department and your insurer within 48 hours of the occurrence. The claim can be reported initially to the Department by telephone (651-284-5041), fax (651-284-5731), or personal notice. The initial notice must be followed by the filing of this form within **seven** days of the occurrence.

Employers are required to complete this form. Each piece of information is needed to determine liability and entitlement to benefits. Failure to complete the form may result in delayed processing and possible penalties. You must file this form with your insurer, and give a copy to the employee and the employee's local union office. You are required to provide the employee with a copy of the Employee Information Sheet, which is available on the Department's web site at www.doli.state.mn.us. Employees are not responsible for completing this form.

SEND REPORT TO INSURER IMMEDIATELY— DO NOT WAIT FOR DOCTOR'S REPORT

SPECIFIC INSTRUCTIONS FOR COMPLETING THIS FORM

- Item 2:   OSHA Case #. Fill in the case number from the OSHA 300 log. This form contains all items required by the OSHA form 301.
- Items 15-20: Fill in all the wage information. If the employee does not work a regularly scheduled work week, attach a 26 week wage statement so your insurer can calculate the appropriate average weekly wage.
- Items 22-24: Be as specific as possible in describing: the events causing the injury; the nature of the injury (cut, sprain, burn, etc.), and the part(s) of body injured (back, arm, etc.); and the tools, equipment, machines, objects or substances involved.
- Item 26: Fill in the first day the employee lost any time from work (including time lost for medical treatment), even if you paid the employee for the lost time.
- Item 27: Check the appropriate box to indicate if there was lost time on the date of injury and whether you paid for that lost time.
- Item 28: Fill in the date you first became aware of the injury or illness.
- Item 29: Fill in the date you became aware that the lost time indicated in Item 26 was related to the claimed injury.
- Item 30: Leave the box blank if the employee has not returned to work by the time you file this form. If the employee has returned to work, fill in the date and notify your insurer if the employee misses time due to this injury after that date.
- Item 39: Fill in your Federal Employment ID number (FEIN). For information on this number, see www.firstgov.gov and click on Employer ID Number under Business.
- Items 40 and 44: Fill in your Unemployment ID number and North American Industry Classification System (NAICS) code which are both assigned by the Minnesota Unemployment Insurance Program (651-296-6141).
- Items 46-54: Your insurer or claims administrator will complete this information.

INSTRUCTIONS TO THE INSURER/CLAIMS ADMINISTRATOR/SELF-INSURED EMPLOYER

The following data elements must be completed on this form prior to filing with the Department of Labor and Industry: employee's name and social security number; date of injury; and the names of the employer and insurer. If any of this information is missing, the First Report will be rejected and returned to you (per Minn. Stat. § 176.275). Providing the name of the third party administrator does not meet the statutory requirement to provide the name of the insurer. NOTE: If the claim does not involve lost time beyond the waiting period or potential PPD, the form does **NOT** need to be filed with the Department.
- Item 46: Fill in the name of the insurance company. If the employer is self-insured, indicate the name of the licensed or public self-insured company or group.
- Items 47-48: Fill in the legal name of the employer who purchased the policy from the insurer (named in Item 46) and the policy number. If the employer is licensed to self-insure, fill in the certificate number.
- Item 49: Fill in the insurer's Federal Employment ID number (FEIN) number.
- Item 51: Fill in the name and address of the company administering the claim (either the insurer or third party administrator). Be sure to mark either the "Insurer" or "TPA" box.
- Item 53-54: Fill in the claims administrator's FEIN and claim number.

This material can be made available in different forms, such as large print, Braille or on a tape. To request, call (651) 284-5030 or 1-800-342-5354 (DIAL-DLI)/Voice or TDD (651) 297-4198.

ANY PERSON WHO, WITH INTENT TO DEFRAUD, RECEIVES WORKERS' COMPENSATION BENEFITS TO WHICH THE PERSON IS NOT ENTITLED BY KNOWINGLY MISREPRESENTING, MISSTATING, OR FAILING TO DISCLOSE ANY MATERIAL FACT IS GUILTY OF THEFT AND SHALL BE SENTENCED PURSUANT TO SECTION 609.52, SUBDIVISION 3.

14.7   When a Third Party Causes the Worker's Injury

When a third party causes the worker's injury, the employer has a right to sue the third party for damages, which will consist of the workers' compensation benefits paid to the injured worker. The question then becomes how does one identify third party claims? Often, it is easy, such as an auto accident caused by a third party injured the employee trucker's back. Premises liability and products liability might also apply. In premises liability, did the owner of property expose the employee entering the property to an unreasonable risk of harm? An example would be a slip-and-fall accident while an employee is making an off-site delivery. For products liability, there will be a machine or product that failed to perform as it was intended to perform. An example would be a broken chair. In these instances, the employer will be able to sue the responsible third party for reimbursement.

Court Clerks
By Robert Moore, Paralegal

Clerks are civil servants. They don't get any more pay for doing more work, and they work for a bureaucracy that is typically understaffed and underfunded. Don't ask them to do something that is not specifically their job. If you ask them to do something that is really your own job, they will almost certainly refuse. Sometimes they will refuse your requests even if it is their job and will direct you to another clerk. In dealing with clerks, always be polite, make sure you are in the right department for your request, and ensure that you have minimized their work. Your request should be necessary and sufficient for the task at hand — no more and no less. If your request involves things to be mailed to your law firm, send pre-addressed, stamped envelopes.

In the unfortunate situation where a clerk refuses to do his job, be polite but persistent. First, make doubly sure that you are in the right place and talking to the right person. Consider eventually making the clerk realize that he/she will have to spend more time and do more work to refuse your request than to grant it. The key is to do it in such a way that the clerk remembers you as a polite professional that needs to be taken seriously in the future, rather than someone he begrudges forever. One technique is persistence via the "unending conversation" where you politely continue to talk about the problem and never leave until the clerk grants your request. Another technique is to "pile on" requests — ask for the clerk's full name, number, email address, organizational structure, points-of-contact in the organizational structure (particularly the clerk's bosses), the services provided by organizational structure, etc., and then start requesting those services from the clerk. The next-to-last technique is to indirectly report the refusal of services to the clerk's boss (or boss's boss), never telling the clerk that you're doing that, and without actually making a formal complaint. Tell the clerk that you are just trying to find out who in the department is supposed to fulfill your request, and then ask to speak to the boss. Usually the clerk won't let things go that far. If you do talk to the boss, politely explain what happened, name the clerk who said that it was not his job, and ask whose job it is. If all else fails and a formal complaint needs to be made, it is better for the senior members of your law firm to do it, rather than you. They can afford to make an enemy of a clerk while you may not.

E T H I C S

Rule 5.5 Unauthorized Practice of Law; Multijurisdictional Practice of Law

(a) A lawyer shall not practice law in a jurisdiction in violation of the regulation of the legal profession in that jurisdiction, or assist another in doing so.[2]

Attorneys can delegate work to a paralegal. If an attorney improperly delegates work to a paralegal, then the attorney will have helped the paralegal commit the unauthorized practice of law. This would be a violation of Rule 5.5, above. However, this rule does not define what the practice of law is. Providing advice to clients is normally considered the practice of law. Paralegals have frequent interaction with clients and clients will often ask the paralegal for legal advice. It is unethical as well as illegal for a paralegal to offer the client advice. One of the other major reasons a paralegal does not want to offer a client advice is the paralegal may be named on a legal malpractice lawsuit, along with the attorney. The lawsuit exposes the paralegal to potentially paying the client legal damages. The best way to handle a request for advice is to remind the client you are not the attorney, but you will be happy to forward the question on to the attorney. Typically, paralegals cannot appear on behalf of clients in court or take depositions.

Unauthorized practice of law means a paralegal cannot represent a client in a court of law. However, workers' compensation is an appeals board, or an administrative hearing board. Paralegals can therefore represent clients in many administrative hearing proceedings. In the state of California, for example, hearing representatives, who are not attorneys, may represent clients.

Chapter Summary

Workers' compensation programs are funded by employers, either through insurance or out of the employer's own pocket. Workers' compensation is an alternative to a negligence lawsuit. The employee will not have to prove the employer was negligent in order to recover compensation under workers' compensation. Thus, workers' compensation is a no-fault system.

Even though the worker will not need to prove the employer was negligent, there are other factors the worker will have to prove in order recover under workers' compensation. The act giving rise to the injury must have occurred within the employer/employee relationship. There must have been a contract for the employment, whether the contract was express, or implied by the parties' conduct. The worker will still have to show proximate cause, i.e., that the injury was caused by the employment. The injury must have taken place during the course and scope of the employment. Course and scope refers to time and place. Typically, injuries occurring while the employee is taking care of his personal comfort (such as going to restroom at the job location) are covered under workers' compensation.

There are many exceptions under which a worker will not be covered by workers' compensation. These exceptions include injuries while the employee is intoxicated, self-inflicted injuries, and injuries that occur while committing a felony. Usually

---

2. Model R. Prof. Conduct 5.5 (ABA 2004).

injuries not occurring at the job location are not covered. The going-and-coming rule holds if the employee is injured while going or coming to/from work, the injury will not usually be covered. If the employee is engaged in horseplay at work, the injury resulting from horseplay is typically not covered by workers' compensation.

While each state has different rules about workers' compensation, there are benefits common to the workers' compensation system. These benefits include medical treatment, permanent disability benefits, temporary disability benefits, and vocational rehabilitation benefits. The employer, once it has determined there was a compensable workers' compensation injury, should pay for the medical treatment. Permanent disability payments come into play when the employee has a lasting injury, even after the employee has reached his maximum level of medical improvement. Temporary disability refers to a disability that can still be improved through further medical care. Vocational rehabilitation is used to help the worker return to the work place after the injury.

If the worker elects to receive compensation under workers' compensation, the worker cannot later sue the employer for negligence. Thus, workers' compensation is known as the "exclusive remedy."

Key Terms

- Assumption of the risk
- Contributory negligence
- Course and scope of employment
- Employee
- Exclusive remedy
- Going-and-coming rule
- Independent contractor
- Independent medical examination
- Insurance
- Medical Provider Network
- Occupational Safety and Health Act ("OSHA")
- Permanent disability
- Proximate cause
- Self-insurance
- Strict liability
- Temporary disability
- Vocational rehabilitation
- Wage replacement
- Workers' Compensation Appeals Board
- Work restrictions
- Workers' compensation

Review Questions

- What is the main purpose of the workers' compensation system?
- What type of activities taking place at work would still not be covered under workers' compensation?
- Does the employee make as much money on temporary disability as she makes while working? If not, then why is this not as inequitable as it sounds?

- How many recoveries does the employee get if she pursues a claim against a third party and her employer?

Web Links

- Further resources on workers' compensation include: www.law.cornell.edu/topics/workers_compensation.html, www.workerscompensation.com, and www.workerscompresource.com.

- www.cdc.gov/. One of the more helpful websites for workers' compensation issues is the Centers for Disease Control's website. The site discusses health issues in the workplace, such as the health risks of electric and magnetic fields. If you go into workers' compensation, many of the workers will have types of injuries you may not be familiar with, and this website is helpful in understanding the workers' condition.

- The United State Department of Labor has a good website (www.dol.gov) to look at when dealing with workers' compensation issues. The Department's Employment Standards Administration's Office of Workers' Compensation Programs (OWCP) runs four different workers' compensation programs. However, if a person is injured by a non-federal employer, then the employee will need to go through his state workers' compensation board. A listing of all the state workers' compensation boards is on this website as well.

Exercises

- Go to the Centers for Disease Control's website. Look in the Workplace Safety and Health section. Read about asbestos ailments. Determine what asbestos is.

- Look up the name, address, phone number, email, and website of the agency in your state responsible for handling workers' compensation claims.

- Which of the following, if any, scenarios occurred within the course and scope of employment?
  - Muhammad is an employee of a city library. He leaves work to go home. As soon as he exits the employee exit, a dead bird falls on his head and he suffers mental anguish as a result.
  - Lucius gets a half-hour for lunch every day. This only allows him time to eat at a hole-in-the-wall deli next to his place of work. He contracts food poisoning from eating at this deli.
  - Randolph races to work in the morning because there are only 50 parking spaces for the 150 employees where he works. He does not get to work in time

to grab one of the employee parking spaces and has to pay to park in a public lot. He is injured in this public lot, which is next door to the building where he works.

○ Franklin is allowed a half-hour for lunch and two 15-minute breaks a day. He uses his first 15-minute break to smoke a cigarette in the designated outside smoking location at this building. While snuffing out his cigarette, he pulls a muscle.

Discovery and Review of Medical Records

"Discharge status: Alive but without permission."[1]

Chapter Outline

15.1   Introduction to Discovery and Review of Medical Records
15.2   Discovery of Medical Records
15.3   Access to Medical Records by the Patient
15.4   Access by Third Parties in Light of the Health Insurance Portability and Accountability Act
15.5   Obtaining Medical Records
15.6   Dealing with Confidentiality of Medical Records
15.7   Why Review Medical Records?
15.8   Tips for Reviewing the Different Components of Medical Records
  a.   Outpatient Records
  b.   Ambulance Records
  c.   Emergency Room Records
  d.   Hospital Records
  e.   History and Physical
  f.   Charting
  g.   Progress Notes
  h.   Laboratory Test Results
  i.   Nursing Notes
  j.   Operative Records
  k.   Anesthesia Records
  l.   Medications
  m.   Discharge Summary

---

1. The quote was taken from an actual medical record, dictated by a physician. *See* http://www.creatingfutures. net/archive/jokes/medicalrecords.htm (accessed April 15, 2008).

Chapter Objectives

- Discuss the discovery of medical records by both the plaintiff and the defendant
- Explain how to deal with confidentiality issues arising from medical record requests
- Demonstrate how to review medical records by chronology and mention topic medical summaries
- Give tips on how to review medical records
- Place emphasis on the importance of medical records to the case in general and at trial in particular

15.1   Introduction to Discovery and Review of Medical Records

Discovery and review of medical records is a very common to most types of personal injury litigation. Medical records are some of the most important evidence in many personal injury cases. Because obtaining medical records is crucial to so many different types of tort litigation, including negligence, medical malpractice, intentional torts, strict liability, products liability, and workers' compensation, this information is placed near the end of the book.

Access to medical records is regulated by law to protect the privacy of the patient. Health care providers can be penalized if the providers release patient information without the proper authorization. Thus, certain procedures must be followed to obtain medical data. This chapter covers the legal ways to obtain access to medical records.

This chapter further discusses why medical records review is so important to a case and focuses on the types of things to look for while reviewing the components of medical records. Helpful methods in organizing the summaries of the records are discussed and a chronological summary is illustrated.

15.2   Discovery of Medical Records

The discovery of medical records is essential to most types of tort litigation. When a plaintiff is injured through negligence, the plaintiff must prove his medical damages. Whenever the plaintiff initiates a medical malpractice claim, some of the first records the attorney will want to obtain are the medical records. If the plaintiff is assaulted and battered (which are intentional torts, see Chapter 9), then the plaintiff needs to show evidence of any physical evidence he suffered. Even if the plaintiff is injured in strict liability (Chapter 12) or under products liability (Chapter 12), the plaintiff has to show evidence of his medical injuries, if any, if the plaintiff wants to be reimbursed. Workers' compensation also requires proof of a plaintiff's work injury through medical records. Medical records are one type of evidence that can prove injury to the plaintiff. Reviewing medical records is normally a paralegal's job. The paralegal needs to review the medical records for important information and summarize the information.

15.3   Access to Medical Records by the Patient

The patient can request his medical records, which normally should be provided to the patient within 30 days. This is a national standard. The medical provider can extend the 30 days to a total of 60 days for good cause. The patient has to pay for the cost of copies and postage. Others who may obtain records are parents of minor children, legal guardians, or an agent (for example, someone designated in a Health Care Power of Attorney).

15.4   Access by Third Parties in Light of the Health Insurance Portability and Accountability Act

Health Insurance Portability and Accountability Act (HIPAA)
a federal standard addressing who can obtain an individual's medical information.

The **Health Insurance Portability and Accountability Act (HIPAA)** is a federal standard addressing who can obtain an individual's medical information. HIPAA was originally drafted in 1996, but Congress asked the United States Department of Health & Human Services (HHS) to amend HIPAA to include regulations regarding medical records privacy and security. These privacy regulations went into effect on April 14, 2003. HIPAA covers personal written, oral, or electronic medical data. In addition, each state may have stricter patient privacy laws.

Nursing and doctors' notes, the patient's medical complaints, any alcohol and drug treatment, mental health counseling, and billing are protected. For example, this information cannot be shared with the patient's employer unless the patient signs an authorization. Information can be passed between medical providers for the patient's treatment; for billing purposes; for the government to check on the standard of care being provided and for nursing home safety; for the government to report on disease; and to report gunshot wounds.

Almost all health care providers must comply with HIPAA, including but not limited to doctors, nurses, medical clinics, hospitals, pharmacies, and nursing homes. In addition, health insurance companies, health management organizations (HMOs), Medicare, and Medicaid must comply with HIPAA.

Due to the new privacy laws enacted by HIPAA, there are only three ways a third party (someone other than the patient) can obtain medical records. The first way is to obtain an authorization from the patient. An authorization is necessary for the disclosure of medical information under HIPAA. An **authorization** is a detailed document giving medical providers the permission to disclose health information to a third party.

Authorization
a detailed document giving medical providers the permission to disclose health information to a third party.

A medical authorization should have the following elements:

- a description of information to be disclosed,
- the medical provider authorized to disclose the information,

■ the person who is receiving the disclosure, and
■ the expiration date of the authorization.

The authorization should discuss the medical information to be released in a "specific and meaningful fashion."[2] If the patient is your client, the patient is usually willing to sign an authorization you, the paralegal, prepare for him. (See Figure 15.1.)

Figure 15.1

Medical Authorization

Medical Authorization

To: Medical Provider

   Re: Dates of Service from _____ to _____

This authorization will serve to allow my attorney, _____, located at _____, to obtain copies of my medical records, including the following checked items:

_____Admission Records

_____Discharge Summary

_____History/Physical Exam

_____Consultation Reports

_____Operative/Procedure Reports

_____Emergency Department Reports

_____Progress Notes (including Nurses' Notes)

_____Laboratory Tests

_____X-ray Reports

_____Photographs, Videotapes, or Other Images

_____Out-patient Records

_____Anesthesia Records

_____Medications

_____Other: _____

In addition, you have my specific authorization to release the following sensitive information:

_____HIV/AIDS tests

_____Psychiatric Treatment

---

2. *See* 45 CFR 164.508(b)(1) and 164.508(c)(1)(i).

_____Alcohol Treatment

_____Drug Abuse Treatment

This medical treatment facility may not further use or disclose this medical information unless I so authorize or such disclosure is required by law. This authorization is effective beginning on the date signed and continuing until either 1) I revoke the authorization in writing or 2) one year expires from the date this authorization is signed.

My attorney will comply with all requirements of the privacy rule under the Health Insurance Portability and Accountability Act of 1996 (45 CFR 160 and 164).

Signature of Patient: _____

Name of Patient: _____

Date of Birth: _____

Social Security Number: _____

Telephone Number: _____

The second way to obtain medical records is to use a subpoena, which may be necessary for defense counsel. Defense counsel may not be able to obtain a medical authorization from the plaintiff. The subpoena must be served on the custodian of the medical records. The third way to obtain medical records, as a defense paralegal, would be to obtain the records from the plaintiff's attorney. However, the more preferable method is to obtain the records directly from the facility because the plaintiff's attorney may not provide the entire medical record to the defendant.

15.5 Obtaining Medical Records

Once you have obtained a medical authorization or subpoena, most law firms have the paralegals work with a specialized legal copy service (called an attorney service) to obtain the medical records. Usually, you will call whichever attorney service your law firm or individual client uses. Some clients have specific contracts with attorney services and want the law firm to use that service for the clients' cases. The attorney service will prepare the request to the medical facilities, take care of any upfront copying charges, and arrange for the copies to be delivered to the law firm's office. While attorney services have greatly increased the efficiency of obtaining records, the paralegal is the one responsible for making sure the attorney service actually obtains the records and properly bills the client or firm.

The following is a starting list of key documents to obtain during medical records discovery:

- Ambulance records
- Emergency room records

- Hospital records, including administrative records, a history and physical, charting, and progress notes
- Admitting records
- Lab results
- Nursing notes
- Operative records
- Medications
- Pharmaceutical bills
- Medical examiner's report
- Death certificate
- X-rays
- MRIs
- CAT scans
- EKG strips
- Physical therapy records and bills
- Insurance policies
- Psychiatric records
- Occupational therapy
- Any alcohol/drug abuse treatment

15.6   Dealing with Confidentiality of Medical Records

The confidentiality of medical records is important to receiving proper medical care. If a patient does not feel safe disclosing medical conditions (such as a sexually transmitted disease or a pregnancy) to her health care provider, then how can the patient receive appropriate medical care? The implementation of HIPAA has increased medical provider's sensitivity to this issue. If a medical provider, without consent or another legally viable reason, lets out confidential information about a patient, the provider could be sued for a breach of confidentiality. Confidential information needs to be obtained during the doctor-patient relationship and should be protected so patients can receive the best care.

Doctor-patient privilege
information related to treatment that is provided by a patient to a treating doctor does not normally have to be disclosed in litigation.

The **doctor-patient privilege** protects the information a patient provides to a treating doctor. The information provided must be related to the treatment of the patient. The doctor-patient privilege holds these communications do not have to be disclosed in the process of litigation. However, the doctor-patient privilege is not an absolute privilege, which can never be waived. The doctor-patient privilege is a qualified privilege, meaning the privilege will not apply when the subject matter of the litigation is the plaintiff's physical injuries, caused by the defendant. In this type of litigation, the information provided by the patient, to the doctor, must be disclosed to prove the plaintiff's case. The privilege does not belong to the doctor, but to the patient. The patient is the one who can waive the doctor-patient privilege.

15.7   Why Review Medical Records?

The first assignment a paralegal in a personal injury law firm may be given is to review medical records and provide a summary of those records. Often, a paralegal is asked to summarize medical records as the records arrive in the office. Some law firms organize medical records into binders or organize the medical records from each health care provider into file folders. Some law firms tab the different sections of the medical records or flag important passages. Depending upon the number of pages, an index of the medical records after Bates stamping the records may be required. Bates stamping is consecutively numbering exhibits, starting at the number one. The numbering is placed on the bottom right hand corner of the page by a stamp called a Bates stamp, by labels, or by Bates numbering software. Frequently, while performing medical record review, the medical records will refer to other treatment the plaintiff had at another facility. Ask the attorney whether he would like you, as the paralegal, to obtain those additional records.

The main goal of medical record review is to ascertain whether the plaintiff's allegations, such as physical injuries, are substantiated by the medical records. If the plaintiff's allegations are substantiated, the next questions are whether the plaintiff's injury is as severe as claimed and whether the plaintiff is claiming the proper amount of medically related damages. The medical bills need to be obtained in addition to the medical records to ensure the plaintiff is claiming the proper amount of medical damages. See Chapter 5 for more information on damages.

Another issue to look for in reviewing medical records is falsified records. Although the majority of cases will not involve falsified medical records, a paralegal should keep an eye out for falsified records during the medical records review. Alteration of medical records can be huge to a plaintiff's case because altered records may provide evidence the defendant knew he was wrong. There are a variety of ways in which to falsify medical records, such as

- late entries,
- falsifying entries,
- making up medical records,
- destroying medical records,
- omitting information, and
- purposefully making medical records impossible to read.

However, there are many changes a medical provider can make to medical records without falsifying those records. Many nurses and doctors make changes to medical records to correct simple writing mistakes. When medical providers make corrections in an improper way, it raises suspicion of wrongdoing, but does not absolutely prove wrongdoing. If a defendant or plaintiff did falsify a medical entry, it is a criminal offense.

To review records for falsification, check that all pages in the medical record have the patient's information on one of the corners. Frequently, even without any intent of wrongdoing, medical records are misfiled and an x-ray or lab from one patient may be inadvertently placed into another patient's file. Another way to determine whether there has been medical record falsification is to look at the medical bills in comparison to a patient's chart. If there are bills for procedures not referenced in the chart, then that may be indication of falsification.

15.8   Tips for Reviewing the Different Components of Medical Records

Paralegals are often expected to review the medical records although they do not have prior medical training. Reviewing Appendix A of this book, An Introduction to Medicine, is a start to becoming more knowledgeable about medicine. While you will not be expected to be a medical expert, you will be expected to summarize the important information within the medical records. The following is a list of tips to help you in figuring out what to look for within the different components of medical records. This list is not exhaustive. This is a general listing and you, as the paralegal, will need to review the complaint and case to determine what the major issues of the case are and then review the medical records with those issues in mind as well.

a.   Outpatient Records

Outpatient records are often organized as follows:

- office notes,
- consults,
- labs,
- consent forms,
- correspondence, and
- bills.

Outpatient records may be more in-depth than hospital records regarding any drug or family problems, and thus are even better to review for those issues than hospital records.

Tips on What to Look for in Outpatient Records

- Determine why the patient went to see this doctor.
- Check whether the doctor performed a detailed history and physical. What information can you obtain about the patient from the history and physical?
- Did the doctor refer the patient to any other health care provider for a consultation? If so, you may need to obtain those additional records.
- Note any medications the patient is taking, along with the dosage, and how long the patient has been taking those medications. Look those medications up and determine what conditions the medications treat.

b.   Ambulance Records

There may or may not be an ambulance record, depending upon how the plaintiff was transported and whether the plaintiff needed emergency medical care. Many times ambulances are used in nonemergency situations, such as transportation to dialysis or transferring nursing home patients.

Tips on What to Look for in Ambulance Records

- Compare how the patient was when the ambulance picked him up, during the ambulance ride, and his status upon admission in the hospital. Was the patient dead on arrival?
- Was the ambulance a basic life support unit or an advanced life support unit? Basic life support units cannot perform all the life saving techniques advanced life support units can.

---

c.   Emergency Room Records

When patients arrive in the emergency room, they are assessed as to how urgent their status is, also known as triage.

Tips on What to Look for in Emergency Room Records

- How imperative was the patient's status considered? Was the patient high on the triage list?
- Determine whether the emergency room saw the patient in a time that was reasonable to the problem.
- Was the emergency room able to treat the patient in the emergency room or was the patient transferred to another part of the hospital?

---

d.   Hospital Records

Administrative records should contain both an admission and discharge sheet. There should be a form with the different primary and secondary diagnoses listed, along with a consent form to hospital treatment when the patient was admitted. The consent form should include a clause for the hospital to release information to the patient's insurance company for payment.

Tips on What to Look for in Administrative Records

■ Find the primary and secondary diagnoses.
■ Figure out the patient's insurance company so you can also request or subpoena the insurance company for records.

e.   History and Physical

The history and physical should have a summary of the patient's entire past medical history (including smoking or drinking), family medical problems, and the current illness.

Tips on What to Look for in the History and Physical

■ What was the patient's primary complaint when entering the facility?
■ Review the patient's medical history to see if his past medical history contributed to his current problem. For instance, make sure to note any drug or alcohol problems, which will strengthen or weaken the case.
■ Did the patient have a family history of this medical problem, which would make him predisposed to having this medical problem?

f.   Charting

Doctor's orders should be in the chart, with a date. Determine what tests and procedures were ordered.

g.   Progress Notes

The doctor's progress notes should be made on a daily basis and should note any changes in the patient's health. Progress notes include test results and responses to treatments.

Tips on What to Look for in Progress Notes

■ Were there any changes in the patient's health?
■ What were the test results?
■ How did the patient respond to treatment?
■ How frequently were progress notes made?

h. Laboratory Test Results

Laboratory test results normally have to be evaluated by a medical professional. However, if you are able to see any abnormal lab results, determine whether the health care provider noticed those abnormal results and treated the patient accordingly.

i. Nursing Notes

In addition to the above-referenced history and physical, nurses also perform their own history and physical upon admission. The nurses are looking to assess the patient's physical abilities (whether the patient is able to walk or use the restroom independently), mental status, and allergies. The nurses also take a list of the patient's medications. Ongoing nurses' notes will include patient's daily complaints, such as pain. In addition, the nurses' notes will discuss IVs and medication.

Tips on What to Look for in Nursing Notes

- What are the patient's abilities?
- Is the patient alert?
- What are the patient's allergies?
- What are the patient's medications?
- Are there indicators of the plaintiff's pain and suffering?

---

j. Operative Records

Operative records include a consent form specific to the particular surgery. The consent will be important if the plaintiff has raised informed consent as an issue.

During the procedure, the nurses or anesthesiologists should note the skin coloration. In simple outpatient procedures, the nurse may note the skin coloration. In the majority of more complex surgeries, the patient is almost completely draped, and it is the anesthesiologist's responsibility to monitor respiratory and circulatory function, including skin coloration. The nursing notes or anesthesiologist's notes will also note the time the procedure began and ended. The operative records may contain notes about whether sponge and instrument counts before and after surgery matched. This is a big issue if a sponge or instrument was left in the patient.

Tips on What to Look for in Operative Records

- Look for the status of the patient upon entering into surgery.
- See if the vital signs were taken and what the signs were.
- Did the patient have anything to eat or drink?
- Did the sponge and instrument count before and after surgery match?

k. Anesthesia Records

The anesthesia records should record what the patient's prior experiences with anesthesia were. They should also include a detailed accounting of the patient's medications so the anesthesiologist can make sure he is using the proper anesthesia.

Anesthesia records are important to summarize if the plaintiff is alleging his condition after surgery is due to the anesthesia, rather than the surgery itself.

l. Medications

Determine whether the patient had reactions to the medication prescribed while he was in the hospital.

m. Discharge Summary

There should be a plan upon discharge, such as whether the patient is to follow up with any specialists upon leaving the hospital.

If correctly drafted, this document will include the dates of the hospitalization, the admitting diagnosis, the treatment, any complications to the treatment, and how the patient is doing upon his discharge. Therefore, if any of this information was not already in prior medical records, the discharge summary is another place to look for the information. Frequently, there will also be included any aftercare instructions to the patient and/or to his family if the patient is unable to execute those instructions by himself.

Tips on What to Look for in the Discharge Summary

- Was the patient referred to any specialists? If so, you may need to obtain those records.
- How is the patient doing upon his discharge?
- Do the discharge instructions state the plaintiff is to refrain from certain activities, such as working?

---

n. Autopsy

The most important issue with autopsy reports is the cause of death, which should be listed in the report. When looking at an autopsy, make sure the toxicology reports, if any, have been included. In addition, the opposing side may try to contest the autopsy by attacking the doctor's methods in performing the autopsy. Look at the tests the doctor performed and research whether the tests are widely accepted in the medical community.

> ## Tips on What to Look for in Autopsy Records
>
> - What is the cause of death?
> - Are there any toxicology reports?
> - What tests did the coroner employ? Are these tests widely accepted in the medical community?

o. Miscellaneous Records

There are a number of medical records that might not be produced when the medical records are requested. These records must be specifically named in order to obtain them. For instance, in an obstetrics case, ask specifically for the fetal heart monitor strips, which are not normally produced with the records. X-rays are common documents that must be mentioned by name. Many times, actual films are not kept; rather the x-rays are on computer disks and must be separately produced. These records are not produced because they are often different shapes and sizes in addition to being kept separately from the patient's file.

Ambulance records will not be included in the emergency room report and need to be obtained separately from the ambulance company. There will also be an audiotape of radio communication between the ambulance and the hospital, which will be separately kept. Autopsy records may be considered separate from the hospital records, in which case the paralegal will have to make another records request.

In order to receive HIV testing results, have the plaintiff sign a special medical records release. This also applies to mental health or substance abuse records. The authorization, earlier, can be used to obtain those records.

15.9 Analyzing Medical Records by Chronology or Topic

The purpose of a medical summary is to condense information. Summaries are often sent to insurance company clients and can be extremely helpful to attorneys who are reviewing the case, preparing to meet with experts, preparing for depositions, or preparing for trial. Medical experts, who normally charge a high rate, may look at the chronologies, although most will review the medical records themselves rather than rely on a summary. Another reason to summarize medical records is to determine the issues and determine what documents will be exhibits at trial. A chronological summary is the most commonly used in the legal field. With a chronological summary, a paralegal summarizes the records in date order and adds the medical provider's name with a short summary of the record. (See Figure 15.2.) In the sample medical summary, be sure to look up the terms which you are unfamiliar with.

A topical or subject matter summary organizes the medical information into specific subjects. For instance, if a plaintiff has more than one physical injury, then different topics could be: the right hand, left knee, and neck.

Figure 15.2

Summary of Medical Records

Medical Provider	Date	Summary
Dr. Remington	4/21/08	Orthopedic consultation. Right shoulder pain since accident. Difficulty with abduction. Pain across right scapula, radiating into right elbow. Pain in left elbow, radiating into left shoulder. No numbness or tingling in left arm. Difficult to dress. Cervical x-rays show spine is relatively straight. Cervical muscle spasms. IMPRESSION: impingement syndrome and tendonitis, right shoulder with adhesive capsulitis; severe chronic sprain and strain superimposed with degenerative disc disease at C4/5 and C5/6; lumbosacral sacroiliac sprain with restricted motion; trigger finger, left middle finger.
X-Ray Report	4/21/08	Moderate severe degenerative disc disease C4/5 and C5/6 with spondylosis; normal osseous study, right shoulder.
Progress Note	5/15/08	Recheck of neck and back. Injection to middle finger not helpful. Decreased pain in left elbow. No locking in left middle finger. Right arm continues to be painful. IMPRESSION: impingement syndrome with bursitis/tendonitis, right shoulder and adhesive capsulitis; severe chronic sprain and strain superimposed with degenerative disc disease of the cervical spine. RECOMMENDATIONS: MRI of right shoulder, Celebrex, bone density study.
MRI	6/14/08	Intermediate signal intensity with supraspinatous tendon suggesting tendinopathy; mild hypertrophy of acromioclavicular joint.
Progress Note	6/24/08	Numbness and tingling in right shoulder. Patient has been seeing a neuromuscular massage therapist who has been working on her trigger points. Patient believes therapy has helped range of motion. She has been working with no restrictions.
Nerve Conduction Study	7/19/08	Normal left median nerve conduction study.

Attorney work product
the ideas, thoughts, and
working papers an attorney
generates while working
on a case.

Make sure to label the summaries as attorney work product so the summaries will not be produced during the discovery phase of litigation. **Attorney work product** includes the ideas, thoughts, and working papers an attorney generates while working on a case. The work product rule also applies to your work on behalf of the attorney on a case.

Despite all your research into the different medical problems and treatments, you are not a nurse or a doctor. Therefore, there will always be sections of the medical records, such as heart monitor strips, that a paralegal will not be able to summarize. Depending on the importance of these strips to the case, the law firm may need to obtain an expert to read those.

If and when you cannot read something contained in the medical records, do not make an educated guess at what the writing states. A better practice would be to ask the copy service to recopy the medical record. If you still cannot read the information, bring the issue up to your attorney, who might want to set the medical provider's deposition. The attorney can then ask the medical provider what the record states at the deposition.

15.10   Medical Records at Trial

Remember, the medical records you request and summarize may be introduced at trial. Even though medical records are considered hearsay, they can still be admitted in court. Hearsay is an out-of-court statement used to prove the truth of the matter asserted in the context of that statement. The Federal Rules of Evidence 803(b) states a hearsay exception is:

> A . . . record . . . of acts, events, conditions, opinions, or diagnosis, made at or near the time by . . . a person with knowledge, if kept in the course of a regularly conducted business activity, and if it was the regular practice of that business activity to . . . record . . . all as shown by the testimony of the Custodian or other qualified witness, unless the source of information or the method or circumstances of preparation indicate lack of trustworthiness (1998).

Business records, such as medical records, are exceptions to the hearsay rule. If the attorney lays a proper foundation, then the medical records, as business records, may be allowed into evidence at trial even though medical records are hearsay. To lay a proper foundation, the attorney has to show the medical record was created near the time of the medical treatment, the person who created the medical record had knowledge of the treatment, and the medical record was a record regularly kept in the course of the medical provider's normal business. The attorney needs the help of the paralegal in obtaining and reviewing the medical records so the attorney can effectively use the records at trial.

Document Review
By Doreen Vega, Paralegal

Going through documents is very time-consuming and extremely important in the field of law. Looking for privileged documents, noting the author of documents, and labeling documents by department are just a few reasons why Excel and other computer programs are so vital. As a paralegal, it is paramount that the value of each document is rightfully noted, and to note this information into the computer as you go through the documents up front, even thought this may lead to additional time. However, on the other end, when information is being requested by the attorneys, the paralegal will be able to obtain the requested information quickly and efficiently.

For example: if you have a document, you note the origination of the document by author, department, and that it supports plaintiff or defendant into the computer. When the attorney is requesting information about plaintiff or defendant, the same information will come up. This cross-referencing is done for you automatically because the effort was made up front when reviewing the documents.

I saw first-hand requests by attorneys to the paralegal that was mentoring me. David Garcia would get a request, go to his computer, type in key words and then the notations regarding the documents would be displayed, including where the original documents were located so that the documents could be retrieved promptly. This documentation in the computer was also essential for David when he would be in meeting with the attorneys regarding a specific case. Many times attorneys would ask specific questions in the meetings and David had the information in front of him. By printing out the information he had downloaded into the computer and taking it to the meeting with him, David was able to answer the questions right on the spot. This not only saved time, it made David invaluable to the attorney.

I was impressed by how quickly David could find the information the attorneys requested, and he knew where the originals were. When David would go through the documents while he was inputting information, he would scan the documents that he felt were important. There is so much paper in our field that knowing where to find a particular piece of information instantly is a valuable asset. David made a difficult task seem easy, and I saw the respect he was given for his quick and efficient responses.

E T H I C S

Model Rules of Professional Conduct
Client-Lawyer Relationship

Rule 1.8 Conflict Of Interest: Current Clients: Specific Rules

  (a) A lawyer shall not enter into a business transaction with a client or knowingly acquire an ownership, possessory, security or other pecuniary interest adverse to a client unless:

    (1) the transaction and terms on which the lawyer acquires the interest are fair and reasonable to the client and are fully disclosed and transmitted in writing in a manner that can be reasonably understood by the client;

    (2) the client is advised in writing of the desirability of seeking and is given a reasonable opportunity to seek the advice of independent legal counsel on the transaction; and

    (3) the client gives informed consent, in a writing signed by the client, to the essential terms of the transaction and the lawyer's role in the transaction, including whether the lawyer is representing the client in the transaction.

(c) A lawyer shall not solicit any substantial gift from a client, including a testamentary gift, or prepare on behalf of a client an instrument giving the lawyer or a person related to the lawyer any substantial gift unless the lawyer or other recipient of the gift is related to the client. For purposes of this paragraph, related persons include a spouse, child, grandchild, parent, grandparent or other relative or individual with whom the lawyer or the client maintains a close, familial relationship.

(d) Prior to the conclusion of representation of a client, a lawyer shall not make or negotiate an agreement giving the lawyer literary or media rights to a portrayal or account based in substantial part on information relating to the representation. . . .

(j) A lawyer shall not have sexual relations with a client unless a consensual sexual relationship existed between them when the client-lawyer relationship commenced.[3]

The attorney is responsible for avoiding conflicts of interest between the paralegal interests and the client.

Loyalty to the client is required of both the paralegal and the attorney. The lawyer and paralegal should be working for the benefit of the client and not a conflicting interest. A **conflicting interest** is an interest that might be considered a higher priority than the client's interest or might compete with the client's interest.

An example of a conflict of interest in a torts case would be the attorney representing both the plaintiff and the defendant. The two parties' interests are opposed. The plaintiff wants to recover monetary damages from the defendant. The defendant wants to avoid paying monetary damages. The lawyer cannot work on both sides and do a proper job for each side.

A conflict of interests check must be done prior to representing any client. The paralegal is often expected to perform the conflict of interest check. This check involves the paralegal reviewing the list of clients to determine that a potential new client's interests are not opposed to any prior clients.

Ethics exercise: Review Model Rules 1.7 through 1.13, which discuss conflicts of interest.

Chapter Summary

One of a paralegal's key jobs in personal injury litigation will be to obtain medical records. If you represent the patient, this is fairly easy. Prepare an appropriate authorization for release of medical records, have the client sign it, and send the authorization to the medical provider so the records will be copied. If you represent the defendant and the plaintiff(s) will not provide an authorization or the medical records themselves, you may have to obtain a subpoena for the records. Either way, you must take into consideration the Health Insurance Portability and Accountability Act, which causes reluctance on the part of health care professionals to freely provide medical records.

Medical records are important in determining the value of a case. The main goal of a medical record review is to verify the plaintiff's allegations of physical injuries. If the plaintiff's allegations are substantiated, then the medical bills also need to be verified against the amount in damages the plaintiff is requesting for medical

---

3. Model R. Prof. Conduct 1.8 (ABA 2004).

expenses. While paralegals are not expected to be medical experts, they are expected to review the records. This chapter provides some tips for you, as a paralegal, in reviewing the records. These tips are general and a paralegal must review the file regarding specific issues to look for while reviewing medical records. Two ways in which to review medical records are by chronology (in the time order of the treatment) and by topic (by body part). Chronological summaries are more common than topical summaries. Medical records are important in proving a case because the records can also be admitted at trial. Therefore, it is important the paralegal properly obtain the records and review the records.

Key Terms

- Attorney work product
- Authorization
- Chart
- Chronological summary
- Conflicting interest
- Confidentiality
- Consent form
- Diagnosis
- Discharge summary
- Doctor-patient privilege
- HIPAA
- Medical history
- Release/medical records release

Review Questions

- What are some ways medical records may be obtained?
- How does doctor-patient confidentiality promote the gathering of accurate information from patients?
- What elements should be contained in a medical authorization?
- What are some ways medical records might be falsified?
- How might a patient's prior medical history influence the strength of his case?
- Give an example of organizing a patient's medical records chronologically.
- Where might the interpretation of records by a medical professional be useful in the summary of the records?

Web Links

- The Centers for Disease Control's website (www.cdc.com) is a wonderful website for learning about different medical conditions.
- www.katsuey.com describes itself as the "consumer's gateway to the law." The material on Katsuey is free. One of the nice features of this website is that it will

link you to acronym finders, which are helpful in reviewing medical records. When you are starting your job search, this is also an important resource to remember as it has a legal jobs directory. Some of the job searches are free and some are fee-based.

■ There is a good listing of prescriptions along with their descriptions located at www.rxlist.com.

Exercises

Review the following medical records and prepare a chronological summary. The medical records are for the same plaintiff.

Results   **Chest X-Ray 2 VW**

Allergies
(Not on File)

Rad Entry information

Entry Date	Entry Time	
4/21/08	3:32 p.m.	Resulting Agency
		UNIVERSITY ANCILLARY SYSTEM

Result Narrative
CHEST PAIN

COMPARISON STUDIES:
None
HISTORY:
41-year-old F; chest pain
TECHNIQUE:
PA and Lateral Chest Radiographs
FINDINGS:
See Impression

Result Impression
IMPRESSION:

1. No acute cardiopulmonary disease.
2. Moderately well expanded lungs. No focal consolidation, edema, or pleural effusion.
3. Unremarkable cardiomediastinal silhouette.
4. No acute bony abnormalities. Mild dextroconvex scoliosis at the lower thoracic spine.

I have reviewed the images and agree with the resident's interpretation.

NM Bone Scan Whole Body   CARSON, NORMA
Final Report
Result type: NM Bone Scan Whole Body
Result date: 18 March 2008 10 a.m. PST
Result status: Auth (Verified)
Verified By: Peterson MD

Final Report*

Reason for Exam
Other (See Special Instructions)
Interpretation
NUCLEAR MEDICINE WHOLE BODY SCAN

History: Scapular pain.

Technique: 27.2 mCi of technetium-99m MDP were administered with anterior and posterior views of the skeletal system three hours post injection.

Findings: The scapula shows symmetric and normal uptake. There are degenerative changes about the acromicoclavicular joints. There is a focal area of increased activity in an anterior lower right rib. There are multifocal areas of increased activity in the cervical, thoracic and lumbar spine. Degenerative changes are present about the great toes bilaterally.

IMPRESSION:
No evidence of abnormal scapular uptake.

Anterior right first rib activity, probably correlating with a fracture in the patient's reported history of a fall.

Multifocal areas of increased activity in the spine, which may be degenerative. Correlation with plain films would be useful.
END OF IMPRESSION.

The Tort Litigation Process Before Trial

Discovery consists of seeing what everybody has seen and thinking what nobody has thought.[1]

Chapter Outline

Chapter Objectives

- Describe the importance of insurance in personal injury lawsuits
- Discuss how policy limits affect settlement amounts
- Introduce the concept of the "duty to defend"
- Explain no fault insurance
- Show how to draft a complaint
- Illustrate how to prepare a deposition summary
- Discuss discovery requests and responses
- Discuss how to prepare clients for their deposition

---

1. Albert Szent-Gyorgyi von Nagyrapolt, *The Scientist Speculates* (1962).

16.1 Introduction to Tort Litigation Before Trial

This chapter covers the practicalities of the job for a paralegal involved in personal injury cases. This chapter gives an account of what a personal injury case entails and what may be expected of the paralegal. While acting in support of an attorney working on a personal injury case, the paralegal will often be involved in

- information gathering through discovery, such as interrogatories and depositions;
- obtaining a court reporter and helping prepare deponents for their depositions;
- summarizing deposition transcripts;
- helping arrange medical treatment and evaluation; and
- searching for medical experts to testify.

Pleading
a document by which the parties make allegations against one another.

> ## *Warning*
>
> The rules regarding the content and form of **pleadings** and discovery documents vary from one jurisdiction to the next. The paralegal must be thoroughly familiar with those rules before drafting pleadings or discovery.

16.2 Insurance

Insured
the holder of the insurance policy.

Typically, a defendant will be insured. Insurance is provided pursuant to a contract between the **insured** (the holder of the insurance policy) and the insurance company. If the insured is sued for a loss covered under the policy (such as the insured causing an automobile accident), then the insurance company frequently has a duty to defend the insured by hiring a lawyer. While the insurance company pays for the attorney, the attorney works for the insured. An insurance company usually has certain attorneys who have agreed to defend the insurance company's insureds. Many personal injury paralegals work for these attorneys.

Plaintiff's attorneys usually will not sue a defendant without insurance, because individual defendants are unlikely to have sufficient assets from which to pay a legal settlement. If a defendant does have insurance, the likelihood of a plaintiff being able to recover money is greater. Car accidents are one area of personal injury where insurance plays a major role. Most drivers have motor vehicle insurance. Many states require registered automobiles to have motor vehicle insurance. There may be a minimum amount of automobile insurance coverage required.

Example

In the state of California, there is a legal requirement that drivers maintain $15,000 of insurance per person, and $30,000 insurance per accident. In addition, if a California driver obtains automobile insurance but later cancels the insurance, the Department of Motor Vehicles is notified of the cancellation.

If there is a car accident and the police respond, the police will often fill out an accident report with information about each driver's insurance. The accident report is thus important to obtain as early as possible because it contains information necessary for contacting the insurance company and information helpful in discovery.

Common types of insurance include the following:

- accident insurance,
- car insurance,
- contractor's insurance,
- homeowners' insurance,
- liability insurance,
- malpractice insurance,
- product liability insurance,
- property insurance, and
- workers' compensation insurance.

Declarations page
page or pages of the insurance policy, which names the insured the covered cars, and the amount of the policy.

The two most common types of insurance are automobile insurance and homeowners' insurance. Automobile insurance policies include a declarations page, a discussion of liability coverage, and a discussion of uninsured or underinsured motorist coverage. The **declarations page** of an insurance policy names the insureds, the covered cars, and the amount of the policy. (See Figure 16.1.)

Figure 16.1

Example of Declarations Page

State: Colorado
Policy Number: 00188 72 82U 0117 7
Policy Period: April 5 2008-October 5 2008
Operators: Wesley Kent & Ned Kent
Name Insured and Address: Wesley Kent, 83211 Coolridge Ave, Thornton, Colorado 80233
Description of Vehicle:

Veh	Year	Brand	Model	Body	Total Mileage	Identification #	Use
1	07	Toyota	Prius	4D	10,000		Work

This vehicle is principally garaged at the above address.

COVERAGES (LIMITS OF LIABILITY)	VEHICLE 1 DEDUCTIBLE	VEHICLE 1 6-MO PREMIUM
Part A — Liability Bodily Injury Each Person $500,000 Each Accident $1,000,000 Property Damage Each Accident $100,000		$91.83 $55.63
Part C Uninsured Motorists Bodily Injury Each Person $500,000 Each Accident $1,000,000 Waiver of collision deductible		$27.15 $4.21
Part D Physical Damage Coverage Comprehensive Loss Actual Cash Value Collision Loss Actual Cash Value Towing & Labor	$500 $500	$20.86 $60.51 $5.88

Vehicle 1 Total Premium for 6 Mo.: $266.07

If an insured causes an accident, the insurance company will pay the person who was injured as part of the insured's liability coverage. Liability coverage includes bodily injury and property loss. Typically, the insurance policy is discussed as one amount per person and a larger amount per accident.

Example

$15,000 might be paid per person, with a total of $30,000 paid per accident. Thus, if three people were injured in one accident, the total recovery would be $30,000, not $45,000.

Uninsured motorist coverage
insurance protection for the insured when she is hit by a driver without insurance.

Underinsured motorist coverage
insurance protection for the insured when she is hit by a driver without enough insurance to pay all the costs of the accident.

Extended coverage
additional insurance.

Despite laws requiring motor vehicle insurance, many drivers do not have insurance. If a woman is hit by a driver who has little to no insurance, her own insurance company may step in to compensate her if she has uninsured motorist coverage. **Uninsured motorist coverage** covers the insured when she is hit by a driver without insurance. Underinsured motorists do not have enough insurance to cover the total cost of the injury. **Underinsured motorist coverage** covers the insured when she is hit by a driver without sufficient insurance to pay all the costs of the accident.

Homeowners' insurance insures the owners of a single-family home. Basic homeowners' coverage may include losses due to fire, lightning, wind, or hail. **Extended**, or additional, homeowners' coverage can provide personal liability protection, or coverage for different types of physical losses. A homeowners' insurance policy usually specifically excludes losses caused by the operation of automobiles. This is one reason why people carry car insurance.

Examples of a Potentially Covered Homeowner's Losses

- The death of one of the family's children in the family swimming pool may be covered by the homeowner's insurance.
- If the family dog bit a guest, the homeowner's insurance may cover this injury.

Liability insurance covers the insured for losses caused by the insured, as outlined by the policy. These losses could include bodily injury or property damages. Intentional injuries are not normally covered by liability insurance. In addition, liability insurance does not often cover punitive damages. If you, as the paralegal, work for an insurance defense firm, the insurance company will most likely be concerned about insurance fraud. One way in which to catch insurance fraud is by using a personal investigator. The following is an example of insurance fraud:

Insurance Fraud Example

Rodney rented a U-Haul-It-Yourself trailer. While in the U-Haul-It-Yourself trailer, Rodney was hit by another truck. He suffered injuries. Rodney instituted a lawsuit against U-Haul-It-Yourself's (he sued the company in addition to the driver, trying to get more money). During the trial against U-Haul-It-Yourself, Rodney worked at a used car lot. On the last day of the trial, while working at the used car lot, Rodney performed a back flip. A private investigator recorded the back flip and the insurance company for U-Haul-It-Yourself argued the back flip proved Rodney was making a false insurance claim. Rodney settled his claim because of the tape of the back flip. The story made the local news. An assistant district attorney saw the news and pursued the matter. Rodney was found guilty of a felony for making a false insurance claim.

16.3 Complaints

Basic Facts Needed to Prepare a Complaint:

The parties' names
The county and state where the parties reside
The facts of the case
The location of the incident

Complaint
the first pleading from the plaintiff, which begins a civil action and consists of the plaintiff's allegations against the defendant.

A complaint begins a civil action and consists of the plaintiff's allegations against the defendant. A **complaint** gives notice to both the defendant and the court of the plaintiff's claims. Prior to writing the complaint, the paralegal needs to obtain sufficient information from the client through a client questionnaire.

See Appendix B for a sample. Each firm has a slightly different version of this document. The questionnaire should at least ask for the following information:

- all of the plaintiff's previously used names and addresses,
- the plaintiff's prior employment,
- education,
- a thorough medical history,
- prior injuries (pay particular attention to prior injuries involving the same body parts), and
- other accidents/insurance claims.

Normally, the paralegal will limit the inquiries on the questionnaire to the last five to ten years. If the client is reluctant to provide this information, take this as a red flag warning. Once the client files a lawsuit her life — even areas supposedly unrelated to the suit — will be scrutinized. If she is not willing to answer the questionnaire, she should imagine the questions the defense will ask.

Most clients cannot immediately recall the above information, so the paralegal should send the questionnaire to the client prior to the initial client meeting. The **initial client meeting** is the first meeting where the client comes to the law office.

At home, the client can then refer to her personal documents (such as address books) to answer the questions. The initial client meeting can be used to clear up any issues raised by the questionnaire. Prior to the meeting, the paralegal should prepare any medical or employment authorizations for the client's signature. This allows you, as the paralegal, to obtain those records much more easily. The Appendix of this book goes into further detail on the actual conduct of the initial client meeting.

Using the information provided in the questionnaire and the initial client meeting, a complaint will be drafted. There are several different sections to a complaint. The part of the complaint below, outlining the court and the parties, is called the caption. After the caption comes the body of the complaint, which consists of general allegations (those allegations before the causes of action) and the causes of action (so labeled). The facts the plaintiff provided will be used to meet the elements of different causes of action. At the end of the complaint is the prayer for damages, where the plaintiff requests damages. Find and identify each section in Figure 16.2.

Initial client meeting
the first meeting where the client comes to the law office.

Figure 16.2

Sample Complaint

Emily Lynch Morissette, Esq.
123 Main Street
Anywhere, Any State

Attorney for Plaintiffs, John and Jane Johnson

IN THE SUPERIOR COURT OF THE STATE OF ANY
STATE IN AND FOR THE COUNTY OF ANYWHERE

JOHN AND JANE JOHNSON,) Plaintiffs,)) vs.)) FRED FLINTS and DOES 1-25, inclusive,)) _____Defendants._____)	Case No.: COMPLAINT FOR PRIVATE NUISANCE AND NEGLIGENCE PER SE

COMES NOW PLAINTIFFS TO FILE THE FOLLOWING CROSS-COMPLAINT AGAINST DEFENDANT AND DOES 1-25, INCLUSIVE, as follows:

1.   Plaintiffs are, and at all times relevant herein were, individuals residing in the County of Anywhere.

2.   Defendant is, and at all times relevant herein was, an individual residing in the County of Anywhere.

3.   The County of Anywhere is the proper venue for this action because the Defendant resides in Anywhere County, was doing business in the County of Anywhere, and the acts complained of in this complaint were committed in Anywhere County.

4.   Plaintiffs are presently unaware of the true names or capacities of Defendants named herein as Does 1-25, inclusive. Plaintiffs will seek leave of Court to allege their true names and capacities after same have been ascertained. Plaintiffs are informed and believe and thereon allege that the Defendants, Does 1-25, inclusive, dispute Plaintiffs contentions and are in some manner legally responsible for the acts and omissions alleged herein, and actually and proximately caused and contributed to the various injuries and damages referred to herein.

5.   At all times herein, Plaintiffs and Defendant are neighbors. Plaintiffs' residence is located directly across the street from Defendant's residence.

6.   Since on or about 2004, Defendant has been using his garage to make furniture for sale to the public. Defendant runs electrically powered equipment at all times during the day and evening. The noise levels from these tools violate local noise control ordinances.

7.   Plaintiffs have been listening to the blaring noise from Defendant's woodworking business since Defendant has been working with this equipment in his garage. Plaintiffs have attempted to discuss this situation with Defendant but Defendant continues to use his garage to build furniture with his power tools.

8.   Plaintiffs have filed many complaints with the police department regarding the noise blaring from defendant's property. To date, none of the police's actions have had any effect on Defendant's actions. Plaintiffs have also sought to enjoin Defendant from creating this noise. The Plaintiffs have obtained temporary restraining orders against Defendant in the past for creating this noise as well as other behaviors by the Defendant stated below.

FIRST CAUSE OF ACTION

PRIVATE NUISANCE

9.   Plaintiffs refer to and incorporate herein by reference paragraphs 1-8 as though fully set forth herein.

10.   The noise from Defendant's power tools and Defendant's actions towards Plaintiffs has created a private nuisance as defined in the Civil Code Section _____. Defendant's acts are injurious to the health of Plaintiffs, offensive to their senses, and/or an obstruction to the free use of their property so as to interfere with the comfortable enjoyment of their lives and/or property.

11.   Defendant's acts have substantially and unreasonably interfered with the interests of Plaintiffs. There is no legal justification for Defendant's actions.

12.   Therefore, Plaintiffs pray for judgments against Defendant for the above-described injuries and losses, as described below.

SECOND CAUSE OF ACTION

NEGLIGENCE PER SE

13.   Plaintiffs refer to and incorporate herein by reference paragraphs 1-12 above as though fully set forth herein.

14.   Defendant has the duty to obey noise ordinances created by local government.

15.   Defendant has breached this duty by running his power saws and power sanders at all times during the day and evening. The noise created by these power tools exceeds the limits proscribed by local government.

16.   Plaintiffs have been damaged by Defendant's breach of duty by having their right of quiet enjoyment ruined by the noise produced by Defendant's power tools and this occurrence is of the nature of which the statute was designed to prevent. The Plaintiffs are among the class of persons for whose protection the statute was adopted.

17.   Defendant's actions and resulting breach of duty is the proximate cause of Plaintiffs' damages.

18.   Since Defendant's negligence has violated a city ordinance, this is negligence per se.

19.   Wherefore, Plaintiffs pray for judgments against Defendant for the above-described injuries and losses, as described below.

PRAYER FOR RELIEF:

PLAINTIFFS PRAY FOR:

1. Damages for pain and suffering according to proof at trial;
2. Medical expenses according to proof at trial;
3. Compensatory damages according to proof at trial;
4. Costs of suit incurred in bringing this action; and
5. Such other and further relief as the Court deems necessary.

Dated this _____ day of September 2007

Respectfully Submitted,

_____

Emily Lynch Morissette, Esq.
Attorney for Plaintiffs

Figure 16.3

Proof of Service

PROOF OF SERVICE
Re: [Case Name]
Case No.:

Certificate of service
a specialized proof of service, used for complaints, which states under the penalty of perjury how the defendant was served.

Proof of service
a document, declaring under penalty of perjury, that the person who signed the document served the document.

Personal service
when a party to the lawsuit is served himself, usually by handing the document to him or by placing the document in his presence.

Substituted service
service on a party to the lawsuit that is not given to the party directly, but usually to another member of the defendant's household and then mailed to the defendant.

Default
the defendant's failure to answer the plaintiff's complaint.

I declare that I am over the age of eighteen, am not a party to this case, and am employed in the county of _____. My business address is _____. I served the Case Management Statement [or other document] by sealing and placing it in the regular course of the U.S. mail with the proper postage affixed, addressed as follows:

[addresses]
Signed at [city], [state]
Dated: January 14, 2008

_____
Emily Lynch Morissette

The complaint must be served within specific time limits, usually within 30 to 60 days. Check your jurisdiction to determine the applicable time limit. Also, in addition to serving the complaint in a timely manner, a certificate of service must be filed. A **certificate of service** is a specialized proof of service, used for complaints, which states under the penalty of perjury how the defendant was served. A **proof of service** is a document, declaring under penalty of perjury, that the person who signed the document served the document.

An example of a proof of service is Figure 16.3. Service can be achieved through a variety of ways. For example, did a process server hand the complaint to the plaintiff, such as is done in **personal service**? Or did the process server use **substituted service**, where service is given to another member of the household and then mailed to the defendant?

The defendant can respond to the complaint by answering the complaint, filing a counter or cross-claim (discussed below), filing a motion, or **defaulting** (failing to answer).

16.4 Answers

Answer
the defendant's response to the complaint, which admits, denies, and/or states the defendant has insufficient knowledge to admit or deny plaintiff's allegations made in the complaint.

General denial
a refusal of all allegations of the complaint.

An **answer** is the defendant's response to the complaint. An answer admits, denies, and/or states the defendant has insufficient knowledge to admit or deny the plaintiff's allegations made in the complaint. A statement of insufficient knowledge to admit or deny must be made in good faith. If the defendant can easily obtain the information, then stating the defendant has insufficient knowledge is not a good faith response. If the defendant does not deny an allegation, then the allegation is considered admitted by the defendant. A **general denial** denies all allegations of the complaint.

Specific denial
a refusal of a particular allegation of the complaint.

Affirmative defense
a new issue, which constitutes a defense to the plaintiff's allegations, even if the plaintiff's allegations are assumed to be true.

Counterclaim
a pleading made by the defendant in opposition to the plaintiff's claims.

Cross-claim
a pleading made by the defendant against a co-defendant.

Venue
the county in where the lawsuit should be brought.

Demurrer
a motion by one party arguing that even if the other party's facts can be proven at trial, those facts do not meet the elements required for the cause of action.

Specific denials are for a certain numbered paragraph in the complaint and respond to just the particular allegation. The answer must parallel the complaint and be organized in paragraphs and by counts.

Affirmative defenses are raised by the defendant in the answer. An affirmative defense is a new issue, which constitutes a defense to the plaintiff's allegations, even if the plaintiff's allegations are assumed to be true. An affirmative defense does not negate an element of a cause of action alleged in the complaint. An affirmative defense can provide justification for the defendant's conduct, such as self-defense. Affirmative defenses are raised in the answer so the plaintiff has a chance to respond.

A defendant also has a right to make a **counterclaim** against the plaintiff. A counterclaim is a pleading made by the defendant in opposition to the plaintiff's claims. The defendant can also raise a **cross-claim**, a claim against a co-defendant. The defendant has the opportunity to file motions for lack of personal jurisdiction, lack of subject matter jurisdiction, or improper venue. **Venue** is the county in where the lawsuit should be brought. The defendant can challenge the complaint by making a demurrer, or motion to dismiss for failure to state a claim. A **demurrer** is a motion by one party arguing that even if the other party's facts can be proven at trial, those facts do not meet the elements required for the cause of action. Finally, the defendant could decide not to respond to the lawsuit at all, which is considered a default. See Figure 16.4 for examples of affirmative defenses.

Figure 16.4

Examples of Affirmative Defenses[2]

Failure to State a Cause of Action

The defendants allege that such complaint, and each and every cause of action alleged therein, fails to state facts sufficient to constitute any cause of action.

Statute of Limitations

The plaintiff's cause of action did not occur within three years before the beginning of this action and is therefore barred by the applicable statute of limitations.

> ### *Warning*
>
> Always calendar the statute of limitations date both in the computer calendar and on the paper calendar. Not all statutes of limitations are uniform. Some statutes of limitations are one year, while others are two or three years. Missing a statute of limitations may mean the plaintiff cannot file a lawsuit.

---

2. Please note not all of the affirmative defenses will be available in every jurisdiction.

Acts of God

As a separate and affirmative defense to the _____ cause of action, defendant alleges that the property damage alleged in the complaint herein, if any, was the result of an irresistible, superhuman cause which could not be foreseeably anticipated and whose effects could not be prevented by reasonable care. This irresistible, superhuman cause was _____ [an example of a superhuman cause would be an earthquake]. It caused the damages to real property alleged in the complaint, if any, by _____.

Consent

The plaintiff was fully informed of the risks inherent in this medical procedure and freely consented to the procedure.

Failure to Mitigate Damages

As a separate affirmative defense to the complaint, the defendant alleges that the plaintiff has failed, refused, and neglected to do all that was reasonable under the circumstances to avoid, minimize, and properly mitigate his damages, if any, which damages are expressly denied, thus barring recovery in whole or in part.

Privilege

The statements made by the defendant, as alleged in the complaint, were privileged.

Unclean Hands

As a separate affirmative defense to the complaint, the defendant alleges that to the extent plaintiff seeks equitable relief, his inequitable conduct constitutes unclean hands and therefore bars the granting of such relief.

Waiver

As a separate affirmative defense to the complaint, the defendants allege that the plaintiff has waived any and all claims made by him in the complaint.

Comparative Fault

If the plaintiff did in fact suffer any injury the injury was directly and proximately contributed to by the negligence, recklessness, fault and conduct of the plaintiffs, and damages of plaintiffs, if any, should be reduced in proportion to the amount of negligence due to the fault of the plaintiffs.

Self-Defense

At the time and place mentioned in the complaint for battery, plaintiff willfully and wrongfully and without just cause or provocation assaulted and battered defendant by coming at the defendant with a knife [or whatever weapon was used] and threatening the defendant, placing the defendant in reasonable fear of his personal safety and life. The defendant responded to this assault by doing only those acts that were reasonably necessary for his self-defense and safety and was justified in doing so.

Truth

The defendant alleges that the statements plaintiff complains of were not false. Rather, the statements were completely truthful.

Assumption of the Risk

As a _____ separate and affirmative defense to the _____ cause of action, defendant alleges that the plaintiff's injuries were proximately caused by her own misconduct, as plaintiff read but failed to obey the signs clearly posted on the animal's cage which warned that "these animals bite and are poisonous." Plaintiff placed herself in a position where she could be seriously injured in that plaintiff stuck her finger into the animal's cage. Plaintiff did this act voluntarily and with full understanding not only of the danger and risk she faced, but also the magnitude of this danger and risk, in that she knew that sticking her finger in the cage might result in the animal's biting her finger, injecting poison, and seriously injuring the plaintiff, both of which events plaintiff alleges occurred. Plaintiff invited the injuries of which she complains by the foregoing misconduct, and plaintiff assumed the risk of the injuries suffered.

Figure 16.5

Sample Answer

SUPERIOR COURT OF _____

COUNTY OF _____

PETER THOMPSON,
    Plaintiffs,
 	
vs.
 	
CLAIRE SIMPSON and DOES
1-25, inclusive,
 	
         Defendants.
	)))))))))))	Case No.:
		
		ANSWER TO COMPLAINT

Defendant, Claire Simpson, answers the complaint of the plaintiff, Peter Thompson, in this action as follows:
1. In regards to paragraph 1, defendant admits that she is an individual residing in this _____County, _____. Defendant denies the remaining allegations in the paragraph.

2.   In regards to paragraph 2, defendant is without sufficient information or belief to admit or deny the allegations in this paragraph. Based on this lack of information or belief, defendant denies the allegations.

3.   In regards to paragraph 3, defendant denies each and every allegation contained therein.

4.   In regards to paragraph 4, defendant admits the allegations contained therein.

5.   In regards to paragraph 5, defendant denies the allegations in this paragraph.

6.   In regards to paragraph 6, defendant denies the allegations in this paragraph.

7.   Admit.

8.   Deny.

FIRST AFFIRMATIVE DEFENSE

Fails to State a Cause of action

9.   The complaint is barred by the plaintiff's failure to state a cause of action.

SECOND AFFIRMATIVE DEFENSE

10.   The plaintiff's injuries and damages were caused by the plaintiff's own negligence, which was the sole proximate cause of any such injuries and damages.

WHEREFORE, the defendant requests judgment as follows:

1.   That the plaintiff take nothing by the complaint, and that the complaint be dismissed.

2.   That the defendant recover from the plaintiff costs in the amount to be proven.

3.   That the Court order further relief as it deems reasonable.

Date:

_____

Leslie Shane, Attorney for
Defendant

16.5   Discovery

Discovery Checklist:

_____ Calendar discovery cut-off dates ordered by the court (cut-off dates are the dates by which discovery must be sent or answered).

_____ Interrogatories

_____ First Request for Production of Documents

_____ Second Set of Interrogatories, if needed

_____ Second Request for Production of Documents, if needed

_____ Depositions

_____ Deposition Summaries

_____ On Site Inspections of Scene, if needed

_____ Reports obtained from both sides' experts
_____ Expert Designations
_____ Requests for Admission

Discovery
the means in which the
opposing parties gather
information on the other side's
facts and evidence

Even after the complaint and answer have been submitted, very little is known about each side's case. Discovery is the part of the case where each side tries to find out as much as possible about the other side's case. **Discovery** is the means in which the opposing parties gather information on the other side's facts and evidence. Discovery allows each side to gather nonprivileged information about the other side's case. If a matter is privileged, then it may not be obtained during discovery. For instance, documents with an attorney-client privilege should not be produced during discovery.

Digital Discovery

95 percent of all corporate business documents are made electronically and 75-80 percent of that information is never printed.[3] Due to the high percentage of electronic-only Information, it is essential paralegals become knowledgeable about obtaining digital discovery.

Types of Electronic Data are

- word processing,
- spreadsheets,
- PowerPoints,
- e-mail,
- instant messaging,
- voice mail,
- internet browsers, and
- the list keeps getting longer as technology evolves.

Meta data
data about data; stored
information which does not
show up on the printed
document, but can be accessed
if someone has the document
electronically.

Meta data is stored information, which does not show up on the printed document, but can be accessed if someone has the document electronically. In other words, meta data is data about data. For instance, when saving a document, word processing programs save information about the document, such as the author of the document. If the document is sent electronically, the recipient can view the information. In addition, if a paralegal uses original documents for a second client, and if the document is sent electronically, the recipient can often find out who was the original client. This is a breach of client confidentiality. Meta data shows information copied over in an electronic document, such as a Microsoft Word document.

---

3. University of California, Berkeley, *How Much Information* (2003 Study).

a. Interrogatories

Interrogatories
written questions answered
under oath.

Interrogatories are written questions answered under oath. Only the defendants and plaintiffs have to answer written interrogatories. Written interrogatories are not sent to witnesses. Unless the opposing party refuses to answer written interrogatories, a court normally does not get involved in written interrogatories, or any type of discovery. If a party refuses to answer interrogatories, then a motion to compel discovery responses may be necessary. The parties start the discovery process themselves, by sending questions to the other party. There are standard interrogatories, called form interrogatories, containing set questions. Special interrogatories allow each party to ask questions that were not covered in the form interrogatories. Special interrogatories contain questions created by each party to the other party. Some jurisdictions limit the number of interrogatories a party may send.

Typically, the interrogatories are sent to the client and the client is asked to answer the interrogatories using her own information. If the law firm is representing a corporation, the person who will be answering the interrogatories on behalf of the corporation needs to be determined. The person answering on behalf of the corporation has to use the information available to the corporation when answering the questions. The client sends the interrogatory responses to her attorney. Usually, the paralegal prepares draft responses with the help of the information sent by the client. Then the paralegal or attorney will meet with the client to go over the responses. The final answers are drafted, along with any objections to the questions. Once the final version is prepared, then the responses are sent to the opposing attorney.

Some proper objections to discovery are irrelevance, privilege, or that the question seeks protected information. Other frequently used objections are vague, overbroad, or burdensome. Additional objections include:

- ambiguous,
- assumes facts not in evidence,
- calls for a legal conclusion,
- calls for an expert witness opinion,
- compound,
- the document speaks for itself,
- the document is the best evidence,
- beyond the scope of allowable discovery,
- attorney-client privilege, and
- attorney work product.

Examples of Discovery Objections

- **Answer to Interrogatory number 3:** The defendant objects to Interrogatory number 3 as the interrogatory asks for irrelevant information, which is unlikely to lead to the discovery of admissible evidence.
- **Answer to interrogatory number 4:** The defendant objects to Interrogatory Number 4 as it asks for information that is protected by the attorney-client privilege.

As a paralegal, you may be expected to prepare form interrogatories and special interrogatories. In order to do this, the paralegal will need a good understanding of the case from having read the file. The following interrogatories are geared more towards a defendant asking the questions of a plaintiff. This list is not an exhaustive list of all the reasons for asking these questions. Commonly asked questions in form interrogatories might include:

- Name: You will need to request the client's full name.
- Date of birth: Date of birth is useful in obtaining the correct medical records for a plaintiff.
- Address: The address is also helpful for accurately identifying the parties. In addition, in some cases (i.e., nuisance) the value of the property may be in issue.
- Social security number: Sometimes a client will hesitate to provide his social security number; however, most records requests now require a social security number to verify the correct records are being produced.
- Relationship: Nowadays, it is not sufficient to ask if someone is married, as many people now cohabitate without being married. However, legally, usually spouses have more rights than cohabitants. This is a good time to ask whether a woman has retained her maiden name or not.
- Information about children: Children may be an important part of a lawsuit if the children depended upon the plaintiff's wages and the plaintiff's wages were reduced after an injury.
- Education: The plaintiff's education is important in determining what jobs the plaintiff may be able to perform after an injury.
- Felonies: Felonies, especially felonies involving a person's veracity (such as forgery or cashing a bad check) can reflect on a person's ability to tell the truth. Felonies can, sometimes, be used to impeach a witness on the stand (impeachment is discussed in the following chapter).
- Hobbies: Hobbies are a good subject matter to broach in interrogatories as well as depositions because often the plaintiff will discuss a hobby she continues to perform that exceeds what she states she currently is able to physically perform or what the doctor indicates the plaintiff should be able to physically perform.
- Injuries: Determine the extent of any injury. Find out the location of pain, along with the duration and the intensity of the pain. Ask when and where treatment was provided. If the plaintiff has the information, ask them to provide the cost of such treatment. Request the names and addresses of all medical providers so medical records can be requested. Determine whether the plaintiff is still receiving medical treatment. In addition to treatment, ask what medications were taken and are being taken.
- Social security, workers' compensation, or disability payments: If working for the defense, ask whether the plaintiff has a disability qualifying for social security disability. Obtain the dates the payments were received, the types of injuries, whether or not there is a current disability, and whether the plaintiff had the

disability at the time of the injury. Repeat the process for workers' compensation payments. Another way to obtain information regarding past medical claims is to ask for the plaintiff's insurance information, and then subpoena those records.

- Income and tax returns: In the chapter on damages, proof of lost wages was discussed. Lost wages need to be verified by looking at income records (such as W-2s) or tax returns.
- Prior hospitalizations: Prior hospitalizations can help reveal any past medical conditions the plaintiff had, particularly to the same body part involved in the injury.
- Information regarding medical providers: Obtaining information about medical providers makes it easier to subpoena medical records.
- Employment history: Past employment is particularly important when a plaintiff will not be able to return to the job she was performing at the time of the accident. The plaintiff may have skills allowing her to find another job. If working for the defense, request the names and addresses of the plaintiff's employers, the dates of employment, a description of the job, wages, and the name of the supervisor. If needed, discovery can later be sent to the supervisor to verify this information.
- Current Employment: To prepare an estimate of the potential damages, ask whether the plaintiff lost any time from work as a result of the accident, the number of days off work, and the amount of any lost wages. Obtaining the name and address of the employer is important so as to separately verify this information.
- Any other out-of-pocket expenses: A defendant needs to know the total amount of all damages being claimed by a plaintiff.

With written interrogatories other than form interrogatories, the paralegal is going to want to know the who, what, when, where, and why regarding the incident. To get an idea of how to prepare these as your firm would like, do a computer search for interrogatories on similar cases and use those interrogatories as examples.

Example of an Interrogatory

Have you taken any medications for the injury which you attribute to the accident? If so, please state the name of the medication, who prescribed the medication, how long you took the medication, and your cost for the medication.

As the paralegal receives and sends interrogatories and responses, she needs to index them so the interrogatories and responses are easily referenced. A discovery index is like a table of contents for the discovery. Look for a prior case with a discovery index to determine how the particular law firm wants the discovery indexes set up. If there is not a discovery index, either in a file or on the computer, use the following as a general guideline. On one side of a file folder will be the index with the requests tabbed. On the other side of the file folder will be the index with the responses tabbed.

Left Side of File Folder:

Tab No.	Date	Request Propounded to Client
1	1/18/08	Form Interrogatories, Set No. 1

Right Side of File Folder:

Tab No.	Date	Responses to Requests
1	2/10/08	Response to Form Interrogatories, Set No. 1

It is also the paralegal's responsibility to calendar discovery due dates. Check your jurisdiction for the time to propound discovery. For instance, if the paralegal propounds (sets forth) discovery to the other side, and the other side has 25 days plus 5 for mailing, then the paralegal needs to calendar the other side's responses for 30 days. If the responses to the requests are not received by the 30-day deadline, the paralegal will need to notify the attorney. The attorney will make a decision on whether a motion to compel discovery responses should be drafted.

b. Depositions

Deposition
oral questions, taken under oath.

Lay Witness
a person who saw the event.

Deponent
the person being deposed.

Depositions are oral questions, taken under oath. Depositions can be taken of the plaintiff, defendant, and witnesses. **Lay Witnesses** include those people who saw the event, such as an accident. Witnesses can also be a medical expert or a doctor who treated the plaintiff. The person being deposed is called the **deponent**. The benefit to depositions is the attorney can ask follow-up questions immediately after an answer. The attorney taking the deposition is the deposing attorney. The attorney for the deponent (who may or may not be a party) is the defending attorney.

Depositions are taken under oath, so if a deponent lies, the deponent can be prosecuted for perjury. Also, like trial testimony, the deposition is typed up by a court reporter. Frequently the paralegal is expected to set up the court reporter. Even though a court reporter is used, depositions do not occur in court. Depositions normally take place in an attorney's conference room. Depositions can be tape recorded, through audio or visual means. Videotaping may be necessary if the deponent may no longer be alive or available at trial. Some clients, such as insurance companies, require the attorney to use a certain court-reporting agency. This is because the insurance company has negotiated rates with the court-reporting agency. When setting up the appointment with the court reporter, make sure the client will pay for the specific court reporter.

Your paralegal responsibilities, in regard to oral depositions, are to schedule when and where the deposition will be if your attorney is the deposing attorney. You need to take into consideration the schedule of the deposing attorney, the defending attorney, and whether the location is available. Once you have found a suitable date, send out notice of the deposition. If you are unable to obtain the schedule for the defending attorney, just set the deposition. This will result in the attorney's office getting back to you if the deposition is not convenient for them.

Figure 16.6 is an example of a notice of deposition. This notice of deposition is specific to California; the paralegal needs to research the code sections on notice of deposition for her state before preparing a notice of deposition for a state other than California.

Figure 16.6

Notice of Deposition

PAUL THORNTON, ESQ. (SBN 123456)
1234 Sunset Road
Los Angeles, CA
Telephone: 945-5000

Attorneys for Defendant, Biotech, Inc.

SUPERIOR COURT OF THE STATE OF CALIFORNIA

COUNTY OF LOS ANGELES

Thomas O'Hare,	)	Case No.: GIC 456789
	)	
Plaintiffs,	)	
	)	NOTICE OF DEPOSITION OF NANCY
	)	DOUGHERTY
	)	
vs.	)	
	)	Dept: 10
Biotech, Inc. and Does 1 through 25,	)	Judge: Winnable
inclusive,	)	
	)	
Defendants.	)	

TO ALL PARTIES AND THEIR ATTORNEYS OF RECORD:

NOTICE IS HEREBY GIVEN pursuant to California Code of Civil Procedure Section 2025 that Defendant Biotech, Inc. will take the deposition upon oral examination of Nancy Dougherty, commencing on July 10, 2006 at 9:00 a.m. at the offices of its counsel, Paul Thornton, 1234 Sunset Road, Los Angeles, CA and continuing from day to day thereafter until completed. **NOTICE IS FURTHER GIVEN** that under California Code of Civil Procedure Section 2025.220(a)(5), the deposition testimony may be recorded by audio and videotape and instant visual display of testimony.

Dated: _____, 2006   By:

_____
PAUL THORTON, ESQ.
Attorneys for Defendant,
Biotech, Inc.

Subpoena duces tecum
a document with the power
of a court behind it
commanding a witness in the
lawsuit to bring documents to
the deposition.

Along with the notice of deposition, you will need to prepare a subpoena duces tecum if the attorney wants the deponent to bring records with the deponent to the deposition. A **subpoena duces tecum** is a document with the power of a court behind it, commanding a witness in the lawsuit to bring documents to the deposition.

If it is the law firm's client who is to be deposed, have the client come to the office before the deposition to prepare for her deposition. Paralegals are often in charge of preparing the client for her deposition. One of the best ways to prepare the deponent is to review questions that will probably be asked of the deponent at the deposition. The paralegal should go over the pleadings, discovery, medical records, and any potential exhibits with the client. The deponent should review any prior statements she made. The paralegal needs to explain to the client what a deposition is and what the deposition procedure is. It is helpful, prior to this process, for a paralegal to sit in on a deposition so the paralegal will be able to fully explain the process. The paralegal should tell the client the defending attorney will make any necessary objections. The client should pause before answering so the defending attorney can make these objections. In addition, the paralegal needs to go over the following guidelines with the client:

- The deponent must tell the truth; otherwise, she is committing perjury.
- The deponent should listen to the questions and make sure she understands the questions before she answers. If she does not understand a question, she should not answer it.
- The deponent should take a moment to think about what she wants to say before she answers.
- It is fine to for the deponent to state she "doesn't know" or "does not remember."
- The deponent should dress as if she is going to church with her Grandma. The other attorney is sizing the deponent up to see how she would look at trial.
- The deponent should not bring any documents to the deposition without first having her attorney look at those documents. The other attorney will ask for the documents at the deposition.
- The deponent should not make jokes. Jokes do not come across well when reread from the deposition transcript, after the deposition.
- The deponent should not volunteer information, as this will lead to additional questioning.
- The deponent should not guess at an answer.

Once you, as a paralegal, receive the transcript, you will often be asked to summarize the transcript. The following is an actual deposition, though the names of the people were changed. The deposition begins with admonitions, which is common in most depositions. **Admonitions** are statements from the deposing lawyer who is taking the deposition to the deponent that discuss the deponent's duties. The admonitions are often similar to the guidelines the paralegal went over with the client prior to her deposition. The foremost duty a deponent has is to tell the truth. The deponent is under oath. The deposing attorney usually also tells the deponent the deposition will be transcribed into a booklet and the deponent will have a chance to

Admonitions
statements from the lawyer
who is taking the deposition to
the deponent that discuss the
deponent's duties.

change her answers after the booklet is sent to the deponent. The deposing attorney will warn the deponent that if she does change her answers, the deposing attorney will potentially comment on those changes.

The attorney will ask the client to speak audibly and not make nonverbal gestures. The deponent will be asked not to interrupt the deposing attorney. The deponent will also be asked whether she feels well enough to testify. (For a sample deposition, see Figure 16.7.)

Figure 16.7

Sample Deposition

SUPERIOR COURT

PAULINE DEVRY,	)	Case No.: GIC 123456
	)	
Plaintiffs,	)	
	)	
vs.	)	
	)	
GREEN HOSPITAL CAFETERIA, INC. and	)	
DOES 1 through 25, inclusive	)	
	)	
Defendants.	)	

Deposition of Pauline DeVry
Monday, April 23, 2007.
Reported by: Carrie Watson

Appearances:
For the plaintiff:

    Law Office of John St. Paul
    Attorney at Law
    123 Main Street
    Anytown, USA

For the defendants:

Brenda Newton
Attorney at Law
125 Main Street
Anytown, USA

Deposition of Pauline DeVry

Taken on behalf of the defendants, pursuant to notice and the applicable sections of the Code of Civil Procedure, commencing at 10:03 a.m., on Monday, April 23, 2007 at 125 Main Street, Anytown, USA before Carrie Watson, Certified Shorthand Reporter, Notary Public in and for the County of Anytown, USA.

1   PAULINE DEVRY having been first duly sworn, was examined and testified as follows:

2   EXAMINATION

3   By Brenda Newton: Would you please state your full name?

4   Pauline Devry.

5   Have you ever had your deposition taken before?

6   Yes.

7   How long ago was that?

8   Approximately 15 years ago.

9   What was the subject of that deposition?

10   I had a fall.

11   Since you have not had your deposition taken in approximately 15 years, I will go ahead and give you the standard admonitions. The court reporter has just administered an oath, and that is the same type of oath that would be administered if you were to testify in court. Do you understand that?

12   Yes.

13   I am going to be asking you a number of questions. If you cannot hear me or do not understand the question, you will tell me, right?

14   Right.

15   To prepare a clear transcript, I need you to wait until I finish my entire question. Do you understand that?

16   Of course.

17   I also ask that you respond to all my questions orally. Do not nod or shake your head as that response does not show up in the transcript. Also, I need you to avoid such expressions as "uh-huh" or "huh-uh." Rather, I need you to make a "yes" or "no" response. Are we on the same page so far?

18   Yep.

19   Is that a yes?

20   Oh, yes.

21   Have you taken any medication today?

22   Yes, I have.

23   Tell me what you took.

24   Tysac, 180 milligrams.

25   Does that medication impair your ability to recall or give accurate testimony?

26   No.

27   What are you taking that medication for?

28   High blood pressure.

29   Do you feel well enough to give accurate and complete testimony today?

30   Yes.

....

1   I am going to ask you questions today that deal with dates, times, and distances. I do want estimates. I do not want a guess. An example of an estimate, which I do want, is if you looked at this conference table and told me how many feet you thought it was. An example of a guess, which I do not want, is if you try to guess the size of my dining room table. You have never been to my house and you have not seen my table, so it is not appropriate for you to speculate as to how long my table is. Do you understand the difference between a guess and an estimate?

2   Yes.

3   After reviewing your medical records, I noted that you have problems with your heart. Is that correct?

4   Yes.

5   Were you having problems with your heart on the day of the incident?

6   No.

7   I would like to go over your interrogatory responses with you and verify that they are correct. Were you born on 12/23/42?

8   Yes.

9   Did you receive medical training in the Women's Army Corps?

10   Yes.

11   Are you planning to offer a medical opinion as to your injuries?

12   No.

13   In your interrogatory responses, you claim a loss-of-earning capacity. What do you base that on?

14   Oh, no, that's wrong. I'm retired. I don't have any lost earnings.

15   So you will not be asking for any loss of income in this case?

16   No, I guess not.

17   Also in your interrogatory responses, you indicated that you had an additional CT scan scheduled. Have you had that CT scan yet?

18   No.

19   Why not?

20   Because I was the one that requested it from my doctor and when my health insurance saw that — that I was going to get a second one, they disagreed and won't pay for it. That's HMOs for you.

21   Did the HMO state why they did not want you to have the CT scan?

22   Yeah, they said that I have reflux and that another CT scan isn't going to fix that.

23   What do you mean by "reflux?"

24   Well, I'm not swallowing right anymore and food gets stuck in my throat. I feel like I'm choking and my heart starts going really fast.

25   Have you had a swallowing test?

26   Yes, I have, but they come out negative! Even applesauce gets stuck in the back of my throat. So I have to relearn how to swallow right. I have to eat a spoon of food at a time and not liquid or solids together. Once I start choking, I get anxiety. I have to put my chin down and swallow. I'm working with the speech therapist, but it has not alleviated the problem.

Page 2

1   This problem with swallowing is something that started since the April 25, 2006 incident happened?

2   Yes.

3   Why did you go to Green Hospital on April 25, 2006?

4   I have a son that's handicapped, and I took him for blood work. He loves to eat in the cafeteria, so we went to the cafeteria to have lunch. I ordered the chicken salad.

5   How often would you go to Green Hospital before the incident?

6   I would go for my son. He had a lot of problems because of the cerebral palsy. He had blood work . . . a sonogram . . . even a kidney removed. So I would go for him, maybe once every two or three months.

7   What does your son like about the cafeteria?

8   He likes the people. He is very social, and he likes the people. And he likes to sit there and visit with the people while we are eating.

9   Are the cafeteria employees friendly to your son?

10   Yes, most everyone is. He is a friendly guy, so everyone is very friendly with him.

11   On the day of the incident, were just your son and you eating the cafeteria?

12   Yes.

13   How many times would you say you had eaten in the cafeteria before this incident?

14   Maybe 12 times.

15   At any time before the April 25th incident, had you had an unpleasant experience in this cafeteria?

16   No.

17   Had you ever felt that the food at this cafeteria was unsafe before April 25th?

18   No.

19   Had you had prior problems with swallowing before this incident happened?

20   No.

21   You are claiming that something got stuck in your throat as a result of the way the chicken salad was prepared at this cafeteria; is that correct?

22   Yes.

23   What do you think you choked on?

24   Somewhere people started to think it was a chicken bone. I never said it was a chicken bone. I said it was a sharp object. I don't know what it was.

25   What did you do when you started to choke on the sharp object?

26   I asked somebody to watch my son, and I went to the emergency. I kept rubbing my throat. I grabbed a glass of water while I was in the emergency. I kept drinking and I said, "Something is stuck in my throat." By the time the ER people got done with the paperwork and asked me all these questions, it went down. I said, "Oh, it went, down," you know. They asked me to sign a release, and I did.

27   Was that a release that stated you decided to leave the emergency room against medical advice?

28   Yep.

Page 3

1   Yes.

2   Did any of the cafeteria employees see you choke?

3   I don't know. I kinda ran past them on the way to emergency. I ran to the emergency, because it felt like something was cutting my throat.

4   Did your son see you start to get something stuck in your throat?

5   Yes, he did, and he got very excited.

6   Where was your son sitting in relation to where you were?

7   Across from me.

8   Did anyone make the chicken salad in front of you?

9   No. It was in a bowl.

10   Can you describe that bowl?

11   No.

12   Was it plastic?

13   I have no idea.

14   Do you remember if it had a lid on it?

15   No, I don't remember.

16   Did you have to unwrap the salad?

17   I know I didn't have to unwrap it.

18   Before you started to eat the chicken salad, did you see anything that shouldn't have been in the chicken salad?

19   No.

20   So you didn't see any sharp objects before you took a bite?

21   No, I didn't.

22   Did you purchase a drink with your chicken salad?

23   Yes.

24   Do you recall what that was?

25   I can't remember.

26   When you started to get the object stuck in your throat, how much liquid was left in your cup, in your drink?

27   I don't remember.

28   Was it half a cup?

29   Oh, no. It was, like, two bites of chicken salad is when I got choked, so it probably was three quarters full, what I was drinking.

30   Did you attempt to get the item out of your throat?

31   No.

32   Did you try to get rid of the item in your throat by taking a drink?
33   Oh, yes. I did drink.
34   Did you try swallowing?
35   Yes, and rubbing my throat, which was probably wrong.
36   How was the lighting in the cafeteria?
37   It was good.
38   You could see your food?
39   Yes.
40   Were you looking at your food before you took each bite?
41   I was talking to my son and eating.

Page 4

1   When you bought the chicken salad, did anyone warn you about sharp objects?
2   No.
3   When the time got lodged in your throat, did you make any noise?
4   I was — Yes. I was trying to clear by throat and swallowing and rubbing my throat on the way to the emergency.
5   Did you waive your arms for help?
6   No. I just went running. I figured if anything was going to happen, it was a good place to happen — in the emergency room.
7   How soon after the item got lodged in your throat would you say that you went to the emergency room?
8   Within three minutes.
9   Where you treated in the emergency room?
10   No.
11   Why not?
12   The reason is, the doctor wanted to do a CT scan at that time. But my son was there, and I knew he would be upset. When I rubbed my throat and drank, it went down, so I wasn't apprehensive about anything. And so I said, "Oh, it went down. I don't need that now." And then I went back and sat down with my son and calmed him down. I told him, "I went to the emergency room, and I'm fine. Now we'll go home."
13   Did you do anything else at the hospital before you went home?
14   I asked if I could speak to someone about the chicken salad, this was in the cafeteria. I wanted to let them know that I swallowed a sharp object and got something stuck in my throat, so they might want to check it. And so I went over and sat down. And when I did, it took an awful long time for me to get anyone to come out for me to tell them that.
15   About how long?
16   Oh, at least 15 to 20 minutes.
17   Who did you speak to?
18   I spoke to two ladies. I don't know their names. I didn't take their names, because I didn't feel it was necessary. I felt my problem was over. And so they asked me if they could pay for my lunch, and I said, "Oh, no, that's not my problem. I just wanted you to know, you know, to check the salad."
19   How did these two women respond?
20   They said, "Well, can we give you something to drink?" I said, "Oh, yes. I'll have a Coke to take with me."
21   Then did you leave the hospital?
22   Yes. But on the way home, something came up in strings, and it was like my throat was bleeding. And so I hurried home. I went into the bathroom, and I didn't spit up any blood, so I thought I'm okay. So I went to bed that night.
23   When did you next have a problem with your throat?
24   When I was lying in bed that night, I felt some irritation. I went to the bathroom and swallowed some water. I thought, there is no blood, so I'm fine. The next day, I thought that it felt a little weird, so I went to go see the doctor.

Page 5

1   Which doctor did you see?

2   I saw Dr. Jacobs. He said, "We have to get an X-ray." And he said, "But I have to get a radiologist to read it, because I am seeing something here." I went on home after telling him to call me if anything was found.

3   What was the next step you took regarding the health of your throat?

4   When I got home, the doctor's office called and said that they had found a sharp object in my throat and for me to go get a CT scan.

5   Did you get the CT scan?

6   Yes, I did. They also told me that they had found a sharp object in my throat and that they didn't know what to do about it. The doctor decided to send me to the ENT doctor.

7   For the record, can we clarify what "ENT" is? Is that an ear, nose, and throat doctor?

8   Yes.

9   What did the ENT doctor tell you?

10 He said, "I don't think there is any sharp object there. Everything is fine." So he put the light down my throat, and he said he didn't see any bleeding or anything. And so he said, "So just go on," you know. "Go on home."

11 What was the ENT doctor's name?

12 Dr. Thompson.

13 What day was it that you went and saw Dr. Thompson?

14 The day after I got the sharp thing stuck in my throat.

15 The accident occurred on the 24th, correct?

16 Yep.

17 What time of day did the accident occur?

18 Approximately 12:00, 12:15. Could you wait a minute? I am getting a little choking here.

19 Yes.

20 Would you like some water or a break?

21 (Off the record.)

22 Did Dr. Thompson tell you anything else?

23 He said, "If you swallowed something, it will pass." He never identified what the object was, whether it was a bone or what it was.

24 Can you describe the two women you spoke with at the cafeteria?

25 They were not thin. They were very nice.

26 Do you remember anything else about them?

27 No, not really.

28 When you left the emergency room, did the personnel ask you to sign a release?

29 Well, they asked me to. And I said, "Oh, yeah, I will sign a medical release." I said, "I feel better. There is nothing wrong."

30 Did that medical release state that the hospital would not be responsible if you left against medical advice?

31 It said "If you sign yourself out, remember, we are not responsible."

32 After you got to the ER, how long was it before you saw someone?

Page 6

1   It was about seven minutes, eight minutes at the most. Unless you are half dead, they don't come to you right away. They have to take some information about you. In the meantime, I am rubbing my throat.

2   Do you know of anyone else who choked in this cafeteria?

3   No.

4   No doctor has formed an opinion as to what was in your throat?

5   "Sharp object" is all they have ever told me.

6   How did the object feel in your throat?

7   Like a knife was cutting me.

8   Did it feel like metal?

9   I don't know.

10 So you can't say with certainty that it was not a chicken bone; correct?

11 No. I can't, no.

12 What was the size of the object? Do you have any estimate of what the size was?

13 No.

14 Did it feel like an inch on your throat that was irritated?

15 It was less than an inch.

16 Half an inch?

17 I don't know.

18 Where did the object lodge on your throat? Can you locate it for me on your throat?

19 (The witness indicated.)

20 For the record, let's note she was rubbing the left side of her throat, upper, maybe an inch below the jaw. Were there any other customers around you when you got the item lodged in your throat?

21 I don't remember. I certainly didn't want to make a scene.

22 Did you speak to anyone else after the incident, other than the emergency room workers and the ladies in the cafeteria?

23 No. I made an incident report. Is it in my file?

24 Yes, I have an incident report.

25 From the time of the incident until now, have you gone back to this particular cafeteria?

26 Yes. I didn't eat any salads.

27 Did you eat other foods there?

28 Yes.

29 So you felt safe going back and eating at the cafeteria?

30 Sure.

31 Did you have any more problems with this cafeteria?

32 No.

33 Are you unable to continue your same activities that you were doing before the incident?

34 When I get the choking feeling and I get the A-fib. I don't drive. I have someone else drive, because I don't know when I might have trouble with the A-fib, but I'm able to do most everything else.

Page 7

....

1 Are there social activities that you have difficulties with since this incident?

2 People kind of stare at me; because when I eat, I am not supposed to take but a teaspoon of food at a time. And then, if I order soup, I eat the soup — the solid — or the liquid first and then the solid, and then — So it's kind of embarrassing, the way I have to eat when I got out.

3 Do you find that you go out to eat less now?

4 Oh, yes. I have lost weight. That's the good side, you know.

5 How much weight have you lost?

6 About 17 pounds.

7 But you are happy about losing that weight?

8 It doesn't bother me, as long as I don't lose any more.

9 When was the last time you have been to the doctor regarding this incident?

10 I paid to go get a consultation from another ENT doctor.

11 You paid for the consultation out of your own pocket?

12 Yes. And that ENT said, "Those guys haven't been doing their job with you." So he is the one that recommended me to have what they call the swallowing test. But, the speech therapist couldn't give it to me because it wasn't recommended by my HMO doctor.

13 How much money did you have to pay for that consultation?

14 Only one hundred dollars. Sometimes I get real hoarse, and sometimes there is a surgery for this, but that's the last resort, of course. What that ENT was concerned about is, if I am not swallowing properly, that it will go down the wrong way and get into my lungs. I have a sheet of paper that tells me how to swallow properly.

15   When is the next time you are going to see Dr. Thompson?

16   Well, he told me to take some antacid. If that didn't work, then he would have to go do something else. So I have taken it, and it doesn't help.

17   Will you be setting up a medical appointment with Dr. Thompson soon?

18   I am going to follow up. I have got another problem. I have got a blood clot, but that's not related to this.

19   Has seeing the speech therapist helped?

20   No. It's like I have this choking in my throat. Normally, when I get this — and excuse me for saying it. I don't know how else to say it. But when I get this, if I can go to the bathroom and, like, gag, it feels like something's there. Gagging seems to relieve it.

21   Has your voice been getting hoarse a lot as a result of the incident?

22   At, times. Sometimes, when I am talking on the phone — I do that a lot — it gets hoarse. Then after about 20 minutes, it goes away.

23   You have been telling me you get A-fib after you choke. Can you explain to me what you think A-fib is?

24   I get excited when I get choked. When I would get excited, then it would start the fast heartbeat.

25   We have to wrap up for today.

26   (Off the record).

Page 8

Figure 16.8 is a sample deposition index of the above deposition transcript. There are traditionally three types of deposition summaries:

■ page/line,
■ topic, and
■ chronological.

The following is a page/line summary. The page/line summary is the most common type of deposition summary. The summary follows the deposition transcript from the first to the last page. The summary of the lines is next to the line numbers so the actual deposition transcript can easily be referenced.

A topic summary summarizes the deposition transcript based upon the topics discussed at the deposition. For instance, if a plaintiff had a neck, left shoulder, and low back injury, then the paralegal could divide the summary by those three main topics. Further topics might include a deponent's education, employment history, medical history, any insurance, other accidents, etc. However, this type of summary is not as easy to prepare as the page/line summary because the attorney frequently bounces from topic to topic during depositions.

The chronological summary follows a timeline order, not the order of the pages in the deposition necessarily.

Figure 16.8

Deposition Summary/Index of Pauline DeVry

Page/Line:	Summary:
1:5-10	Ms. DeVry had her deposition taken 15 years ago, when she had a fall.
1:21-28	Pauline took 180 mg of Tysac for her high blood pressure before her deposition. This will not impair her ability to give accurate testimony.
2:3-7	Ms. DeVry was not having heart problems on the day of the incident.

2:9-10	She was born on 12/23/42.

2:9-10 She was born on 12/23/42.
2:11-14 She did receive medical training in the Women's Army Corps, but does not plan on offering a medical opinion.
2:15-18 She is retired and does not have any lost earnings.
2:19-24 Ms. DeVry requested the second CT scan, which the HMO did not agree to.
2:25-26 By reflux, Pauline means that she is not swallowing right, gets food stuck in her throat, and starts to choke.
2:27-28 Her swallowing test came out negative. She must eat solids and liquids separately. Once she starts choking, she becomes anxious. She has to put her chin to her chest.
3:2-3 The deponent went to Green Hospital to take her son for blood work. They ate in the cafeteria afterward.
3:4-5 Due to her son's cerebral palsy, they would go to the hospital once every 2-3 months.
3:6-9 Her son likes the cafeteria because he is very social. The cafeteria employees were friendly to her son.
3:11-12 She had eaten at the cafeteria maybe 12 times before.
3:19-20 She is claiming that something got stuck in her throat as a result of the way the chicken salad was prepared.
3:21-22 She does not know what she choked on.
3:23-30 When she started to choke, she went to the emergency room. She kept drinking and rubbing her throat. However, before she could be seen, the object went down. She signed an against medical advice release. She was able to run to the emergency room.
4:5-14 The chicken salad was in a bowl. It was not made in front of her. She did not have to unwrap it.
4:36-39 She was talking at her son and eating.
5:3-4 She was able to make noise once the item became lodged in her throat.
5:7-8 She was in the ER within three minutes after starting to choke.
5:9-12 She was not apprehensive after the item went down. She did not feel she needed a CT scan, especially with her son still in the cafeteria.
5:13-14 She spoke to someone in the cafeteria so they would check the salad.
5:15-20 She had to wait 15-20 minutes to speak to two ladies. The ladies offered to pay for her lunch. She said no. She was offered a drink, which she accepted.
5:21-22 She then left the hospital, but on the way home, "something came up in strings." She thought her throat was bleeding, but once she checked it at home, she was fine.
5:23-24 She felt some irritation in her throat that night.
5:25-6:3 She saw Dr. Jacobs. He recommended an X-ray. The radiologist found a sharp object in her throat. The doctor told her to get a CT scan.
6:4-7 The CT scan also showed a sharp object. She was referred to an ear, nose and throat doctor.
6:8-11 The ENT doctor, Dr. Thompson, told her that everything was fine.
6:31-32 Once she got to the ER, it was about 7-8 minutes before she saw someone.
7:6-21 The object felt like a knife was cutting her. It affected less than an inch of her throat.
7:25-32 She had gone back to the cafeteria since this incident happened. She felt safe going back to eat there and has not any more problems with the cafeteria.
7:33-34 When she gets the "choking feeling," then she gets A-fib.
7:35-8:6 People stare at her when she goes out to eat. She goes out to eat less and has lost 17 pounds. Losing that weight does not bother her.

8:7-12   She paid to get a consultation form another ENT doctor. That doctor stated that she should have a swallowing test. She paid $100 out of pocket for that consultation.

8:13-16   Dr. Thompson told her to take some antacid, but that does not help.

8:17-18   Gagging helps.

8:21-end She would like to know if this incident is the reason she now has A-fib. A-fib means a fast heartbeat to her.

c. Request for Production of Documents (RFPDs)

Request for documents
a formal request for documents in the opposing party's control and the request is made to the opposing party.

A **request for documents** is a formal request for documents in the opposing party's control and the request is made to the opposing party. Requests for production of documents ("RFPDs") are only sent to parties. Commonly requested documents include:

- income tax returns and W-2s (these documents substantiate a lost wages claim),
- medical bills,
- expert witnesses,
- witness statements,
- correspondence,
- medical records,
- photographs, and
- pharmacy records.

Other documents the paralegal should consider requesting are:

- driving records, including driver's license and vehicle registration,
- credit history,
- police reports,
- 911 calls, and
- criminal history.

Requests for production of documents allow the defendant to request copies of the other insurance policies to determine whether or not there are other potential defendants.

As a paralegal, you will need to prepare a draft copy of RFPDs for the attorney to review and sign. In addition, you will need to direct an attorney copy service to copy those documents. As with form interrogatories, do not forget to index these documents and to calendar dates.

Examples of Requests

Psychological:

- Any and all records, notes (whether typed, handwritten, or electronic), reports, psychological tests, and any results. Any and all psychological evaluations, correspondence (again, whether typed, handwritten, or electronic) of the plaintiff. Any and all therapy notes. Any and all progress notes.

Medical Records:

- Any and all documentation of any type regarding the patient care and treatment of Sally Thompson (Date of Injury: January 27, 2007), including, without being limited by, medical records, and treatment records including any and all calls and/or nurse records as described as follows:
- Any and all medical records or reports, diagnosis reports, and reports regarding any and all medical treatment provided by Chicago General staff regarding the plaintiff.
- Any and all labs or tests regarding the plaintiff.
- Any and all x-rays and CT scans regarding the plaintiff.
- Any and all ambulance medical records regarding the plaintiff.
- Any and all nurses notes, medication records, and progress notes regarding the plaintiff.

Witnesses:

- The names, phone numbers (including home, work and cell phone numbers), and addresses of each witness you will call at trial that is set for _____[date].

    Photographs:

- Any and all photographs (whether Polaroids, film or digital), film, audio tapes, and videotapes that relate to this case.

Example of a Response to an RFPD

Response to Plaintiff's No. 9 Request for Production of Documents: The defendant agrees to produce the documents requested in plaintiff's request no. 9 at the offices of the plaintiff's attorney on or before March 27, 2008.

d.   Requests for Admission (RFAs)

Requests for admission
questions where one party asks the other party the truth of allegations.

Requests for admission are questions where one party asks the other party the truth of allegations. Each allegation must be either admitted or denied — or a statement must be provided explaining why the allegation can neither be admitted nor denied. It is extremely important to respond to requests for admissions. If the requests are not responded to, then the requests will be deemed admitted. To determine what the other side should be asked to admit, the paralegal needs to look at allegations in the complaint, police or accident reports, interrogatory answers, and depositions.

Example of Requests for Admission

1. You are requested to admit that each of the attached documents is genuine (and then list the documents).

2. You are requested to admit that each of the following statements is true (and then list the statements).

Example of a Response to RFA

The information known or readily obtainable is insufficient to enable this party to admit or deny the matter.

e.   Defense Medical Evaluation (DME)

Defense medical examination when the defendant asks the plaintiff to be evaluated by the defendant's choice of doctor, and the plaintiff undergoes the evaluation.

The plaintiff is normally evaluated by her own doctor. The defense can request the plaintiff see a doctor chosen by the defense, which is known as a defense medical evaluation. A **defense medical examination (DME)** can be obtained by stipulation between both parties, a request for one, or by court order if necessary. A request for medical examination takes place when the defendant asks the plaintiff to be evaluated by the defendant's choice of doctor. The request should state when and where the exam is to occur, the name of the doctor who will be conducting the exam, and a short description of what will be evaluated in the exam.

Typically, the defense's paralegal arranges the appointment. The location of the examination should be reasonably close to where the plaintiff lives. If allowed in the state, the plaintiff's attorney should be present to make sure the defense's medical doctor asks only proper questions.

To obtain a DME by court order, good cause must be shown. Good cause means the exam must be relevant, and there is a need for the exam because there is not another way to obtain the information. A DME by court order is more likely to occur where the defendant requests a mental health evaluation.

The defense medical examination evaluates the condition, its causes, and the likelihood of the patient becoming better. The examination must be chronicled in a written report by the doctor, which discusses the medical findings, test results, diagnoses, and conclusions. The defense needs to write a letter to the defense doctor, prior to the exam, providing a little background information on the case. The letter also outlines the questions the defense would like the doctor to address. See Figure 16.9.

Figure 16.9

Sample Letter to Independent Medical Examiner

December 27, 2007

Dr. Simon Latham
100 Main Avenue
City, State 22356

Re: Austin Sena v. Big Corporation, Date of Birth 9/14/1980

Dear Dr. Latham:

This office represents the defendant, Big Corporation, against Mr. Sena in his claims for injuries regarding an automobile accident which occurred on or about March 21, 2007.
You are asked to prepare a medical evaluation of Mr. Sena, and to specifically answer the following questions:

- What is Mr. Sena's current diagnosis?
- Are the injuries that Mr. Sena complains of caused by the March 21, 2007 automobile accident?
- What is the future prognosis for Mr. Sena?
- Does Mr. Sena need any further medical treatment? If so, please indicate.
- Does Mr. Sena have any work restrictions?
- Have any of Mr. Sena's injuries resulted in a permanent disability?

Sincerely,
Attorney for Big Corporation

The Judicial Road to Recovery: Steps to a Lawsuit
By Jennifer Mashini, Paralegal

To file a lawsuit, one must move through the intricate processes of our legal system. Without knowledge of the rules and procedures of the court system, this progression can be quite complicated and daunting. Paralegals are trained in starting the judicial journey of what we know as a lawsuit from an administrative perspective; naturally then, the first few steps often start with them.

Usually the paralegal would first become familiar with the initial action that jumpstarts the lawsuit, which is referred to as the cause of action. There can be numerous causes of action but in a civil suit, it is typically a contractual issue or one of torts. Torts are breaches of some sort of legal duty or obligation. They are broken into three categories: the first being negligence, the second intentional torts and the third strict liability.

Once the paralegal understands the causes of action, the next step is to fill out the complaint. The complaint is the legal document needed to outline the cause of action, basic information regarding the plaintiff and defendant, and details of what happened. Also located in the complaint is the prayer. The prayer portion of the complaint is where it outlines what the plaintiff is asking for as a result of the causes of action. The amount of the relief sought will determine what type of classification the case will be. If the amount sought is for over twenty five thousand dollars then the case would be filed as an unlimited civil case. If the relief is for twenty five thousand dollars or less then it would be filed as a limited civil case. Finally if the case is worth five thousand dollars or less, it would be filed in small claims court, where plaintiffs represent themselves. [Check your jurisdiction to determine whether your state divides lawsuits into these categories.]

After the proper classification of case is defined, proper venue must be decided. Venue is the county or designation where the case may be heard in court. Venue for damages to real property usually lies in the county where the land is located. All other actions however, have venue where any defendant resides, where the contract is entered into or performed, or where the cause of action took place.

Upon completion of the complaint, a paralegal should be equipped with at least three conformed copies and a fee when entering the court for processing.

One copy stays with the firm for recording purposes, one stays with the court for their file and the other will be served on the defendant. All three must bear an original signature which should be in blue ink, to avoid any confusion later as to whether the signatures are original or copied.

When serving the defendant, time is of the essence. In state court cases one usually has sixty days to serve and file proof. In federal cases, one would have one hundred twenty days. Anyone who is a competent adult and not a party to the action could serve the defendant so long as they state what the document is that they are serving. Many firms have companies they use specifically for this purpose. Those that may receive service besides the defendants themselves are parents or guardians for minors, agents that act on behalf of individuals or entities or officers or designated agents acting on behalf of corporations.

There are also different manners of service of process to be considered. The most valued and concrete would be through personal service. This entails giving it directly to the person or officer and would make service effective immediately upon its delivery. If that effort fails then one could try substituted service which involves leaving a copy of the summons and complaint at the dwelling place with a competent member of the home or at the usual place of business and with someone in charge. If this service is used then a copy of the summons and complaint must also be mailed at the location it was left at. The next effort would be to use service by mail. The summons and complaint would be mailed to the defendant along with two copies of the notice and acknowledgement form. One copy is for them to keep and one is to mail back in the stamped return envelope that also needs to be provided. If the defendant signs and mails it back, service is effective the date on which they signed the documents. If the defendant does not comply after twenty days, then they are responsible for any other service costs. The final exertion would be through service by publication. This requires a court order first and proof of a reasonable effort through other methods of service. It calls for a publishing in the local paper. [Verify all these types of service are acceptable in your jurisdiction.]

As anyone in the legal community could tell, the path to the courtroom is one that could very well be mangled with confusion. So long as the paralegal moves with careful attention to detail, dates, rules and procedure, the road to recovery will be far more accessible.

E T H I C S

Electronic discovery is rife with potential ethics violations. For instance, according to the Federal Rules of Civil Procedure, Rule 26(f), as soon as possible, the parties are supposed to discuss how to preserve electronic discovery and neither party should hide discovery. Further, per FRCP Rule 26(a)(1)(B), electronic discovery must be produced even before a discovery request. Once it is reasonable that litigation will ensue, there is a litigation hold put on all electronically stored information (ESI) so the information will not be destroyed. Interestingly, there is also a clawback provision if privileged material is produced in ESI discovery. FRCP Rule 26(b)(5)(B) states the party who receives the privileged material must "return, sequester or destroy" the information and "may not use or disclose the information until the claim is resolved." How do you think this rule will work in conjunction with the zealous representation an attorney should provide his client? Seemingly in contradiction to these rules, there is a safe harbor provision in FRCP Rule 37(f): "a court may not impose sanctions under these rules on a party for failing to provide electronically stored information lost as a result of the routine, good-faith operation of an electronic information system." Do you think there is a potential for abuse of the safe harbor provision?

Chapter Summary

Insurance is a contract between the holder of the insurance policy and the insurance company. The policyholder pays premiums so if there is an accident, the insurance company will indemnify the policyholder against losses. The insurance company will often have to provide an attorney to its client if the client is sued. This is known as the duty to defend. Plaintiff's attorneys look for insurance, as most individual defendants do not have sufficient personal assets to pay damages.

The two most common types of insurance are automobile insurance and homeowner's insurance. If a person is hit in an automobile accident by someone without insurance, the person may still be covered through her insurance policy for uninsured motorists. If a person is hit by someone without sufficient insurance to cover all of the injury, the person may still be covered through her insurance policy for underinsured motorists.

A complaint starts the lawsuit and puts the defendant on notice of the plaintiff's allegations. To prepare the complaint, the client needs to be interviewed first. Using the information from the client, the complaint will then be prepared.

The defendant then responds to the complaint by answering the complaint. The answer admits, denies, or states the defendant has insufficient knowledge to admit or deny the plaintiff's allegations. Affirmative defenses are raised by the defendant at this time. An affirmative defense provides a justification for the defendant's conduct. Examples of affirmative defenses include not filing a complaint within the statute of limitations, the plaintiff's consent to the defendant's conduct, or even self-defense.

After the complaint and answer are filed, the discovery process begins. Discovery is the means in which the opposing parties gather information on the other side's facts and evidence. Discovery can be implemented by interrogatories, which are written questions, made under oath. There are also depositions, which are oral questions, made under oath. The paralegal sets up the time and place of the deposition, along with a court reporter. The paralegal may also be responsible for preparing the client for his deposition. After the deposition is taken, a transcript is sent to the parties. One of a paralegal's major tasks is to summarize deposition transcripts.

There are three types of deposition summaries: page/line, topic, and chronological. The page/line summary is the most common and it summaries the deposition next to the line numbers of the deposition so the actual transcript can be easily referenced. A topical summary divides the deposition into the different subject matters discussed during the deposition. Finally, a chronological summary puts the information into order.

Another discovery device is requests for production of documents, which is a formal request for documents in the opposing party's control. Requests for admission are questions where one party asks the other party the truth of certain allegations. Another discovery device is a defense medical evaluation. The defense may request a defense medical evaluation, where the plaintiff sees a doctor and is evaluated by a doctor chosen by the defendant.

Key Terms

- Affirmative defense
- Answer
- Cause of action
- Certificate of service
- Complaint
- Counterclaim
- Cross-claim
- Declarations page
- Default
- Defendant
- Demurrer
- Deponent
- Deposition
- Deposition transcript
- Defense medical examination
- Digital discovery
- Discovery
- Extended coverage
- General denial
- Indemnify
- Initial client meeting
- Injunction
- Interrogatory
- Insurance premium
- Meta data
- Negligence
- Personal service
- Physical and mental examination
- Plaintiff
- Pleading
- Policy
- Policyholder
- Proof of service
- Request for admissions
- Request for production of documents
- Specific denial
- Statute of limitations
- Subpoena duces tecum
- Substituted services
- Underinsured motorist coverage
- Uninsured motorist coverage
- Waiver

Review Questions

- What are the obligations of a policyholder and insurance company with regards to the insurance contract?
- Why are defendants with insurance more likely to be sued than defendants without insurance?
- Explain what underinsured motorist coverage is.
- How does underinsured motorist coverage differ from uninsured motorist coverage?
- What is the insurance company's duty to defend its insured?
- Explain how a cause of action and an affirmative defense are different.
- Why is it important for a defendant to have the affirmative defenses in the answer?
- Define statute of limitations.
- Name the different types of discovery.
- What are reasons to object to discovery requests?
- How should you prepare a client for his deposition?
- How can a defendant respond to a complaint?
- What is an interrogatory?

- Who does not have to answer an interrogatory?
- What are some commonly asked questions in interrogatories?
- Who may answer a deposition?
- What is a request for production of documents?
- What are some types of electronic data that may be included in digital discovery?

Web Links

- If you find yourself in a job dealing with insurance, go to www.insurance.com to become more savvy about insurance terms and how insurance works. Use the insurance learning center.
- If the client is having difficulty in getting his insurance company to pay on a claim, a good place to obtain more information is www.badfaithinsurance.org. Bad faith insurance involves insurance claims by the insured person against the insurance company when it wrongfully denies the insurance claim.
- www.iii.org. This is the Insurance Information Institute's website. This website has a glossary of insurance terms.

Exercises

- Make a flow chart of the events before, during, and after trial.
- What is the minimum amount of automobile insurance coverage required in your state?
- Research which affirmative defenses outlined above are not available in your state.
- When must a complaint be served in your state?
- Determine when the responses are due in your state and the number of requests for each of the following:

Interrogatories

Response Due   Limits on Number

Request for Production of Documents

Response Due   Limits on Number

Requests for Admissions

Response Due   Limits on Number

Oral Depositions

Timing   Objections

Medical Examinations

Response Due   Limits on Number

The Tort Litigation Process During Trial

Preparation is the be-all of good trial work. Everything else — felicity of expression, improvisational brilliance — is a satellite around the sun. Thorough preparation is that sun.[1]

Chapter Outline

Chapter Objectives

- Show how to schedule witnesses and experts for trial
- Discuss preparation of trial exhibits
- Explain the steps in a trial
- Describe how the paralegal assists an attorney at trial

---

1. Louis Nizer.

17.1 Introduction to Tort Litigation During Trial

One of the most important elements of a trial is the evidence that will be presented. There are different types of evidence, but all evidence must be relevant, meaning the evidence must be in some way related to the trial and tend to prove something related to the trial. A paralegal helps in trial preparation by instructing the witnesses on what to expect at trial and by going over the witness's previous discovery with the witness. A trial has several steps. Pre-trial includes getting ready for presenting the evidence to the jury. Prior to the start of the trial, the jury must also be selected. Once the jurors are selected and sworn in, each party has an opportunity to summarize the evidence they are about to present through the use of an opening statement. In the middle of the trial, witnesses are questioned by both parties. At the end of the trial, closing arguments are made and before the jury goes into the deliberation room, they are given some instructions.

In addition to preparing witnesses, another major way in which the paralegal assists with a trial is by preparing a trial notebook. The trial notebook puts all the important and necessary information to the case into handy and easily accessible notebooks.

17.2 Evidence

Direct evidence
evidence a witness can ascertain through his senses, such as sight, hearing, smell, or touch.

Circumstantial evidence
evidence that can be inferred from other facts.

Direct evidence is evidence a witness can ascertain through his senses, such as sight, hearing, smell, or touch. An example of direct evidence is a witness actually seeing an automobile accident. **Circumstantial evidence** is evidence that can be inferred from other facts. An example of circumstantial evidence would be the witness hearing something sounding like a crash, turning around, and seeing two cars speeding away from one another. Even though the witness heard the crash, he had to infer there was a crash since he did not actually see the crash. Circumstantial evidence is not as strong of evidence as direct evidence. In the example of an accident, it would have been better testimony if the witness had actually seen the accident.

Federal Rules of Evidence state for evidence to be admissible, the evidence must be relevant.[2] This rule is typically the rule in each state as well. Rule 401 states relevant evidence is "evidence having any tendency to make the existence of any fact that is of consequence to the determination of the action more probable or less probable than it would be without the evidence." This rule can be broken into two parts. First, relevant evidence has to prove something. Second, what the evidence proves must be related to the lawsuit.

17.3 Witness Preparation

When preparing a witness to testify, let the potential witness know the opposing attorney will attempt to make him defensive or angry. The witness needs to be polite

---

2. Fed. R. Evid. 402.

even when the opposing attorney is not. Polite witnesses make a positive impression on a jury and/or the judge. Provide the witness with the same list of instructions as were provided to a deponent. Counsel the witness on appropriate dress for the courtroom. Remind the witness to carefully listen to what is being asked and only answer what is being asked. If the witness does not understand a question, he should ask for the question to be rephrased. The witness should not talk over the attorney. The witness should state he does not recall if he does not.

Witnesses should be interviewed prior to trial. Each witness should review his prior testimony (including depositions and answers to written discovery). Go over the questions the attorney plans to ask the witness on direct examination. However, avoid having the witness sound as if he has rehearsed his answers. In addition to direct examination questions, the witness should review potential cross-examination questions. The paralegal should review with the witness where he will be sitting in the courtroom. If the witness is not a plaintiff or defendant to the lawsuit, then the paralegal must subpoena the witness so he is required to appear at the trial.

17.4 Other Pre-Trial Matters

Usually, the parties will have a pre-trial conference with a judge (who often is not the judge who will hear the case). The purpose of this conference is to attempt to settle the case one last time before trial. If the case is not settled, the issues for trial will be narrowed down at the pre-trial conference.

A large number of cases literally settle on the courthouse steps. Once each side sees the other side has fully prepared for trial, there is an impetus to settle, rather than risk the uncertainty of a trial. If the trial is a jury trial, there is the potential the jury could award a large verdict to the plaintiff. At the pre-trial conference, the parties each exchange witness lists. Written motions, called motions in limine, may also be discussed at the pre-trial conference. **Motions in limine** are pre-trial motions on the evidence. Motions in limine resolve evidence issues so the issues do not have to be taken up with the jury.

Motions in limine
pre-trial motions on the evidence.

17.5 Trial

Step in a trial:	Corresponding Trial Checklist:
Pre-trial conference	Motions in limine Pre-trial orders
The jury is selected	Jury list Voir dire already prepared
Opening Statements are made	Opening statement already prepared
The witnesses are questioned and cross-examined	Already prepared: • Witness questions • Arranged for each witness to appear at trial

	• Subpoenaed witnesses
	• Alerted experts as to trial dates and time
Closing arguments are made	Closing argument already prepared
The jury is given their instructions	Jury instructions prepared ahead of time
The jury deliberates	
The verdict is given	

Caution

Trial notebooks are prepared prior to the start of trial and during the trial. Although trial notebooks are discussed along with trial, paralegals should not wait until trial to start preparing a trial notebook. Trial notebooks should be prepared throughout the case.

17.6   Trial Notebooks

"Nothing so undermines the confidence of a court or jury in a lawyer as his constant groping and fumbling."[3] The trial notebook ensures that everything necessary for successfully litigating the case is within easy reach and is easily found. Preparing trial notebooks is perhaps the greatest way in which paralegals help attorneys with trials. Phases of trial are discussed in this chapter in conjunction with the corresponding section of the trial notebook. While each attorney has a personal preference of what he would like to include in his trial notebook and the order in which those items should be, there are general items most attorneys would like to see in the trial notebooks the paralegal prepares for them.

Typically, a trial notebook is a three-ring binder holding size 8½-by-11-inch paper. Use the tabs preferred by the attorney to separate the different sections of the notebook. If the tabs are easy to see, most lawyers will not require a separate table of contents. However, a table of contents might more easily organize the material.

a.   Pre-Trial Motions

Motions in limine, discussed earlier, should be placed at the start of the trial notebook, along with trial briefs, and any pleadings to be discussed at trial.

b.   The Law

One of the first sections of the trial notebook should be the law upon which the attorney is relying to win the case. The law the attorney is relying on is normally the

---

3. J. Appleman, ed., *Successful Jury Trials 100* (1952).

case law, but it may also be statutory law. Whatever law the attorney is relying upon should be one of the first items in the trial notebook.

c. Jury Selection

Voir dire

a Latin term meaning to speak the truth; the jury selection process.

Preemptory challenges

each side at trial is allowed to dismiss jurors without stating a reason, up to a certain number, as dictated by the state.

Typically, there is a section in the trial notebook for voir dire, or jury selection. **Voir dire** is a Latin term meaning to speak the truth. Voir dire occurs when the court verifies jurors are going to be impartial in listening to and deciding the case. Potential jurors can be stricken for cause by the judge. Cause for striking a juror could be because the juror is biased against the plaintiff or defendant. There are also **preemptory challenges**, which allow each side to dismiss a juror without stating a reason.

Many courts provide a chart of blank jury boxes, in which the attorney can fill in each prospective juror's name and information. Note in the sample below that there are twelve boxes, one box per juror.

Sample Jury Chart

The paralegal should still provide multiple blank copies of a jury chart (blown up and horizontally oriented) in the trial notebook in case the court does not. Under each of the juror's names, the attorney will jot notes on how the juror answered questions and what his impression of the juror is.

The attorneys and/or judge ask potential jurors questions. The more common procedure today is for the judge to ask a set of predetermined questions to limit the time spent on voir dire.

Sample Voir Dire Question

Does Juror Number 10 know any of the parties or attorneys involved in the lawsuit?

Is Juror Number 4 an attorney or closely related to any attorney?

The predetermined questions will probably include:

- age,
- occupation,
- marital status,
- children,
- spouse's employment, and
- prior jury service.

If the case has been in the news a lot, then voir dire questions might include whether the potential juror has already made up his mind about the case from the news.

Once the jurors have been chosen, the judge will normally tell the jurors how they are to conduct themselves during trial. The judge will say something similar to what follows:

- Do not talk to anyone about this case. This includes family members, friends, people you work with, psychologists, psychiatrists, and ministers. You are not even to talk to your fellow jurors until you are instructed to deliberate on the case as directed by the judge.
- You may not independently speak with any of the attorneys, the parties, witnesses, or the judge.
- While the trial is in progress, you many not watch information about the trial on television, listen to information about the trial on the radio, or even read trial information on the internet or printed media.
- Do not perform any research regarding the trial on your own.
- You are not to visit the scene of the incident unless specifically directed to do so by the judge.

The judge will also usually provide the jurors with a brief overview of the trial process. The judge states the trial begins with opening statements, if the parties choose to give one. An opening statement is not required and it is not considered evidence. The plaintiff presents his evidence first, after the opening statements. Once the plaintiff has finished putting on his case, then the defense presents its evidence. Each side asks questions of its own witnesses. Once the plaintiff is finished questioning each of his witnesses, the defendant is allowed to cross-examine the plaintiff's witness. Once the defendant is finished questioning each of his witnesses, the plaintiff is allowed to cross-examine the defendant's witness. The attorneys summarize their evidence through a closing argument. Finally, after the judge discusses the steps in a trial, the judge may give the jurors a brief statement on what the case is about.

d.   Opening Statement

Opening statement
a statement made by each side's attorney at the beginning of trial.

Many of the items to be placed in the trial notebook by the paralegal will have to first be prepared by the attorney. One of these items is an opening statement. An **opening statement** is a statement made by each side's attorney at the beginning of trial. Whichever party has the burden of proof (normally the plaintiff) will make the first opening statement. A defendant can present his opening statement right after the plaintiff's, or wait until the beginning of his presentation of the evidence before giving the opening statement. In an opening statement, each attorney presents his view of the case and the evidence he plans to submit to prove his case. The opening statement is an introduction of the case to the jury.

The attorney will have notes from which he will speak when giving the opening statement. Those notes should be placed in the trial notebook. Do not expect to receive these notes until shortly before trial. An opening statement is best prepared after all the discovery is completed, and sometimes even after the attorney has had a chance to evaluate the jurors.

e. Witnesses

An imperative item in the trial notebook, prepared by a paralegal, is the witness list. The witness list must have the addresses and all available telephone numbers for the witness. Frequently, witnesses do not show up on time or it is necessary to call the witnesses earlier than anticipated. The paralegal's job is to contact the witness and get him into court as soon as possible. When subpoenaing the witnesses before trial, the paralegal should be gathering their contact information so it will be much easier to compile this information when trial arrives. Along with the contact information for witnesses, the paralegal should maintain contact information for opposing counsel, the judge (including the judge's clerks), and the client.

Example of Witness Contact Information

Witness	Telephone Numbers	Addresses	Email
Jenny Love	• Work: (615) 235-9873 • Home: (615) 378-9682 • Personal: (615) 278-1963	Home: 3782 Laurel Avenue Work: N/A	Love@yahoo.com

f. Exhibits

Exhibit
something other than testimony tending to prove the facts.

Real evidence
exhibits that can be touched.

Demonstrative evidence
exhibits representing real objects such as photographs or charts.

Frequently, when a case goes to trial there are hundreds of exhibits. An exhibit is something other than testimony. An **exhibit** can be a document, but the document must tend to prove the facts. For instance, a contract could tend to prove there was an agreement to buy and sell property. The paralegal is expected to take the exhibits to trial and keep track of them.

Real evidence exhibits are types of evidence that can be touched. Physical objects, such as a gun, can be used as exhibits. Exhibits representing real objects can be used, such as photographs and charts. These types of exhibits are called **demonstrative evidence**.

Example of Demonstrative Evidence

The case is a lawsuit for battery caused by striking the plaintiff on the head with the butt of a gun. The gun will most likely be at the trial. However, usually jurors are not allowed to touch the actual gun and do not get very close to the gun. If the defendant wants to show the gun used in the battery lawsuit was not the gun found at his home, he will probably have blown-up photographs of the gun showing the difference between the two guns. Thus, the gun in the photograph would be demonstrative evidence whereas the actual gun would be real evidence. See Figure 17.1.

Figure 17.1

Photograph Used as Demonstrative Evidence

Each exhibit must be proven to be the item it is being held out as. Therefore, the attorney must show at trial that a photograph of the gun, used as an exhibit, is indeed a photograph of the gun.

A wide variety of writings can be used as exhibits. For instance, a rental agreement can be used as an exhibit to show the parties did have an agreement. Finally, business records can also be used as exhibits, if the records qualify.

The exhibits should be organized in the order the exhibits will be appearing at trial. Exhibits are generally marked with letters and/or numbers depending upon whether the exhibit is the plaintiff's or defendant's exhibit.

If your attorney plans on using demonstrative evidence for the trial, these exhibits should be prepared in advance and those exhibits that physically can should go into the trial notebook.

The exhibits, depending upon the size, may need to go into a separate book. Many judges want their own exhibit book, which will be prepared by both the plaintiff and defendant. Typically, the exhibit will state which party or parties plan to use the exhibit.

Figure 17.2

Example Exhibit Tabs

As the paralegal receives exhibits during the trial process, she should be keeping a list as follows:

Record of Potential Exhibits

Document Title	Date Received	Received from
Police Report	11/3/07	Defendant's RFPDs
Five Photographs of Plaintiff's Injuries	Taken 11/3/07	Plaintiff

g.   Examination of the Witnesses

Expert witness
a person designated as highly knowledgeable about a subject matter due to his education or experience.

A witness is a person called to testify at trial. There are two types of witnesses: expert witnesses and lay witnesses. An **expert witness** is so designated by his education or experience, which makes him an expert about a subject. Experts are qualified in certain areas, such as heart medicine. Experts testify when the jury does not have knowledge about a subject matter. Try to get excerpts of prior testimony of both your and the opposing counsel's experts to place in the trial notebook and look up any publications by the experts prior to trial. Determine whether the expert's opinion is consistent throughout the publications. In addition, the paralegal will need to get a copy of the expert's curriculum vitae (resume), and verify the degrees, schooling, awards, and memberships the expert has. This review of the expert's qualifications needs to occur prior to the start of trial. If the expert should be licensed (i.e., an attorney or doctor), the paralegal needs to verify the expert is licensed and the license is current with the state. In addition, experts normally have different rates for pretrial and trial work. Trial, when the expert will be testifying, is usually more expensive. Therefore, it is important to minimize the time the expert will be waiting and charging the client. This is another instance where the witness contact list becomes important, so the paralegal can call and notify the expert witness if he will be testifying at a later or an earlier time than previously anticipated.

Lay witness
a person who saw the incident in question.

A lay witness is an ordinary person, who does not have to have any special training to testify. A **lay witness** discusses the incident he saw. A lay witness is also known as a fact witness. For instance, if a person saw an accident occur, the person could potentially be a lay witness at trial and testify as to what he saw. The witness would have been located through the police report, during discovery. A witness is qualified to testify if he understands he must tell the truth and has knowledge of what he is going to testify about.

As the paralegal prepares a deposition summary of each witness's deposition transcript, the paralegal needs to place the summaries into the trial notebook. Having the summaries in the trial notebook helps the attorney reference passages in the depositions quickly.

The order in which witnesses are examined is as follows:

- direct examination,
- cross-examination,
- redirect examination,
- re-cross examination, and
- rebuttal examination.

Direct examination
occurs when the attorney calling the witness questions the witness.

Cross-examination
occurs when a party questions a witness the party did not call as a witness.

Impeachment
occurs when an attorney attempts to show a witness is not being truthful.

Direct examination occurs when the attorney calling the witness questions the witness. The trial notebook should have a copy of the questions the attorney plans to ask each witness on direct examination. Make a tab for these questions so the attorney can place his questions in the binder once he has prepared the questions. **Cross-examination** occurs when a party questions a witness the party did not call as a witness. Once these questions are prepared, the trial notebook should include a copy of the questions the attorney plans to ask the witnesses he did not call. The attorney may try to impeach the witness's testimony on cross-examination. **Impeachment** occurs when an attorney attempts to show a witness is not being truthful.

Example of Impeachment

Q: Go to your response to Interrogatory 8. Read your response to yourself.
A: Alright, I've read it.
Q: Do you agree that the response to this interrogatory was made closer in time to the accident?
A: Yes.
Q: Did you make the response under oath?
A: Yes.
Q: Now, in your response to the interrogatory, you stated you did not see the accident, you only heard the accident, correct?
A: Yes.
Q: Therefore, after looking at your response to interrogatories, do you wish to change your earlier testimony here today?
A: Well, yeah, I guess. I mean . . . I think . . . I know what happened from hearing the accident and coming out of my house and seeing the two wrecked cars, but I didn't actually see the accident.

Redirect examination provides both sides with the chance to clarify any previously asked questions. Since redirect examination will be based upon the answers of the witnesses at trial, these questions do not need to be placed in the trial notebook.

Once each party has finished putting on his case, then the other party can call additional witnesses to trial to discredit the first witnesses. These witnesses are known as rebuttal witnesses, meaning the new witnesses' statements will show the first witnesses' statements not to be true.

h.   Closing Argument

Closing arguments
each side's final statement or
summary of the evidence.

Closing arguments are each side's final statement or summary of the evidence. The summary includes a discussion of what each side proved along with what was not proved by other side. An attorney for the plaintiff will slant the summary of the case in the most positive light for the plaintiff. An attorney for the defense will slant the summary of the case in the light most positive for the defendant. The closing argument will also explain to the judge or jury why they should rule in favor of the plaintiff's or defendant's side. Your attorney will probably not prepare the closing argument until the end of the trial. However, notes the attorney takes during trial can be placed in the trial notebook to help prepare him for the closing argument.

i.   Jury Instructions

Jury instructions are directions to the jury on the law and on the conduct each juror should follow while fulfilling his jury duty service. Each state has different instructions because the law is different from state to state. Jury instructions are usually phrased in plain English, so the instructions can be understood by someone without a legal background. The jury instructions have to be discussed with opposing counsel and the judge before the instructions can be presented to the jury. However, when preparing the case, the attorney will ask the paralegal to print all the jury instructions related to the case. The attorney will then select the instructions he would most like to be adopted for the jury. Place the instructions selected by the attorney in the trial notebook. As the instructions are changed with the input of opposing counsel and the judge, update the jury instructions. See Figure 17.3 for sample jury instructions.

Figure 17.3

Sample Jury Instruction

- Express Assumption of the Risk: The defendant is claiming the plaintiff cannot receive any damages because the plaintiff signed a document before the accident stating the plaintiff would not hold the defendant responsible for any accident which occurred to the plaintiff as a result of _____. If the defendant is able to prove there was a signed written agreement and the agreement applies to the accident which occurred, then you, the jury, must find the defendant is not responsible for the plaintiff's injuries.
- Speeding: A driver must drive at a reasonable speed, which is determined by traffic conditions, including number of people on the road, weather, and the condition of the road. If a driver was driving at an unreasonable speed, causing danger to another person, then you, the jury, must find the defendant negligent.

Snapshot of Being a Paralegal
By Nicole Winn, Paralegal

I am currently employed with a mid-size insurance defense firm. We have three offices, Las Vegas, Los Angeles and San Diego. I have been at this firm for six years and during this time I have had a myriad of experiences ranging from visiting inmates in the county jail to attending a concert for investigative purposes. Some personal benefits have also included dinner cruises, major league football and baseball games, and being rewarded with holiday bonuses. Most law firms also have wonderful health insurance benefits and 401(k) plans. Salaries vary depending on the size of the firm and the practice area. I look forward to a long career with the firm as a paralegal. Good luck in your career!

E T H I C S

In preparing for trial, a paralegal frequently prepares a witness or plaintiff to testify on the stand. One of the reasons it is important to prepare people for testifying is testifying makes many people nervous. The paralegal can help calm the witness down by explaining the process to the witness. Explaining the process includes letting the witness know she will be sworn in and questioned by both parties. Preparing the witness for her testimony on the stand also includes going over the witness's prior testimony, for instance, from a deposition. Once the process has been explained to the witness, hopefully the witness will calm down and give her best testimony. However, the paralegal should never tell the witness exactly what to say on the stand. Emphasis should be placed upon the absolute necessity of telling the truth while testifying under oath.

Chapter Summary

After the discovery is completed, if the parties have not settled or gone to alternative dispute resolution, a trial will be held. There are different types of evidence that can be presented at trial. Direct evidence is evidence a witness can ascertain through his senses. Circumstantial evidence is evidence inferred from other facts. All evidence presented must tend to prove a fact and be related to the lawsuit.

During trial, paralegals also aid in witness preparation, which is similar to preparing a person for his deposition.

The responsibilities of the paralegal can be extensive and can be invaluable to the success of the attorney at trial. Perhaps the most important aid the paralegal provides is the preparation of a trial notebook. At the beginning of the book, information about the selection of jurors will be placed. After the jury selection information comes the opening statement information. The opening statement is a speech made by each side's attorney, normally held at the beginning of trial. The witness list is crucial to the success of the trial. The paralegal needs to amass all the contact information for the witnesses so the witnesses can be kept abreast of when they should appear at trial. There are two types of witnesses: expert witnesses and lay witnesses. Expert witnesses are designated as such because of their education or experience about a subject matter. Lay witnesses saw the event in question. Exhibits are frequently voluminous at trial and the paralegal is instrumental in keeping the exhibits updated and organized. At the end of trial, the closing argument sums up each party's take on the case. Before the jury goes to the jury room, they are read instructions on the law. The paralegal prepares those instructions, in draft format, together and places them in the trial notebook.

Key Terms

- Admonitions
- Circumstantial evidence
- Closing argument
- Cross-examination
- Demonstrative evidence
- Direct evidence
- Direct examination
- Document
- Exhibit
- Expert witness
- Jury chart
- Jury instructions
- Lay witness
- Motion
- Motions in limine
- Opening statement
- Preemptory challenge
- Pre-trial motions
- Real evidence
- Trial notebook
- Voir dire
- Witness

Review Questions

- What is your role as a paralegal in the litigation process?
- How can a witness be impeached?
- How do you effectively organize trial materials?
- What is direct questioning?
- What is cross-examination?
- What is redirect questioning?

Web Links

- www.depoconnect.com/. TrialSmith bills itself as the nation's largest on-line deposition bank for plaintiff's attorneys. This site is extremely valuable when you are asked to research an expert witness to determine how the expert has testified in the past. You can search for the expert by name in over 300,000 depositions. This is also a helpful site for determining the amount of money juries in similar cases have been awarding plaintiffs.

■ www.GrandVoirDire.com allows the attorneys and paralegals on a case to keep track of all the information gathered in voir dire on a laptop, rather than using the jury chart in the chapter.

Exercises

■ Previously, the emphasis was on obtaining information from clients. In this chapter, the emphasis was on preparing witnesses for trial. To properly prepare witnesses for trial, the paralegal needs to have interviewed the witness prior to trial. Preparing for a witness and a client interview is very similar. Make sure you have reviewed the file and understand the case well before setting up the witness interview. You will want to have a list of questions prepared before the witness arrives. Prepare a generic list of questions for a witness to an accident. You will want to use this list as a general guide in preparing real cases and then tailor the guide to those individual cases. To tailor the questions to an individual case, look at any depositions previously taken from the witness. The following are some questions to get you started.

   ○ What is your full name and how do you spell it?
   ○ Have you gone by another names?
   ○ What is your current address?
   ○ What was the date of the injury you witnessed?
   ○ What was the time?
   ○ Where did the accident take place?
   ○ How did the injury occur?
   ○ Did you see any physical injuries to either party?
   ○ Did you report this injury to anyone?
   ○ Where there any other witnesses to the injury?

■ Practice the parts of a witness interview that are common to all witness interviews:
   ○ Greeting the client: If the witness comes to the law office, make sure to have the conference room set up with some basic beverages, such as coffee and water. In many law offices, the receptionist or file clerk is responsible for setting up the conference room (i.e., making sure the conference room is clean, the chairs are set up properly, and that there are beverages).
   ○ Thank the witness for coming.
   ○ Let the witness know you are a paralegal, not an attorney.
   ○ Get background information on the witness, such as witness's contact information so you will have it when it comes to preparing the trial notebook.

APPENDIX

An Introduction to Medicine

Be careful about reading health books. You may die of a misprint.[1]

Introduction

Appendix A: An Introduction to Medicine presents a short introduction to medical terms, basic anatomy, common prescription drug types, and medical tests that may be encountered when reviewing personal injury medical records. A familiarity with these fundamentals will assist the paralegal in understanding and preparing for a personal injury case. Knowing Latin prefixes, roots, and suffixes will help the paralegal figure out the meaning of words not defined here. This appendix is a jumping-off point for the paralegal, who will have to learn much more about medicine if she decides to work in personal injury. This appendix is by no means an exhaustive review of the medical information a paralegal working in torts law will need to know. In the body of this appendix and at the end of this appendix, there are additional sources for further information. For instance, the Physician's Desk Reference and Medline Plus are invaluable tools for further research.

Note

In the majority of medical malpractice causes, the existence of medical malpractice, or the connection between the malpractice and the injury is not obvious and will have to be determined by a medical expert.

For other types of personal injuries, a paralegal needs a working knowledge of medical terminology, anatomy, and medical procedures. It is recommended the paralegal also study separate texts on these topics.

---

1. Mark Twain, American writer (1835-1910).

Medical Vocabulary

Prefixes	
AMBI-	Both
ANTE-	Before
ANTI-	Against
ARTHO-	Joint
BI/DI-	Two
CARDIO-	Heart
CEREBRO-	Brain
CERVICO-	Neck
CIRCUM-	Around
DACTYL-	Finger/toe
DENT-	Tooth
DERMA-	Skin
DIGIT-	Finger/toe
ENDO-	Inside
HYPER-	Above
HYPO-	Below
HYSTER-	Womb
INTER-	Between
INTRA-	Within
ISO-	Equal
LABI-	Lip
MAL-	Bad
MED-	Middle
OCUL-	Eye
PED-	Foot
PERI-	Around
POD-	Foot
POLY-	Many

POST-	After
PRE-	Before
PRO-	Before
PSEUD-	False
SUPRA-	Above
TACHY-	Fast
THORAC-	Chest

Word Roots	
ARTHO	Joint
BIO	Life
CARDI	Heart
CRANIO	Skull
GASTRO	Stomach
HEM	Blood
MYO	Muscle
NEURO	Nerve
OSTEO	Bone
PATHO	Disease

Suffixes	
-ALGIA	Pain
-ECTOMY	Excision
-ITIS	Inflammation
-LOGY	Study
-PATHY	Disease
-TROPY	Growth

Medical Terminology

Terminology for positions of the body	Definition
Anterior	Front
Posterior	Back
Ventral	Front
Dorsal	Back
Proximal	Towards
Distal	Away
Superior	Above
Inferior	Below

Terminology for positions of the body	Definition
Abduction	Away from the center of the body
Adduction	Towards the center of the body
Flexion	Bending
Extension	Straightening
Supination	Turns up
Pronation	Turns down

Medical Abbreviations[2]

ADL	Activities of daily living
ADR	Adverse drug reaction
Afib	Atrial fibrillation
AIDS	Acquired immunodeficiency syndrome
A&P	Anterior and posterior
ASA	Aspirin
Bid	Twice a day
BLS	Basic life support
BMP	Basic metabolic panel

2. Medical abbreviations are constantly evolving, so keep a list of any new ones you come across.

BP	Blood pressure
BPM	Beats per minute
CBC	Complete blood count
CC	Chief complaint
C/O	Complaint of
COPD	Chronic obstructive pulmonary disease
C-spine	Cervical spine
DC	Discharge
DNR	Do not resuscitate
DOA	Dead on arrival
DX	Diagnosis
ETOH	Alcohol
Fx	Fracture
F/U	Follow up
GI	Gastrointestinal
HBP	High blood pressure
HIV	Human immunodeficiency virus
H&P	History & physical
H/O	History of
HTN	Hypertension
Hx	History
LBP	Low back pain
L-spine	Lumbar spine
MVA	Motor vehicle accident
OR	Operating room
PE	Physical exam
PRN	As needed
PT	Physical therapy
Qid	Four times a day
R/O	Rule out
ROM	Range of Motion
Sob	Shortness of breath
T-spine	Thoracic spine
URI	Upper respiratory infection

Anatomy

The following diagrams illustrate parts of the body commonly affected in personal injury cases. While a paralegal is not expected to be a medical expert, a paralegal should familiarize herself with these body parts as these body parts will frequently be referred to throughout the medical records.

a. Cranium

Figure A.1

Cranial Bones

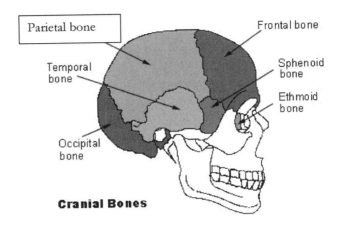

The cranium diagram (Figure A.1)[3] most importantly shows the frontal, temporal, and occipital bones in the skull. In an extreme accident, a plaintiff could suffer a fracture to part of his skull. However, usually if a plaintiff suffers an injury to a part of his skull, it will be to his face, as the bones and cartilage in the face are weaker than the rest of the skull. For instance, if a plaintiff were in a car accident and went through the windshield, and if he was unable to duck his head, he would probably hit and break his nose. However, if the plaintiff did duck his head while going through a windshield, the frontal bone would be the portion of the skull most likely impacted. Luckily, the frontal bone is extremely strong in adults and it would be unlikely to suffer a fracture.

Bones to know for the skull:

Frontal
Temporal
Parietal
Occipital
Maxilla
Mandible

---

3. National Cancer Institute, Divisions of the Skeleton, *Cranial Bones*, http://training.seer.cancer.gov/module_anatomy/unit3_5_skeleton_divisions.html# (last accessed Feb. 17, 2007).

b.   Upper Extremity Bones

Figure A.2

Upper Extremity

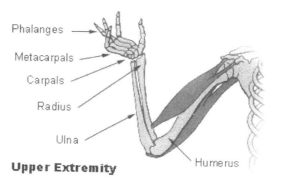

Upper Extremity

The upper extremity diagram (Figure A.2)[4] pinpoints the location of the upper extremity bones. With the upper extremity, some of the more common ailments you will see in medical records will be a fracture of usually the radius or ulna and then repetitive motion injuries, such as carpal tunnel syndrome.

Bones to know for the upper extremity	Definition
Clavicle	Collar bone
Scapula	Shoulder blade
Humerus	The upper arm bone
Ulna and radius	The two bones of the lower arm
Carpals	Eight wrist bones
Metacarpals	Bones of the hand
Phalanges	Finger bones

Bones to know for the upper trunk	Definition
Ribs	Twelve pairs of curved bones

4. National Cancer Institute, Divisions of the Skeleton, *Upper Extremity*, http://training.seer.cancer.gov/module_anatomy/unit3_5_skeleton_divisions.html# (last accessed Feb. 17, 2007).

Mighty muscles in the trunk	Definition
Trapezius	Muscle at the back of neck and upper truck
Pectoralis	Muscles located on the chest
Deltoid	Shoulder muscle
Triceps	Muscle on the back of the upper arm
Biceps	Muscle on top of the upper arm

c.   Shoulder

Figure A.3

Shoulder Diagram

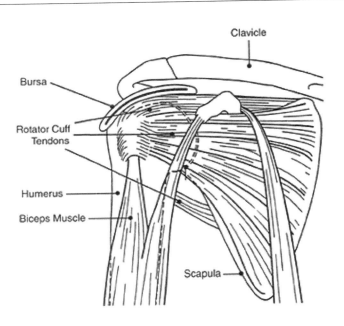

The shoulder diagram (Figure A.3)[5] shows the clavicle, bursa, rotator cuff, tendons, humerus, biceps, and scapula. Rotator cuff tears are a common personal injury. The bursa will often become inflamed. Due to the large amount of muscle, tissue, and bone in the shoulder, the shoulder is susceptible to inflammation, which may be cured by an injection into the area. However, if injections or physical therapy do not work, then rotator cuff surgery may be necessary to reduce shoulder problems and decrease any prior loss in movement.

---

5. National Institute of Arthritis and Musculoskeletal and Skin Diseases, Health Topics, *What Are Shoulder Problems?, Fast Facts: An Easy-to-Read Series of Publications for the Public,* http://www.niams.nih.gov/hi/topics/shoulderprobs/ff_shoulder_problems.htm (last accessed Nov. 2006).

d.   Back

Figure A.4

Side View of Spine

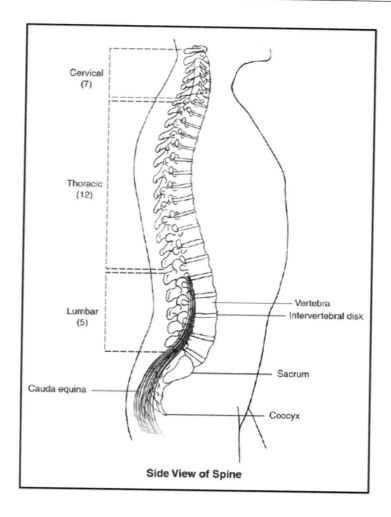

Side View of Spine

The back diagram (Figure A.4)[6] illustrates the cervical, thoracic, lumbar, sacrum and coccyx areas of the spine. Medical records regarding these areas will commonly refer to these areas as C-3 for instance. C-3 means the third vertebrae in the cervical area of the spine. Neck injuries are common in personal injury; think of whiplash. The lumbar spine is also a commonly affected area of the spine in personal injury. When you obtain the read-outs corresponding to the MRIs and X-rays, check whether the problems the patient is having are due to degenerative disk disease (a natural aging process) or some other cause, attributable to the incident.

---

6. National Institute of Arthritis and Musculoskeletal and Skin Diseases, Health Topics. *Handout on Health: Back Pain*, http://www.niams.nih.gov/hi/topics/pain/backpain.htm (last accessed Sep. 2005).

Bones to know for the back	Definition
Cervical	Consists of seven vertebrae
Thoracic	Consists of twelve vertebrae
Lumbar	Consists of five vertebrae
Sacrum	Consists of five fused vertebrae
Coccyx	Tail bone

Figure A.5

Normal Vertebra

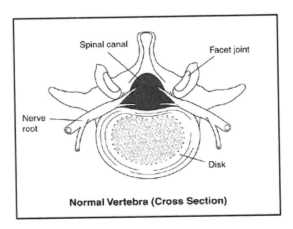

The normal vertebra diagram (Figure A.5)[7] illustrates the spinal canal, facet joint, nerve root, and disk in a normal vertebra. Plaintiffs often experience extreme pain if there is impingement on the nerve root.

e.   Lower Extremities

Bones to know for lower extremities	Definition
Pelvis	
Acetabulum	Socket into which the femur fits
Femur	Upper leg bone
Patella	Kneecap
Tibia and fibula	Bones of the lower leg
Tarsals	Seven bones in the ankle
Metatarsals	Five bones in the foot
Phalanges	Toe bones

7. National Institute of Arthritis and Musculoskeletal and Skin Diseases, Health Topics. *Handout on Health: Back Pain,* http://www.niams.nih.gov/hi/topics/pain/backpain.htm (last accessed Sep. 2005).

f.   Knee

Figure A.6

Lateral View of the Knee

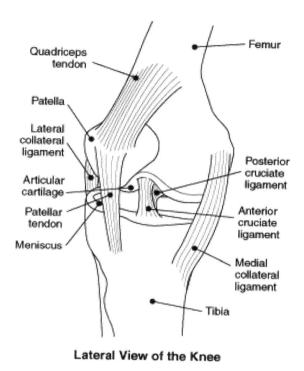

Lateral View of the Knee

The knee diagram (Figure A.6)[8] demonstrates the position of the tendons, cartilage, ligaments, patella, femur, tibia, and meniscus. Knee problems are another common injury in personal injury law. Some of the more frequent injuries to the knee that a paralegal will likely see are a torn meniscus or an anterior cruciate ligament (ACL) tear.

8. National Institute of Arthritis and Musculoskeletal and Skin Diseases, Health Topics: *What are Knee Problems, An Easy-to Read Series of Publications for the Public,* http://www.niams.nih.gov/hi/topics/kneeprobs/ffknee.html (last accessed March 2006).

g. The Respiratory System

Figure A.7

Respiratory Tract

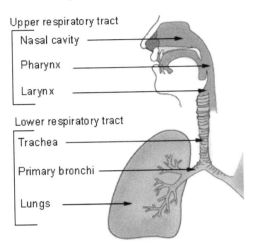

Conducting Passages

Upper respiratory tract
- Nasal cavity
- Pharynx
- Larynx

Lower respiratory tract
- Trachea
- Primary bronchi
- Lungs

The respiratory tract diagram (Figure A.7)[9] illustrates the location of the nasal cavity, pharynx, larynx, trachea, primary bronchi, and lungs. Respiratory illnesses commonly seen in personal injury law include upper respiratory tract infections. With an upper respiratory tract; the infection stops before reaching the bronchi and lungs. Thus, an upper respiratory tract infection is not an as severe a condition as bronchitis and then pneumonia, which enter into the lower respiratory tract. Many patients, while in the hospital for another condition, will contract pneumonia. Especially in older patients, pneumonia can be fatal. The patient's family then may try to make a claim against the hospital for the death caused by pneumonia. If the patient was already in a weakened condition and, because the risk of infection in a hospital is high, the patient's family will probably have a difficult time recovering on this basis.

Principle parts of the Respiratory System	Function
Nose	Breathing and smelling
Pharynx	Air passage between the nose, mouth, and larynx, used for breathing and eating-
Larynx	Used for talking and swallowing

9. National Cancer Institute, *Respiratory System, Conducting Passages*, http://training.seer.cancer.gov/module_anatomy/unit9_4_resp_passages.html (last accessed Feb. 16, 2007).

Trachea	
Bronchi	Carry air from the trachea into the lungs-
Lungs	
Diaphragm	Main muscle used in breathing-

h.   The Digestive System

Figure A.8

Digestive System

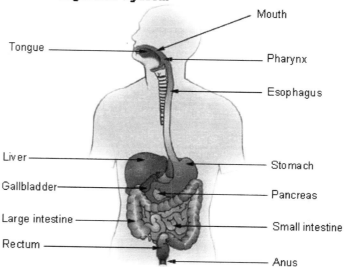

The digestive diagram (Figure A.8)[10] covers the mouth, tongue, pharynx, esophagus, liver, stomach, gallbladder, pancreas, large intestine, small intestine, rectum, and anus. With the digestive system, medical records today are increasingly showing cancers of the esophagus, stomach, pancreas, and colon. However, it is a difficult case for the plaintiff to prove his cancer was the result of the defendant's acts. Normally, a paralegal will see these types of cases with communities that live under power lines.

---

10. National Cancer Institute, Regions of the Digestive System, http://training.seer.cancer.gov/module_anatomy/unit10_3_dige_regions.html (last accessed Feb. 16, 2007).

Principle Parts of the Digestive System	Function
Mouth	Taking in food
Pharynx	Breathing and eating
Esophagus	Connects the pharynx to the stomach
Stomach	Digests food
Small intestine	Digests food
Large intestine	Digests food

i. Exterior of Heart

Figure A.9

Heart

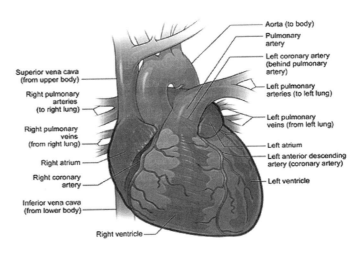

The exterior of the heart diagram (Figure A.9)[11] includes the aorta, arteries, atrium, ventricle, vena cava, and veins. A few of the most commonly referenced parts of the heart exterior, in personal injury medical records, are the pulmonary arteries, atriums, aortas, coronary arteries and ventricles. The arteries frequently become clogged and prevent flow into the heart itself, which may result in a heart attack.

---

11. National Heart Lung and Blood Institute, *How the Heart Works, Anatomy of the Heart*, http://www.nhlbi. nih.gov/health/dci/Diseases/hhw/hhw_anatomy.html (last accessed Feb. 16, 2007).

j.   Interior of Heart

Figure A.10

Interior of the Heart

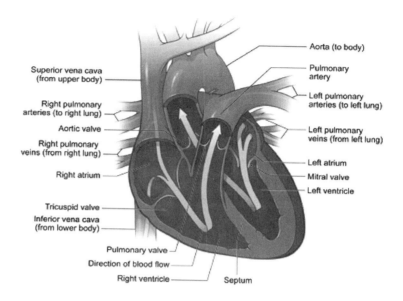

The interior of the heart diagram (Figure A.10)[12] covers many of the same items as the exterior of the heart diagram. However, there are additional items to learn with the interior heart, such as the mitral valve and tricuspid valve. The interior view of the heart allows you to see the flow of oxygen and blood to and from the heart.

Common Medical and Surgical Procedures

The following list of common medical and surgical procedures will get you, as the paralegal, started on a basic understanding of some of the different medical and surgical procedures common to personal injury law.

a.   Arthroscopy

A knee arthroscopy allows a doctor to use a device to see inside the knee joint with a light and project the image to a television monitor. The doctor can use this view to look at the anterior and posterior cruciate ligaments of the knee.

---

12. National Heart Lung and Blood Institute, *How the Heart Works, Anatomy of the Heart*, http://www.nhlbi.nih.gov/health/dci/Diseases/hhw/hhw_anatomy.html (last accessed Feb. 16, 2007).

b. Biopsy

With a biopsy, the medical practitioners are taking tissue samples to examine under a microscope.

c. Colonoscopy

A colonoscopy procedure allows doctors to insert a small viewing device into the rectum and inspect the lining of colon.

d. Complete Blood Count (CBC)

A CBC is a laboratory test checking on both red and white blood cells, along with platelets. Blood is drawn from the patient and sent to the laboratory to be analyzed.

e. Computerized Axial Tomography (CAT or CT Scan)

A CT scan uses computers to take multi-dimensional views of the human body. An X-ray is more limited in it can only take a two-sided view into the human body.

f. Defibrillation

Defibrillation is an electric shock to the heart. The purpose is to restart a regular heartbeat.

g. Discectomy

When a disk is ruptured or herniated, there is frequently pain, which radiates down into the leg. The discectomy is performed to remove material from the disk that is pressing on the nerve and causing the pain.

h. Electrocardiogram (EKG/ECG)

The purpose of an electrocardiogram is to check the electrical activity in the heart.[13] With an EKG, a medical professional can determine how fast the heart is beating. This test can help detect a heart attack or other potential heart problems.

i. Magnetic Resonance Imaging (MRI)

A Magnetic Resonance Imaging (MRI) uses radio waves, magnetic fields, and computers to generate multidimensional views of soft tissues and bones.

---

13. National Heart Lung and Blood Institute, Diseases and Conditions index, *Electrocardiogram*, http://www.nhlbi.nih.gov/health/dci/Diseases/ekg/ekg_what.html (last accessed July 2006).

j. Spinal Fusion

Spinal fusion fuses two or more vertebrae together. Once the fusion is completed, the patient will suffer a loss of movement, but hopefully will have a reduction in pain.

k. Stent

A stent is placed into a blood vessel, for instance, to help keep that blood vessel open.

l. Transcutaneous Electric Nerve Stimulation (TENS)

The TENS procedure is often combined with physical therapy for treatment of pain. Low doses of electrical currents are applied to the skin with electrode patches.

m. Ultrasound/Sonogram

An ultrasound or sonogram is the use of high-frequency sound waves to provide images of organs.

Types of Prescription Drugs

Unfortunately, plaintiffs in extreme pain can become addicted to pain medication, which can also be very costly. The medical field is becoming increasingly sensitive to the issues of prescription pain medication addiction. However, a few patients do go from one hospital to the next to obtain these medications and may even attempt to forge a prescription (which, due to increased security procedures, has become more difficult). There are certain elements of a prescription you should check to verify it is a valid prescription.

Figure A.11

Sample Prescription

Phone: (858) 111-0000   DEA #: AB 1234567

Dr. Joe Schmoe

111 B St.

San Diego, CA 92120

Name_____   Age_____

Address_____

Date_____/_____/_____

Rx

Refill_____

_____MD

Note the Drug Enforcement Agency (DEA) number on the above sample prescription. Forgetting to put a DEA number on a prescription is one of the major ways a prescription forger will slip up in preparing his phony prescription.

a. Types of Medications

Analgesics are pain relief drugs. Some of the commonly prescribed analgesics are:

- Acetaminophen
- Tylenol
- Ultracet
- Cymbalta
- Neurontin.

A handful of the pain medications that are classified as narcotics and are addictive are:

- Darvocet
- Oxycontin
- Percocet
- Tylenol with Codeine
- Vicodin.

A short list of the Nonsteroidal Anti-Inflammatory Drugs (NSAIDs), which reduce swelling and inflammation:

- Bextra
- Celebrex
- Motrin
- Naprosyn
- Toradol
- Vioxx
- Aspirin.

A couple of the medications that are used as muscle relaxers are:

- Flexeril
- Soma.

Psychotherapeutic medications are divided into three main categories: antianxiety, antidepressants, and antipsychotic (which are not discussed). A few of the antianxiety drugs are:

- Valium
- Xanax
- Effexor

- Paxil (this drug is also used to treat obsessive-compulsive disorder)
- Zoloft (this drug is also used to treat obsessive-compulsive disorder).

The drug companies are constantly marketing new or different versions of anti-depressants; here are some of the current ones:

- Cymbalta
- Effexor
- Prozac (Prozac is prescribed for a variety of reasons, including obsessive-compulsive disorder and as an antipanic agent)
- Wellbutrin.

Selective serotonin reuptake inhibitors (SSRI) are a category of antidepressants that includes:

- Celexa
- Lexapro
- Paxil (Paxil is also used as antipanic agent)
- Zoloft (Zoloft is also used as an antipanic agent).

b. The Physician's Desk Reference and Physician GenRX

The above listing of drugs is a very small portion of the medications available. If a law firm does a significant amount of medically related law, the firm should have a physician's desk reference. With this reference, the paralegal will be able to look up all the drugs in the above-referenced categories and more. The Physician's Desk Reference is helpful when a plaintiff is making a medical malpractice case based on side effects.

In addition, the Internet has a wealth of information on medicine; just be sure to verify you are seeking the information from a reliable source. The National Institutes of Health has their own extensive reference on almost all things medical. This online source is called Medline Plus. Medline Plus is also a good starting point for referrals to other websites with more specialized information. Medline is located at http://www.nlm.nih.gov/medlineplus/. Medline covers over 700 tropics on diseases, including pictures, treatment options, links to other websites, links to specialists in that disease, etc. There is also a drug look-up on Medline, along with a medical encyclopedia and dictionary. A consumer can use Medline to find doctors.

Another online source that is excellent for explaining different types of medical conditions is the Centers for Disease Control's website, located at www.cdc.com.

Other resources:

- www.mayohealth.org
- www.themedengine.com
- www.medscape.com
- www.nih.gov
- www.osha.gov
- www.innerbody.com

Initial Client Meeting Form

Plaintiffs' paralegals often interview clients initially, especially if the paralegal is at a workers' compensation firm. As the paralegal, you should either take notes during a client interview or tape-record a client interview. As clients tend not to be as forthcoming when they are being recorded, taking notes is the preferred method.

When scheduling the client interview, consider what documents the client should bring to the initial client meeting. The client needs to come to the interview with all the paperwork she has regarding the incident. If the client is the defendant in the lawsuit, then the client will have been served a complaint that he will need to bring to the meeting. If the client is the plaintiff, the person may have medical bills from an injury, which she will need to bring to the meeting.

When calling the client to schedule the meeting, the paralegal must identify herself as a paralegal. While talking to the client on the phone, make sure to provide the client with directions to the law office. The initial client meeting is when the client normally signs the attorney-client fee agreement. The attorney must actually sign the agreement along with the client; the paralegal cannot sign the agreement. Therefore, at some point during the initial client interview, the paralegal will need to call the attorney into the conference room to sign the fee agreement.

Prior to the meeting, make sure to prepare a list of questions to ask the client. If the law firm does not have a general client questionnaire, you can use the following questionnaire. Add questions raised by the client's first phone call to the law firm.

The meeting normally takes place in the conference room, which should be clean. Make sure the chairs are set up in a configuration that is comfortable to both you and the client. In addition, offering the client basic beverages, such as coffee or water is a good way to start the interview. Start the questioning by asking background information. Starting with neutral topics will help put the client at ease and might bring up some important information. Background information includes the client's education and past and current employment. Another way to put the client more at ease is to explain the interview process to the client prior to beginning the process. The interview process is to obtain the facts the attorney will need if the attorney takes the case.

Ask the client to give a general overview of the reason why she came to the law office. For instance, was this an automobile accident? You can let the client begin to tell his story and if he gets too far off topic, you can ask follow-up questions.

Let the client know the attorney needs all the facts, not just the facts that paint the client in a positive light. For instance, the client needs to be forthcoming about any prior criminal convictions. Prior criminal convictions are a topic the client might not think to mention, but a topic the other side will ask through interrogatories or at a deposition.

Before concluding the interview, let the client know you will provide the information to the attorney and the attorney will contact the client. The paralegal should put the facts obtained at the client interview into a memo to the attorney.

INITIAL CLIENT INTERVIEW

Date of Meeting:_____

File No._____

Statute of Limitations:_____

Background Information

- The client's full name_____
  - What does client prefer to be called?_____

- If client is a minor, who is the client's guardian?_____
- Any other names the client is known by_____
_____

- Past and current addresses for the last five-ten years (note if mailing address is different from physical address)_____
_____
_____

- Telephone numbers:
  - Home:_____
  - Work:_____
  - Cell phones:_____

- Fax numbers:_____
- Email addresses:_____
- Social Security Number:_____
  - Have you ever had another Social Security Number?_____

- Date of Birth:_____
- Where were you born?_____
- Driver's license:_____

- Marital status:_____
   - ○ How many times have you been married?_____
- Does your significant other work?_____
   - ○ If so, where?_____
- Names of family members_____

   _____

- What are the ages of your family members?_____

   _____

- Have you ever been convicted of a felony?_____
   - ○ If you have been convicted of a felony, what was the felony?_____

   _____

Education

- Do you have a high school diploma?_____
- What is the highest level of education you have?_____
- When did you last go to school?_____
- If you went to college, what was your major?_____
- Did you go to trade school?_____
- Do you have any certificates or licenses?_____

Military

Do you have any military service?_____

Navy, Army, Airforce, or Coast Guard?_____

What was your job?_____

Employment Information

- Current Employer:_____
- Work address:_____
- Job title and duties:_____

   _____

   _____

   _____

- Length of employment/Date employed:_____

- Supervisor's name:_____

- Last day of work before the date of injury ("DOI"):_____

- Compensation or salary:_____

- Has the client returned to work?_____

- Heath Insurance Company & policy number:_____

_____

The Incident

- DOI:_____

- Location of the incident:_____

- Weather conditions on DOI, if applicable:_____

- Police report:_____

  ○ Was the client or defendant cited for breaking any laws?_____

  ○ If so, what?_____

- Description of the incident:_____

_____

_____

_____

_____

_____

- Description of the injuries:_____

_____

_____

_____

- Diagrams of the incident, if applicable:_____

_____

- Where there any other parties involved?_____

Questions Applicable to Automobile Accidents

- Description of automobiles, if the incident is a car accident (Vehicle 1, client's car; Vehicle 2, defendant's car)

- ○ Vehicle 1
  - ● Make/Model:_____
  - ● Year:_____
  - ● Owner:_____
- ○ Vehicle 2
  - ● Make/Model:_____
  - ● Year:_____
  - ● Owner:_____

■ Damages:_____

_____

■ Any photos of the injuries and damages:_____

■ Vehicle 1 auto insurance company and address:_____

_____

- ○ Policyholder's name:_____
- ○ Policyholder's status (i.e., driver):_____
- ○ Policy number:_____
- ○ Policy limits:_____
- ○ Claim number:_____
- ○ Adjuster:_____

■ Vehicle 2 auto insurance company and address:_____

_____

- ○ Policyholder's name:_____
- ○ Policyholder's status (i.e., driver):_____
- ○ Policy number:_____
- ○ Policy limits:_____
- ○ Claim number:_____
- ○ Adjuster:_____

Workers' Compensation

■ Ask whether the incident was an on-the-job injury.:_____

The Defendant's information (if not an automobile injury)

- Name:_____
- Address:_____
- Driver's License Number:_____
- Insurance Company:_____
- Policy Number:_____
- Policy Limits:_____
- Have the adverse parties made recorded statements?_____
- Any additional defendants (repeat above questions as needed)

Witnesses

- Name, address, and phone numbers of any witnesses:_____
  _____
  _____

Injuries

- Persons injured:_____
- Description of each injury:_____
  _____
  _____
  _____

- The cost of medical bills (and the actual bills if the client has them):_____
- Hospital visits and the dates:_____
  _____
  _____

- Doctors seen and the dates:_____
  _____
  _____

- Physical therapy and the dates:_____
  _____
  _____

- Prior injuries and medical history, including medications:_____

  _____

- Prognosis:_____
- Permanent disabilities:_____
- Medication prescribed as a result of the injury:_____

  _____

  _____

- Description of pain and suffering:_____

  _____

  _____

  _____

Lost Wages

- Did the caller lose any time from work?_____
  - Wage loss?_____

Miscellaneous

- Loss of Consortium claim:_____

  _____

  _____

- Arrests:_____
- Bankruptcy:_____
- Ever represented by another attorney?_____

Documents provided by client:

Source of Document	Type of Document	Description of Document	Any Comments

Documents needed:

Source of Document	Type of Document	Description of Document	Any Comments

Glossary

Absolute privilege: a privilege which provides complete protection from liability. (Chapter 9)

Act: a voluntary movement. (Chapter 9)

Actual cause: another term for cause-in-fact. (Chapter 4)

Actual malice (in defamation): making a statement with knowledge of its falsity or with reckless disregard of whether the statement was true or false. (Chapter 9)

Administrative law: law handed down from the administrative agencies that are part of the executive branch (e.g., presidential branch) of our government. (Chapter 1)

Admonitions: statements from the lawyer who is taking the deposition to the deponent that discuss the deponent's duties. (Chapter 16)

Affirmative defense: even if what is alleged in the complaint is true, this defense (such as contributory negligence) is a defense to the complaint; a new issue which constitutes a defense to the plaintiff's allegations, even if the plaintiff's allegations are assumed to be truthful. (Chapters 7, 11, and 16)

Agent: a person who agrees to perform tasks for another. (Chapter 6)

Aggressor: the person who starts a fight. (Chapter 11)

Annotated statutes: statutes along with references to cases that interpret the statutes. (Chapter 1)

Answer: the defendant's response to the complaint, which admits, denies, and/or states the defendant has insufficient knowledge to admit or deny plaintiff's allegations made in the complaint. (Chapter 16)

Appreciable amount of time: a significant amount of time. (Chapter 9)

Apprehension: an anticipation or awareness of something. (Chapter 9)

Appropriation: the use of someone's name or likeness (a photograph, a drawing, or a cartoon) without her permission and usually for commercial advertising. (Chapter 9)

Arbitration: when a case is taken in front of a neutral third party, often a retired judge, for a final and binding decision. (Chapter 8)

Artificial condition: a condition placed on the land by man, rather than a naturally occurring condition. (Chapter 6)

Assault: an act committed with the intent to harmfully or offensively touch another, which does cause the other person to be apprehensive he is about to be harmfully or offensively touched. (Chapter 1 and 10)

Assumption of the risk: when a plaintiff knowingly takes a chance he will be injured, the plaintiff takes responsibility for the consequences of his actions. (Chapter 7)

Attorney work product: the ideas, thoughts, and working papers an attorney generates while working on a case. (Chapter 15)

Attractive nuisance: a visible object enticing to children and potentially harmful to children. (Chapter 6)

Battery: a harmful or offensive contact with a person, caused by the defendant's intent to cause the harmful or offensive contact. (Chapter 1 and 10)

Breach of duty: the use of unreasonable actions towards a third party to whom a defendant owes a duty of care. (Chapter 3)

Breach of warranty: a theory under which a plaintiff can sue in products liability; combines tort and contract law to provide a remedy for a plaintiff. (Chapter 12)

But-for test: one test for determining the cause-in-fact of an injury; stated as but-for the defendant's negligence, the plaintiff would not have been injured. (Chapter 4)

Cause-in-fact: without the defendant's action or inaction, the incident would not have happened. (Chapter 4)

Causes of action: legally acceptable reasons for bringing about a lawsuit. (Chapter 9)

Caveat emptor: A Latin phrase meaning "let the buyer be aware." (Chapter 12)

Certificate of service: a specialized proof of service, used for complaints, which states under the penalty of perjury how the defendant was served. (Chapter 16)

Chattel: personal property. (Chapter 10)

Child: for legal purposes, a child is a person who is generally too young to appreciate the dangers in a situation. (Chapter 6)

Circumstantial evidence: evidence that can be inferred from other facts. (Chapter 17)

Closing arguments: each side's final statement or summary of the evidence. (Chapter 17)

Collateral source rule: rule prohibiting the defendant from mentioning in court that the plaintiff has already had his medical treatment provided by his insurance company. (Chapter 5)

Commission: an act. (Chapter 2)

Common law: hundreds of years of judicial law making; started in England and then carried over to the United States of America. (Chapter 1)

Comparative negligence: allows the plaintiff to obtain a recovery from the defendant even if the plaintiff is partially responsible for his injury; plaintiff's recovery will be reduced by the percentage of his own negligence. (Chapter 7)

Complaint: the first pleading from the plaintiff, which begins a civil action and consists of the plaintiff's allegations against the defendant. (Chapter 16)

Concurrent causes: causes acting together to cause the injury, although each cause by itself would not have caused the injury. (Chapter 4)

Conflicting interest: an interest that might be considered a higher priority than the client's interest or might compete with the client's interest. (Chapter 15)

Consent: an agreement to allow an event to occur or not occur. (Chapter 9); a voluntary agreement to a tort or a willingness to undergo a tort made with a full understanding of the consequences. (Chapter 11)

Constitutional law: law consisting of the constitution, the amendments to the constitution, and all the cases interpreting the constitution. (Chapter 1)

Consulting expert: expert who reviews the file and helps the attorney prepare for trial. (Chapter 8)

Continuing nuisance: a nuisance that can be discontinued at any time. (Chapter 13)

Contribution: when a defendant who paid the plaintiff the entire settlement amount seeks at least partial reimbursement from the other defendant who also caused the injury. (Chapter 4)

Conversion: when a defendant deprives the personal property owner of her chattel, without consent, and then puts the property to his own use so the property owner is completely unable to use her property. (Chapter 10)

Counterclaim: a pleading made by the defendant in opposition to the plaintiff's claims. (Chapter 16)

Course and scope of employment: the behavior an employer expects of an employee as part of her job duties.

Cross-claim: a pleading made by the defendant against a co-defendant. (Chapter 16)

Cross-examination: occurs when a party questions a witness the party did not call as a witness. (Chapter 17)

Damage: a loss, frequently monetary. (Chapter 5)

Dangerous activity: an activity with a substantial degree of likelihood of causing injury to people or property, and this likelihood cannot be eliminated with due care. (Chapter 12)

Declarations page: page or pages of the insurance policy, which names the insureds, and the amount of the policy. (Chapter 16)

Defamation: a spoken or written falsehood about another, which causes injury to the person's character or reputation. (Chapter 9)

Defamatory language: statements causing a plaintiff to be hated, treated with contempt, or subjected to ridicule. (Chapter 9)

Default: the defendant's failure to answer the plaintiff's complaint. (Chapter 16)

Defendant: the party from whom compensation is sought for the injury or damage. (Chapter 1)

Defense medical examination: when the defendant asks the plaintiff to be evaluated by the defendant's choice of doctor, and the plaintiff undergoes the evaluation. (Chapter 16)

Defense of property: a limited right to defend one's property form damage or possession by another. (Chapter 11)

Demonstrative evidence: exhibits representing real objects such as photographs or charts. (Chapter 17)

Demurrer: a motion by one party arguing that even if the other party's facts can be proven at trial, those facts do not meet the elements required for the cause of action. (Chapter 16)

Deponent: the person being deposed. (Chapter 16)

Deposition: oral questions, taken under oath. (Chapter 16)

Design defect: a product is not safe for its intended or reasonably foreseeable use; all products in a line have a design feature making them unreasonably unsafe. (Chapter 12)

Direct evidence: evidence a witness can ascertain through his senses, such as sight, hearing, smell, or touch. (Chapter 17)

Direct examination: occurs when the attorney calling the witness questions the witness. (Chapter 17)

Discovery: the means in which the opposing parties gather information on the other side's facts and evidence. (Chapter 16)

Discretionary functions: policy-making decisions. (Chapter 11)

Dispossess: to take away. (Chapter 10)

Doctor-patient privilege: information related to treatment that is provided by a patient to a treating doctor does not normally have to be disclosed in litigation. (Chapter 15)

Domesticated animals: animals conditioned to live among humans. (Chapter 12)

Duress: a defendant's defense to committing an intentional tort based on his own physical safety being threatened. (Chapter 11)

Duty: an obligation for a person to meet a certain standard of care. (Chapter 2)

Duty of reasonable care: the duty to exercise the same care a reasonably prudent person under similar circumstances would to avoid or lessen the risk of harm to others. (Chapter 2)

Eggshell plaintiff theory: a defendant is liable for an injury caused to a particularly sensitive plaintiff, even if the injury would have been much less to a normal person. (Chapter 4)

Element: an element is part of a rule making up a cause of action. (Chapter 9)

Emergency: a situation threatening life or property, which requires an immediate response. (Chapter 11)

Emergency treatment exception: if a person is unconscious and unable to given consent in an emergency, then consent does not need to be obtained. (Chapter 8)

Emotional distress damages: damages awarded for mental anguish. (Chapter 5)

Exhibit: something other than testimony tending to prove the facts. (Chapter 17)

Expert witness: a person designated as highly knowledgeable about a subject matter due to his education or experience. (Chapter 17)

Express consent: consent verbally stated or written and not implied by conduct. (Chapter 11)

Express assumption of the risk: the plaintiff signs a written waiver of the risk or verbally states she accepts the risk. (Chapter 7)

Extended coverage: additional insurance. (Chapter 16)

Fair market value: the value of a good on the open marketplace. (Chapter 5)

False arrest: false imprisonment committed by a person who appears to have the authority to confine the victim. (Chapter 9)

False imprisonment: a person is confined through physical or emotional restraints, such as threatening to harm another. (Chapter 9)

False light in the public eye: occurs when a defendant publicly attributes offensive statements or actions to the plaintiff. (Chapter 9)

Family purpose doctrine: if a member of the family is driving a family car with permission from the head of the household, then the head of the family is vicariously liable for the driver's negligence. (Chapter 6)

Family relationship rule: a rule allowing a bystander who is closely related to the victim to recover under negligent infliction of emotional distress. (Chapter 6)

Federal Tort Claims Act: law providing immunity to the federal government from certain types of lawsuits. (Chapter 11)

Foreseeable risk: a risk a reasonable person could have anticipated. (Chapter 2)

Frolic and detour: when the employee's behavior so deviates from the employer's business purpose that the employer will not be found vicariously liable. (Chapter 6)

Fraud: any act or omission which hides the breach of a duty or material fact. (Chapter 9)

General consent form: a consent to medical care. (Chapter 8)

General denial: a refusal of all allegations of the complaint. (Chapter 16)

Going and coming rule: an employer is not vicariously liable for accidents occurring to an employee on his way to and from work. (Chapter 6); if the employee is injured either going or coming to work, the injury is typically not covered by workers' compensation. (Chapter 14)

Good Samaritan: a person who aids another when he is under no legal obligation to help. (Chapter 3)

Gross negligence: the failure to exercise care or to act with so little care as to show indifference to the safety of others. (Chapter 1)

Harmful contact: a contact causing physical damage or pain. (Chapter 9)

Health Insurance Portability and Accountability Act (HIPAA):   a federal standard addressing who can obtain an individual's medical information. (Chapter 15)

Holistic treatment: treatments considered outside of traditional Western medicine, such as acupuncture. (Chapter 5)

Immunity: a protection from liability provided to the defendant based upon the defendant's status. (Chapter 11)

Impact rule: there must be a physical impact to the bystander in order for the bystander to make a claim for negligent infliction of emotional distress. (Chapter 6)

Impeachment: occurs when an attorney attempts to show a witness is not being truthful. (Chapter 17)

Implied assumption of the risk: when a plaintiff shows by his conduct he has accepted a risk. (Chapter 7)

Implied consent: nonverbal consent, inferred from conduct. (Chapter 11)

Independent contractor: a person hired for a specific job, who has control over how the job is performed, and is not an employee. (Chapter 6)

Informed consent: a patient understanding and making a decision based upon the information provided by a health care provider who discloses material information. (Chapter 8)

Infra: below. (Chapter 6 and 7)

Initial client meeting: the first meeting where the client comes to the law office. (Chapter 16)

Injunction: an order from a court telling the defendant to refrain from or stop performing certain act(s). (Chapter 1)

Instructions: a discussion on how to safely and effectively use a product. (Chapter 12)

Insured: the holder of the insurance policy. (Chapter 16)

Intent: want or purpose for a result to happen or knowing to a substantial certainty that a result will happen. (Chapter 9)

Intentional infliction of emotional distress: when a defendant's extreme and outrageous conduct disturbs the plaintiff's peace of mind. (Chapter 9)

Intentional tort: the defendant acts with the intent to cause the injury or with substantial certainty the injury will occur. (Chapter 1)

Interrogatories: written questions answered under oath. (Chapter 16)

Intervening cause: a cause occurring after the tortfeasor's negligent act that contributes to the victim's injury. (Chapter 4)

Intra-family tort: when a family member commits a tort against another family member. (Chapter 11)

Invasion of privacy: when a defendant places the plaintiff's private life into the public in an intrusive manner. (Chapter 9)

Invitee: a person on the land for a business purpose or for a purpose for which the land is open to the public. (Chapter 6)

Involuntary intoxication: a rare defense to intentional torts, which occurs when a person becomes intoxicated without knowing it or intending to become intoxicated. (Chapter 11)

Joint and several liability: two or more defendants being held responsible for the plaintiff's injury. (Chapter 4)

Joint tortfeasors: two or more defendants who all contributed through their acts to cause the injury to the plaintiff. (Chapter 4)

Known or discovered trespasser: those trespassers the possessor of the premises knows about. (Chapter 6)

Last clear chance: if a defendant could have avoided the harm at the last minute, but did not, then the defendant will be found liable to the plaintiff even though the plaintiff contributed to her own injury. (Chapter 7)

Lay witness: people who saw the event. (Chapter 16); a person who saw the incident in question. (Chapter 17)

Learned Hand Formula: a formula which weighs the burden of taking precautions versus the likelihood and potential severity of an injury, to determine whether the conduct was negligent. (Chapter 3)

Lessee: renter. (Chapter 6)

Lessor: landlord. (Chapter 6)

Libel: written defamation. (Chapter 9)

Libel per se: written statements, which by their very nature are considered libel. (Chapter 9)

Licensee: a person on the land for her own purposes. (Chapter 6)

Locus in quo: Latin phrase meaning the place where the accident occurred. (Chapter 3)

Loss of consortium: the loss of benefits of the marital relationship because the injured spouse is not well enough to prove those benefits; examples of benefits include date nights, household help, and sex. (Chapter 5)

Malicious prosecution: a cause of action for malicious prosecution arises when the defendant misuses the court system unjustly to retaliate against the plaintiff. (Chapter 9)

Malice in malicious prosecution: the plaintiff brought the charge against the plaintiff with the knowledge the charge was false. (Chapter 9)

Manufacturer: maker of the product that caused injury to the consumer. (Chapter 12)

Manufacturing defect: a product which does not conform to the rest of the products in a line due to something occurring in the manufacturing process which damages the product. (Chapter 12)

Material fact: a fact important to an event or transaction, usually between the parties. (Chapter 9)

Material information: information essential to the patient's determination of whether to undergo treatment. (Chapter 8)

Medical authorization: a detailed document giving medical providers the permission to disclose health information to a third party. (Chapter 15)

Medical malpractice: the failure of a medical professional to act as a reasonable medical professional would to comply with the applicable standards of care under the circumstances. (Chapter 8)

Meta data: data about data; stored information which does not show up on the printed document, but can be accessed if someone has the document electronically. (Chapter 16)

Ministerial functions: functions which carry out policy decisions; the government is not given immunity for ministerial functions. (Chapter 11)

Minor: a person under the age of 18. (Chapter 8)

Mitigation of damages: the obligation of plaintiffs to lessen their potential injuries through prompt medical treatment or other actions a reasonable person would have performed under similar circumstances. (Chapter 5)

Modified comparative negligence: when a plaintiff has equal or greater than an amount of negligence as compared to the defendant, then the plaintiff cannot recover. (Chapter 7)

Motions in limine: pre-trial motions on the evidence. (Chapter 17)

Necessity: the privilege of using an innocent person's property to prevent greater harm. (Chapter 11)

Negligence: actions that cause unreasonable risk of harm to another person. (Chapter 1)

Negligence per se: negligence in and of itself; conduct which is inarguably negligence because it is either a violation of a statute or it is obvious reasonable care was not used. (Chapter 2)

Negligent infliction of emotional distress: a claim for the emotional trauma suffered when one person sees another person injured. (Chapter 6)

Nominal damages: small amounts of money (frequently $1.00) awarded to the plaintiff when the defendant's actions have caused little to no harm. (Chapter 5)

Nuisance: the unreasonable or unlawful use of real property so as to interfere with the plaintiff's interest in the real property. (Chapter thirteen)

Offensive contact: a contact that would offend the dignity of a reasonable person. (Chapter 9)

Omission: failing to act. (Chapter 2)

One's person: a body and items so closely attached or associated with one's body as to be identified with one's body. (Chapter 9)

Opening statement: a statement made by each side's attorney at the beginning of trial. (Chapter 17)

Out-of-pocket expenses: those expenses the plaintiff already paid or is going to have to pay. (Chapter 5)

Outrageous behavior: behavior so outside normal behavior, it is actionable. (Chapter 9)

Permanent disability: the disability left after a worker has reached his maximum medical improvement. (Chapter 14)

Permanent nuisance: a nuisance where one act causes a lasting injury and the damages can be assessed once and for all. (Chapter 13)

Personal service: when a party to the lawsuit is served himself, usually by handing the document to him or by placing the document in his presence. (Chapter 16)

Physical manifestations rule: the plaintiff must show the emotional distress caused physical injury in order to recover under negligent infliction of emotional distress. (Chapter 6)

Plaintiff: the party who files the lawsuit. (Chapter 1)

Pleading: a document by which the parties make allegations against one another. (Chapter 16)

Preemptory challenges: each side at trial is allowed to dismiss jurors without stating a reason, up to a certain number, as dictated by the state. (Chapter 17)

Premises liability: law governing when a person in possession of land is responsible for injuries incurred by people on those premises. (Chapter 6)

Presumption: an inference tending to prove the truth of or falsehood of a fact. (Chapter 2)

Prima Facie: Latin term meaning, "on its face." (Chapter 1)

Primary authority: the most persuasive type of legal authority; includes statutes and is the first place a paralegal should look to answer a legal question. (Chapter 1)

Principal: a person for whom the agent performs tasks. (Chapter 6)

Private necessity: a qualified privilege, which allows a defendant to damage the plaintiff's property to prevent a greater harm to his own property but still requires the defendant to pay the plaintiff for the harm caused to the plaintiff's property. (Chapter 11)

Private nuisance: an invasion of another's interest in his private use and enjoyment of land through means other than a physical entry onto the real property. (Chapter 13)

Privilege: allows a person to act in a way adverse to another person's right without being subjected to tort liability. (Chapter 11).

Products liability law: law involving cases against manufacturers or sellers of items that injure people. (Chapter 12)

Proof of service: a document, declaring under penalty of perjury, that the person who signed the document served the document. (Chapter 16)

Proprietary function: a function performed by the government that could have been performed by a private corporation, which is provided immunity. (Chapter 11)

Pro rata: proportionate. (Chapter 4)

Prosecutor: the person who brings and pursues a criminal action against a criminal defendant on behalf of the government. (Chapter 1)

Proximate cause: an uninterrupted sequence, which causes an injury and without this cause, the injury to the plaintiff could not have happened. (Chapter 1); a cut-off of the defendant's liability when the defendant is only a remote cause of the injury. (Chapter 4)

Public figure: a person with power or whose reputation is known in the community. (Chapter 9)

Public nuisance: an unreasonable interference with a right common to the general public. (Chapter 13)

Publication: the communication of the information to a third party. (Chapter 9)

Public disclosure of private facts: a defendant's communication of private information about the plaintiff to the public, without the plaintiff's permission, which a reasonable person would find offensive. (Chapter 9)

Public necessity: an absolute privilege allowing a defendant a complete defense to injure private property to protect the community. (Chapter 11)

Punitive damages: non-compensatory damages that punish the defendant and act to deter others from the same or similar conduct. (Chapter 5)

Pure comparative negligence: no matter how great the plaintiff's degree of fault, she is allowed a recovery so long as she is 99% or less at fault. (Chapter 7)

Real evidence: exhibits that can be touched. (Chapter 17)

Reasonable person: an ordinarily prudent person who avoids injuring other people by using reasonable care. (Chapter 3)

Reasonable person standard: a test to evaluate whether the defendant acted as a reasonable person under similar circumstances and with similar abilities to the defendant, would have acted. (Chapter 3)

Reasonable use of force: the force necessary to stop an attack. (Chapter 11)

Recapture of chattel: owners of personal property have a limited right or privilege to repossess their property. (Chapter 11)

Request for documents: a formal request for documents in the opposing party's control; the request is made to the opposing party. (Chapter 16)

Requests for admission: questions where one party asks the other party the truth of allegations. (Chapter 16)

Res ipsa loquitur: a tort which would not have ordinarily occurred without negligence. (Chapter 4)

Respondeat superior: the doctrine an employer is responsible for the harm the employer causes while working within the course and scope of her employment. (Chapter 6)

Restatement of Torts: a set of reference books on the principles of tort law which many courts refer to when formulating decisions. (Chapter 1)

Restatement (Second) of Torts' Risk-Utility Test: an act is negligent if the magnitude of risk caused by the act outweighs the utility of the act. (Chapter 3)

Risk-utility test: a formula used to weigh the risk versus utility of conduct, to determine whether the conduct was negligent. (Chapter 2)

Scope of duty: the people to whom one has a duty. (Chapter 2)

Self-defense: the privilege to use force to protect one's self against unprivileged acts a person reasonably believes will physically harm him. (Chapter 11)

Seller: the party who makes defective products available to the public. (Chapter 12)

Sine qua non: also known as the but-for test; a Latin phrase meaning "a necessary requirement." (Chapter 4)

Slander: oral defamation. (Chapter 9)

Slander per se: oral statements, which by their very nature are considered slander. (Chapter 9)

Sovereign immunity: a governmental right including the prevention of suing the government without the government's consent. (Chapter 11)

Special or economic damages: actual monetary damages particular to the plaintiff. (Chapter 5)

Special relationship: a relationship where the parties are in a position of trust with one another. (Chapter 9)

Specific consent form: a consent to a specific procedure, usually medically-related. (Chapter 8)

Specific denial: a refusal of a particular allegation of the complaint. (Chapter 16)

Standard of care: the amount of care required under the particular circumstances. (Chapter 3)

Statutes of limitations: the time frame in which a tort lawsuit can be brought. (Chapter 1 and 7)

Statutory law: law made by politicians. (Chapter 1)

Strict liability: a tort where fault is not the issue; conduct which has liability imposed upon it even if there was no intent or negligence in committing the conduct. (Chapter 1); abnormally dangerous activities for which a defendant has liability, without regard to the defendant's negligence. (Chapter 12)

Subpoena duces tecum: a document with the power of a court behind it commanding a witness in the lawsuit to bring documents to the deposition. (Chapter 16)

Substantial factor test: test that asks was the defendant a big contributor in causing the injury to the plaintiff? (Chapter 4)

Substituted service: service on a party to the lawsuit that is not given to the party directly, but usually to another member of the defendant's household and then mailed to the defendant. (Chapter 16)

Superseding cause: an act of negligence occurring after the first defendant's negligent act, which overshadows the original act of negligence. (Chapter 4)

Temporary disability: an impairment that can be cured or greatly improved with the proper medical care. (Chapter 14)

Testifying expert: an expert who testifies at trial. (Chapter 8)

Therapeutic exception: a doctor does not have to provide information when he believes the information would be harmful to the patient or prevent the patient from healing. (Chapter 8)

Tort: a wrong done by one person (A) to another (B) that results in injury to the other person (B) or B's property, and involves obtaining monetary compensation for the injury or damage. (Chapter 1)

Tort damages: the losses a plaintiff suffers due to the actions of the defendant. (Chapter 5)

Tortfeasor: the person who causes the harm, also known as the defendant. (Chapter 1)

Transferred intent: a defendant's intention to injure one plaintiff may be transferred to the plaintiff who was actually injured; a defendant's intention to commit one tort may be transferred to the tort the defendant actually committed. (Chapter 9)

Trespassing: entering another's land without permission and without having a legal privilege for being on the land. (Chapter 6)

Trespass to chattel: when a person harms or interferes with the plaintiff's use of personal property. (Chapter 10)

Trespass to land: occurs when a person enters a landowner's real property without consent. (Chapter 10)

Ultimate user: the party who ends up using the product, who may not be the person who originally bought the defective product. (Chapter 11)

Unavoidable accident: a freak accident, not caused by the defendant. (Chapter 1)

Underinsured motorist coverage: insurance protection for the insured when she is hit by a driver without enough insurance to pay all the costs of the accident. (Chapter 16)

Uniform Commercial Code: a statute governing sales. (Chapter 12)

Uninsured motorist coverage: insurance protection for the insured when she is hit by a driver without insurance. (Chapter 16)

Unreasonable intrusion: a tort action for a high-level of offensive intrusion into the privacy of another. (Chapter 9)

Venue: the county in where the lawsuit should be brought. (Chapter 16)

Vicarious liability: occurs when one person is held liable for another person's negligence. (Chapter 6)

Vocational rehabilitation benefits: assistance in finding another type of employment, taking into consideration the employee's work limitations caused by an employment-related accident. (Chapter 14)

Voir dire: a Latin term meaning to speak the truth; the jury selection process. (Chapter 17)

Waiver: a failure to claim a right. (Chapter 16)

Warning: a discussion of dangers. (Chapter 12)

Warranty of fitness for a limited purpose: a seller telling the buyer a product can be used for a purpose other than the purpose the item is normally used for. (Chapter 12)

Warranty of merchantability: an item must be fit and safe for its ordinary purpose. (Chapter 12)

Wrongful death action: a legal action for damages due to the death of another person. (Chapter 5)

Zone of danger rule: a bystander witnessing an injury to a third party must be immediately threatened by the negligent action of the defendant to recover damages. (Chapter 6)

Index